Children's Rights in America:

U.N. Convention on the Rights of the Child Compared with United States Law

Edited by
Cynthia Price Cohen
Howard A. Davidson

American Bar Association
Center on Children and the Law
A Program of the ABA Young Lawyers Division

Defense for Children International-USA

Nothing herein shall be construed as representing the opinions, policies or actions of the American Bar Association, or Defense for Children International-USA.

© American Bar Association 1990

ISBN 0-89707-641-9

Table of Contents

Preface iii
Biographical Profiles of Authors vii
U.N. Convention on the Rights of the Child xi

SECTION I—GENERAL CONSIDERATIONS

Chapter 1: The Best Interests of the Child
Articles 3, 9, 18 and 40
Jane Ellis 3

Chapter 2: The Child's Evolving Capacities
Articles 5 and 14
James Garbarino 19

Chapter 3: A Guide to Linguistic Interpretation of the
Convention on the Rights of the Child
Articles 1, 4, 41 and 45
Cynthia Price Cohen 33

Chapter 4: Federal-State Implications of the Convention
Lawrence L. Stentzel, II 57

SECTION II—SUBSTANTIVE ISSUES

Chapter 5: The Child, Parents and the State
Articles 3, 5, 9, 10, 11, 18, 19, 34 and 36
John E.B. Myers 87

Chapter 6: Anti-Discrimination and Identity Rights of the
Child
Articles 2, 7, 8, 22 and 30
Daniel L. Skoler 109

Chapter 7: Civil Rights of the Child
Articles 13, 14, 15 and 16
Robert E. Shepherd, Jr. 135

Chapter 8: The Child's Right to be Heard and Represented
Article 12
Howard A. Davidson 151

Chapter 9:	Educating the Child for a Productive Life *Articles 28 and 29* Susan H. Bitensky	167
Chapter 10:	Assuring an Adequate Standard of Living for the Child *Articles 26 and 27* James Weill	197
Chapter 11:	Assuring Adequate Health and Rehabilitative Care for the Child *Articles 6, 23, 24 and 25* Kay A. Johnson/Molly McNulty	219
Chapter 12:	Promoting the Dignity of the Child Through Mental Health Services *Articles 23, 25 and 39* Gary B. Melton	239
Chapter 13:	The Child's Rights in Adoption and Foster Care *Articles 20 and 21* Joan Heifetz Hollinger/Alice Bussiere	259
Chapter 14:	The Child's Access to Diverse Intellectual, Artistic and Recreational Resources *Articles 13, 17, 28, 31 and 32* Martin Guggenheim	289
Chapter 15:	Preventing Exploitation of the Child *Articles 32, 33, 34, 35, 36 and 39* James B. Boskey	303
Chapter 16:	Rights of the Child Charged With Violating the Law *Articles 37 and 40* Merril Sobie	315
Chapter 17:	Involvement of the Child in Armed Conflict *Article 38* Thomas A. Johnson	325
Afterword:	Sanford N. Katz	335
Appendix:	Guide to Chapters Containing References to Articles of the Convention on the Rights of the Child	341

Preface

The Convention on the Rights of the Child was unanimously adopted by the General Assembly of the United Nations on November 20, 1989. The signing ceremony was held on January 26, 1990 and, having obtained more than the required ratification by twenty nations, the Convention went into force on September 2, 1990. Not even the Convention's most enthusiastic supporters could have predicted the extent to which it has been embraced by the international community or the speed with which it has become a legally binding treaty.

Drafting of the Convention on the Rights of the Child was undertaken at the behest of the Polish government as part of the celebration of the 1979 International Year of the Child (IYC). The purpose of the Convention was to put into treaty form the values contained in the 1959 United Nations Declaration of the Rights of the Child, which IYC had been organized to commemorate. It took nearly ten years to complete the Convention, which has emerged as a comprehensive compilation of rights—including civil-political, economic-social-cultural, and humanitarian—which all nations of the world have agreed are the minimum rights that governments should guarantee to children. Interestingly, the text of the Convention is drafted in language which strongly emphasizes the rights of the individual child, rather than the child as member of a family or group. In the words of James Grant, executive director of UNICEF, the Convention on the Rights of the Child is truly a "magna carta for children."

At the time that this book goes to press, more than one hundred countries, well over half of the Member States of the United Nations, have signed the Convention on the Rights of the Child. The only obligation incurred by signing the Convention is a State's promise to review the treaty with an eye toward future ratification. Thus far, fifty-six countries have ratified (or acceded to) the Convention. Sadly, the United States is not among either the signers or ratifiers of the Convention. Shortly before this book went to press, both the U.S. Senate and the House of Representatives passed resolutions urging the prompt submission of the Convention to the Senate for its advice and consent to ratification.

Considering the United States' distressing record on international human rights treaty ratification, it concerns us that some are suggesting that the U.S. ratification of the Convention on the Rights of the Child might not take place at any time in the near future. The comprehensiveness of the Convention's text, coupled with the fact that many of the Convention's rights ordinarily fall within the the jurisdiction of state rather than federal law, raises the possibility that Senate review and debate over the Convention could get bogged down interminably.

This collection of essays was undertaken in the hope that a general overview of the relationship between existing United States law and the standards of the Convention would help to minimize confusion about the treaty's content and that it would provide a basis for facilitating discussion and dialogue among legislators and within the Administration. It should be noted, however, that the importance of the Convention on the Rights of the Child to children's rights advocates and activists does not hinge on United States ratification of the treaty. The Convention is the result of agreement among all nations of the world. To that extent, it also stands as a set of international norms which can guide the efforts of all those who work with children.

The publication of this book is the result of the editors' personal belief that people in the United States, especially child advocates and attorneys, should be informed about the important international human rights standards set forth in the Convention on the Rights of the Child and, further, that the United States should ratify this new human rights treaty as soon as possible. A request for assistance in this endeavor brought an enthusiastic response from members of the American legal and child advocacy community. Authors were asked to take a group of articles from the Convention and to write a brief analysis of the extent to which United States national and state laws and social policies conform to the Convention's standards. Most of the authors are specialists in the fields about which they are writing. Few had extensive prior familiarity with the Convention on the Rights of the Child.

We are most grateful to the authors of these essays for the time they spent, given their busy schedules, in studying the Convention and its relationship to American law. We are also deeply indebted to Cheryl A. Hinton for her vital assistance in preparing the manuscript of the book, as well as to Kay Castelle, Executive Director of Defense for Children International-USA, for her careful proofreading of the text and her guidance in the style and design of the completed book. Finally, for helping us produce this book, we are most appreciative of the financial support provided by the ABA Fund for Justice and Education, as well as grants awarded by the Administration for Children, Youth and Families, Office of Human Development Services, U.S. Departmen of Health and Human Services.

Cynthia Price Cohen

Howard A. Davidson

Biographical Profiles of Authors

SUSAN H. BITENSKY is Associate Professor of Law, Detroit College of Law. She teaches Constitutional Law, Evidence, and Education Law. She was formerly Associate Counsel for the New York City Board of Education.

JAMES B. BOSKEY is Professor of Law at Seton Hall University Law School in Newark, NJ. He serves as President of the Association for Children of New Jersey, a member of the Board of Directors of the New Jersey Division of Youth and Family Services and of Parents Anonymous, Inc. He is the Faculty Director of the Seton Hall Family Law Clinic.

ALICE BUSSIERE is a staff attorney at the National Center for Youth Law (NCYL) in San Francisco. NCYL is a national support center which specializes in legal issues that affect poor children.

CYNTHIA PRICE COHEN is the United Nations Representative for Human Rights Internet, a Research Consultant for Defense for Children International-USA and a Research Associate with the Ralph Bunche Institute on the United Nations of the City University of New York. Ms. Cohen was a member of the Ad Hoc NGO Group on the Drafting of the Convention on the Rights of the Child, a group of about thirty non-governmental organizations concerned with children's rights. She participated in the drafting of the Convention from 1983 until its final adoption by the United Nations General Assembly on November 20, 1989. Ms. Cohen has written and lectured extensively on the human rights of children.

HOWARD A. DAVIDSON is Director of the Washington, DC-based American Bar Association Center on Children and the Law. He has directed that program, previously called the National Legal Resource Center for Child Advocacy and Protection, since its inception in 1979. Prior to that, he was involved in the full-time representation of children in the Boston area. He is co-editor of the book *Legal Rights of Children* (1984) and an active speaker and writer on child protection legal issues.

JANE ELLIS served as editorial assistant to Professor Joseph Goldstein and his co-authors on *In the Best Interests of the Child*. Before obtaining her law degree in 1983, she trained in and practiced family therapy. She joined the faculty at the University of Washington School of Law in 1987, after clerking at the United States Court of Appeals for the Second Circuit and practicing law in California. She teaches and writes about family and criminal law.

JAMES GARBARINO is President of the Erikson Institute for Advanced Study in Child Development, a graduate school and research center located in Chicago, Illinois. Among his recent books dealing with child development are *What Children Can Tell Us* (1989) and *The Psychologically Battered Child* (1986). In 1989, he received the American Psychological Association's award for Distinguished Contributions to Public Service.

MARTIN GUGGENHEIM is Professor of Clinical Law and Director of Clinical and Advocacy Programs at New York University School of Law. He has litigated many cases involving children's rights and is the author of numerous scholarly articles and books on the rights of children and parents.

JOAN HEIFETZ HOLLINGER is Professor of Law at the University of Detroit. She has held visiting appointments at a number of law schools, including Michigan, Stanford and UC Hastings, is the editor and principal author of *Adoption Law & Practice* (Matthew Bender 1988; Supp. 1990), and Reporter for the NCCUSL Uniform Adoption Act project. After a stint on the national board of the Planned Parenthood Federation, she is currently on its Legal Advisory Council.

KAY A. JOHNSON is Director of the Health Division for the Children's Defense Fund. Ms. Johnson is co-author of the CDF Maternal and Child Health Databooks and a variety of reports and articles on child and adolescent health policy issues.

THOMAS A. JOHNSON is with the Office of the Legal Advisor, U.S. Department of State. He served as the Counselor for Legal Affairs at the United States Mission to International Organizations in Geneva, Switzerland from 1985-1990. Mr. Johnson was the U.S. Representative to the U.N. Working Group on the Convention on the Rights of the Child from 1980 to 1983, and also to the U.N. Commission on Human Rights from 1986 to 1989.

SANFORD N. KATZ is Professor of Law at Boston College Law School. He has served as Editor-in-Chief of the *Family Law Quarterly*, Chairman of the Family Law Section of the American Bar Association and President of the International Society of Family Law. He has authored, co-authored or edited many books on family law including *American Family Law in Transition*.

MOLLY MCNULTY is Senior Health Specialist with the Children's Defense Fund, specializing in federal health policy and health law issues. Prior to joining CDF, she held a Revson Women's Law & Public Policy Fellowship at the National Health Law Program, where she specialized in women's health issues.

GARY B. MELTON is Carl Adolph Happold professor of psychology and law, and Director of the Law/Psychology Program and the Center on Children, Families, and the Law at the University of Nebraska-Lincoln. He is president of the American Psychology-Law Society and a past president of the Child, Youth, and Family Services Division of the American Psychological Association (APA). Professor Melton recently was a Fulbright scholar at the Norwegian Center for Child Research, where he examined the implications of the U.N. Convention for Norwegian law, and he studied the use of an ombudsman for children as a mechanism for ensuring the fulfillment of children's rights.

JOHN E.B. MYERS is professor of law at the University of the Pacific, McGeorge School of Law in Sacramento, California. Professor Myers writes extensively on legal aspects of child abuse and neglect. His many published works include *Child Witness Law and Practice* (Wiley, 1987).

ROBERT E. SHEPHERD, Jr. is Professor of Law and former Director, Youth Advocacy Clinic, University of Richmond Law School. He is the former Chair, Juvenile Justice Committee, Criminal Justice Section, American Bar Association and current Chair, Virginia Bar Association, Commission on the Needs of Children.

DANIEL L. SKOLER is Director of Continuing Education and Training, Federal Judicial Center. He chairs the Committee on Children's Rights of the American Bar Association's Section of Individual Rights and Responsibilities. His previous posts have included Executive Director of the National Council of Juvenile and Family Court Judges and Deputy Associate Commissioner with the Social Security Administration's Office of Hearings and Appeals. He has published extensively in the juvenile justice and children's rights areas.

MERRIL SOBIE is Professor of Law at Pace University, where he teaches Family Law, Juvenile Justice, Children's Rights, Criminal Procedure and Judicial Administration. He has served as Executive Officer of the Family Court, New York City and Assistant to the Director of Administration of the Courts, First Department (NY). His publications include the book *The Creation of Juvenile Justice: A History of New York's Children's Laws* (New York Bar Foundation, 1987), and numerous articles. He is also the official commentator to several parts of the New York Domestic Relations Law and Family Court Act (McKinney's, West Publishing).

LAWRENCE L. STENTZEL, II is Of Counsel in the Business and Finance Section of the Morgan, Lewis and Bockus law firm's Washington office. After 23 years in private practice, in 1975 he joined USAir, Inc., where he served as General Counsel and Senior Vice President (1975-1982) and then Executive Vice President (1983-1986). He formerly served as a Director and President of the Washington Metropolitan Area Corporate Counsel Association and as a Director and Member of the Executive Committee of the American Corporate Counsel Association.

JAMES D. WEILL is General Counsel of the Children's Defense Fund, where he previously was Program Director. From 1969 to 1982 he was with the Legal Assistance Foundation of Chicago as Deputy Director for supervising federal litigation and special projects, and litigated, among others, *Trimble v. Gordon*, 430 U.S. 762 (1977) and *Miller v. Youakim*, 440 U.S. 125 (1979).

U.N. Convention on the Rights of the Child

Preamble

The States Parties to the present Convention,

- *CONSIDERING that in accordance with the principles proclaimed in the Charter of the United Nations, recognition of the inherent dignity and of the equal and inalienable rights of all members of the human family is the foundation of freedom, justice and peace in the world,*

- *BEARING IN MIND that the peoples of the United Nations have, in the Charter, reaffirmed their faith in fundamental human rights and in the dignity and worth of the human person, and have determined to promote social progress and better standards of life in larger freedom,*

- *RECOGNIZING that the United Nations has, in the Universal Declaration of Human Rights and in the International Covenants on Human Rights, proclaimed and agreed that everyone is entitled to all the rights and freedoms set forth therein, without distinction of any kind, such as race, colour, sex, language, religion, political or other opinion, national or social origin, property, birth or other status,*

- *RECALLING that, in the Universal Declaration of Human Rights, the United Nations has proclaimed that childhood is entitled to special care and assistance,*

- *CONVINCED that the family, as the fundamental group of society and the natural environment for the growth and well-being of all its members and particularly children, should be afforded the necessary protection and assistance so that it can fully assume its responsibilities within the community,*

- *RECOGNIZING that the child, for the full and harmonious development of his or her personality, should grow up in a family environment, in an atmosphere of happiness, love and understanding,*

- *CONSIDERING that the child should be fully prepared to live an individual life in society, and brought up in the spirit of the ideals proclaimed in the Charter of the United Nations, and in particular in the spirit of peace, dignity, tolerance, freedom, equality and solidarity,*

- *BEARING IN MIND that the need for extending particular care to the child has been stated in the Geneva Declaration on the Rights of the Child of 1924 and in the Declaration of the Rights of the Child adopted by the United Nations in 1959 and recognized in the Universal Declaration of Human Rights, in the International Covenant on Civil and Political Rights (in particular in articles 23 and 24), in the International Covenant on Economic, Social and Cultural Rights (in particular in its article 10) and in the statutes and relevant instruments of specialized agencies and international organizations concerned with the welfare of children,*

- *BEARING IN MIND that, as indicated in the Declaration of the Rights of the Child adopted by the General Assembly of the United Nations on 20 November 1959, "the child, by reason of his physical and mental immaturity, needs special safeguards and care, including appropriate legal protection, before as well as after birth",*

- *RECALLING the provisions of the Declaration on Social and Legal Principles relating to the Protection and Welfare of Children, with Special Reference to Foster Placement and Adoption Nationally and Internationally; the United Nations Standard Minimum Rules for the Administration of Juvenile Justice (The Beijing Rules); and the Declaration on the Protection of Women and Children in Emergency and Armed Conflict,*

- *RECOGNIZING that in all countries in the world there are children living in exceptionally difficult conditions, and that such children need special consideration,*

- *TAKING DUE ACCOUNT of the importance of the traditions and cultural values of each people for the protection and harmonious development of the child,*

- *RECOGNIZING the importance of international co-operation for improving the living conditions of children in every country, in particular in the developing countries,*

Have agreed as follows:

Part I

ARTICLE 1

For the purposes of the present Convention, a child means every human being below the age of 18 years unless, under the law applicable to the child, majority is attained earlier.

ARTICLE 2

1. States Parties shall respect and ensure the rights set forth in the present Convention to each child within their jurisdiction without discrimination of any kind, irrespective of the child's or his or her parent's or legal guardian's race, colour, sex, language, religion, political or other opinion, national, ethnic or social origin, property, disability, birth or other status.

2. States Parties shall take all appropriate measures to ensure that the child is protected against all forms of discrimination or punishment on the basis of the status, activities, expressed opinions, or beliefs of the child's parents, legal guardians, or family members.

ARTICLE 3

1. In all actions concerning children, whether undertaken by public or private social welfare institutions, courts of law, administrative authorities or legislative bodies, the best interests of the child shall be a primary consideration.

2. States Parties undertake to ensure the child such protection and care as is necessary for his or her well-being, taking into account the rights and duties of his or her parents, legal guardians, or other individuals legally responsible for him or her, and, to this end, shall take all appropriate legislative and administrative measures.

3. States Parties shall ensure that the institutions, services and facilities responsible for the care or protection of children shall conform with the standards established by competent authorities, particularly in the areas of safety, health, in the number and suitability of their staff as well as competent supervision.

ARTICLE 4

States Parties shall undertake all appropriate legislative, administrative, and other measures for the implementation of the rights recognized in this Convention. In regard to economic, social and cultural rights, States Parties shall undertake such measures to the maximum extent of their available resources and, where needed, within the framework of international co-operation.

ARTICLE 5

States Parties shall respect the responsibilities, rights, and duties of parents or, where applicable, the members of the extended family or community as provided for by local custom, legal guardians or other persons legally responsible for the child, to provide, in a manner consistent with the evolving capacities of the child, appropriate direction and guidance in the exercise by the child of the rights recognized in the present Convention.

ARTICLE 6

1. States Parties recognize that every child has the inherent right to life.

2. States Parties shall ensure to the maximum extent possible the survival and development of the child.

ARTICLE 7

1. The child shall be registered immediately after birth and shall have the right from birth to a name, the right to acquire a nationality, and, as far as possible, the right to know and be cared for by his or her parents.

2. States Parties shall ensure the implementation of these rights in accordance with their national law and their obligations under the relevant international instruments in this field, in particular where the child would otherwise be stateless.

ARTICLE 8

1. States Parties undertake to respect the right of the child to preserve his or her identity, including nationality, name and family relations as recognized by law without unlawful interference.

2. Where a child is deprived of some or all of the elements of his or her identity, States Parties shall provide appropriate assistance and protection, with a view to speedily re-establishing his or her identity.

ARTICLE 9

1. States Parties shall ensure that a child shall not be separated from his or her parents against their will, except when competent authorities subject to judicial

review determine, in accordance with applicable law and procedures, that such separation is necessary for the best interests of the child. Such determination may be necessary in a particular case such as one involving abuse or neglect of the child by the parents, or one where the parents are living separately and a decision must be made as to the child's place of residence.

2. In any proceedings pursuant to paragraph 1, all interested parties shall be given an opportunity to participate in the proceedings and make their views known.

3. States Parties shall respect the right of the child who is separated from one or both parents to maintain personal relations and direct contact with both parents on a regular basis, except if it is contrary to the child's best interests.

4. Where such separation results from any action initiated by a State Party, such as the detention, imprisonment, exile, deportation or death (including death arising from any cause while the person is in the custody of the State) of one or both parents of the child, that State Party shall, upon request, provide the parents, the child or, if appropriate, another member of the family with the essential information concerning the whereabouts of the absent member(s) of the family unless the provision of the information would be detrimental to the well-being of the child. States Parties shall further ensure that the submission of such a request shall of itself entail no adverse consequences for the person(s) concerned.

ARTICLE 10

1. In accordance with the obligation of States Parties under article 9, paragraph 1, applications by a child or his or her parents to enter or leave a State Party for the purpose of family reunification shall be dealt with by States Parties in a positive, humane and expeditious manner. States Parties shall further ensure that the submission of such a request shall entail no adverse consequences for the applicants and for the members of their family.

2. A child whose parents reside in different States shall have the right to maintain on a regular basis save in exceptional circumstances personal relations and direct contacts with both parents. Towards that end and in accordance with the obligation of States Parties under Article 9, paragraph 1, States Parties shall respect the right of the child and his or her parents to leave any country, including their own, and to enter their own country. The right to leave any country shall be subject only to such restrictions as are prescribed by law and which are necessary to protect the national security, public order (*ordre public*), public health or morals or the rights and freedoms of others and are consistent with the other rights recognized in the present Convention.

ARTICLE 11

1. States Parties shall take measures to combat the illicit transfer and non-return of children abroad.

2. To this end, States Parties shall promote the conclusion of bilateral or multilateral agreements or accession to existing agreements.

ARTICLE 12

1. States Parties shall assure to the child who is capable of forming his or her own views the right to express those views freely in all matters affecting the child, the views of the child being given due weight in accordance with the age and maturity of the child.

2. For this purpose, the child shall in particular be provided the opportunity to be heard in any judicial and administrative proceedings affecting the child, either directly, or through a representative or an appropriate body, in a manner consistent with the procedural rules of national law.

ARTICLE 13

1. The child shall have the right to freedom of expression; this right shall include freedom to seek, receive and impart information and ideas of all kinds, regardless of frontiers, either orally, in writing or in print, in the form of art, or through any other media of the child's choice.

2. The exercise of this right may be subject to certain restrictions, but these shall only be such as are provided by law and are necessary:

(a) For respect of the rights or reputations of others; or

(b) For the protection of national security or of public order (*ordre public*), or of public health or morals.

ARTICLE 14

1. States Parties shall respect the right of the child to freedom of thought, conscience and religion.

2. States Parties shall respect the rights and duties of the parents and, when applicable, legal guardians, to provide direction to the child in the exercise of his or her right in a manner consistent with the evolving capacities of the child.

3. Freedom to manifest one's religion or beliefs may be subject only to such limitations as are prescribed by law and are necessary to protect public safety, order, health, or morals or the fundamental rights and freedoms of others.

ARTICLE 15

1. States Parties recognize the rights of the child to freedom of association and to freedom of peaceful assembly.

2. No restrictions may be placed on the exercise of these rights other than those imposed in conformity with the law and which are necessary in a democratic society in the interests of national security or public safety, public order (*ordre public*), the protection of public health or morals or the protection of the rights and freedoms of others.

ARTICLE 16

1. No child shall be subjected to arbitrary or unlawful interference with his or her privacy, family, home or correspondence, nor to unlawful attacks on his or her honour and reputation.

2. The child has the right to the protection of the law against such interference or attacks.

ARTICLE 17

States Parties recognize the important function performed by the mass media and shall ensure that the child has access to information and material from a diversity of national and international sources, especially those aimed at the promotion of his or her social, spiritual and moral well-being and physical and mental health. To this end, States Parties shall:

(a) Encourage the mass media to disseminate information and material of social and cultural benefit to the child and in accordance with the spirit of article 29;

(b) Encourage international co-operation in the production, exchange and dissemination of such information and material from a diversity of cultural, national and international sources;

(c) Encourage the production and dissemination of children's books;

(d) Encourage the mass media to have particular regard to the linguistic needs of the child who belongs to a minority group or who is indigenous;

(e) Encourage the development of appropriate guidelines for the protection of the child from information and material injurious to his or her well-being bearing in mind the provisions of articles 13 and 18.

ARTICLE 18

1. States Parties shall use their best efforts to ensure recognition of the principle that both parents have common responsibilities for the upbringing and development of the child. Parents or, as the case may be, legal guardians, have the primary responsibility for the upbringing and development of the child. The best interests of the child will be their basic concern.

2. For the purpose of guaranteeing and promoting the rights set forth in the present Convention, States Parties shall render appropriate assistance to parents and legal guardians in the performance of their child-rearing responsibilities and shall ensure the development of institutions, facilities and services for the care of children.

3. States Parties shall take all appropriate measures to ensure that children of working parents have the right to benefit from child care services and facilities for which they are eligible.

ARTICLE 19

1. States Parties shall take all appropriate legislative, administrative, social and educational measures to protect the child from all forms of physical or mental violence, injury or abuse, neglect or negligent treatment, maltreatment or exploitation including sexual abuse, while in the care of parent(s), legal guardian(s) or any other person who has the care of the child.

2. Such protective measures should, as appropriate, include effective procedures for the establishment of social programmes to provide necessary support for the child and for those who have the care of the child, as well as for other forms of prevention and for identification, reporting, referral, investigation, treatment, and follow-up of instances of child maltreatment described heretofore, and, as appropriate, for judicial involvement.

ARTICLE 20

1. A child temporarily or permanently deprived of his or her family environment, or in whose own best interests cannot be allowed to remain in that environment, shall be entitled to special protection and assistance provided by the State.

2. States Parties shall in accordance with their national laws ensure alternative care for such a child.

3. Such care could include, *inter alia*, foster placement, *Kafala* of Islamic Law, adoption, or if necessary placement in suitable institutions for the care of children. When considering solutions, due regard shall be paid to the desirability of continuity in a child's upbringing and to the child's ethnic, religious, cultural and linguistic background.

ARTICLE 21

1. States Parties which recognize and/or permit the system of adoption shall ensure that the best interests of the child shall be the paramount consideration and they shall:

> (a) Ensure that the adoption of a child is authorized only by competent authorities who determine, in accordance with applicable law and procedures and on the basis of all pertinent and reliable information, that the adoption is permissible in view of the child's status concerning parents, relatives and legal guardians and that, if required, the persons concerned have given their informed consent to the adoption on the basis of such counselling as may be necessary;

> (b) Recognize that intercountry adoption may be considered as an alternative means of child's care, if the child cannot be placed in a foster or an adoptive family or cannot in any suitable manner be cared for in the child's country of origin;

> (c) Ensure that the child concerned by intercountry adoption enjoys safeguards and standards equivalent to those existing in the case of national adoption;

> (d) Take all appropriate measures to ensure that, in intercountry adoption, the placement does not result in improper financial gain for those involved in it;

> (e) Promote, where appropriate, the objectives of this article by concluding bilateral or multilateral arrangements or agreements and endeavour, within this framework, to ensure that the placement of the child in another country is carried out by competent authorities or organs.

ARTICLE 22

1. States Parties shall take appropriate measures to ensure that a child who is seeking refugee status or who is considered a refugee in accordance with applicable international or domestic law and procedures shall, whether unaccompanied or

accompanied by his or her parents or by any other person, receive appropriate protection and humanitarian assistance in the enjoyment of applicable rights set forth in the present Convention and in other international human rights or humanitarian instruments to which the said States are Parties.

2. For this purpose, States Parties shall provide, as they consider appropriate, co-operation in any efforts by the United Nations and other competent intergovernmental organizations or non-governmental organizations co-operating with the United Nations to protect and assist such a child and to trace the parents or other members of the family of any refugee child in order to obtain information necessary for reunification with his or her family. In cases where no parents or other members of the family can be found, the child shall be accorded the same protection as any other child permanently or temporarily deprived of his or her family environment for any reason, as set forth in the present Convention.

ARTICLE 23

1. States Parties recognize that a mentally or physically disabled child should enjoy a full and decent life, in conditions which ensure dignity, promote self-reliance and facilitate the child's active participation in the community.

2. States Parties recognize the right of the disabled child to special care and shall encourage and ensure the extension, subject to available resources, to the eligible child and those responsible for his or her care, of assistance for which application is made and which is appropriate to the child's condition and to the circumstances of the parents or others caring for the child.

3. Recognizing the special needs of a disabled child, assistance extended in accordance with paragraph 2 shall be provided free of charge, whenever possible, taking into account the financial resources of the parents or others caring for the child, and shall be designed to ensure that the disabled child has effective access to and receives education, training, health care services, rehabilitation services, preparation for employment and recreation opportunities in a manner conducive to the child's achieving the fullest possible social integration and individual development, including his or her cultural and spiritual development.

4. States Parties shall promote in the spirit of international co-operation the exchange of appropriate information in the field of preventive health care and of medical, psychological and functional treatment of disabled children, including dissemination of and access to information concerning methods of rehabilitation education and vocational services, with the aim of enabling States Parties to improve their capabilities and skills and to widen their experience in these areas. In this regard, particular account shall be taken of the needs of developing countries.

ARTICLE 24

1. States Parties recognize the right of the child to the enjoyment of the highest attainable standard of health and to facilities for the treatment of illness and rehabilitation of health. The States Parties shall strive to ensure that no child is deprived of his or her right of access to such health care services.

2. States Parties shall pursue full implementation of this right and, in particular, shall take appropriate measures:

   (a) To diminish infant and child mortality,

   (b) To ensure the provision of necessary medical assistance and health care to all children with emphasis on the development of primary health care,

   (c) To combat disease and malnutrition, including within the framework of primary health care, through *inter alia* the application of readily available technology and through the provision of adequate nutritious foods and clean drinking water, taking into consideration the dangers and risks of environmental pollution,

   (d) To ensure appropriate pre- and post-natal health care for expectant mothers,

   (e) To ensure that all segments of society, in particular parents and children, are informed, have access to education and are supported in the use of, basic knowledge of child health and nutrition, the advantages of breast-feeding, hygiene and environmental sanitation and the prevention of accidents,

   (f) To develop preventive health care, guidance for parents, and family planning education and services.

3. States Parties shall take all effective and appropriate measures with a view to abolishing traditional practices prejudicial to the health of children.

4. States Parties undertake to promote and encourage international co-operation with a view to achieving progressively the full realization of the right recognized in this article. In this regard, particular account shall be taken of the needs of developing countries.

ARTICLE 25

States Parties recognize the right of a child who has been placed by the competent authorities for the purposes of care, protection, or treatment of his or her physical or mental health, to a periodic review of the treatment provided to the child and all other circumstances relevant to his or her placement.

ARTICLE 26

1. States Parties shall recognize for every child the right to benefit from social security, including social insurance, and shall take the necessary measures to achieve the full realization of this right in accordance with their national law.

2. The benefits should, where appropriate, be granted taking into account the resources and the circumstances of the child and persons having responsibility for the maintenance of the child as well as any other consideration relevant to an application for benefits made by or on behalf of the child.

ARTICLE 27

1. States Parties recognize the right of every child to a standard of living adequate for the child's physical, mental, spiritual, moral and social development.

2. The parent(s) or others responsible for the child have the primary responsibility to secure, within their abilities and financial capacities, the conditions of living necessary for the child's development.

3. States Parties in accordance with national conditions and within their means shall take appropriate measures to assist parents and others responsible for the child to implement this right and shall in case of need provide material assistance and support programmes, particularly with regard to nutrition, clothing and housing.

4. States Parties shall take all appropriate measures to secure the recovery of maintenance for the child from the parents or other persons having financial responsibility for the child, both within the State Party and from abroad. In particular, where the person having financial responsibility for the child lives in a State different from that of the child, States Parties shall promote the accession to international agreements or the conclusion of such agreements as well as the making of other appropriate arrangements.

ARTICLE 28

1. States Parties recognize the right of the child to education, and with a view to achieving this right progressively and on the basis of equal opportunity, they shall, in particular:

   (a) Make primary education compulsory and available free to all;

(b) Encourage the development of different forms of secondary education, including general and vocational education, make them available and accessible to every child, and take appropriate measures such as the introduction of free education and offering financial assistance in case of need;

(c) Make higher education accessible to all on the basis of capacity by every appropriate means;

(d) Make educational and vocational information and guidance available and accessible to all children;

(e) Take measures to encourage regular attendance at schools and the reduction of drop-out rates.

2. States Parties shall take all appropriate measures to ensure that school discipline is administered in a manner consistent with the child's human dignity and in conformity with the present Convention.

3. States Parties shall promote and encourage international co-operation in matters relating to education, in particular with a view to contributing to the elimination of ignorance and illiteracy throughout the world and facilitating access to scientific and technical knowledge and modern teaching methods. In this regard, particular account shall be taken of the needs of developing countries.

ARTICLE 29

1. States Parties agree that the education of the child shall be directed to:

(a) The development of the child's personality, talents and mental and physical abilities to their fullest potential;

(b) The development of respect for human rights and fundamental freedoms, and for the principles enshrined in the Charter of the United Nations;

(c) The development of respect for the child's parents, his or her own cultural identity, language and values, for the national values of the country in which the child is living, the country from which he or she may originate, and for civilizations different from his or her own;

(d) The preparation of the child for responsible life in a free society, in the spirit of understanding, peace, tolerance, equality of sexes, and friendship among all peoples, ethnic, national and religious groups and persons of indigenous origin;

(e) The development of respect for the natural environment.

2. No part of this article or article 28 shall be construed so as to interfere with the liberty of individuals and bodies to establish and direct educational institutions, subject always to the observance of the principles set forth in paragraph 1 of this article and to the requirements that the education given in such institutions shall conform to such minimum standards as may be laid down by the State.

ARTICLE 30

In those states in which ethnic, religious or linguistic minorities or persons of indigenous origin exist, a child belonging to such a minority or who is indigenous shall not be denied the right, in community with other members of his or her group, to enjoy his or her own culture, to profess and practise his or her own religion, or to use his or her own language.

ARTICLE 31

1. States Parties recognize the right of the child to rest and leisure, to engage in play and recreational activities appropriate to the age of the child and to participate freely in cultural life and the arts.

2. States Parties shall respect and promote the right of the child to fully participate in cultural and artistic life and shall encourage the provision of appropriate and equal opportunities for cultural, artistic, recreational and leisure activity.

ARTICLE 32

1. States Parties recognize the right of the child to be protected from economic exploitation and from performing any work that is likely to be hazardous or to interfere with the child's education, or to be harmful to the child's health or physical, mental, spiritual, moral or social development.

2. States Parties shall take legislative, administrative, social and educational measures to ensure the implementation of this article. To this end, and having regard to the relevant provisions of other international instruments, States Parties shall in particular:

(a) Provide for a minimum age or minimum ages for admissions to employment;

(b) Provide for appropriate regulation of the hours and conditions of employment; and

(c) Provide for appropriate penalties or other sanctions to ensure the effective enforcement of this article.

ARTICLE 33

States Parties shall take all appropriate measures, including legislative, administrative, social and educational measures, to protect children from the illicit use of narcotic drugs and psychotropic substances as defined in the relevant international treaties, and to prevent the use of children in the illicit production and trafficking of such substances.

ARTICLE 34

States Parties undertake to protect the child from all forms of sexual exploitation and sexual abuse. For these purposes,

States Parties shall in particular take all appropriate national, bilateral and multilateral measures to prevent:

(a) The inducement or coercion of a child to engage in any unlawful sexual activity;

(b) The exploitative use of children in prostitution or other unlawful sexual practices;

(c) The exploitative use of children in pornographic performances and materials.

ARTICLE 35

States Parties shall take all appropriate national, bilateral and multilateral measures to prevent the abduction, the sale of or traffic in children for any purpose or in any form.

ARTICLE 36

States Parties shall protect the child against all other forms of exploitation prejudicial to any aspects of the child's welfare.

ARTICLE 37

States Parties shall ensure that:

(a) No child shall be subjected to torture or other cruel, inhuman or degrading treatment or punishment. Neither capital punishment nor life imprisonment without possibility of release shall be imposed for offences committed by persons below 18 years of age;

(b) No child shall be deprived of his or her liberty unlawfully or arbitrarily. The arrest, detention or imprisonment of a child shall be used only as a measure of last resort and for the shortest appropriate period of time;

(c) Every child deprived of liberty shall be treated with humanity and respect for the inherent dignity of the human person, and in a manner which takes into account the needs of persons of their age. In particular, every child deprived of liberty shall be separated from adults unless it is considered in the child's best interest not to do so and shall have the right to maintain contact with his/her family through correspondence and visits, save in exceptional circumstances;

(d) Every child deprived of his or her liberty shall have the right to prompt access to legal and other appropriate assistance, as well as the right to challenge the legality of the deprivation of his or her liberty before a court or other competent, independent and impartial authority and to a prompt decision on any such action.

ARTICLE 38

1. States Parties undertake to respect and to ensure respect for rules of international humanitarian law applicable to them in armed conflicts which are relevant to the child.

2. States Parties shall take all feasible measures to ensure that persons who have not attained the age of 15 years do not take a direct part in hostilities.

3. States Parties shall refrain from recruiting any person who has not attained the age of 15 years into their armed forces. In recruiting among those persons who have attained the age of 15 years but who have not attained the age of 18 years, States Parties shall endeavour to give priority to those who are oldest.

4. In accordance with their obligations under international humanitarian law to protect the civilian population in armed conflicts, States Parties shall take all feasible measures to ensure protection and care of children who are affected by an armed conflict.

ARTICLE 39

States Parties shall take all appropriate measures to promote physical and psychological recovery and social re-integration of a child victim of: any form of neglect, exploitation, or abuse; torture or any other form of cruel, inhuman or degrading treatment or punishment; or armed conflicts. Such recovery and re-integration shall take place in an environment which fosters the health, self-respect and dignity of the child.

ARTICLE 40

1. States Parties recognize the right of every child alleged as, accused of, or recognized as having infringed the penal law to be treated in a manner consistent with the promotion of the child's sense of dignity and worth, which reinforces the child's respect for the human rights and fundamental freedoms of others and which takes into account the child's age and the desirability of promoting the child's re-integration and the child's assuming a constructive role in society.

2. To this end, and having regard to the relevant provisions of international instruments, States Parties shall, in particular, ensure that:

(a) No child shall be alleged as, be accused of, or recognized as having infringed the penal law by reason of acts or omissions which were not prohibited by national or international law at the time they were committed;

(b) Every child alleged as or accused of having infringed the penal law has at least the following guarantees:

i) To be presumed innocent until proven guilty according to law;

ii) To be informed promptly and directly of the charges against him or her, and if appropriate through his or her parents or legal guardian, and to have legal or other appropriate assistance in the preparation and presentation of his or her defence;

iii) To have the matter determined without delay by a competent, independent and impartial authority or judicial body in a fair hearing according to law, in the presence of legal or other appropriate assistance and, unless it is considered not to be in the best interest of the child, in particular, taking into account his or her age or situation, his or her parents or legal guardians;

iv) Not to be compelled to give testimony or to confess guilt; to examine or have examined adverse witnesses and to obtain the participation and examination of witnesses on his or her behalf under conditions of equality;

v) If considered to have infringed the penal law, to have this decision and any measures imposed in consequence thereof reviewed by a higher competent, independent and impartial authority or judicial body according to law;

vi) To have the free assistance of an interpreter if the child cannot understand or speak the language used;

vii) To have his or her privacy fully respected at all stages of the proceedings.

3. States Parties shall seek to promote the establishment of laws, procedures, authorities and institutions specifically applicable to children alleged as, accused of, or recognized as having infringed the penal law, and in particular:

(a) The establishment of a minimum age below which children shall be presumed not to have the capacity to infringe the penal law;

(b) Whenever appropriate and desirable, measures for dealing with such children without resorting to judicial proceedings, providing that human rights and legal safeguards are fully respected.

4. A variety of dispositions, such as care, guidance and supervision orders; counselling; probation; foster care; education and vocational training programmes and other alternatives to institutional care shall be available to ensure that children are dealt with in a manner appropriate to their well-being and proportionate both to their circumstances and the offence.

ARTICLE 41

Nothing in the present Convention shall affect any provisions that are more conducive to the realization of the rights of the child and that may be contained in:

(a) The law of a State Party; or

(b) International law in force for that State.

Part II

ARTICLE 42

States Parties undertake to make the principles and provisions of the Convention widely known, by appropriate and active means, to adults and children alike.

ARTICLE 43

1. For the purpose of examining the progress made by States Parties in achieving the realization of the obligations undertaken in the present Convention, there shall be established a Committee on the Rights of the Child, which shall carry out the functions hereinafter provided.

2. The Committee shall consist of 10 experts of high moral standing and recognized competence in the field covered by this Convention. The members of the Committee shall be elected by the States Parties from among their nationals and shall serve in their personal capacity, consideration being given to equitable geographical distribution as well as to the principal legal systems.

3. The members of the Committee shall be elected by secret ballot from a list of persons nominated by States Parties. Each State Party may nominate one person from among its own nationals.

4. The initial election to the Committee shall be held no later than six months after the date of the entry into force of the present Convention and thereafter every second year. At least four months before the date of each election, the Secretary-General of the United Nations shall address a letter to States Parties inviting them to submit their nominations within two months. The Secretary-General shall subsequently prepare a list in alphabetical order of all persons thus nominated, indicating the States Parties which have nominated them, and shall submit it to the States Parties to the present Convention.

5. The elections shall be held at meetings of the States Parties convened by the Secretary-General at United Nations Headquarters. At those meetings, for which two-thirds of the States Parties shall constitute a quorum, the persons elected to the Committee shall be those who obtain the largest number of votes and an absolute majority of the votes of the representatives of States Parties present and voting.

6. The members of the Committee shall be elected for a term of four years. They shall be eligible for re-election if renominated. The term of five of the members elected at the first election shall expire at the end of two years; immediately after the first election the names of these five members shall be chosen by lot by the Chairman of the meeting.

7. If a member of the Committee dies or resigns or declares that for any other cause he or she can no longer perform the duties of the Committee, the State Party which nominated the member shall appoint another expert from among its nationals to serve for the remainder of the term, subject to the approval of the Committee.

8. The Committee shall establish its own rules of procedure.

9. The Committee shall elect its officers for a period of two years.

10. The meetings of the Committee shall normally be held at the United Nations Headquarters or at any other convenient place as determined by the Committee. The Committee shall normally meet annually. The duration of the meetings of the Com-

mittee shall be determined, and reviewed, if necessary, by a meeting of the States Parties to the present Convention, subject to the approval of the General Assembly.

11. The Secretary-General of the United Nations shall provide the necessary staff and facilities for the effective performance of the functions of the Committee under the present Convention.

12. With the approval of the General Assembly, the members of the Committee established under the present Convention shall receive emoluments from the United Nations resources on such terms and conditions as the Assembly may decide.

ARTICLE 44

1. States Parties undertake to submit to the Committee, through the Secretary-General of the United Nations, reports on the measures they have adopted which give effect to the rights recognized herein and on the progress made on the enjoyment of those rights:

> (a) Within two years of the entry into force of the Convention for the State Party concerned,

> (b) Thereafter every five years.

2. Reports made under this article shall indicate factors and difficulties, if any, affecting the degree of fulfilment of the obligations under the present Convention. Reports shall also contain sufficient information to provide the Committee with a comprehensive understanding of the implementation of the Convention in the country concerned.

3. A State Party which has submitted a comprehensive initial report to the Committee need not in its subsequent reports submitted in accordance with paragraph 1(b) repeat basic information previously provided.

4. The Committee may request from States Parties further information relevant to the implementation of the Convention.

5. The Committee shall submit to the General Assembly of the United Nations through the Economic and Social Council, every two years, reports on its activities.

6. States Parties shall make their reports widely available to the public in their own countries.

ARTICLE 45

In order to foster the effective implementation of the Convention and to encourage international co-operation in the field covered by the Convention:

(a) The specialized agencies, UNICEF and other United Nations organs shall be entitled to be represented at the consideration of the implementation of such provisions of the present Convention as fall within the scope of their mandate. The Committee may invite the specialized agencies, UNICEF and other competent bodies as it may consider appropriate to provide expert advice on the implementation of the Convention in areas falling within the scope of their respective mandates. The Committee may invite the specialized agencies, UNICEF and other United Nations organs to submit reports on the implementation of the Convention in areas falling within the scope of their activities;

(b) The Committee shall transmit, as it may consider appropriate, to the specialized agencies, UNICEF and other competent bodies, any reports from States Parties that contain a request, or indicate a need, for technical advice or assistance along with the Committee's observations and suggestions, if any, on these requests or indications;

(c) The Committee may recommend to the General Assembly to request the Secretary-General to undertake on its behalf studies on specific issues relating to the rights of the child;

(d) The Committee may make suggestions and general recommendations based on information received pursuant to articles 44 and 45 of the present Convention. Such suggestions and general recommendations shall be transmitted to any State Party concerned and reported to the General Assembly, together with comments, if any, from States Parties.

Part III

ARTICLE 46

The present Convention shall be open for signature by all States.

ARTICLE 47

The present Convention is subject to ratification. Instruments of ratification shall be deposited with the Secretary-General of the United Nations.

ARTICLE 48

The present Convention shall remain open for accession by any State. The instruments of accession shall be deposited with the Secretary-General of the United Nations.

ARTICLE 49

1. The present Convention shall enter into force on the thirtieth day following the date of deposit with the Secretary-General of the United Nations of the twentieth instrument of ratification or accession.

2. For each State ratifying or acceding to the Convention after the deposit of the twentieth instrument of ratification or accession, the Convention shall enter into force on the thirtieth day after the deposit by such State of its instrument of ratification or accession.

ARTICLE 50

1. Any State Party may propose an amendment and file it with the Secretary-General of the United Nations. The Secretary-General shall thereupon communicate the proposed amendment to States Parties with a request that they indicate whether they favour a conference of States Parties for the purpose of considering and voting upon the proposals. In the event that within four months from the date of such communication at least one-third of the States Parties favour such a conference, the Secretary-General shall convene the conference under the auspices of the United Nations. Any amendment adopted by a majority of States Parties present and voting at the conference shall be submitted to the General Assembly of the United Nations for approval.

2. An amendment adopted in accordance with paragraph (1) of this article shall enter into force when it has been approved by the General Assembly of the United Nations and accepted by a two-thirds majority of States Parties.

3. When an amendment enters into force, it shall be binding on those States Parties which have accepted it, other States Parties still being bound by the provisions of the present Convention and any earlier amendments which they have accepted.

ARTICLE 51

1. The Secretary-General of the United Nations shall receive and circulate to all States the text of reservations made by States at the time of ratification or accession.

2. A reservation incompatible with the object and purpose of the present Convention shall not be permitted.

3. Reservations may be withdrawn at any time by notification to this effect addressed to the Secretary-General of the United Nations who shall then inform all States. Such notification shall take effect on the date on which it is received by the Secretary-General.

ARTICLE 52

A State Party may denounce the present Convention by written notification to the Secretary-General of the United Nations. Denunciation becomes effective one year after the date of receipt of the notification by the Secretary-General.

ARTICLE 53

The Secretary-General of the United Nations is designated as the depositary of the present Convention.

ARTICLE 54

The original of the present Convention, of which the Arabic, Chinese, English, French, Russian and Spanish texts are equally authentic, shall be deposited with the Secretary-General of the United Nations.

In witness thereof the undersigned plenipotentiaries, being duly authorized thereto by their respective Governments, have signed the present Convention.

Done at...this...day of...19....

Section I
General Considerations

CHAPTER 1

The Best Interests of the Child
Articles 3, 9, 18 and 40

Jane Ellis

Introduction

The United Nations Convention on the Rights of the Child is premised on a belief in the importance, in all actions concerning children, of the "best interests of the child." Thus, Article 3 states that whether an action is "undertaken by public or private social welfare institutions, courts of law, administrative authorities or legislative bodies, the best interests of the child shall be a primary consideration."

This chapter presents a brief overview of the role of the "best interests of the child" standard in American jurisprudence. It describes how the Convention's use of the phrase is consonant with this country's basic legal precepts governing children, and how the Convention might serve as a model for improving, on paper and in practice, the laws governing the fate of a child.

For over one hundred years, American courts have expressed and reiterated the special attention given to children by our legal system with the words "best interests of the child." The case most commonly credited for introducing the notion of the child's interest is an 1889 Kansas opinion, *Chapsky v. Wood*.[1] The case is alive and well in this century:

> Without question, the paramount concern of courts in child custody proceedings is the welfare of the child. Beginning with the early cases written by Mr. Justice Brewer [including] . . . Chapsky v. Wood . . . this court has consistently adhered to the rule that when a controversy arises as to the custody of a minor child, the primary question to be determined by the court is what is for the best interest of the child.[2]

Best Interests

The phrase has an equally long history in state statutes. Thus, for example, the Revised Codes of the Territory of Dakota referred as early as 1877 to "what appears to be for the best interests of the child" as the first of three factors a court was to consider in awarding the custody of a minor, or in appointing a guardian.[3]

Today the words appear in many thousands of state and federal court opinions covering a broad range of issues concerned with children.[4] The legislation of all fifty states contains statutes incorporating the phrase as well. These laws cover areas as diverse as adoption, dependency (abuse and neglect) proceedings, foster care, termination of parental rights, child support obligations of divorced, separated, and never-married parents, aid to families with dependent children, divorce custody, other custody proceedings, non-parental visitation, jurisdiction, juvenile delinquency, education, labor, evidence, and surrogate parenthood.[5] The standard also appears in numerous sections of important federal Acts (including, for example, the Child Abuse Prevention and Treatment and Adoption Reform Act of 1978, the Juvenile Justice & Delinquency Prevention Act, and the Indian Child Welfare Act). Numerous federal regulations refer to the "child's best interests."[6]

The phrase "best interests of the child" has been legitimately criticized, because of its breadth and indeterminacy, as a rule for resolving specific disputes.[7] The difficult problem of arriving at a consensus concerning the precise content that should be poured into the words in any given context will not easily disappear. Nevertheless, the phrase has rightfully retained its place in American law as an expression of the need to keep the interests and perspective of the child foremost in the minds of adult decisionmakers. It embodies an aspiration against which policy and doctrine must be measured as the law grapples with specific dilemmas and as it integrates knowledge of the needs of growing children in different circumstances. The Convention's reliance on the "best interests of the child" thus echoes the attempt, in American law, never to lose sight of the perspective of that most vulnerable and dependent member of the human family, the child.

In addition to taking the "best interests of the child" as a basic premise, the Convention uses the phrase in the specific articles concerned with the relations of parents, children and the state; foster care; and juvenile delinquency.

None of these references conflict with American law, and some may serve as useful reminders for individual state legislatures as they work to improve their laws concerning children and their professional training for those who will implement those laws. Each of these references will be examined in turn.

■ PROTECTION AGAINST ABUSE AND NEGLECT: ARTICLE 9

A. Abuse & Neglect

Children may be legally separated from their parents against the will of those parents because such intervention is deemed necessary by the State to protect the child. Article 9 requires that no such separation shall occur unless a competent authority, acting in accord with established and reviewable legal principles, decides such intervention is necessary for the child's best interests. In so doing, it echoes a basic assumption in American culture and American family law: absent evidence to the contrary, a child's interests are best served by protecting the integrity of the child's family unit.[8] Thus the first principle articulated by the Joint Commission on Juvenile Justice Standards of the Institute of Judicial Administration and the American Bar Association in its Model Standards Relating to Abuse and Neglect states:

> 1.1 *Family autonomy* Laws structuring a system of coercive intervention on behalf of endangered children should be based on a strong presumption for parental autonomy in child rearing.[9]

This preference has been expressed by many leading scholars.[10] It is found in the statutes and case law of many states.[11] And it has been recognized and advocated by the United States Congress in the 1980 Adoption Assistance and Child Welfare Act, requiring agencies to make "reasonable efforts" to keep children in their family homes and, when separations are necessary, to reunify parent and child as soon as possible.[12] Programs around the country, like Homebuilders in Seattle, Washington, have been designed to assure care for the child while allowing that child to stay in the parental home.[13] There is still a great need, however, for implementation of such an approach in other locations. The Convention will assist in that important effort.[14]

In spite of the importance of family integrity, there are instances where a child's needs require separation of the child from his or her parents. American law's response to that need is described in this book's chapter on The Child, Parents and the State (Chapter 5). The Convention, like the Model Standards cited above, considers the child's interests paramount where such separation is necessary.[15] The challenge for lawmakers, of course, is articulating when such separation does, in fact, serve the child's best interests. The nature of the standards that strike the correct balance between the need for intervention in the family and the need not to intervene for the sake of the child has been, and will likely continue to be, a subject of controversy among scholars and policymakers.[16] Many of the state statutes that authorize separation of parent and child, do refer to the child's "best interests," yet are too vague to ensure those interests will be met. Leading scholars, as well as the ABA Model Standards, have urged that all such state statutes, whether substantive or procedural, be drafted with as much specificity and clarity as possible.[17] The Convention's reference to "applicable law and procedure" provides an important reminder that while "best interests" is a necessary basis for removing a child from a family, it is not a sufficient basis.

Article 9(3) provides that a child who is separated from his or her parents has a right to maintain a relationship with those parents except if "contrary to the child's best interests." This phrase accords with the experience of experts that "[v]isitation between parent and child has been shown in numerous studies to be one of the most important, if not *the* most important, reunification service."[18] The Convention therefore reflects the importance, for agencies overseeing temporary separations, of making every reasonable effort to assist in maintaining parent-child contact during the time the child must be apart from parents, subject to the need of the child to be protected from that contact. One commentator has recommended clear guidelines on required "reasonable efforts" to ensure these visits.[19] Such guidelines, along with unambiguous statements concerning when a child's best interest is not met by visits, would further goals set by Congress in the Adoption Assistance and Child Welfare Act. The Convention's language will help any legislative or judicial attempt to implement these goals.

Not all separations are temporary, however. A state may act to sever permanently a child's relationship with his or her parent or parents in accord with child protection laws. In those cases, involving "termination of parental rights", all contact with the parent ceases.[20] The substance of the laws governing such termination of parental rights, including constitutionally required protections for parents, is discussed in another chapter of this book. For purposes of this chapter, however, it is important to note that while the statutes assign a central role to the "best interests of the child" in the termination decision, that ideal is not always realized in practice. Thus, as one scholar has noted:

> Many courts continue to require exact proof of the statutory grounds for termination [e.g. abandonment, serious physical harm], refusing to terminate parental rights on the ground of the child's best interest, even though the refusal may subject the child to instability, very poor home conditions, or life in a succession of foster homes. . . On the other hand in some states parental rights may be terminated solely on the ground that this will serve the child's best interests. . . [B]ut even in these cases evidence of serious parental neglect or harm is usually found.[21]

Work, therefore, remains to be done to ensure that the child's best interests are a primary consideration when separation from parents is more than temporary. Once again, the most important need is for clear legal guidance concerning both the standards for termination and standards for the amount of time that the state may keep a child separate from his or her parents without freeing that child for the possibility of adoption into a stable home.

Improved legal standards, however, cannot alone guarantee that decisions to intervene in a family on behalf of a child or permanently remove a child from his or her family are properly administered. The "best interests of the child" also require "competent authorities": well-trained and humane professionals in both the public and private sectors. Child placement professionals from different disciplines tread many thin lines as they attempt to fulfill the mandate of a child's "best interests".

> [T]he tragic situations that [child placement professionals] often confront in child placement cases tend to blur their awareness of their own limitations and the limits of their assignments. Their personal experiences and sympathies sometimes interfere with their

professional judgment. And their effort to maintain a purely professional stance carries with it the risk that they may become wooden and lose the humanity that is essential to good work with children and their families.[22]

While professionals must be ever vigilant against losing sight of their own limitations and their proper roles in assisting children and families, they sometimes fail in this hard task. They take on, for example, the role of parent when they are not and will never be the child's parent. Or, in their efforts to protect children they take on tasks for which they are not professionally qualified.[23] Continued education for these important professionals must remain a high priority if the rhetoric of "best interests of the child" is to be made and remain a reality.

Finally, systems to check intentional or unintentional departures from the letter and spirit of the law must be in place. The Convention's stricture against separation of parent and child absent a determination by competent authorities "subject to judicial review" therefore provides an additional safeguard to the child's interests. The requirement that the process of separation be a visible and accountable one helps to ensure that decisions about a particular child's "best interests" are not the result of misreading or misuse of the child protection laws by professionals who have temporarily lost sight of their proper roles.[24]

B. Parental Divorce or Separation

Article 9(1) also reflects the reality that children may become separated from a parent because of the fact that a child cannot live simultaneously with both parents following a separation or divorce. Article 9(3) reinforces the right of the child to maintain contact with the other parent in such situations. Every state in the country recognizes a parent's right of "visitation," or the semantic equivalent, following divorce where visitation will not endanger the child.[25]

Here again, the Convention advocates that the child's interest be a primary consideration. The proper balance between meeting that interest by ordering visits and protecting the child against visits, where necessary for his or her best interests, requires a conscientious weighing of values and attention to

Best Interests

evolving knowledge about children of divorced or separated parents. Most state statutes on visitation are framed in general terms.[26] A notable exception is the recent Washington State Parenting Act which spells out those situations in which visitation may be contrary to the child's best interests.[27] While the Convention in no way contradicts current American law, it may help to generate more specific policymaking concerning the meaning of the child's "best interests" in the divorce and separation arena as well as in the child abuse and neglect arena.

C. Separation from the Unwed Father

Recognition of the family unit's integrity is not dependent on the marital status of the child's parents. As noted in the chapter in this book on The Child, Parents and the State, the protections accorded the parent-child relationship derive "from the emotional attachments that arise from the intimacy of daily association."[28] Thus, the United States Supreme Court has held that an unwed father who raised his children was no less entitled to procedural protections against the state taking away those children than were married parents.[29] The American law concerning the rights of unwed fathers in relation to their children is complex and constantly evolving. In almost all cases, however, where unwed fathers have a "developed parent-child relationship",[30] that relationship, in the person of the father, has been accorded constitutional protection.[31] The child, as a member of that relationship is also a beneficiary of that law.

The plain language of article 9, referring to a "separation", implies that an actual physical and emotional relationship exists between parent and child for the article to apply. This interpretation is consonant with the fact that the U.S. Supreme Court has never accorded constitutional protection to unwed fathers by virtue of biological parenthood alone. Thus, Justice Stewart has written, "Parental rights do not spring full-blown from the biological connection between parent and child. They require relationships more enduring."[32] Furthermore, those state statutes that accord rights and responsibilities to unwed fathers require the jurisdiction to consider the child's "best interests" in deciding whether even to permit a father-child relationship where one has never before existed.[33] The child's needs are thus recognized as a "primary consideration."

■ COMMON RESPONSIBILITY OF PARENTS: ARTICLE 18

Article 18 describes the importance of State recognition of the responsibilities of both parents for their growing children, along with the fact that parents have the primary responsibility for raising their children in accord with the child's best interests. In American culture it is assumed, again absent evidence to the contrary, that both parents will be guided by a deep and abiding concern for their children's needs. The law, as discussed above in connection with article 9, reflects this belief in its attempt to protect the child's best interests first and foremost by protecting the integrity of the child's family.

At the same time, the law is explicit about certain of the responsibilities that go hand-in-hand with parenthood. Both mother and father (or legal guardian) are, for example, responsible for financial support of their child during, after, or outside of marriage.[34] Furthermore, unwed fathers, assuming proof of paternity and absent any termination of their parental rights and responsibilities, are obligated to contribute to the support of their children.[35]

■ SEPARATION FROM FAMILY: ARTICLE 20

The reference to "best interests" in this subsection of the Convention reiterates article 9's insistence that a child not be removed from the care of his or her intact family unless his or her interests so require. The nature of the special protection and care described in the remainder of the article are described in the chapter on foster care and adoption (Chapter 13).

■ RIGHTS OF THE ACCUSED CHILD: ARTICLE 40

Article 40 addresses issues concerning the child accused of a crime, and articulates the right of that child to have his or her parents or legal guardians present at proceedings, unless that presence "is considered not to be in the best interest of the child."

In the United States when a juvenile is accused of a crime, he or she is entitled, along with his or her parents, to "timely notice, in advance of the hearing, of the specific issues that they must meet."[36] Parents have a statutory right to attend proceedings and customarily do attend, although they are not necessarily required to do so.[37] Those rights and customs recognize the importance for the child of retaining his or her parents' protection in a state proceeding. "Protection of the family, protection of the child from the state—not from his parents—is central to the holding in *Gault*."[38]

The Convention thus recognizes the child's need for parental presence. It also recognizes, however, that there may be unusual situations when that presence may not be in the child's best interest. For example, a parent may be disruptive at a hearing or a judge may ask an older child for a candid explanation of certain behavior, and that explanation might implicate parental behavior (e.g. violence or abuse) that the child might be afraid to relate in the presence of the parents. This writer could find no law holding that a judge would not have discretion to ask parents to leave a proceeding in such an unusual situation.[39] Furthermore, even if a court were to hold that parents had a constitutional right to be present or that the child had such a right to their presence, that court might find that those rights should give way in exceptional cases where the child's needs clearly so require.[40] Thus, in a recent case concerning child victims in sex abuse trials and a criminal defendant's sixth amendment right to confront the child witness, the United States Supreme Court reiterated that "'[W]e have sustained legislation aimed at protecting the physical and emotional well-being of youth even when the laws have operated in the sensitive area of constitutionally protected rights.'"[41] Such an approach is even more likely in a setting designed to consider the special needs of juveniles.

In this arena, however, as in the abuse and neglect area, the child's need for parental protection and guidance must not be forgotten. The Convention recognizes this fact, and the Convention's concern for the child's needs should become the occasion for carefully delineating those rare situations in which parents can and should be excluded from juvenile proceedings. Once again, professionals in this area must learn to tread that fine line between looking out for the child's interest and trying, inappropriately, to take the place of the child's parents.[42]

Best Interests

One commentator, having documented "an escalating punishment cycle with respect to youth . . . [and] distorted perceptions of an epidemic of youth crime," has written that:

> [A]dvocates must continue to press for fairness, sensitivity, individualized justice, habilitative services and innovation on behalf of the youth coming before the nation's juvenile and family courts—and must wait for the inevitable shift in political tide from punishment to compassion.[43]

Article 40 of the Convention will assist in this process, and will emphasize, as do the laws of many states, that a basic principle of the juvenile justice system in this country has always been the "best interests of the child."[44]

Footnotes

[1] 26 Kan. 650 (1889).

[2] Perrenoud v. Perrenoud, 206 Kan. 559, 480 P.2d 749 (1971).

[3] Rev. Codes of the Territory of Dakota Section 127 (1877), *cited in* LaFave, *Origins and Evolution of the "Best Interests of the Child" Standard*, 34 S.D.L. REV. 459, 470 (1989).

[4] A Lexis search for references to "best interests w/5 child!" totalled 19,171 state court opinions and 543 federal court opinions.

[5] A survey of state statutes revealed that legislation concerning adoption in at least 43 states referred explicitly to the child's best interests. With respect to the other categories mentioned in the text the minimum numbers of states making use of the phrase are: dependency proceedings - 40; foster care - 32; termination of parental rights - 38; support obligation of never married parents - 27; support obligations of divorced parents - 29; aid to families with dependent children - 20; divorce custody - 41; other child custody proceedings - 25; non-parental visitation - 32; jurisdiction (Uniform Child Custody Jurisdiction Act) - 50; delinquency - 42; education - 25; child labor - 5; evidence - 6; surrogacy - 3.

[6] *See, e.g.*, 45 C.F.R. § 232 (1989); 45 C.F.R. § 1340.14 (1989).

7 *See, e.g.*, GOLDSTEIN, FREUD & SOLNIT, BEYOND THE BEST INTERESTS OF THE CHILD (1973) 53-60; Mnookin, *Child Custody Adjudication: Judicial Functions in the Face of Indeterminacy*, 39 LAW & CONTEMP. PROBS. 226 (Summer 1975).

8 Parental marriage is not essential to recognition of a parent-child family unit. *See infra* note 28 and accompanying text.

9 IJA-ABA JOINT COMMISSION ON JUVENILE JUSTICE STANDARDS, STANDARDS RELATING TO ABUSE AND NEGLECT 15 (1981).

10 *See, e.g.*, GOLDSTEIN, FREUD & SOLNIT, BEFORE THE BEST INTERESTS OF THE CHILD 4 (1979). The authors write:

> [W]e believe that a child's need for continuity of care by autonomous parents requires acknowledging that parents should generally be entitled to raise their children as they think best, free of state interference. This conviction finds expression in our preference for "minimum state intervention" and prompts restraint in defining justifications for coercively intruding on family relationships.

See also Mnookin, *Foster Care—In Whose Best Interest?*, 43 HARV. EDUC. REV. 599, 600 (1973) ("Most American parents raise their children free of intrusive legal constraints or major governmental intervention. Although compulsory education and child labor laws indicate there are some conspicuous legal limitations on parents, it is the family, not the state, which has primary responsibility for child rearing."); Wald, *State Intervention on Behalf of "Neglected" Children: Standards for Removal of Children From Their Homes, Monitoring the Status of Children in Foster Care, and Termination of Parental Rights*, 28 STAN. L. REV. 623 (1976). ("The proposed standards derive from a strong preference for 'family autonomy' in childrearing. By this I mean that the state should be required to justify clearly any coercive intervention in a parent-child relationship and to demonstrate the likely efficacy of such intervention.")

11 *See, e.g.*, WASH. REV. CODE § 13.34.020 (1989):

> The legislature declares that the family unit is a fundamental resource of American life which should be nurtured. Toward the continuance of this principle, the legislature declares that

> the family unit should remain intact unless a child's right to conditions of basic nurture, health, or safety is jeopardized. When the rights of basic nurture, physical and mental health, and safety of the child and the legal rights of the parents are in conflict, the rights and safety of the child should prevail.

See also N.Y. SOC. SERV. LAW § 384-b (1)(a)(iii) (McKinney 1983):

> (a)The legislature hereby finds that...
> (iii)the state's first obligation is to help the family with services to prevent its break-up or to reunite it if the child has already left home...

For an example of the many hundreds of cases that recognize the importance of family autonomy for the child's sake, *see In re Juvenile Appeal*, 455 A.2d 1313, 1318-19 (Conn. 1983):

> Studies indicate that the best interests of the child are usually served by keeping the child in the home with his or her parents. "Virtually all experts, from many different professional disciplines, agree that children need and benefit from continuous, stable home environments." ... Even where the parent-child relationship is "marginal," it is usually in the best interests of the child to remain at home and still benefit from a family environment.

Accord, Hamilton v. State, 410 So. 2d 64, 66 (Ala. Civ. App. 1982):

> In recognition of [the right to maintain family integrity], the Alabama courts indulge a presumption that parental custody will be in the best interests of a child.... The ultimate consideration... is, of course, the welfare of the child.... The prima facie right of a natural parent to custody of his or her child is therefore overcome where it is shown that such custody would be contrary to the child's best interest.

[12] Adoption Assistance and Child Welfare Act of 1980, Pub.L. No. 96-272, Stat. 500 (1981), (codified as amended) at 42 U.S.C. § 620 et seq. (1989).

[13] *See* A. NORMAN, KEEPING FAMILIES TOGETHER: THE CASE FOR FAMILY PRESERVATION (1985).

14 For an excellent discussion of the fate of the "reasonable efforts" provision of the Act, see Shotton, *Making Reasonable Efforts in Child Abuse and Neglect Cases: Ten Years Later*, 26 CAL. W.L. REV. 223 (1990). Shotton notes that efforts to use an in-home approach to abuse and neglect problems are cost-effective and that the federal legislation provides an economic incentive to states by permitting them to transfer any unused foster care funds into such services. *Id.* at 224 and 254.

15 Standard 1.5 of the Model Standards states:

> *Child's interests paramount.* State intervention should promote family autonomy and strengthen family life whenever possible. However, in cases where a child's needs as defined in these standards conflict with his/her parents' interests, the child's needs should have priority.

16 See, e.g., Wald, *Thinking About Public Policy Toward Abuse and Neglect of Children: A Review of "Before the Best Interests of the Child"*, 78 MICH. L. REV. 645 (1980) (*criticizing* standards recommended by Goldstein, Freud & Solnit in BEFORE THE BEST INTERESTS OF THE CHILD).

17 See, e.g., authorities cited *supra* note 10. Congress joined this call for better statutory guidance in legislation requiring that federal funding for child abuse and neglect prevention and treatment programs be contingent on "comprehensive definitions of child abuse and neglect." S. Rep. No. 167, 95th Cong. 2d Sess., *reprinted in* 1978 U.S. CODE CONG. & ADMIN. NEWS 557, 575. Congress may wish, in accord with the recognized need for statutory improvement, to require comprehensive and, to the extent possible, precise statutes and regulations to guide those professionals who must make the difficult decision whether it is in a child's best interests to separate him or her from his or her parents.

18 Shotton, *supra* note 13, at 249.

19 *Id.*

20 *But see* Garrison, *Why Terminate Parental Rights?*, 35 STAN. L. REV. 423, 425 (1983) (proposing that parental visitation rights only be terminated "after a judicial finding that the child will otherwise suffer specific, significant harm and that any alternative short of termination will not avert that harm.") Were this suggestion to be adopted it would

[21] CLARK, THE LAW OF DOMESTIC RELATIONS IN THE UNITED STATES 893-894 (2d ed. 1988).

[22] GOLDSTEIN, FREUD & SOLNIT, IN THE BEST INTERESTS OF THE CHILD 5 (1986).

[23] These problems and others against which well-meaning child placement professionals must struggle are described and illustrated in GOLDSTEIN, FREUD & SOLNIT, IN THE BEST INTERESTS OF THE CHILD (1986).

[24] GOLDSTEIN, FREUD & SOLNIT, *supra* note 10, at 18. ("It is equally important to establish procedures for intrusion which make highly visible the function, nature, and degree of intrusion that is justified at each point of decision.")

[25] CLARK, *supra* note 21, at 812.

[26] *See, e.g.*, MICH. COMP. LAWS § 722.27a (1989):
> (3) A child shall have a right to visitation with a parent unless it is shown on the record by clear and convincing evidence that it would endanger the child's physical, mental, or emotional health.

LA. CIV. CODE ANN. art. 146.1 (West Supp. 1990):
> A parent not granted custody or joint custody of a child is entitled to reasonable visitation rights unless the court finds, after a hearing, that visitation would not be in the best interest of the child.

[27] WASH. REV. CODE § 26.09.191 (1989).

[28] Lehr v. Robertson, 463 U.S. 248, 261 (1983), *quoting* Wisconsin v. Yoder, 406 U.S. 205 (1972).

[29] Stanley v. Illinois, 405 U.S. 645 (1972).

[30] Lehr v. Robertson, *supra* note 28, at 261.

[31] *But see* Michael H. & Victoria D. v. Gerald D., 109 S. Ct. 2333 (1989) (unwed father who had relationship with child not accorded parental rights where child's mother was married to another man at child's birth and, after period of separation, returned, with the child, to live permanently with her husband).

32 Lehr v. Robertson, *supra* note 28, at 260, citing Justice Stewart's opinion in Caban v. Mohammed, 441 U.S. 380 (1979).

33 *See, e.g.*, WASH. REV. CODE § 26.26.130(6) and 26.09.002 (1989).

34 CLARK, *supra* note 21, at 259. For examples of statutory authority, *see, e.g.*, N.Y. FAM. CT. ACT § 413 (McKinney Supp. 1990):

> 1, (a) [T]he parents of a child under the age of twenty-one years are chargeable with the support of such child and if possessed of sufficient means or able to earn such means, shall be required to pay for child support a fair and reasonable sum as the court may determine.

35 *Id.* at 174. For examples of statutory authority, *see, e.g.*, IOWA CODE ANN. § 675.1 (West 1987):

> The parents of a child born out of wedlock and not legitimized (in this chapter referred to as "the child") owe the child necessary maintenance, education and support. . . .

CAL. CIV. CODE § 7012 (West Supp. 1990):

> (a) If existence of the father and child relationship is declared, or paternity or a duty of support has been acknowledged or adjudicated under this part or under prior law, the obligation of the father may be enforced in the same or other proceedings by the mother, the child, the public authority that has furnished or may furnish the reasonable expenses of pregnancy, confinement, education, support, or funeral, or by any other person, including a private agency, to the extent he has furnished or is furnishing these expenses.

W. VA. CODE § 48A-6-4 (Supp. 1989):

> If the defendant, by verified responsive pleading shall admit that the man is the father of the child and owes a duty of support, or if after a trial on the merits, the court or jury shall find, by clear and convincing evidence that the man is the father of the child, the court shall order support in accordance with the provisions of this chapter.

36 *In re* Gault, 387 U.S. 1, 34 (1967).

37 *See* Bird, Conlin & Frank, *Children in Trouble: The Juvenile Justice System* 461, 485 in LEGAL RIGHTS OF CHILDREN (HOROWITZ & DAVIDSON eds. 1984); 79 HARV. L. REV. 775, 789 (1966).

[38] GOLDSTEIN, FREUD & SOLNIT, *supra* note 10, at 129.

[39] "[T]here is no hard and fast rule governing the needs for the parents to be present during the adjudicatory hearing" in a juvenile case. Bird, Conlin & Frank, *supra* note 37, at 485.

[40] *See* Standard 6.5(B) and Commentary thereto, IJA-ABA JOINT COMMISSION ON JUVENILE JUSTICE STANDARDS, Standards Relating to Pretrial Court Proceedings 110-116 (1980). In its reference to the child's age, the article also implicates the complex issue of whether a child may waive any right he or she may have to parental presence at a hearing. This writer could find no definitive law that conflicts with this approach by the Convention. Common sense dictates at a minimum, however, that any waiver by a juvenile be accompanied by rigorous safeguards.

[41] Maryland v. Sandra Ann Craig, 111 L Ed 2d 666 (1990), *quoting* New York v. Ferber, 458 U.S. 747, 756-757 (1982).

[42] GOLDSTEIN, FREUD & SOLNIT, IN THE BEST INTERESTS OF THE CHILD, *supra* note 22, at cover page ("The professional participants in the child placement process do not, either separately or together, make up or make up for a parent").

[43] *See* Fink, *Juvenile Delinquency Legislation: Punishment in Vogue* 263, 264 and 286 in AMERICAN BAR ASSOCIATION, LEGAL ADVOCACY FOR CHILDREN AND YOUTH: REFORMS, TRENDS, AND CONTEMPORARY ISSUES (1986).

[44] *See, e.g.,* ALASKA STAT. § 47.10.082 (1984); MICH. COMP. LAW § 712A.4 (1989); UTAH CODE ANN. § 78-3A-25 (1987). As one court has stated:

> The common thread running throughout the Juvenile Code is that the court must consider the child's best interests in making all placements whether at the dispositional hearing or the review hearing.

In re Loretta Diane Shue, 63 N.C. App. 76, 303 S.E.2d 636 (1983), *modified on other grounds*, 311 N.C. 586, 319 S.E.2d 567 (1984).

CHAPTER 2

The Child's Evolving Capacities
Articles 5 and 14

James Garbarino

Introduction

Article 5 of the Convention on the Rights of the Child calls upon nations to approach children developmentally—i.e., "in a manner consistent with the evolving capacities of the child." U.S. policy has made progress in this regard in recent decades. Several examples make this clear. First, the American legal system has come to regard children as neither automatically competent nor incompetent. Rather, legal system participants are encouraged to match practices to the specific capacities of the child at a particular point in that child's developement.

Second, policy and practice with regard to children with disabilities has moved to a similar recognition that the child's maturing capacities constitute the principal criterion for determining appropriate education, therapy, and support. Third, a broad national awareness is coming into being, i.e., that there are many crucial opportunities to promote development in the early years of a child's life.

This increased awareness dictates a range of programs and policies designed to ensure that families respect and nurture the child as capacities evolve and develop. But all these improvements—which are very much in the spirit of the Convention—rest upon our understanding of child development, of the child's evolving capacities.

This chapter addresses "the evolving capacities of the child." What are these capacities that should govern the way adults provide guidance and direction? What does it mean to act "in a manner consistent with" these evolving capacities? The key to answering this question is a model of child development that illuminates the role of the adult as a teacher in the life of the child, it lies in understanding what it means to approach a child developmentally.[1]

19

■ WHAT IS CHILD DEVELOPMENT?

What is child development? In the broadest sense, of course, it is the process of becoming fully human.[2] A child's experiences combine with a child's biological givens, and from this mixture emerges a complete person, ready for the challenges of day-to-day life— as a student, as a worker, as a friend, as a family member, and as a citizen. To succeed in these roles children need to be rooted in the basic skills of modern life. They need to become socially competent. They must know who they are. They must have a secure and positive sense of their own identity. They must become proficient in thinking and speaking clearly. They must learn to understand the many ways people communicate with one another. The foundation of this understanding is the child's emergent capacity to *know* in the broadest sense of the word, for everything else is tied to this capacity.

■ THE MEANING OF COGNITIVE DEVELOPMENT

When we speak of cognitive development, we are interested in changes in the way children acquire and use knowledge. There are two major themes in the study of cognitive development.[3] Both have something to say about a child's knowledge. The first, however, is most often concerned with measuring the speed and power of the child as an information processor. Why and how are some children more effective and efficient in processing, storing, and discerning patterns in the information available from their senses? This has been the organizing question for intelligence testing. The second theme, in contrast, emphasizes the styles of knowing that people exhibit in their ideas about the world. How do ideas and the ability to generate and use ideas arise? This is the second theme's central question. Of course, a concern for the whole child incorporates both themes: ideas without calculation are chaotic; calculation without substance is sterile.

Research and theory about cognitive development has matured substantially in recent decades, in both thematic areas. The Nineteenth Century saw the development of tests to measure an individual's intellect. In the late 1800's Sir Francis Galton prepared a battery of tests to determine how effective different individuals were in discriminating among sights, sounds and other sensory input.[4] Within a few decades, derivatives of these tests were being used by the military and other institutions to categorize and classify people, and to place them in different jobs or schools. In the Twentieth Century researchers and testers have placed great emphasis on an individual's score in relation to standardized expectations for his or her age—the Intelligence Quotient (IQ score). A score of 100 indicates a match of performance with age; most scores are found between 90 and 110. Several instruments for measuring IQ have come to dominate the field, among them the Stanford-Binet test and the Wechsler Intelligence Scales.[5]

One of the important issues in research and theory dealing with intelligence is the degree to which intelligence is a general characteristic or attribute vs. a collection of abilities.[6] This is an area in which the field has shown a great deal of maturing in recent years. Early in the Twentieth Century the dominant view was that intelligence consisted of an inherited general factor that indicated a person's ability to think abstractly and to verbalize. Louis Terman proposed this view and labelled this factor "g" (general). Later Charles Spearman hypothesized that a second factor exists ("s") that accounts for mathematical and spatial reasoning.[7] As the decades have passed, "g" and "s" have been the subject of many empirical studies, and subject to theoretical critique.

Today, most experts recognize that intelligence includes many different abilities, abilities that may develop independently of each other. Intelligence is thus "multidimensional." While at some level there may be a foundation for learning and intellectual function that is general, the best picture of the human intellect portrays a set of characteristics and abilities, not one or two. James Guilford, for example, postulated 120 distinct intellectual abilities.[8] Some of these involve generating multiple alternatives to a stated problem (divergent thinking). Others exemplify arriving at a prespecified single solution to a problem (convergent thinking).

■ A NEW MODEL OF INTELLIGENCE

Perhaps the most highly evolved among current efforts to understand intelligence is the work of Robert Sternberg.[9] Sternberg's approach takes the concept of intelligence from an abstract quality to a feature of real life situations, and in so doing recognizes that there are several strategies for making sense of the world. He concludes that the best model contains three themes (a "triarchic" theory). The first is raw analytical power. He calls this "componential" to refer to the fact that it concerns the whole set of components contained in "traditional" thinking about intelligence. It refers to what goes on inside a person's head when thinking to solve problems, criticize hypotheses, make sense of sensory data, etc. This is information processing in the image of a computer. The second theme is "experiential," and refers to the ability to combine the knowledge and ideas at hand creatively and insightfully. The emphasis here is creating new arrangements of what one has experienced or learned as a way of mastering the world.

The third theme Sternberg calls "contextual" in the sense that it represents the ability to understand a particular environment's expectations and arrange to meet or change them. Here the emphasis is on reading the social realities and mastering them as a way to solve problems. Sternberg points out that conventional tests of intelligence play to the componential theme. Guilford's approach, with the addition of creativity, allows the identification of the experiential. But "life" offers an opportunity for the contextual to show its stuff. One of the important implications of Sternberg's approach is this principle: you only know as much about a person's intelligence as you permit yourself to know by the range of assessments you make. A narrow look at information processing may only permit expression of the componential, just as a test confined to creativity and insight will only be good for uncovering the experiential. And, only assessing situationally defined competence (be it on the streets or in the school) will only measure the contextual.

The details of each theme and its origins are explored in Sternberg's 1985 book *Beyond IQ*.[10] He reports that modern assessments of IQ do a pretty good job on componential intelligence, but that once someone is in the normal range (100 or higher) IQ differences don't account for much in life success. However, this conclusion heightens the importance of preventing IQ deficiencies of the sort associated with early deprivations. Sternberg finds that three abilities comprise the experiential: being able to see what is the relevant information about a puzzling situation ("selective encoding"), being able to put a set of facts together in a way that sheds light in a consistent manner ("selective combinations"), and being able to see new analogies between objects or events previously thought to be unconnected or dissimilar ("selective comparison"). What is more, Sternberg finds that instruction can boost experiential intelligence (as it can componential and contextual as well, to some degree).

Sternberg's approach to contextual intelligence is based on how well people understand possible matches between situations and self. It involves seeing how social realities are organized and how to make them work towards one's goals (which may include reshaping or redirecting those social realities). Of course, the real thrust of Sternberg's approach is to argue that each person needs to do as much as possible to enhance all three themes and arrange life to play to strengths and shield weaknesses. In a diverse environment there are many opportunities to accomplish this. The keys are to avoid a debilitating deficiency of componential intelligence, to be encouraged to develop experiential intelligence, and to have access to opportunities to learn "the ropes" of social realities that offer important material and psychic rewards and resources. The threats are thus early deprivations that suppress componential intelligence, repressive environments that stultify creativity and foster rigid thinking, and being sidetracked or dead-ended into settings that are cut off from a society's principal resources. As we shall see, the purpose of early intervention programs to improve cognitive development is to deal with these risks in the lives of high risk poor children. At present all three threats are real, and disturbingly common for poor children, whether they be in rural poverty or the urban underclass. But, before turning to these intervention issues, we should recognize that the underpinning for such intervention is a broadly based commitment to promoting "the whole child." Cognitive development is rooted in the success of the child's overall progress.

Beyond the demands of everyday social competence, children need a sense of wonder to sustain cognitive development. They need to appreciate the wonder of being alive. We want them to do more than just learn to read. We want them to experience the joy of great literature and the pleasure of reading just for fun. We want them to do more than just cope with human relationships. We want them to know love and friendship. They need to be able to do more than just exist. We want them to know and appreciate the miracles of existence around us—in a flower, in a painting, in a blue sky, in a poem, in a tree, in a dance, in a creative moment. We want our children to spread their wings and fly, just as we want them to take root and live socially responsible lives. We want them to develop in all three domains of intelligence.

How is all this to happen? First and foremost, we must recognize that it is not going to happen automatically. If it is going to happen, it is going to be because the adults who care for children approach children "developmentally."

What does it mean to approach children developmentally?

- It means that we recognize the child's changing capacity. As children develop, their intellectual, physical, and emotional potentials change. The range of what is possible increases and alters. These changes in the child's capacity are what child development is all about. Many experts believe these changes take place in a regular sequence, in which the child faces first one, then another issue. Erik Erikson, for example, described eight "stages," beginning in infancy and extending through old age.[11] FIGURE 1 outlines the first four, the stages that apply to childhood in Erikson's approach; and the key developmental issues that the child faces along the way. Facing these issues is bound up in cognitive development to be sure. The child's capacity to experience "trust" depends upon the ability to recognize continuity and regularity in care and caregivers. To *feel* the world is a regular and safe place the child must be able to *know* the difference. To become autonomous the child must *know* who she or he is—and who not. To become confident about fantasy and reality the child must *know* the difference. To take on the role of student the child must *know* the basic behaviors required for mastery. The point in all this is that the processes of knowing are inextricably bound to the processes of feeling. Children develop as children, not as computers being reprogrammed as new software becomes available.

- It means that we recognize the capacity for change.[12] The child's life is not fixed in some unalterable genetic code that predetermines what and who the child will be. Each child contains the potential to be many different children, and caring adults can do much to shape which of those children will come to life. The worst thing that we can do is to assume that all is fixed. For example, when genetically identical twins are raised together or in very similar communities, they grow up to be very similar, even to the extent of having very similar IQ scores. However, when genetically identical twins grow up in very different environments, their IQ scores are likely to be much less similar. One study reported a correlation of .85 for identical twins reared separately but in similar communities, but only .26 for identical twins reared separately in dissimilar communities.[13] While recognizing that genetic heritage can (and usually does) make an important contribution to cognitive development, we must recognize that other biological influences can be powerful as well—e.g. nutrition that affects brain growth. What is more, we *must* recognize that the social environment a community provides will go a long way toward determining whether biological potential will bloom or wither, whether the biological underpinnings of cognitive development will be fulfilled or denied by experience.[14]

- It means that we recognize that development is the process by which the child forms a picture or draws a map of the world and his or her place in it. As children draw these maps they move forward on the paths they believe exist. If a child develops a map of the world which depicts people and places as hostile, and the child as an insignificant speck relegated to one small corner, we must expect troubled development of one sort or another: a life of suspicion, low self esteem, self denigration, and perhaps violence and rage. We can also expect a diminution of cognitive development, most likely in the experiential and contextual domains.

■ PRECONDITIONS FOR OPTIMAL DEVELOPMENT

What does it take for a child to form a realistic and positive map of the world, a map that will lead outward into the world with confidence and sympathy for love, trust, responsibility and beauty? It takes a world that offers to each family the means to meet a child's basic needs.[15] Such a family has access to health care so that children can grow strong and healthy. Early deprivation (including malnutrition) can suppress brain development and cognitive functioning. The child needs a family that has access to adequate employment and income. This provides the basis for *pro-social* contextual intelligence. And, it provides day-to-day stability in important caregiving relationships for the child. Such stability is crucial, in the early years most of all.

Whether or not children experience these essential ingredients is critical to their development. Threats to the physical health of a child can jeopardize mental and emotional development. Poverty can stunt intellectual development and impose stress that undermines social development. Instability of child care arrangements can threaten the child's sense of security and continuity.

Beyond these roots, what does the child need to develop experiential intelligence? It takes adults, parents, teachers, caregivers—who recognize the processes of development at work in the life of the child and who seize upon occasions to interact with the child and thus create an environment in which the development of creativity can go forward, so that experiential intelligence can flourish.

Much of our thinking about how children develop intellectually relies upon the pioneering work of the Swiss psychologist Jean Piaget.[16] Piaget's view of development is based upon the idea that children form concepts that represent reality. As their brains mature and they experience the world, they either fit these experiences into existing concepts (a process that Piaget called "assimilation") or they adjust or change the schemes to make sense of new or incongruous ideas (a process that Piaget labelled "accommodation"). Thus, for example, the child develops a scheme "dog" to cover four-legged furry creatures, and is able to accept the fact that German Shepherds, Collies, and Dachshunds are all dogs. But the child must alter his or her concept of "dog" to acknowledge the fact that some four-legged furry creatures are not dogs, but rather are horses, cows, cats, or llamas.

But, Piaget is not the whole story. The child does not, will not, can not develop in a social vacuum. There is more to development than maturation. Development is a social process, for it is through relationships with people that the child learns about the world and how it works.[17] Who points out that this four-legged, furry creature is not a dog but is rather a cat? Who reassures the child when he or she is frightened? Who affirms the child's need to play and daydream? Who guides and helps the child in learning society's rules and beliefs? Who encourages the child to think creatively— to engage in selective encoding, selective combination, and selective comparison?

Child development proceeds through and because of social relationships. The earliest and most important of these are the early social relationships between infant and parents (and others who care for the child). These "attachment" relationships are the training ground and the foundation for subsequent social relationships. Problems in early attachments tend to translate into general social problems, cognitive deficiencies, and emotional difficulties. Deprive the child of crucial social relationships and the child will not thrive and move forward developmentally, but will fall back, regress, stop.

What the child needs are responses that are *emotionally validating but developmentally challenging*.[18] This is what moves development forward. When the child says, "Car go," she needs the person who responds with a smile, "Yes, honey. That's right, the car is going. And where do you think the car is going?" The child needs people to teach him how to be patient, how to follow through, how to behave responsibly, as well as how to tell dogs from cats, A's from B's, and 1's from 2's. A child needs people who care for *that* child, know *that* child, and who validate *that* child emotionally.

The psychologist Lev Vygotsky went beyond Piaget's concept of development to emphasize the role of the adult as a teacher in the child's development.[19] The good teacher understands the distance between what the child can accomplish alone and what the child can do when helped by an adult or a more competent peer. Vygotsky called this "the zone of proximal development." It is the critical territory for interventions that seek to stimulate and support the child's cognitive development. When a child's environment does not do these things "naturally," intervention is needed to change that fact, hopefully, by changing the child's permanent environment rather than by trying to inoculate the child against that environment (a strategy of dubious validity and very limited success). The key is to shift the child's environment into operating effectively in the zone of proximal development. This means shaping the behavior of adults in the child's life.

TEACHING AS THE KEY TO DEVELOPMENT

Indeed, it is not so much our capacity for learning that distinguishes humans from other species, but rather our capacity to teach. All animals can learn. But only humans consciously set out to teach as a way of facilitating development. Human beings construct elaborate and sophisticated cultures and teach them to children in ways that are a marvel to behold. It is because we teach that we do not need to reinvent the wheel each generation or discover fire over and over again. Children learn from adults in many ways, some of which are inadvertent on the adult's part. Deliberate teaching plays a special role in this learning process, however.

What does all this mean for understanding child development, and "the evolving capacities of the child?" Children aren't simply pre-programmed computers. Their development will not move forward most efficiently if we simply turn them loose with the message "go forth and learn!" nor if we totally plan every detail in their experience. Children need to be treated like honored dignitaries from a foreign land who do not yet understand the language and know the customs. They need to be respected but also to be taught the ropes.

What else do we need to know to assess the role of early intervention in cognitive development? We need to know that the development of children reflects a mixture of forces and influences, some conscious, some not. Unconscious forces play an important role in the child's life. Early evidence of unconscious processes comes from the toddler's sudden resistance to going to sleep, acquiring imaginary playmates, having nightmares, and the invention of monsters, ghosts, witches, and bogeymen. Fantasy and play (and particularly pretend play) are vital to a child's development. Through them, children have a chance to explore the meaning of the world around *and inside* them. In this sense, play is the child's vocation. It serves both the need to work through unconscious forces and the need to practice basic life skills.[20]

This is what we mean by child development, by "the evolving capacities of the child." The U. N. Convention on the Rights of the Child mandates that governments do all they can—consistent with local conditions —to encourage and support parents and other adults to approach children developmentally. This means that adults view their task as one of preserving a child's options by doing all that is within their means to provide a nurturant and supportive environment in which cognitive and affective development can proceed. It means that they seek to gradually empower the child to fulfill his or her rights in ever broader ways. Thus, while a young child will probably make few if any major decisions about issues of residence, education, or employment, an older child will be permitted to participate in this process of decision-making (*at a level commensurate with his or her abilities*). The capacity of children to be empowered in the matter of exercising their rights changes. That is the essence of development, and the fundamental meaning of the Convention's mandate that children be treated in a manner compatible with their evolving capacities. Research has identified a wide range of threats to the evolving capacities of children—malnutrition and health care deficiencies, violence, lack of stimulation, lack of responsiveness to the child's exploratory and early verbal behavior, etc. How do these deficiencies impede the child from exercising his or her rights? As a function of modernization, the key is the child's ability to exercise the right to an adequate education (articles 28 and 29).

Many children start school below the minimum level of componential intelligence (IQ of less than 90), but the biggest problem seems to be cultural, in the sense that many children haven't been immersed in the "academic culture" because they don't see people reading, don't have models of success in school, aren't familiar with the kinds of things that happen in school.[21]

Being thus out of sync with school, they fall behind, more and more as the years pass and their paths of cognitive development (often in all three domains) become less and less attuned to school success. How does school failure perpetuate the cycle in which children are denied their fundamental rights? In modern societies school failure usually signals lack of the credentials that are used to screen entrants to the work force, a pattern of socialization that makes someone out of touch with the style needed for job success (and thus deficient in the contextual intelligence relevant to job success, no matter how useful it is "on the streets"), and even some deficiencies in conventional (i.e. componential) intelligence. Thus, school failure perpetuates the cycle of deprivation in several ways, with cognitive development being directly involved particularly from a perspective informed by a triarchic model of intelligence.

Conclusion

The United Nations Convention on the Rights of the Child challenges societies to approach children developmentally. In a modern society like the United States, the focal point for this challenge lies in the matter of school success. The high demands made by the modern economy for educational success make it incumbent upon public and private institutions to support the child's "right to an education" in a broad and far-reaching manner. It demands that each child's right to be treated in a developmentally appropriate manner—from birth onward—receive a high priority in policy and practice.

At present, many children do not receive this early support. The problems of child maltreatment and poverty translate into developmentally inappropriate treatment of children, treatment that stunts growth and development. Taking steps to ensure developmentally appropriate treatment for each child in the first years of life is a vital piece of any effort to meet the challenge of the Convention. Early development sets the stage and lays the foundation for school success—the principal modern context in which the child's evolving capacities do get recognized.

■ FIGURE 1: STAGES OF CHILD DEVELOPMENT [ERIK ERIKSON (1950)]

Stage I: Infancy Basic Trust vs. Mistrust (birth to 18 months)

The infant needs to develop a sense of security, feeling that the world is a trustworthy place. This comes from establishing a safe and nurturing relationship with primary caregivers—most notably parents (and usually the mother). This period emphasizes basic sensory and intellectual growth.

Stage II: Toddler Autonomy vs. Shame (18 to 36 months)

The toddler needs to develop a sense of being able to do things on his or her own. This includes walking well alone and beginning to master basic communication through words and gestures.

Relationships with parents, brothers and sisters, and caregivers are important in providing opportunities for learning and demonstrating these basic skills. Learning to control bodily functions is very important. Piaget observed the emergence of basic intellectual operations through the senses of touch, sight, smell, and hearing in this period.

Stage III: Preschool Initiative vs. Guilt (3 to 5-1/2 years)

The preschooler needs to become confident about testing the limits of individual freedom and group responsibility, of fantasy and reality, of what feels good and what is permissible. Intellectual skills become more sophisticated and language matures rapidly. There is need to come to terms with social reality in a significant way, but in a manner that does not frighten the child from believing in self worth.

Stage IV: Elementary School Industry vs. Inferiority (5-1/2 to 12 years)

This is the time when children take up the important tasks of becoming an active participant in the culture beyond the family. School means learning basic academic skills, basic skills in making and keeping friends, and learning how to live in groups with adult guidance. Children develop their characteristic style for working on projects and for presenting themselves to the world. This is a time of consolidating the child's inner life in preparation for the special challenges that adolescence brings. Piaget identified important maturing of the child's ability to think and reason, thus laying the foundation for more fully adult-like reasoning, the task to be mastered in adolescence. Freud called this period the Latency Stage, to indicate that the powerful urges of infancy and early childhood were under control, while the sexual impulses of puberty were yet to come to the surface.

Footnotes

[1] J. Garbarino, *Early Intervention in Cognitive Development as a Strategy for Reducing Poverty*, in GIVING CHILDREN A CHANCE (G. MILLER, ed. 1989).

[2] J. Garbarino and Associates, Children and Families in the Social Environment.

[3] R. J. Sternberg, Beyond IQ, (1985).

[4] *Id.*

[5] *Id.*

[6] *Id.*

[7] *Id.*

[8] Guilford, *Creativity*, 5 Am. Psychologist 444 (1965). 9. *See supra* note 3.

[10] *Id.*

[11] E. Erikson, Childhood and Society (1950).

[12] *See supra* note 2.

[13] Bronfenbrenner, *The Ecology of the Family as a Context for Human Development Research Perspectives*, 22 Dev. Psychology 7 (1986).

[14] Bronfenbrenner, Moen, & Garbarino, Families and Communities. In Review of Child Development Research. (R. Park ed. 1984).

[15] J. Garbarino, The Future as if It Really Mattered. (1988)

[16] *See supra* note 2.

[17] L. Vygotsky, Thought and Language. (1986)

[18] J. Garbarino, E. Guttman, and J. Seeley, The Psychologic Battered Child. (1986).

[19] *See supra* note 17.

[20] V. Paley, Boys and Girls: Superheroes in the Doll Corner (1987).

[21] J. McLane, and G. McNamee, Early Literacy. (1990)

CHAPTER 3

A Guide to Linguistic Interpretation of the Convention on the Rights of the Child
Articles 1, 4, 41 and 45

Cynthia Price Cohen

Introduction

Ultimately, no law, whether it is local, national or international, can be understood until it has been interpreted and applied to a given set of circumstances by some "authoritative source."[1] The authoritative source could be an arbitration panel, an administrative hearing or other similar body, as long as the source is recognized as having the authority to interpret the text of the legal material it is reviewing.

In the case of the Convention on the Rights of the Child,[2] that authoritative source will be the Committee on the Rights of the Child. The Committee will be made up of ten "experts of high moral standing and recognized competence in the field" covered by the Convention.[3] They will be elected from among the nationals of States Parties to the Convention and will act in their personal capacities, not as representatives of their governments.[4] Once the Convention on the Rights of the Child goes into force, States Parties have two years in which to submit their first reports.[5] Only then can there be a definitive statement as to the meaning of the many rights, phrases and clauses in the Convention.

While an authoritative source is usually free to interpret the text before it in any way that seems reasonable or in any manner that is logical, where it is practicable, the interpretation is usually based upon the legislative history of the text, with reference to existing legal precedents. The Convention on the Rights of the Child is a long and somewhat complicated treaty. Most of the text is the result of carefully negotiated compromises among delegations from extremely diverse backgrounds.[6] Despite the fact that many of the rights are contained in other international human rights treaties, these rights have been reinterpreted by the United Nations Working Group, which drafted the Convention, in order to make them clearly applicable to children. Moreover, the Convention protects rights that have never, previously been included in an international human rights treaty.[7] Undoubtedly, the intent of the drafters contained in the Convention's legislative history, known as the *"travaux preparatoire"*, will be of singular importance in guiding the work of the Committee on the Rights of the Child.

While every paragraph of the Convention on the Rights of the Child has a significance of its own, certain articles and paragraphs were more controversial than others and, consequently, required lengthy negotiations.[8] Some articles contain phrases and clauses which were taken from other treaties and, therefore, already have a settled meaning.[9] However, much of the Convention's text is made up of concepts and language that is new in intentional law. It is the purpose of this chapter to point out what can be referred to as "obligatory words" and "limitation clauses," so as to give the reader a better understanding of the significance of certain provisions in the Convention and, in addition, to provide the reader with a brief glimpse into the deliberative process.

After a short introduction to linguistic subtleties contained in the texts of human rights treaties, in general, and how these effect interpretation of the Convention, articles 1, 4, 41 and 45 will be used as models of the deliberative process. While articles 1, 4 and 41 are part of the substantive portion of the Convention, they do not guarantee rights, but address technical matters having to do with States Parties' application of the Convention. Article 45 is purely procedural. Since they do not deal directly with rights, none of these articles have been discussed by the other authors in this book.

■ OBLIGATORY WORDS AND LIMITATION CLAUSES

A. Obligatory Words in Human Rights Treaties

In ratifying a human rights treaty, States Parties bind themselves to observe certain standards concerning the rights protected by the treaty. The extent of the States Parties' treaty obligation is indicated in the text by such words as "ensure," "respect" and "recognize." In the Convention on the Rights of the Child these words are almost always prefaced by a phrase such as "States

Linguistic Analysis

Parties shall...," the word which follows indicates what the State must do or not do to protect that right.

In the accepted hierarchy of treaty terminology, a State Party's promise to "ensure" a right denotes the highest degree of obligation. The word "ensure" requires more than mere non-interference with the exercise of a right; it requires a State Party to take positive measures, legislative and otherwise, to make sure that the right can be effectively exercised.[10] The only treaty language which is stronger than the promise to "ensure" a right, is the statement of a right in a form that is absolute. For example, article 6, paragraph 1 of the International Covenant on Civil and Political Rights states:

Every human being has the inherent right to life. This right shall be protected by law. No one shall be arbitrarily deprived of his life.[11]

All of the rights in that Covenant are written in this assertive, absolute fashion.

By contrast, none of the rights in the International Covenant on Economic, Social and Cultural Rights are stated as absolute. All of those rights are written in the form which begins "States Parties to the present Covenant...."[12] Of the ten rights protected, only one binds States Parties to "ensure" a right.[13] The majority of articles in this Covenant require States Parties merely to "recognize" the right.

It should be noted that the word "recognize" is considered to be among the weakest of the obligatory words used in human rights treaties.[14] Unless followed by specific set of clearly stated obligations, which it is in the Covenant on Economic, Social and Cultural Rights, it only obligates the States Parties to refrain from obstructing exercise of the protected right. Somewhere between the criteria of "recognize" and "ensure" lies the obligatory word "respect." Although generally considered to demand more than mere "recognition" of a right, it does not require States Parties to take the positive steps toward guaranteeing the exercise of a right that are inherent in the word "ensure."[15]

B. Obligatory Words in the Convention on the Rights of the Child

Unlike the two human rights covenants, each of which have a distinctly different textual style, all of the various linguistic drafting forms mentioned above can be found in the Convention on the Rights of the Child. This is not surprising, since the Convention protects the full range of human rights: civil-political, economic-social-cultural and humanitarian. What is curious is that, in the Convention, the civil and political rights are not uniformly stated as absolutes. In fact, with few exceptions, articles in the Convention on the Rights of the Child have been written in the "States Parties..." format. One rather surprising exception to this rule is article 16, which protects the child's right to privacy.[16] This is the only article which was drafted in the absolute fashion of the rights protected by the Covenant on Civil and Political Rights. Just why article 16 was drafted in a style so affirmative and so different from the rest of the Convention is far from clear. Yet, this strong guarantee of the child's right to privacy has resulted in the child's being given a right which positively and unquestionably supports his or her individual dignity. It is a right which is not always guaranteed to adults.[17]

Of the three obligatory words described above, the one which appears most frequently in the Convention on the Rights of the Child is the word "ensure." It was used thirty-two times in the substantive portion of the Convention[18] and its frequency reflects the degree of seriousness and commitment that delegates gave to the rights of the child. "Recognize" appears in seventeen places[19] and "respect" in ten.[20] Obligatory words are almost always included in the first paragraph of an article and then are altered or repeated in subsequent paragraphs.

Unfortunately, the task of interpreting the Convention on the Rights of the Child will be more complicated than it might seem from the simple explanation of obligatory words above. These words are rarely used alone. More frequently, they appear in conjunction with other words, which may either strengthen or weaken the obligation. For example, "States Parties *shall* respect" carries a slightly stronger degree of obligation than does the basic phrase "States Parties respect." On the other hand, addition of the word *undertake*, as in "States Parties *undertake* to respect," would indicate a lesser degree of obligation, since the promise to "undertake" an obligation, arguab-

Linguistic Analysis

ly, requires only a good faith effort for a State Party to be in compliance, and does not necessarily require success.

Interestingly, there are many places in the Convention where States Parties are not directly obliged to give effect to a particular right, but are nonetheless obliged to act in a way which supports that right. This obligation is usually couched in terms of what a State Party "shall" do. For example, an article may contain a paragraph which states that "States Parties *shall* promote," "protect," "pursue" or "encourage" something.[21] Note, also that the word "shall," here, as when it is in combination with "ensure," creates a high degree of obligation to do that something. One interesting use of the word "shall" can be found in article 30, where it is said that a right "*shall not* be denied."

Finally, one peculiarity of the Convention on the Rights of the Child is the frequency with which the word "appropriate" appears. This is not a word which is common to international human rights treaties.[22] Yet, in the substantive portion of the Convention there are forty-three places where the word "appropriate" has been utilized to convey what is, arguably, a measurable, but imprecise, standard.[23] This proliferation of the word "appropriate" can be viewed two ways. First, it can be seen as a reflection of the degree to which the language of the Convention is built on compromises. Second, it can be seen as a practical device, capable of evaluation and application, which, because of its flexibility, will be amenable to application over a period of years in which theories of children's rights may change the expectation of what is "appropriate". Moreover, it can also lend itself to an individualized State-by-State analysis of treaty compliance. In other words, given the extremes of cultural diversity, what is "appropriate" in one country may well be "inappropriate" elsewhere.[24]

It should be remembered that the Convention on the Rights of the Child is the product of ten years of negotiation.[25] During that period of time, delegates came and went. Participating governments changed, as did the internal politics and policies within those governments which were continuously represented. Compromises were hammered out, often ending, however, in an unexplained and uneven use of obligatory words.

Linguistic Analysis

The Working Group's "second reading" deliberations, a process through which the original text of a treaty is reviewed and changes are made, led to the correction of most of these inconsistencies. However, any failures or omissions on the part of the Working Group could reasonably be attributed to the fact that it was simply not possible for governments to satisfactorily renegotiate and redraft every paragraph in the Convention on the Rights of the Child within the short period of time allotted to the participants. Any remaining discrepancies or weaknesses will undoubtedly have to be worked out by the Committee on the Rights of the Child, through its capacity as textual interpreter.

C. Limitation Clauses in Human Rights Treaties

No linguistic analysis of human rights treaties would be complete without drawing attention to limitation clauses. A limitation clause is a statement in an article that outlines the circumstances under which a particular right may be denied.[26] In other words, a right which is followed by a limitation clause is never absolute.

There are limitation clauses in most human rights treaties, but unlike the limitation clause in the second paragraph of article 29 in the Universal Declaration of Human Rights, no human rights treaties have limitation clauses which are applicable to the entire text. This is rather curious, since the language of these individual clauses is modeled after that of the Universal Declaration, which states:

> *In the exercise of his rights and freedoms, everyone shall be subject only to such limitations as are determined by law solely for the purpose of securing due recognition and respect for the rights and freedoms of others and of meeting the just requirements of morality, public order and the general welfare in a democratic society.*[27]

Limitation clauses in human rights treaties have been confined to specific areas: freedom of movement, expression, religion, assembly and association.[28]

Linguistic Analysis

The limitation clauses of the Covenant on Civil and Political Rights, which are found in the articles on freedom of assembly and association, are roughly identical:

> *No restrictions may be placed on the exercise of this right other than those which are necessary in a democratic society in the interests of national security or public safety, public order (*ordre public*), the protection of public health or morals or the protection of the rights and freedoms of others.*[29]

Freedom of movement is similar, having only slight differences in the introductory language.[30] By contrast, the text of the article on freedom of religion[31] not only omits references to a "democratic society", but also to "national security" and replaces the words "public order (*ordre public*)" with the single word "order" and makes a similar deletion of the word "public" in reference to "public health." The article on freedom of expression, on the other hand, does include "national security" and "public order (*ordre public*)" and "public health", but omits the "fundamental rights and freedoms of others," inserting instead a phrase protecting the "rights or reputations" of others.[32]

D. Limitation Clauses in the Convention on the Rights of the Child

To a major extent, limitation clauses in the Convention on the Rights of the Child replicate those of the Covenant on Civil and Political Rights. There are limitations on the right to freedom of movement, to free expression, religion, assembly and association. These articles have some minor, insignificant, variations in wording, that are probably due to Working Group oversight, rather than any grand scheme to alter the language of the Covenants. The most important difference between the limitation clauses of the Covenants and those in the Convention is that in the Convention there are only four limitation clauses,[33] whereas in the Convenant there are five. This is because freedom of assembly and association appear in the same article of the Convention.

39

■ MODELS OF THE DELIBERATIVE PROCESS

The text of each article in the Convention on the Rights of the Child has its own individual history. Some articles can trace their origins to a draft Convention, presented to the Commission on Human Rights in 1979 by the government of Poland and used as a model text by the Working Group.[34] Other articles were the result of drafts tabled by government delegations,[35] while still others were sponsored by non-governmental organizations [NGOs].[36] Most articles were altered to some extent during the first reading deliberative process, as delegates sought to modify texts to comply with the standards of their national laws. Examination of the Working Group's second reading textual review reveals that a few articles sparked intense debate, while others were amended somewhat haphazardly.[37]

None of the articles to be examined as examples of the deliberative process directly protects a child's rights. Instead, they are either definitional, administrative or procedural. Each of the articles to be discussed has in some way been modified during the course of the drafting process. Articles 4 and 41 were relatively uncontroversial, and caused correspondingly little debate. Article 45 brought much discussion, along with unclear, heated opposition from Venezuela.[38] As might be expected article 1, which defines the word "child", was a source of conflict and disagreement throughout the drafting process and continues to provoke intense differences of opinion among those States which have already signed or ratified the Convention.[39]

A. Article 1 and the Rights of the Unborn Child

Drafting of the Convention on the Rights of the Child was undertaken in conjunction with the 1979 United Nations International Year of the Child [IYC]. As a part of this celebration, which honored the twentieth anniversary of the 1959 Declaration of the Rights of the Child,[40] the Polish government proposed that a treaty should be created which would put into legally-binding form the ideals of the 1959 Declaration.

The Polish government submitted two draft models of the Convention on the Rights of the Child to the Commission on Human Rights, which was the U.N. branch charged with drafting the Convention. The first model was a virtual replication of the Declaration, with the addition of a simple implementation mechanism.[41] This model was highly criticized, not only because its language was too general, but also because it lacked a definition of the word "child."[42]

The second Polish model Convention was much longer and worded in language which was more specific. This model became the basis for all deliberations by the Working Group to which the Commission on Human Rights had assigned the task of drafting this new human rights treaty.

The second Polish model defined the word "child" in the following manner:

According to the present Convention a child is every human being from the moment of his birth to the age of 18 years unless, under the law of his state, he has attained his age of majority earlier.[43]

Working Group debates over article 1 focused on three areas: the beginning of childhood, the upper age of childhood and the matter of majority.[44] As for the beginning of childhood, States with laws protecting the child from the moment of conception objected vigorously to limiting the rights of the Convention to those children which had already been born. Other States, those with liberal abortion laws, just as strenuously opposed any definition of the word "child" which would clash with their national legislation on this matter. This conflict was resolved by the Working Group when it agreed to a proposal by the Moroccan government to simply delete from the text the words "from the moment of his birth."[45] This agreement, in effect, left the beginning of childhood to be defined by each individual State Party.

Positions regarding the highest age limit on childhood varied. A few delegations sought to lower the age to fifteen to correspond to the upper limit of IYC.[46] Other delegations objected to this on the basis of their national legislation, which placed the age at eighteen.[47] There was also some concern about reference to the age of majority. Some Working Group members informally discussed the possibility of introducing concept of "full legal capacity" or some form of consistent maximum age. However, since under most national legislation the age of majority varies depending on the subject matter, the final text as adopted at the 1980 drafting session, and thus the text of the "first reading," was the same as that in the Polish model, but for the deletion discussed above. Second reading review brought no textual

Linguistic Analysis

changes, except for a tightening of the section regarding the concept of minority.[48]

During the second reading of the Convention, the matter of article 1 and the rights of the unborn child was raised again and was again rejected by the Working Group.[49] Malta and Senegal, supported by the observer from the Holy See, proposed that new language be added referring to the "moment of conception."[50] The negative sentiment in the Working Group was so intense and opposition to the proposals so strong that they were quickly withdrawn by those governments.[51]

All drafting of the Convention was done on the basis of consensus, a process which does not so much denote support, as it does a lack of objection. Objection by even one delegation would have been enough to bring about a proposal's defeat.[52] Rather than face long, wrangling, non-productive debates, it was the general practice for governments to voluntarily withdraw their unpopular proposals.

The Maltese-Senegalese willingness to give up the fight over article 1 was, to a certain extent, the outcome of an earlier agreement in the Working Group to include a quotation from the Declaration of the Rights of the Child in the ninth paragraph of the Convention's preamble. The quoted part of the Declaration reads:

> ...the child, by reason of his physical and mental immaturity, needs special safeguards and care, including appropriate legal protection before as well as after birth.[53]

Even though it is a well-recognized rule of international law that the preamble of a treaty has no binding effect,[54] members of the Working Group were so concerned that this language might be interpreted as protecting the rights of the fetus that they only agreed to its inclusion on the grounds that the *travaux preparatoire* would contain the following statement:

> In adopting this preambular paragraph, the Working Group does not intend to prejudice the interpretation of article 1 or any other provision of the Convention by States Parties.[55]

This statement was, obviously, intended to support and maintain the position of the Working Group that the beginning of childhood was to be defined according to national law.

The inclusion in this statement of the words "any other provision" indicates that the statement is also meant to apply to the right to life provisions of article 6, as well. In interpreting article 6 it should be remembered that the right to life language replicates the wording of the Covenant on Civil and Political Rights.[56] Note, too, its use of the weakest obligatory term "recognize" rather than the strongest, "ensure."[57] This, coupled with the word "inherent," supports the notion that the drafters did not in any way intend that this right should be absolute or that it should apply to the fetus. Moreover, linking the paragraph 1 right to life with the second paragraph on "survival and development" leads to the conclusion that article 6 was meant to protect only the living child.[58]

B. Article 4 and Progressive Implementation

Article 4 began its life as the second paragraph of the article on discrimination in the second Polish model Convention.[59] It set forth the rule that all States Parties:

> shall undertake appropriate measures individually and within the framework of international cooperation, particularly in the areas of economy, health and education for the implementation of the rights recognized in this Convention.

According to the *travaux preparatoire*, at the time it was adopted there was very little debate on this text in the Working Group. It was decided that this should be a separate article, that the types of "appropriate measures" should be clarified and that references to particular "areas" should be deleted. The new text of what was then numbered as article 5 was:

> The States Parties to the present Convention shall undertake all appropriate administrative, legislative and other measures, in accordance with their available resources, and where needed, within the framework of international cooperation, for the implementation of the rights recognized in this Convention.[60]

Linguistic Analysis

The hidden problem, which was not adequately addressed by this first draft, is the difference between the implementation standards applied to civil-political rights and those applied to economic-social-cultural rights. Civil-political rights can never be linked to a national economic standard, since, unlike health and education, such rights as freedom of speech or religion cannot be said to involve a State in a major financial commitment. However, the way the first reading draft was worded, all rights, including civil-political, would have been contingent upon a nation's available resources.

The civil-political rights problem of article 4 was reopened for debate during the second reading. Several Western delegations, including the United States, proposed simple deletion of the phrase dealing with "available resources," on the ground that its inclusion in the text would weaken international standards already set by the Covenant on Civil and Political Rights. Taking an opposing position, delegations from less developed countries asserted that, if the phrase were to be deleted, their economic difficulties would interfere with their ability to totally comply with the Convention's requirements. Finally, a small drafting group, composed of the United States, Senegal, India and Sweden was able to devise compromise language which took into consideration the concerns of all delegations.[61] The article was divided into two sentences. The first sentence stated a basic rule for implementation of the entire Covention. The second sentence, however, modified the first, in that it addressed the different standards to be applied to economic, social and cultural rights:

> *States parties shall undertake all appropriate legislative, administrative, and other measures for the implementation of the rights recognized in this Convention. In regard to economic, social and cultural rights, States Parties shall undertake such measures to the maximum extent of their available resources and, where needed, within the framework of international cooperation.*[62]

This second sentence, as well as the modifying phrases protecting the rights of the disabled child in article 23(4), the right to health in article 24(4) and the right to education in article 28(4) embody a principle known as "progressive implementation." This principle will enable countries, which are economically unable to comply fully with their treaty obligations, to ratify the Convention despite this obstacle. As long as a good faith effort is made, considering national resources, to implement the Convention over a period of time (i.e., progressively), incomplete compliance will not be a breach of the treaty.

C. Article 41 and Customary International Law

Unlike the two articles discussed above, the roots of article 41 cannot be traced to the second Polish model Convention. Article 41 is a direct result of concern among non-governmental organizations and government delegations that the final version of the Convention on the Rights of the Child might in some way weaken existing standards of law applicable to the child.[63] In effect, article 41 was devised as what might be called a "savings clause."

The original proposal for article 41 came from the delegation of Canada. After considerable discussion as to the importance of customary international law and the fact that the Canadian proposal did not make any reference to it, the article was adopted virtually as tabled, without resolving this issue:

> Nothing in this Convention shall affect any provisions that are more conducive to the realization of the rights of the child and may be contained in:
>
> (a) The law of a State Party; or
> (b) Any other international convention, treaty or agreement in force for that State.[64]

Customary international law is the name given to those practices which are so consistently followed by sovereign States that they can be said to comprise a body of unwritten law. No treaties need be involved, no ratification is necessary for a country to be brought to task for a violation of customary international law.[65]

As might be expected, there is no clear agreement among scholars as to the exact extent of the customary international law of human rights. Some scholars argue that the entire Universal Declaration of Human Rights has now been given sufficient international recognition to be considered applicable to all nations.[66] Other scholars are less expansive in their view.

However, there is little disagreement over the fact that, at the very least, there are now customary international norms against torture, discrimination and genocide.[67]

Since it was considered important for customary international law to be covered by the Convention's savings clause, this issue was addressed again during the second heading. The problem was how to add it without complicating the text. One suggestion was to draft a third clause, "c," which would separately specify customary international law.[68] Another proposal completely redrafted the entire article to achieve the same result.[69] Although there was little agreement within the Working Group as to how article 41 should be reworded, there was complete consensus that the purpose of the article was "to ensure that the Convention established a minimum standard of rights to be enjoyed by children."[70]

Interestingly, the compromise solution did not make any additions to the first reading text of article 41, but, rather, deleted most of the details of paragraph (b). In the final version of the Convention paragraph (b) of article 41 simply refers to "international law in force for that State."[71] The words "international law" were seen as including all forms of international law, whether in a formal written form or as custom.

D. Article 45 and Hidden Meanings in the Convention's Implementation

At first glance the implementation portion of the Convention on the Rights of the Child looks substantially like any other reviewing committee implementation procedure. States Parties elect members of the Committee, who then act in their own capacities and review the reports submitted by States Parties.[72] The Committee meets regularly and adopts its own rules of procedure.[73] Articles 43 and 44 have little that is new. The number of Committee members, the frequency of elections, meetings and reports are merely variations of the previously accepted scheme of other human rights treaties. The Convention's implementation innovations are to be found in article 45, which covers the sources from which the Committee may receive information.

Linguistic Analysis

The implementation mechanism of most human rights treaties makes no formal provision for the reviewing committee to receive any information on States Parties' treaty compliance, other than that submitted by the States Parties themselves or by other States Parties. Although it is clear that without some source of outside verification, a reviewing committee cannot accurately evaluate the States Parties' reports, only the Convention on the Elimination of all Forms of Discrimination Against Women has a procedure through which its Committee may obtain materials from United Nations specialized agencies.[74]

To correct this shortcoming, the reviewing committees of both the Covenant on Economic, Social and Cultural Rights[75] and the Convention Against Torture[76] drafted their rules of procedure to allow the Committee to receive outside information from NGO's and specialized agencies, even though no such provision is contained in those treaties' texts. Although it is rather early to begin speculation, it is considered likely that the Committee on the Rights of the Child will make similar arrangements in their rules of procedure. The reason for this optimism is that there is special wording in article 45, which is intended to make it clear that NGO's are expected to play a role in monitoring the Convention.

The Working Group's constructive interaction with the NGO Group[77] led to a proposal that paragraphs (a) and (b) of article 45, while including the United Nations Children's Fund (UNICEF) and other branches of the United Nations, should also specify future NGO activities relating to the Convention's implementation. In fact, one of the early Working Group proposals itemized the group of implementation participants as "UNICEF, specialized agencies and non-governmental organizations."

There was much discussion of this paragraph, most of it having to do with the singling out of UNICEF by name, since other United Nations branches, such as the International Labour Organisation, also have a commitment to children's rights. The ensuing debate revealed that the International Labour Organisation and the World Health Organization are "specialized agencies" of the United Nations, but that UNICEF, the United Nations High Commissioner for Refugees (UNHCR) and the International Committee of the Red Cross (ICRC) are not and, therefore, would be omitted from the monitoring process if not specifically named.[78]

Linguistic Analysis

While the Working Group was willing to name UNICEF in the text of the Convention, it was not willing to list other names. Reluctantly, despite the fact that it would have been a landmark both for NGOs and for treaty drafters, the Working Group deleted from the text the direct reference to NGO's. Instead, the compromise language makes reference to "other competent bodies." The *travaux preparatoire* clearly shows that, in addition to the UNHCR and ICRC, "other competent bodies" was also intended to encompass non-governmental organizations.[79]

The role outlined for NGO's and other monitoring participants is not just one of "watch dog," but it is also one of assistance. The information from NGOs, allowed for in their paragraph (a) role, will function to ensure that States Parties' reports are reliable and responsible.[80] The NGO's role under paragraph (b), on the other hand, is to provide the necessary aid and "technical assistance" which will maximize States Parties' ability to carry out their treaty obligations.[81] In this role NGO's may be asked to do such tasks as providing States Parties with legal assistance in redrafting their existing legislation to bring it into line with the requirements of the Convention. They may also be asked to offer other services, such as helping to set up schools and health facilities.[82]

The most significant aspect of article 45 is that, unlike other human rights treaties, where the implementation is somewhat accusatory or punitive, the theme of the implementation mechanism of the Convention on the Rights of the Child is based on the premise that all States Parties intend to honor the rights of children, but that in some cases they may have difficulty in doing so. The implementation mechanism of the Convention seeks to remedy this situation and, therefore, its emphasis is on facilitation.

Conclusion

The text of the Convention on the Rights of the Child reflects the fact that it is the product of many compromises. In some places it is merely a replication of the language of other international human rights treaties in a form applicable to children; in others the language is entirely new. In some instances it is clearly worded; in others it can be called linguistically unartful at best. One can only wonder at how such phrases as the article 34, "exploitative use of children in prostitution or other unlawful sexual practices" remained unaltered by the second reading. Surely, there cannot be an "unexploitative" form of child prostitution!

Of course, many of these anomalies can be linked to problems of translation and the fact that the official text must be produced in six different languages. One interesting outcome of this complicated process can be seen in article 39, which was originally proposed as an article on "rehabilitation." During the debates on article 39 the Soviet delegate objected to the use of the word "rehabilitation", saying that it has a special connotation in Russian. He explained that in his language the word "rehabiliation" was explicitly applied to cases of unlawful arrest, where, after what might have been extensive incarceration, the person was released and the ensuing reentrance into society was known as "rehabilitation." The attendant search by the drafters for alternative language ended in agreement on the phase "physical and psychological *recovery* and social *reintegration.*"[83]

Because of the general nature of most of the language of the Convention, the Committee on the Rights of the Child will have ample opportunity to interpret the text and to take into consideration evolving theories of child development, education and individual rights. The implementation portion of the Convention, since it includes a role for non-governmental organizations, makes it possible for the Committee to receive useful information from a wide variety of sources. This information will undoubtedly be important to the Committee's linguistic interpretation and clarification of the text of the Convention.

Footnotes

[1] *See* E. W. PATTERSON, JURISPRUDENCE: MEN AND IDEAS OF THE LAW (1953), 117-126.

[2] Convention on the Rights of the Child, U.N. Doc. A/Res/44/23 (1989).

[3] *Id.*, article 43(2).

[4] *Id.*

[5] *Id.*, article 44.

[6] *See* C.P. Cohen, *United Nations Convention on the Rights of the Child, Introductory Note*, 28 I.L.M. 1448 (1989) [hereinafter *I.L.M. note*]. Also

see Cohen and Naimark, *United Nations Convention on the Rights of the Child: Individual Rights Concepts and Their Significance for Social Scientists*, 46 AM. PSYCHOLOGIST, ____(1991) (in press).

[7] *I.L.M. note supra* note 6.

[8] *Supra* note 6.

[9] For a review of Comments by the Committee on Human Rights, which monitors the Covenant on Civil and Political Rights, concerning rights which are also contained in the Convention on the Rights of the Child, *see* Cohen, *General Comments by the Committee on Human Rights Regarding Articles of the International Covenant on Civil and Political Rights with Related Articles from the Convention*, INDEPENDENT COMMENTARY: UNITED NATIONS CONVENTION ON THE RIGHTS OF THE CHILD (C.P. Cohen, ed. 1988).

[10] *See* Buergenthal, *To Respect and Ensure: State Obligations and Permissible Derogations* in THE INTERNATIONAL BILL OF RIGHTS 77-78 (L. Henkin, ed. 1981).

[11] International Covenant on Civil and Political Rights, Dec. 16, 1966, 94 U.N.T.S. 171, G.A. Res. 2200 (xix), U.N. GAOR Supp. (No. 16) at 52, U.N. Doc. A/6316 (1966), article 6(1).

[12] *See* International Covenant on Economic, Social and Cultural Rights, G.A. Res. 2200 (xix), 21 U.N. GAOR Supp. (No. 16) at 49, U.N. Doc. A/6316 (1966), articles 6-15.

[13] *Id.* article 8.

[14] *See* Cohen, *Elasticity of Obligation and the Drafting of the Convention on the Rights of the Child*, 3 CONN J. INT'L. L. 71 (1987) at notes 29-32 and accompanying text.

[15] *Supra* note 10.

[16] *Supra* note 2, article 16.

[17] *Compare, id. with supra* note 11 at article 17 and Griswold v. Connecticut, 381 U.S. 479 (1965).

[18] In the Convention on the Rights of the Child the word "ensure" can be found in approximately eleven different modifying combinations of words. It is never alone, but is always accompanied by a modifying word or phrase. It is most frequently preceded by "shall take all ap-

propriate measures to" or merely by the word "shall," the former being somewhat weaker than the latter. Perhaps the two most unusual combinations of modifying words are the article 24 "shall *strive* to ensure" and the article 20 "shall *use their best efforts* to ensure recognition of." *See supra* note 2, articles 2(a), 2(2), 3(2), 3(3), 6(2), 7(2), 9(1), 9(4), 10(1), 17(1), 18(1), 18(3,) 20(2), 21(2), 21a, 21(c) 23(2), 23(3), 24(1), 24(2-b), 24(2d), 24(2e), 28(2), 32(2), 32(2c), 37, 38(1), 38(2), 40(2-a), 40(2b).

19 *Supra* note 2 at articles 6(1), 15(1), 17(1) 21, 21(b), 23(1), 23(2), 23(3), 24(1), 25, 26(1), 27(1), 28(1), 31(1), 32(1), 40(1).

20 *Supra* note 2, articles 2(1), 5, 8(1), 9(3), 10(2), 14(1), 14(2), 31(2), 38(1).

21 *Supra* note 2, articles 11(2), 23(4), 27(4), 28(3); 24(2); 4(2), 36 and 23(2).

22 The word "appropriate" was not used at all in the International Covenant on Civil and Political Rights. It appears but a few times in the Convention Against Torture and Other Cruel, Inhuman or Degrading Treatment or Punishment and the International Covenant on Economic Social and Cultural Rights and in the International Convention on the Elimination of All Forms of Racial Discrimination. It is only in the Convention on the Elimination of All Forms of Discrimination Against Women that one can find a similar repeated employment of the word "appropriate." In this treaty the repeated use of "appropriate" occurs eighteen times in sixteen articles.

23 *See supra* note 2, articles 2(2), 3(2), 4(1), 5, 8(2), 9(4), 12(2), 17, 18(2), 19(1), 19(2), 21(c), 21(d), 22(1), 22(2), 23(2), 23(4), 24(2), 24(2d) 24(3), 26(2), 27(3), 27(4), 27(4), 28(1b), 28(2), 31(1), 31(2), 32(2b), 32(2c), 33(1), 34, 35, 37(b), 39, 40(2bii), 40(2biii), 40(3d), 40(4). In most instances "appropriate" is the word which elaborates what States Parties are obligated to do. That is, "States Parties shall take all appropriate measures to..." But, it is also linked to numerous other words. Where States Parties are required to do something for which there is no specific standard, the word "appropriate" has been used. Thus, there are requirements of "appropriate guidance," "appropriate information," "appropriate arrangements," "appropriate opportunities" and there are requirements which apply "where appropriate," "if appropriate" or "as they consider appropriate."

[24] *See I.L.M. note, supra* note 6 at 1450-1451.

[25] The United Nations Working Group met for one week each year from 1979 to 1987, just prior to the full session of the Commission on Human Rights, of which it was a part. In 1988 the Working Group met twice for two weeks, the first session was held in January-February to complete the first draft of the Convention and the second session was during November-December to review the text in what is known as a "second reading."

[26] These are also known as "restriction" clauses. *Compare*: Kiss, *Permissible Limitations on Rights* in THE INTERNATIONAL BILL OF RIGHTS, (L. Henkin ed. 1981); Hartman, *Derogation from Human Rights Treaties in Public Emergencies*, 22 HARV. INT'L. L.J. 4-7 (1981); Higgins, *Derogations Under Human Rights Treaties*, 1976-1977, BRIT. Y.B. INT'L. 281; and Questiaux, *Question of the Human Rights of Persons Subjected to Any Form of Detention or Imprisonment*, 35 U.N. ESCOR, Comm. on Human Rights (Provisional Agenda Item 10) at 10-11, U.N. Doc. E/CN.4/Sub.2/1982/15 (1982).

[27] Universal Declaration of Human Rights, G.A. Res. 217(A), U.N. Doc. A/810, article 7 (1948).

[28] *See supra* note 11, articles 12, 18, 19, 21 and 22.

[29] *See supra* note 11, articles 21 and 22.

[30] *See supra* note 11, article 12.

[31] *Id*. at article 18.

[32] *Id*. at article 19.

[33] *Supra* note 2, articles 10, 13, 14 and 15.

[34] U.N. ESCOR Supp. (No.16); U.N. Doc. E/CN.4/1349 (1979), for a discussion of early stages in drafting the Convention *see* Cohen, *The Human Rights of Children*, 12 CAP. U.L. REV. 369 (1983).

[35] For history of proposals see Working Group Reports U.N. Doc. E/CN.4/1981)L.1575 (1981); U.N. Doc. E/CN.4/1982/L.41 (1982); U.N. Doc. 3/CN.4/1983/62 (1983); U.N. Doc. E/CN.4/1984/78 (1984); U.N. Doc. E/CN.4/1985/64 (1985); U.N. Doc. E/CN.4/1986/ (1986); U.N. Doc. E/CN.4/1987/25 (1987); U.N. Doc. E/CN.4/1988/28 (1988) and U.N. Doc. E/CN.4/1989/48 (1989).

36 For details of non-governmental activities *see* Cohen, *The Role of Non-Governmental Organizations in the Drafting of the Convention on the Rights of the Child*, 12 HUM. RTS. Q. 137 (1990). *See also* Cohen, *Juvenile Justice Provisions of the Draft Convention on the Rights of the Child*, 7 N.Y.L. SCH. J. HUM. RTS. 1 (1989).

37 *See supra* note 6.

38 *See* U.N. Doc. E/CN.4/1989/48 (1985) at paras. 660-666. *See also* U.N. Doc. E/CN.4/1988/28 (1988).

39 *See* U.N. Doc. E/CN.4/1989/48 (1989) at paras. 75-85. *See also* ratification document of the Holy See (1990).

40 Declaration of the Rights of the Child, 14 U.N. GAOR Supp. (No. 16); U.N. Doc. A/4054 (1959).

41 U.N. ESCOR Supp. (No. 4); U.N. Doc. E/CN.4/1292 (1978).

42 For a discussion of article 1 *see* P. Alston, *The Unborn Child and Abortion Under the Draft Convention on the Rights of the Child*, 12 HUM. RTS. Q. 156 (1990).

43 U.N. Doc. E/CN.4/B49 (1979), *supra* note 34.

44 *See* U.N. Doc. E/CN.4/L.1542 (1980) paras. 28-36.

45 *Id.* at paras. 30-31.

46 *Id.* at paras. 32-33.

47 *Id.* at paras. 32-36.

48 *Compare*, *supra* note 44 *with* U.N. Doc. E/CN.4/1989/WG1/WP.2 (1989).

49 *See* U.N. Doc. E/CN.4/1989/48 (1989) paras. 75-85. *See also supra* note 42.

50 U.N. Doc. E/CN.4/1989/48 (1989), paras. 76-77.

51 *Id.*

52 For an example of the problems involved in obtaining consensus *see id.* at paras. 600-622 and 732.

53 *See supra* note 50, paras. 32-47.

54 *See supra* note 50, paras. 165-172.

55 *Supra* note 50, para. 43.

[56] *See supra* note 11, article 6(1).
[57] *See supra* notes 10-15 and accompanying text.
[58] *See supra* note 42, 173-175.
[59] *Supra* note 34.
[60] For final text of first draft *see* U.N. Doc. E/CN.4/1989/WG.1/WP.2 (1989).
[61] *See* U.N. Doc. E/CN.4/1989/48 (1989) at paras. 170-177.
[62] *Supra* note 2.
[63] *See* U.N. Doc.E/CN.4/1986/39 (1986) at paras. 146-151 for Working Group debate.
[64] *See* U.N. Doc. E/CN.4/1989/48 (1989) at paras. 623-636.
[65] *See, among others*, L. HENKIN, R. C. PUGH, O. SCHACHTER AND H. SMITH, INTERNATIONAL LAW (1980) at 5-8, 12-17, 36-69.
[66] For background information relating to the importance of customary international law, sometimes refered to as *jus cogens, see* Vienna Convention on the Law of Treaties, U.N. Doc. A/CONF. 39/27 (1969) at article 53 and the Commentary of the International Law Commission contained in Documents of the Conference on the Law of Treaties 1968-1969, U.N. Doc. A/CONF/39/11 Add. 2 at 7 and 68. *See also* South West Africa Cases, 1966 I.C.J. 296-300 and Barcelona Tradition, Light and Power Co., Ltd., opinion of Judge Ammoun, 1970 I.C.J. 1 at 302-306.
[67] *See* Cohen, *International Fora for the Vindication of Human Rights Violated by the United States at Mexico City*, 21 N.Y.U. J. OF INT'L. L. & POL. 241 (1987).
[68] *Supra* note 63 at para. 623.
[69] *Id.* at para. 624.
[70] *Id.* at para. 631.
[71] *Id.* at paras. 633-636.
[72] *Supra* notes 3-5.
[73] *Id.*

Linguistic Analysis

[74] The Convention on the Elimination of All Forms of Discrimination Against Women, G.A. Res. 180, 34 U.N. GAOR Supp. (No. 46) at 193, U.N. Doc. A/34/46 (1979), article 22.

[75] *See* Rule 69, Provisional Rules of the Committee on Economic, Social and Cultural Rights, U.N. Doc. E/1989/L.9 (1989).

[76] *See* Rule 62, Provisional Rules of the Committee Against Torture, U.N. Doc. CAT/C/3 (1988).

[77] *Supra* note 36.

[78] *See* U.N. Doc. E/CN.4/1988/28 (1988).

[79] *Id.*

[80] *See supra* note 2, article 45(a).

[81] *Id.* at article 45(b).

[82] Many children's rights NGOs already have ongoing health and education programs in underdeveloped countries. These would provide a mutual starting point for a cooperative relationship with a State Party.

It should be noted that paragraph (d) also, impliedly, gives NGOs the right to make recommendations to the Committee which can be transmitted to the General Assembly.

[83] *See supra* note 78.

CHAPTER 4

Federal-State Implications of the Convention

Lawrence L. Stentzel, II

Introduction

The Convention on the Rights of the Child is the latest in a series of United Nations multilateral human rights treaties that have been proposed for U.S. ratification.[1] Most of these treaties have encountered opposition which has prevented or substantially delayed ratification by the United States. A recurring theme of opposition to such treaties is that they apply to certain matters that opponents believe lie primarily within the jurisdiction of the states under our federal system of government. A so-called "federal-state clause" is sometimes used as a means of modifying treaty obligations to take account of the federal character of some ratifying States and thereby to counter such opposition.[2] A federal-state clause is occasionally included in the original text of a treaty. In other instances, it may be used by a ratifying Party as a unilateral qualification to that State Party's adherence to the treaty. This latter, unilateral qualification, usually takes the form of a federal reservation.[3]

Uniform application of a multilateral treaty, in its entirety, among all Parties is not required under general principles of international law.[4] As set forth in article 51 of the Convention, however, a reservation incompatible with the object and purpose of the treaty will not be permitted.[5] A State proposing a reservation not acceptable to certain other Parties may, nevertheless, become a Party to the treaty.[6] The treaty will take effect, as between the reserving State and any objecting State, but the provisions to which the reservation relates will not apply as between those States, to the extent of the reservation.[7]

On the basis of experience with comparable human rights treaties, it appears likely that, if the Convention is signed by the President and transmitted to the Senate, a federal reservation will be included.

FEDERAL RESERVATIONS: PAST PRACTICE

Federal reservations are sometimes proposed by States with federal systems, such as the United States, to take account of the differences between the legal effects of treaty ratification in federal and unitary States. When a unitary State enters into a treaty (and adopts enabling legislation for this purpose, if required under its legal system), the treaty obligations become fully binding on that State, and any subdivisions within such State, both under its domestic law and under international law.[8]

Adoption of a treaty by the central government of a federal State is binding on its constituent units (*i.e.*, states) for international law purposes. However, under the national constitution and laws of those States, adoption may or may not, automatically, cause the treaty to supersede conflicting provisions of the laws of the constituent units, for domestic law purposes. Even where, under the federal State's constitution and laws, the treaty would take precedence over the laws of the constituent units, overriding laws of the constituent units could well be politically unpalatable.[9] In an attempt to deal with this issue, certain treaties contain a federal-state clause.[10] When a federal-state clause is not included in the text of the treaty, federal States sometimes condition their ratification of treaties upon a federal reservation. Federal States have varying divisions of authority between the State and its constituent units, with respect to particular subject matters regulated by law. As a consequence, such federal reservations take various forms and have differing legal effects. For example, the United States, a frequent proponent of federal-state clauses,[11] has signed the Torture Convention[12] and is currently seeking the advice and consent of the Senate with respect to ratification.[13] The U.S. explanatory "treaty package" sent to the Senate contains the following proposed federal reservation:

> The United States shall implement the Convention to the extent that the Federal Government exercises legislative and judicial jurisdiction over the matters covered therein; to the extent that constituent units exercise jurisdiction over such matters, the Federal Government shall take appropriate measures, to the end that the competent authorities of the constituent units may take appropriate measures for the fulfillment of the Convention.[14]

The summary of the Torture Convention sent to the Senate states with respect to the federal reservation issue:

> [G]iven the decentralized distribution of police and other governmental authority at federal, state, and local levels, it is desirable to make ...[a] federal reservation...[15]

Some human rights treaties contain provisions specifically addressing the federal question in a manner diametrically opposed to the proposed U.S. federal reservation to the Torture Convention quoted above. Thus, the International Covenants on Civil and Political Rights (CCPR) and on Economic, Social and Cultural Rights (CESCR), sent to the Senate by President Carter in 1978, both contain the following anti-federal clause:

> The provisions of the present Covenant shall extend to all parts of federal states without any limitations or exceptions.[16]

Presumably for the purpose of counteracting this anti-federal clause in the CCPR, the treaty package of proposed reservations, declarations and understandings sent to the Senate by President Carter with the CCPR contained the following qualifying federal reservation:

> The United States shall implement all the provisions of the Covenant over whose subject matter the Federal Government exercises legislative and judicial jurisdiction; with respect to the provisions over whose subject matter constituent units exercise jurisdiction, the Federal Government shall take appropriate measures, to the end that the competent authorities of the constituent units may take appropriate measures for the fulfillment of this Covenant.[17]

The treaty package with respect to the CESCR contained a proposed reservation identical to that quoted above, except that the word "progressively" appears before the word "implement."[18]

The text of the Convention does not contain any anti-federal clause similar to article 50 of the CCPR or article 28 of the CESCR.[19] This might suggest that a qualifying federal reservation to the Convention need not and will not be proposed since it is not needed to override an anti-federal clause. There are several countervailing factors, however, that lead to a contrary conclusion. First, article 29 of the Vienna Convention on the Law of Treaties provides that "[u]nless a different intention appears from the treaty or is otherwise established, a treaty is binding upon each party in respect of its entire territory."[20] While not ratified by the United States, the Vienna Convention is widely acknowledged as an authoritative basis for interpreting treaties and has been frequently cited with approval by the United States. Article 29, above, suggests that in the absence of a federal reservation the Convention would be interpreted to be binding on all parts of federal States, even though the Convention does not contain an anti-federal clause.

Second, attempts by the United States and other nations to include federal-state clauses in numerous treaties and reservations suggest that such clauses are often considered by Federal States to be necessary to exclude the application of treaties to matters within the jurisdiction of their constit-uent units.[21] Thus, the text of the Torture Convention did not contain an anti-federal clause, but the U.S. Administration nevertheless proposed the qualifying federal reservation quoted above. The text of the American Convention on Human Rights (American Convention) promulgated by the Organization of American States contains a federal-state clause similar to the qualifying federal reservations proposed by the United States with respect to the Torture Convention, the CCPR and the CESCR.[22] The United States proposed the inclusion of this clause in the American Convention. Finally, during the 1987 meetings of the U.N. Working Group which produced the Convention, the United States representative proposed a federal-state clause similar to those contained in the U.S. treaty packages for the CCPR and CESCR.[23] The proposal was not accepted by the Working Group.[24]

Past actions of the United States with respect to proposed human rights treaties suggest that a qualifying federal reservation, similar to those attached to the Torture Convention, the CCPR and the CESCR, will be included in the "treaty package," if the President signs the Convention and sends it to the Senate for ratification.

The remainder of this paper will address the following questions: Is such a qualifying federal reservation legally required? What is the legal effect of such a clause as a matter of international law? As a matter of domestic law?

If U.S. ratification is made contingent on a federal reservation, how should the reservation be worded?

■ IS A QUALIFYING FEDERAL RESERVATION WITH RESPECT TO THE CONVENTION REQUIRED UNDER UNITED STATES LAW?

The answer is unequivocally no.[25]

The question implies the possibility that the reserved powers clause or some other provision of the Constitution may proscribe the making of federal law (either by treaty or federal statute or decisional law) which deals with subjects customarily within the jurisdiction of state or local governmental authority. As succinctly stated by a leading authority on U.S. constitutional and international law:

> [T]he argument that the United States is without power under the Constitution to adhere to such [human rights] treaties has no basis whatever—in the language of the Constitution, in its *travaux preparatories*, in the institutions it established, in its principles of federalism or of separation of powers, in almost two centuries of constitutional history, or in any other consideration relevant to constitutional interpretation.[26]

The Constitution confers the power to make treaties upon the President, with the advice and consent of the Senate.[27] It provides that treaties made "under the Authority of the United States, shall be the supreme Law of the Land."[28] Nowhere does the Constitution impose specific limitations on the treaty power[29] and no treaty has ever been held to be unconstitutional by the Supreme Court.[30] Nevertheless, treaties may not conflict with constitutional limitations such as those contained in the Bill of Rights.[31]

At least since the 1920 Supreme Court decision in *Missouri v. Holland*,[32] the principle has been well-understood that whatever is within the treaty power is not reserved to the states by the tenth amendment.[33] Matters customarily regulated by state law domestically are nevertheless subject to the treaty power of the President and the Senate so far as international agreements are concerned. Thus, the Supreme Court "has consistently upheld the validity and supremacy of treaty provisions dealing with matters as local as the right to inherit or to engage in local trade."[34]

Furthermore, since *Missouri v. Holland*, the reach of federal authority, independent of the treaty power, has been greatly expanded, with the result that today there are few, if any, subjects in either economic or civil rights realms reserved exclusively to state control.[35] Even the Department of State, in defending its proposed federal qualifying reservations to the CCPR and the CESCR, acknowledged that "[i]t is true that most of the rights recognized by the Covenants are plausibly within federal jurisdiction . . ."[36] Hence, the State Department in effect conceded that the federal reservations proposed with respect to these two human rights covenants were not legally required. They were proposed because "[t]he Departments of State and Justice want to make clear... that they are not trying to federalize areas of state human rights law or to circumvent the traditional division of competence between the federal and state governments with respect to human rights by way of a treaty."[37]

Since a federal qualifying reservation is not required by the U.S. Constitution or other federal law, its apparent purposes are (i) to facilitate the advice and consent of the Senate in the ratification process, and (ii) to leave to the discretion of the states whether to comply with treaty obligations with respect to matters traditionally regulated by the states.[38] Hence, such a reservation performs a largely political function and can be dispensed with if the Administration chooses to give less effect to traditional lines of demarcation between state and federal authority and believes ratification is achievable without the reservation.

■ WHAT IS THE LEGAL EFFECT UNDER INTERNATIONAL LAW OF A QUALIFYING FEDERAL RESERVATION?

In order to assess the legal effect of a federal reservation, it is necessary to address specific language and available evidence of the intent of the Administration in proposing the reservation. The present Administration has given no indication whether it will propose a federal reservation or, if so, how the reservation will be worded. However, the close similarity of the federal reservations proposed with respect to the CCPR, the CESCR and the Torture Convention, and the federal-state clause contained in article 28 of the American Convention (which clause was included in that treaty at the specific urging of the United States), strongly suggests that a federal reservation as to the Convention would follow the same pattern. For purposes of this analysis, it is assumed that the language will be similar to that of the Torture Convention, the CCPR and the CESCR, which are quoted above. It is also assumed that the reasons advanced by the Department of State for the federal reservations in the Torture Convention, the CCPR and the CESCR probably will be advanced by the Administration in support of a similar reservation to the Convention.

It is submitted that the United States' federal reservations, with respect to the Torture Convention, the CCPR and the CESCR, are at least potentially ambiguous and susceptible of either of two conflicting interpretations as a matter of international law.[39] Read literally, each of these reservations could be viewed as an international commitment that those treaty obligations over which the Federal Government typically exercises legislative and judicial jurisdiction will be fulfilled by the United States, but that fulfillment of those treaty obligations, with respect to which the states typically exercise legislative and judicial jurisdiction, will ultimately be left to the discretion of the states (and therefore perhaps will not be fulfilled). An alternative interpretation is that these reservations could be viewed as an international commitment of the United States that certain of the treaty obligations (involving matters over which the Federal Government, exercises legislative and judicial jurisdiction) will be fulfilled by the Federal Government, and the remainder (over which its constituent units exercise jurisdiction) will be fulfilled by these units (*i.e.*, states).

The latter, alternative view, is the one that would be desired by other Parties to the treaty. This reading necessitates construing "may" to mean "shall" in the second clause of the reservations quoted above. Only under this reading would the United States undertake obligations commensurate with those assumed by unitary States and by federal States not making such a reservation, *i.e.*, a commitment to fulfill all treaty obligations, other than ones covered by a specific reservation or declaration of non-adherence. Some commentators, albeit a minority, have either ascribed this meaning to the federal reservation

Federal-State

in the CCPR treaty package or have concluded that the language is unclear and this is a permissible interpretation.[40]

However, several factors militate against acceptance of this alternative reading of the federal-state clause. There is a vast area of concurrent state and federal jurisdiction under U.S. law.[41] Even if federal jurisdiction dependent solely upon the treaty power is disregarded, the remaining federal jurisdiction is so broad that the potential overlap remains substantial.[42] Because of this overlap of federal and state jurisdiction, both actual (with respect to powers actually exercised) and potential (with respect to unexercised powers), the alternative interpretation produces a situation in which it is difficult to determine where responsibility rests for fulfilling those specific treaty obligations which are not already met by existing federal or state law.

A more formidable obstacle to adopting the alternative interpretation stems from the reasoning advanced by the Administration for proposing the reservation, *i.e.*, the desire to avoid "federalizing" through the treaty process additional subject matters traditionally regulated by the states.[43] The U.S. intention to defer to the states in such areas, arguably, is incompatible with a reading of the clause that would impose an international obligation on the United States to ensure that every treaty commitment will be fulfilled, either by the Federal Government or by the states.

To interpret the federal-state clause as preserving the prerogative of the states to conform to treaty obligations or not in areas over which they exercise jurisdiction appears to be more consistent with the intent of the United States.[44] The problem with this interpretation, however, is that by deferring to the discretion of the states in areas in which they have traditionally exercised jurisdiction, the United States, in effect, avoids any meaningful commitment to fulfill certain treaty obligations. The problem is compounded by the difficulty of determining which treaty obligations are the subject of a firm U.S. commitment and which are not, because of the extensive jurisdictional overlap.

One possible approach to sorting out federal and state areas of jurisdiction is to rely on the fact that the language of the reservation deals with "exercise"[45] of jurisdiction by the Federal Government and the states, rather than the power to exercise such jurisdiction. This may suggest that the meaning of the federal reservation, in terms of allocating responsibility for compliance with treaty obligations between the Federal Government and the states, is to be determined by looking at the actual assertion of jurisdiction to regulate a matter that is the subject of a treaty obligation. Using this approach, matters within the constitutional regulatory power of the Federal Government that are, however, typically regulated by the states would be treated as prerogatives of the states. This would reduce (but not eliminate) the overlap between federal and state jurisdiction and increase the scope of permissible noncompliance with treaty obligations.

Under this construction, there is still another uncertainty inherent in the federal reservation. The Federal Government possesses two separate sources of jurisdiction to implement treaty obligations. One is the treaty power inherent in article II, section 2 of the Constitution which authorizes the United States, by treaty, to remake the law of the land, even in areas otherwise exclusively regulated by the states.[46] The other is the inherent power of the Federal Government, under the commerce clause, the thirteenth, fourteenth, fifteenth and nineteenth amendments and other provisions of the Constitution, to regulate matters otherwise traditionally regulated by the states.[47] The breadth of the latter regulatory jurisdiction has grown substantially as the Supreme Court has sustained a broad range of federal regulation of economic, civil and political interests. The consequence of this dramatic growth of federal jurisdiction with respect to human rights, completely apart from the treaty power, is that the reach of the federal treaty power may include little, if anything, in the domain of human rights which could not today be regulated by the Federal Government under its other constitu-tional powers.

United States ratification of a treaty constitutes exercise of treaty power jurisdiction. Hence, without the federal-state clause,[48] treaty ratification would create "treaty law" implementing each of the treaty obligations not already implemented by pre-existing federal or state law. Two commentators have suggested that the federal reservation under discussion may be susceptible of interpretation as an attempt to renounce federal jurisdiction under the treaty power to the extent that such jurisdiction exceeds federal power derived solely from other constitutional sources.[49]

Federal-State

This construction perhaps could be derived from the reservation language to the effect that "the Federal Government exercises legislative and judicial jurisdiction."[50] Such an interpretation would differentiate treaty power jurisdiction from "legislative and judicial jurisdiction." Under this analysis, it can be contended that the Federal Government has sought to affirm, by means of the reservation, the U.S. commitment to all treaty obligations, except any obligation which could be federally regulated under the treaty power as interpreted in *Missouri v. Holland*, but which would be beyond the reach of the Federal Government under its other constitutional powers.[51] Under this analysis, the language of the reservation would be viewed as an attempt to disclaim any "exercise" of "jurisdiction" as a result of using the treaty power to cause the United States to become a party to the Convention. This reading of the reservation, theoretically, could be deemed to enlarge the category of treaty obligations left to the discretion of the states. However, as noted above, it appears that the reach of the treaty power may embrace very little which could not be regulated by the Federal Government pursuant to its other constitutional powers.

Whatever tortuous analytical path is followed, leaving compliance or noncompliance with material treaty obligations within the discretion of the states, as a result of a blanket federal reservation, raises a substantial question whether such a reservation is compatible with the object and purpose of the treaty, as a matter of international law.[52] As previously noted, article 51 of the Convention provides that a reservation incompatible with the object and purpose of the treaty is not permitted.

Under international law, a State proposing a treaty reservation unacceptable to another Party may, nevertheless, become a Party to the treaty.[53] The treaty will take effect between the reserving State and the objecting State except with respect to the provision to which the reservation relates.[54] Furthermore, one observer of the extensive reservations to the CCPR by the United States concluded as follows:

> Given the Vienna Convention's prohibition of reservations contrary to the purpose of a treaty, the federal-state reservation might be considered objectionable by other states party to the Covenant. As a practical matter, however, such an objection might never be made, in which case the validity of the reservation as a matter of

international law would never be brought into question. . . . If the parties desire the United States to accede to the treaty and feel that it will never do so without the reservations, they may forego an objection they otherwise would have the right to make.[55]

There is little judicial authority on the law of reservations. Only one decision, the *Belilos Case*[56] focuses on the effect of an invalid reservation on the validity of adherence to the treaty by a State Party. Under that decision, unless a State has made clear that a reservation was an essential condition of its consent to be bound by the treaty, the State will be obligated by the treaty, irrespective of the invalidity of the reservation.[57]

The difficulty of ascertaining the legal effect of the federal reservation under international law simply highlights the problem noted by several international law experts concerning the CCPR and CESCR federal reservations recommended by the Administration. These experts have concluded that the United States sought to ratify the Covenants without incurring a commitment to make any change in U.S. federal or state law or practice.[58]

■ WHAT IS THE LEGAL EFFECT OF A QUALIFYING FEDERAL RESERVATION UNDER DOMESTIC LAW?

For purposes of United States domestic law, the legal effect of the federal reservation under consideration depends upon the threshold question whether each specific treaty obligation is self-executing or not self-executing. The United States treaty packages for the CCPR, the CESCR, the Torture Convention and the American Convention all contained sweeping declarations that all of the substantive provisions of such treaties are deemed by the United States to be not self-executing.[59] For purposes of this analysis, it has been assumed that the Administration will propose a similar declaration with respect to the Convention.

When all obligations contained in a treaty are declared to be not self-executing, compliance with the treaty obligations may take the following forms: (i) existing federal or state domestic law that already embodies the obligations; (ii) new federal law; or (iii) new state law. Treaty obligations covered by clause (i) pose no problem with respect to their legal effect under domestic law. Such obligations are already in force in the ratifying State.

With respect to all other treaty obligations, prior to implementation through legislation or other action by the appropriate federal or state authorities, treaty obligations would not be legally binding as a matter of domestic law.[60] Until such implementation, treaty obligations would not be domestic law of the United States and, hence, could not be enforced in U.S. courts.[61] Failure to implement such obligations within a reasonable time could nevertheless place the United States in breach of its treaty obligations as a matter of international law.

■ HOW SHOULD A QUALIFYING FEDERAL RESERVATION BE WORDED?

As noted above, a qualifying federal reservation is not legally required. These reservations have apparently been utilized by previous Administrations to preserve the division of powers between the Federal Government and the states, to counter anticipated political objections and to facilitate ratification. In contrast with the United States, Canada is a State which faces a severe legal obstacle with respect to federalism issues when ratifying human rights and other multilateral international agreements. Under the Canadian Constitution, the treaty-making and treaty-implementing power is divided among the federal and provincial executive and legislative bodies.[62] As one Canadian authority has observed, "[I]n the United States the federal power to make treaties has evolved with great strength and can override state law and congressional acts. On the other hand, in Canada, the treaty power is limited with no ability in itself to affect the distribution of legislative power."[63] Nevertheless, Canada ratified the CCPR without any federal reservation or declaration.[64]

It is the view of several U.S. international law and constitutional law scholars that attaching broad reservations and declarations to human rights treaties is both unnecessary, as a matter of law and, if the U.S. wishes forthrightly to subscribe to the treaty obligations, undesirable as a matter of policy.[65] Yet, the United States has had great difficulty in obtaining the Senate's consent to ratification of human rights treaties.[66] To facilitate ratification, and perhaps to give effect to the Administration's views as to the proper balance between federal and state powers, it appears probable that the Administration treaty package for the Convention will include a qualifying federal reservation. If so, it is in the interest of the Federal Government, the states and other States Parties to the Convention that the reservation be phrased in unambiguous terms and be compatible with the object and purpose of the Convention.

As discussed above, the scope and effect of the federal reservations proposed by the Administration with respect to the CCPR, CESCR and the Torture Convention (as well as the federal-state clause embodied in the American Convention) are not clearly defined. Further, if the reservation is given its broadest possible interpretation, it could be read as imposing few obligations of any significance upon the United States.

In contrast, the ratification by Australia of the CCPR was accompanied by the following declaration, which addresses treaty obligations simply and clearly:

> Australia has a federal constitutional system in which legislative, executive and judicial powers are shared and distributed between the Commonwealth and the constituent States. The implementation of the Treaty throughout Australia will be effected by the Commonwealth, State and Territory authorities having regard to their respective constitutional powers and arrangements concerning their exercise.[67]

This declaration points out the federal nature of Australia's legal system and indicates that the duty to implement treaty obligations will be shared by the Commonwealth and its constituent states. The Australian declaration leaves no doubt that treaty obligations are binding upon the Commonwealth and will be fulfilled by the appropriate Commonwealth entities.

Another approach, that would achieve the same result, was proposed by the Lawyers Committee on International Human Rights with respect to U.S. ratification of the CCPR and the CESCR. Their suggested federal reservation was:

Federal-State

> The United States will implement its obligations under this [Convention] by legislative, executive and judicial means, federal or state, as appropriate.[68]

This reservation recognizes the federal nature of our legal system but does not equivocate as to the assumption of the treaty obligations. From the point of view of clarity, either the Australian clause or the Lawyers Committee proposal would be preferable to the federal reservations proposed by the United States in the CCPR, the CESCR and the Torture Convention. Either could serve as a model, if the United States chooses to make the Convention obligations fully binding on the states, as well as on the Federal Government.

If it were deemed advisable, in the interest of "states' rights," to limit the obligations imposed on the states, there are other possible courses of action. One approach would be to add a provision that direct federal implementation[69] will not exceed the limits on federal power under constitutional provisions other than the treaty power. Such a qualification might assuage the concerns of those who object to extension of federal jurisdiction (and contraction of state jurisdiction) solely via the treaty power. However, because of the extensive reach of federal authority under the commerce clause, the thirteenth, fourteenth, fifteenth and nineteenth amendments and other constitutional provisions, such a qualification would not significantly limit the power or duty of the Federal Government to implement the Convention treaty obligations.

Another approach would be to design the treaty package to combine one of the federal-state clauses recommended above with separate reservations or declarations of non-adherence with respect to those few situations in which state laws important to the national interest conflict with specific treaty obligations.

Conclusion

A qualifying federal reservation to the Convention is not required by the Constitution. The scope and meaning of the federal-state clauses contained in the text of the American Convention and in proposed United States reservations to the CCPR, the CESCR and the Torture Convention are not entirely clear as a matter of international law. They probably were intended, however, to avoid incurrence of international law treaty obligations by the United States with respect to matters generally considered within the purview of the states, to the extent that state laws negate or do not embody such obligations.

There are few specific instances in which United States domestic laws, important to our national interest, may conflict with provisions of the Convention. These could appropriately be dealt with by means of specific reservations, declarations or understandings. This would obviate the need for a blanket federal-state clause, which may conflict with the object and purpose of the Convention. If a federal-state clause is, nevertheless, deemed necessary to facilitate consent to ratification by the Senate, a clearer clause, and one not so broad as to negate any significant obligations beyond existing domestic law, is desirable. To this end, the approach followed by Australia in ratifying the CCPR would be preferable to the traditional United States approach to federal-state clauses pertaining to human rights treaties.

Footnotes

[1] *See* Convention on the Rights of the Child, *opened for signature* Jan. 26, 1990, A/RES./44/25 [hereinafter Convention].

[2] *See* RESTATEMENT (THIRD) OF THE FOREIGN RELATIONS LAW OF THE UNITED STATES, § 302 reporter's note 4 (1986) [hereinafter RESTATEMENT OF FOREIGN RELATIONS], which states:

Federal-state clauses. Federal states such as Canada or Switzerland sometimes have sought special provisions in international agreements to take account of constitutional restrictions on the power of their central government to deal with some matters by international agreement. For international agreements of the United States, such provisions are not required by the Constitution. . . Constitutional requirements apart, federal states, including the United States, have, for domestic political reasons, sometimes sought provisions modifying their obligations so as to take account of their federal character. . .

³ For the definition of "reservation" *see* the Vienna Convention on the Law of Treaties, *opened for signature* May 23, 1969, art. 2(1)(d), 1155 U.N.T.S. 331 (*entered into force* Jan. 27, 1980) [hereinafter Vienna Convention]. Unilateral qualifications are sometimes embodied in declarations or understandings. However, *see* comment (g) to RESTATEMENT OF FOREIGN RELATIONS, *supra* note 2, § 313, which states:

> a state may make a unilateral declaration that does not purport to be a reservation. Whatever it is called, it constitutes a reservation in fact if it purports to exclude, limit or modify the state's legal obligation.

⁴ *See* RESTATEMENT OF FOREIGN RELATIONS, *supra* note 2, § 313(3) which provides:

> (3) a reservation established with regard to another party in accordance with Subsection (2)(c) modifies the relevant provisions of the agreement as to the relations between the reserving and accepting state parties but does not modify those provisions for the other parties to the agreement *inter se.*

Similarly, article 21 of the Vienna Convention, *supra* note 3, provides:

> *1. A reservation established with regard to another party in accordance with articles 19, 20 and 23:*
> *(a) modifies for the reserving State in its relations with that other party the provisions of the treaty to which the reservation relates to the extent of the reservation; and*
> *(b) modifies those provisions to the same extent for that other party in its relations with the reserving State.*
> *2. The reservation does not modify the provisions of the treaty for the other parties to the treaty* inter se.

⁵ Convention, *supra* note 1, art. 51.

⁶ *See* RESTATEMENT OF FOREIGN RELATIONS, *supra* note 2, § 313(2)(c).

⁷ *Id.* § 313(3); *see also* Vienna Convention, supra note 3, art. 21.

⁸ *See,* RESTATEMENT OF FOREIGN RELATIONS, *supra* note 2, § 302 reporter's note 4, which states, in pertinent part:

A "federal-state clause" is likely to render a federal State's commitment under an international agreement less onerous than that of unitary states. Such clauses are therefore more likely to be acceptable in multilateral agreements reflecting common purposes than in those containing reciprocal exchanges.

9 *See* RESTATEMENT OF FOREIGN RELATIONS, *supra* note 2, § 302 reporter's note 4.

10 For an example of a federal clause contained in the body of a treaty, see the American Convention on Human Rights, *opened for signature* Nov. 22, 1969, art. 28, 1144 U.N.T.S. 123 (*entered into force* July 18, 1978) [hereinafter American Convention].

11 As long ago as 1947, the United States proposed such a clause to the working group on a U.N. convention on human rights. The concluding sentence of the proposal stated:

In respect of Articles which the federal government regards as appropriate under its constitutional system, in whole or in part, for action by the constituent States, Provinces or Cantons, the federal government shall bring such provisions, with a favorable recommendation, to the notice of the appropriate authorities of the States, Provinces or Cantons.

Liang, *Notes on Legal Questions Concerning the United Nations*, 45 AM. J. INT'L L. 108, 123 (1951) (quoting U.N. ESCOR Supp. (No. 1) at 29.).

12 Convention Against Torture and Other Cruel, Inhuman or Degrading Treatment or Punishment, *opened for signature* Dec. 10, 1984, G.A. Res. 39/46 Annex, 39 U.N. GAOR Supp. (No. 51), U.N. Doc. A/39/51 (*entered into force* June 26, 1987).

13 *See* President's Message to the Senate Transmitting Convention Against Torture, 24 WEEKLY COMP. PRES. DOC. 642, 642 (May 20, 1988).

14 DEPARTMENT OF STATE, MESSAGE FROM THE PRESIDENT OF THE UNITED STATES, S. TREATY DOC. 100-20, 100th Cong., 2d Sess. 2-3 (1988).

15 *Id.*

16 International Covenant on Civil and Political Rights, *opened for signature* Dec. 19, 1966, art. 50, 999 U.N.T.S. 171 (*entered into force* Mar.

23, 1976) [hereinafter CCPR]; International Covenant on Economic, Social and Cultural Rights, *opened for signature* Dec. 19, 1966, art. 28, 933 U.N.T.S. 3 (*entered into force* Jan. 3, 1976)[hereinafter CESCR].

[17] STATE DEPARTMENT, MESSAGE OF THE PRESIDENT TRANSMITTING FOUR TREATIES PERTAINING TO HUMAN RIGHTS, S. EXEC. DOC. C, D, E, AND F NO. 95-2, 95th Cong., 2d Sess. at XIV (1978) [hereinafter FOUR TREATIES PERTAINING TO HUMAN RIGHTS].

[18] *Compare id.* at XIV (reservation to article 50 of the CCPR), *with id.* at X (reservation to article 28 of the CESCR.)

[19] *See generally* Convention, *supra* note 1.

[20] Vienna Convention, *supra* note 3, art. 29.

[21] However, in contrast to the declaration included in the United States' treaty packages on the CCPR and CESCR, the Australian declaration to the CCPR expressly provides that the treaty will be implemented by the state as well as the federal governments of Australia. *See infra* note 67 and accompanying text.

[22] Article 28 of the American Convention, *supra* note 10, states:

1. Where a State Party is constituted as a federal state, the national government of such State Party shall implement all the provisions of the Convention over whose subject matter it exercises legislative and judicial jurisdiction.

2. With respect to the provisions over whose subject matter the constituent units of the federal state have jurisdiction, the national government shall immediately take suitable measures, in accordance with its constitution and its laws, to the end that the competent authorities of the constituent units may adopt appropriate provisions for the fulfillment of this Convention.

[23] The text of the U.S. proposal was as follows:

1. Where a State Party is constituted as a federal State, the national Government of such State Party shall undertake appropriate measures to implement the provisions of this Convention in so far as it exercises legislative and judicial jurisdiction over the subject matter thereof. In so far as the subject matter of the provisions of this Convention falls within the jurisdiction of the constituent units of the federal

State, the national Government shall take suitable measures, in accordance with its constitution and its laws, to the end that the competent authorities of the constituent units may take appropriate measures for the fulfillment of this Convention.

Report of the Commission on Human Rights, Working Group of the Convention on the Rights of the Child, U.N. Doc. E/CN.4/1987/25 (1987).

[24] *Id.*

[25] International agreements are subject to constitutional limitations. *See* RESTATEMENT OF FOREIGN RELATIONS, *supra* note 2, § 302 comment b, which states:

Treaties and other international agreements are subject to the prohibitions of the Bill of Rights and other restraints on federal power, such as those relating to suspension of the writ of habeas corpus or prohibiting the grant of titles of nobility...

[26] Henkin, *The Constitution, Treaties, and International Human Rights*, 116 U. PA. L. REV. 1012, 1014-15 (1968).

[27] U.S. CONST. ART. II, § 2, cl. 2.

[28] *Id.* at art. VI, § 2, cl. 2.

[29] *See* RESTATEMENT OF FOREIGN RELATIONS, *supra* note 2, § 302 reporter's note 3, which states:

The Tenth Amendment implies no limitations on the subject matter of treaties or other international agreements. . . . There are dicta suggesting particular hypothetical "States' rights" limitations on the subject matter of international agreements, *e.g.*, that a treaty cannot modify a State's form of government or cede State territory to a foreign government without the State's consent. . . . Constitutional limitations protecting States' rights against invasion by the federal government presumably would apply as well to any such invasion by treaty or other international agreement, for example, the limitations in the Eleventh Amendment, or those implied in the guarantee of a republican form of government in Article IV, Section 4. . . .

[30] L. HENKIN, FOREIGN AFFAIRS AND THE CONSTITUTION at 137 (1972); RESTATEMENT OF FOREIGN RELATIONS, *supra* note 2, § 721 reporter's note 1. (Additional research has not revealed any instance in which the U.S. Supreme Court has held a treaty to be unconstitutional.)

[31] *Id.*

[32] 252 U.S. 416 (1920).

[33] L. HENKIN, *supra* note 30, at 146 ("Since the Treaty Power was delegated to the Federal Government, whatever was within it was not reserved to the States by the Tenth Amendment. Many matters, then, may be 'reserved to the States' as regards domestic legislation but not as regards inter-national agreement. They are, one might say, left to the States subject to defeasance if the United States should decide to make a treaty about them."). *See also* RESTATEMENT OF FOREIGN RELATIONS, *supra* note 2, § 302 commented:

> Consequently, the Tenth Amendment, reserving to the several States the powers not delegated to the United States, does not limit the power to make treaties or other agreements. . . .

[34] L. HENKIN, *supra* note 30, at 146. *See also* RESTATEMENT OF FOREIGN RELATIONS, *supra* note 2, § 302 comment c:

> The Constitution refers to treaties and to other agreements or compacts with foreign powers. . ., but it does not define such agreements or intimate any limitations as regards their purpose or subject matter. Contrary to what was once suggested, the Constitution does not require that an international agreement deal only with "matters of international concern." . . . Inter-national law knows no limitations on the purpose or subject matter of international agreements, other than that they may not conflict with a peremptory norm of international law. . . States may enter into an agreement on any matter of concern to them, and international law does not look behind their motives or purposes in doing so. Thus, the United States may make an agreement on any subject suggested by its national interests in relations with other nations.

[35] *Id.* at 147; RESTATEMENT OF FOREIGN RELATIONS, *supra* note 2, § 302; *International Human Rights Treaties: Hearings on Ex. C, D, E and F, 95-2—Four Treaties Relating to Human Rights Before the Senate Com-*

mittee on Foreign Relations, 96th Cong., 1st Sess. 52 (1979) [hereinafter *Hearings*] (statement of the Lawyers Committee for International Human Rights); Bitker, *The Constitutionality of International Agreements on Human Rights*, 12 SANTA CLARA L. REV. 279, 283 (1972) ("Under the Constitution, the power to enter into treaties and subject matters that may be covered appear almost unlimited").

36 *Hearings, supra* note 35, at 55 (response by Department of State to critique by Lawyers Committee).

37 *Id.*

38 Coccia, *Reservations to Multilateral Treaties on Human Rights*, 15 CAL. W. INT'L L.J. 1, 42 (1985); Skelton, *The United States Approach to Ratification of International Covenants on Human Rights*, 1 HOUS. J. INT'L L. 103, 117 (1979) (reservation viewed as "effort to defuse potentially controversial provisions prior to their review and debate by the Senate..."); Weissbrodt, *United States Ratification of the Human Rights Covenants*, 63 MINN. L. REV. 35, 77 (1978) (reservation designed to ease ratification).

39 *See Hearings, supra* note 35, at 302 (supplementary statement of Oscar M. Garibaldi) & at 279 (responses to questions of Senator Javits by Oscar Schachter).

40 *See Hearings, supra* note 35, at 168, in which Professor Anderegg testified:

> The word "may" often enough in American jurisprudence has been read to mean "must." I believe that the force of this reservation is that the Congress will find itself committed to use the taxing power and spending power to make grants to the states on the condition that they shall implement the provisions of these various treaties, even in matters which absent the treaties, would be within the power of the States. I think this is profoundly wrong.

See also id. at 302, in which Professor Garibaldi testified that the proposed reservation presents a "fundamental ambiguity." He stated:

> It may be interpreted literally, as saying that some of the obligations undertaken by the United States in the treaty would be implemented by the Federal Government and (by

positive implication) that some others would be implemented by the states, with the announcement that the Federal Government would try to persuade the latter to comply with the treaty.

In a footnote to the above quoted language, Professor Garibaldi stated that "[i]t may be argued in support of this interpretation, that by using the word 'fulfillment' of the Covenant by state authorities, it is acknowledged that there is a preexisting international obligation to be fulfilled." *Id.*

In response to the question whether the treaty with a federal reservation and a not self-executing declaration, would commit the U.S. Government to passing legislation that would conform to the treaties, Professor Henkin stated:

> Probably. The proposed language is not very clear or meaningful but in any event virtually all of the provisions of all the agreements are provisions 'over whose subject matter the Federal Government exercises legislative and judicial jurisdiction...' The United States would be committed to passing legislation that would make it possible for the authorities and courts to fulfill the obligations of the agreements, whether by specific legislation on particular subjects, or by legislation which gives effect to the treaty provisions generally (i.e., legislation that undoes the effect of the declaration that they shall not be self-executing).

Id. at 288.

[41] *Hearings, supra* note 35, at 302 (supplementary statement of Oscar M. Garibaldi).

[42] *See* L. HENKIN, *supra* note 30, at 149 ("under contemporary views of the powers of Congress there is little—or nothing—that is dealt with by treaty that could not also be the subject of legislation by Congress.").

[43] *See* Hearings, *supra* note 35, at 40 (statement of Jack M. Goldklang) & at 55 (response by Department of State to critique by Lawyers Committee).

[44] *See supra* note 11.

45 *See* footnotes 11-18 and accompanying text for the text of the federal reservations with respect to the Torture Convention, the CCPR and the CESCR.

46 *See supra* note 33.

47 *See* Weissbrodt, *supra* note 38, at 65-66, in which the author concludes:
> In view of the civil rights legislation of the past twenty years, it is clear that the federal government has the power under the commerce clause, as well as the enforcement clauses of the thirteenth, fourteenth and fifteenth amendments to legislate in areas covered by the [human rights] Covenants. Only where the federal government attempts to interfere in 'integral governmental functions of [state] bodies,' such as the relations between a state and its employees, would there now be any question of federal legislative authority.

48 As noted below, human rights treaties signed by the United States have frequently been submitted to the Senate with a declaration that all substantial provisions of the treaty are deemed "not self-executing." *See* FOUR TREATIES PERTAINING TO HUMAN RIGHTS, *supra* note 17, at VIII, XI, XV and XVIII. Such a declaration has no effect under international law. It establishes the intent of the ratifying party that treaty obligations not already met by existing domestic law will be met within a reasonable time after ratification, except to the extent that applicable reservations may provide for non-adherence to particular treaty provisions. The combination of a not self-executing declaration and a federal reservation may result in disavowal by the ratifying party of a broad spectrum of treaty obligations. Furthermore, due to ambiguous wording of federal reservations and the uncertain line of demarcation between federal and state jurisdiction, it may be difficult to determine which treaty obligations are negated.

49 *Hearings, supra* note 35, at 303 (supplementary statement of Oscar M. Garibaldi). *See also* Craig, *The International Covenant on Civil and Political Rights and United States Law: Department of State Proposals for Preserving the Status Quo*, 19 HARV. INT'L L.J. 845, 874 (1978) (author assumes that the CCPR federal reservation "is meant to restrict Congress' power to implement the Covenant to its constitutional limits *absent* the necessary and proper authority to implement treaties.").

[50] *See* FOUR TREATIES PERTAINING TO HUMAN RIGHTS, *supra* note 17, at XIV & X (reservation to article 50 of the CCPR and to article 28 of the CESCR).

[51] One constitutional law scholar has concluded that there may be no difference between the reach of the Treaty Power and Congress' authority to legislate on matters of "international concern" under its other constitutional powers.
Henkin, *The Treaty Makers and the Law Makers: The Law of the Land and Foreign Relations*, 107 U. PA. L. REV. 903, 922 (1959).

[52] *Hearings, supra* note 35, at 302 (supplementary statement of Oscar M. Garibaldi); *see also* Weissbrodt, *supra* note 38, at 64 (author questions whether the federal reservation with respect to the CCPR and CESCR may be unacceptable as "vitiating an essential component of the treaty.").

[53] *See supra* note 4.

[54] *See supra* note 4.

[55] Craig, *supra* note 49, at 871.

[56] 132 Eur. Ct. H.R. (Ser. A)(1988), reprinted in 10 Eur. Hum. Rts. Rep. 466 (1988).

[57] Sir Hersch Lauterpacht analyzes this issue, in greater depth than the Belilos decision, in a dissenting opinion in the Interhandel Case (Switz. v. U.S.), 1959 I.C.J. 6, 95. Judge Lauterpacht states:
> If that reservation is an essential condition of the Acceptance in the sense that without it the declaring State would have been wholly unwilling to undertake the principal obligation, then it is not open to the Court to disregard that reservation and at the same time to hold the accepting State bound by the Declaration.

For an analysis of this decision, see *The Belilos Case*, 29 VA. J. INT'L L. 347 (1989).

[58] *Hearings, supra* note 35, at 49 (critique of Lawyers Committee for International Human Rights); Skelton, *supra* note 38, at 125; Weiss-brodt, *supra* note 38, at 77. *See also Hearings, supra* note 35, at 38 (State Department's witness, Jack M. Goldklang, acknowledged that if treaty

was accepted with proposed reservations no new legislation would be necessary). *See also* note 65, *infra*.

[59] *See, e.g.*, FOUR TREATIES PERTAINING TO HUMAN RIGHTS, *supra* note 17, at VI ("With such declarations, the substantive provisions of the treaties would not of themselves become effective as domestic law.").

[60] *Hearings, supra* note 35, at 301 (Oscar M. Garibaldi stated that "[i]t follows from what has been said that if the proposed declarations are adopted, a lawsuit brought before an American court solely on the basis of the treaties could not prevail.").

[61] *But see id.* at 301 (Professor Garibaldi notes that "even if the treaties are rendered non-self-executing, it would be possible, in my view, to invoke them in domestic legal proceedings, as elements to be taken into account by the courts in the interpretation of the rights guaranteed by domestic law ...").

[62] Leal, *Federal State Clauses and the Conventions of the Hague Conference on Private International Law*, 8 DALHOUSIE L.J. 257, 258 (1984).

[63] *Id.* at 259.

[64] MULTILATERAL TREATIES DEPOSITED WITH THE SECRETARY GENERAL, STATUS AS AT DECEMBER 1988, at 131, U.N. Doc. ST/LEG/SER.E/7, U.N. Sales No. E.89.V.06 (1989).

[65] Several witnesses testified to this effect with respect to the CCPR and CESCR. *See Hearings, supra* note 35, at 249 (Norman Redlich: "We do not agree . . . with the State Department position that we should reserve to ourselves a right to set a lower standard than is set forth in a treaty. There are few instances . . . in which the treaties do set a higher standard than we have under American law, and we think that there is no reason why we should demand of other countries that they raise their standard to the treaty level but insist that we should be able to lower ours below the treaty level.") & at 349 (Richard B. Lillich: "I think these [not self-executing] declarations are unfortunate. If we do go into these treaties, they will not change U.S. law very much at all . . . . [I]n certain areas they may uplift it. Let us let the courts decide . . . whether a particular article of a particular convention is, or is not, self-executing.") & at 175 (David Weissbrodt: "The President's letter of February 23, 1978 . . . expressly proposes to secure ratification of the human

rights treaties without the need to change any U.S. laws. This approach should not be accepted by the Senate. Instead, the Foreign Relations Committee should take pride in advising the minimum possible reservations and understandings . . .") & at 114 (Bruno V. Bitker: "I am for the treaties, but I am for the treaties only with those reservations, understandings, or declarations which deal with constitutional questions. These other matters . . . subvert or attempt to subvert the basic principle that treaties are the supreme law of the land.") & at 120 (Covey T. Oliver: "we can . . . accept these treaties as the 'supreme law of the land' without the necessity of general reservations stating the treaties to be non-self-executing and certainly without outrageously misleading Federal-State clauses that purport to freeze the power of the Federal Government . . . vis-a-vis the States below the maximum level of Federal supremacy under article XI.") & at 52 (Lawyers Committee for International Human Rights: "[N]o such [Federal-state clause] is necessary or desirable.") & at 279 (Oscar Schachter: "Its [Federal-state clause] effect will be to delay, perhaps indefinitely the fulfillment of some of the treaty provisions and therefore to place the United States in default of its obligations.") & at 95 (Thomas J. Farer: "[I]f [the Administration] had not felt constrained by a long tradition of senatorial obstructionism, they would not have proposed this almost illusory form or ratification. To avoid endless debate over every provision that may require some change in U.S. law or practice, they have ground the convention into a perfect facsimile of our status quo. This tactic may win ratification, but my fear is of a consequently empty victory.") & at 92 (Louis B. Sohn: "[I]t seems to me that practically all of the reservations, declarations, and understandings really are unnecessary. It would be a tremendous encouragement to the cause of human rights around the world if the United States would ratify this covenant in a clear manner, without reservations which would detract from its unambiguous character.") & at 260 (Morton H. Sklar: "The reservations pro-posed to the treaties amount to an abrogation of the treaties' human rights standards and an abrogation of our Helsinki Agreement commitments in many areas, almost as great as the failure to ratify itself.").

[66] *See* Craig, *supra* note 49, at 845 (1978); Weissbrodt, *supra* note 38, at 38 n.45; Coccia, *Reservations to Multilateral Treaties on Human Rights*, 15 CAL. W. INT'L L.J. 1, 18-19 (1985).

[67] MULTILATERAL TREATIES DEPOSITED WITH THE SECRETARY GENERAL, STATUS AS AT DECEMBER 1988, *supra* note 64, at 131.

[68] *Hearings, supra* note 35, at 52 (critique of Lawyers Committee for International Human Rights).

[69] Such direct federal implementation is to be differentiated from indirect federal initiatives, such as matching grants, to encourage state compliance with treaty obligations.

Section II
Substantive Issues

CHAPTER 5

The Child, Parents and the State
Articles 3, 5, 9, 10, 11, 18, 19, 34 and 36

John E. B. Myers

Introduction

The family is the foundation of American society, and children are its future. The role of the federal and state governments in supporting families and children is complex and evolving. In many respects, government is deeply involved in the family. For example, the government provides a wide range of services and facilities for children and families. At the same time, however, American law and tradition firmly support the primacy of family autonomy and parental freedom to raise children without government intervention. Judges, legislators, and policy-makers continually struggle to strike the proper balance between government intervention in the family and respect for parental rights and family privacy. The sometimes competing interests of parents and government are not the only factors that require consideration, however, for children have rights too. Thus, a tripartite relationship exists between children, parents, and the State. Fortunately, the tension arising from this complex relationship generates creative solutions to the many challenges facing American's children and their families.

This chapter discusses five fundamentally important aspects of American law, and describes the many ways in which American law is consistent with the United Nations Convention on the Rights of the Child. Ratification and implementation of the Convention will nurture traditional principles of American law, and will strengthen the ability of our society to provide all children with the special care and assistance that is their due. The chapter begins with an overview of American law protecting parental rights and family privacy. From there, attention shifts to government programs designed to support children and families. The third topic relates to protection of children from abuse and neglect. Fourth, the chapter outlines American law designed to combat international child abduction by parents locked in custody disputes. Finally, the chapter concludes with discussion of the family reunification principles undergirding American immigration law.

■ RESPECT FOR PARENTAL RIGHTS AND FAMILY PRIVACY

Several international human rights documents recognize the importance of the family. The International Covenant on Economic, Social and Cultural Rights states that "[t]he widest possible protection and assistance should be accorded to the family, which is the natural and fundamental group unit of society . . ."[1] The International Covenant on Civil and Political Rights speaks in similar terms.[2] Article 5 of the United Nations Convention on the Rights of the Child echoes the requirements of international law by requiring States Parties to respect the rights and duties of parents to provide direction and protection for their children. Article 18 of the Convention recognizes that parents "have the primary responsibility for the upbringing and development of the child." United States law is consistent with the basic tenets of the Convention and international human rights law.

A. The Right to Marry

The United States Supreme Court and state supreme courts have long recognized the fundamental importance of marriage and the family. In an 1888 decision, the United States Supreme Court referred to marriage as "the foundation of the family and of society, without which there would be neither civilization nor progress," and as "the most important relation in life. . . ."[3] The right to marry is "one of the 'basic civil rights of man', fundamental to our very existence and survival."[4]

B. The Expanding Meaning of Family

In contemporary American society, the word "family" has multiple meanings. The term includes more than the traditional nuclear family. In *Stanley v. Illinois*,[5] the Supreme Court upheld the parental rights of unwed parents. In striking down a statute which, in effect, presumed that all unwed fathers are unfit to have custody of their children, the Court wrote that "the interest of a parent in the companionship, care, custody, and management of his or her children 'come[s] to this Court with a momentum for respect lacking when appeal is made to liberties which derive merely from shifting economic arrangements.'"[6] In *Moore v. City of East Cleveland*,[7] a plurality of the Court invalidated a zoning ordinance which limited occupancy of single-family dwellings to immediate family members, and which prohibited a grandmother from residing with her grandchildren. The plurality wrote:

> Our decisions establish that the Constitution protects the sanctity of the family precisely because the institution of the family is deeply rooted in this Nation's history and tradition. It is through the family that we inculcate and pass down many of our most cherished values, moral and cultural.
>
> Ours is by no means a tradition limited to respect for the bonds uniting the members of the nuclear family. The tradition of uncles, aunts, cousins, and especially grandparents sharing a household along with parents and children has roots equally venerable and equally deserving of constitutional recognition.[8]

In a 1983 decision discussing the rights of fathers of children born out of wedlock, the Supreme Court emphasized that the meaning of "family" comes not from the marital status of parents, but "from the emotional attachments that derive from the intimacy of daily association, and from the role it plays 'promot[ing] a way of life' through the instruction of children . . . ."[9] Whatever its composition, it is clear that the family retains its central role in American society.

C. Parental Rights and Responsibilities

The right to have children is protected by the Constitution,[10] and when a child is born, parents assume important responsibilities, rights, and duties. An unbroken line of United States Supreme Court decisions make clear that parental rights are fundamental, and are entitled to protection under the Constitution. In its 1923 decision in *Meyer v. Nebraska*,[11] the Court wrote glowingly of "the right of the individual . . . to marry, establish a home and bring up children . . . ."[12] Two years later, in *Pierce v. Society of Sisters*,[13] the Court struck down a statute that prohibited parents from sending their children to private schools. The Court could discern no justification for state interference with the right of parents to direct their children's education. The Court wrote that "[t]he child is not the mere creature of the State; those who nurture him and direct his destiny have the right, coupled with the high duty, to recognize and prepare him for additional obligations."[14] Later decisions reiterate the Supreme Court's respect for the family and for parental rights. In *Ginsburg v. New York*,[15] for example, the Court wrote that the right of parents to make decisions for their children is "basic in the structure of our society."[16] And in *Wisconsin v. Yoder*,[17] the Court noted that "[t]he history and culture of Western civilization reflect a strong tradition of parental concern for the nurture and upbringing of their children. This primary role of the parents in the upbringing of their children is now established beyond debate as an enduring American tradition."[18] Finally, in *Prince v. Massachusetts*,[19] the Court wrote that "[i]t is cardinal with us that the custody, care and nurture of the child reside first in the parents, whose primary function and freedom include preparation for obligations the state can neither supply nor hinder."[20] The Constitution creates a "private realm of family life which the state cannot enter."[21]

D. Limitations on Parental Rights

While parental rights are fundamental, they are not absolute. The state has a "wide range of power for limiting parental freedom and authority in things affecting the child's welfare."[22] Government authority to intervene in the family to protect children derives from two sources: *parens patriae* power and the police power. The *parens patriae* power is the inherent government authority to protect persons, including children, who are incapable of self-protection. The Supreme Court has written that "the state as parens patriae may restrict the parent's control by requiring school attendance, regulating or prohibiting the child's labor and in many other ways."[23]

The police power is the authority of the state to protect the health, safety, morals, and general welfare of the public. Under the police power the state has authority to protect children from abuse and exploitation, whether perpetrated by parents or others. For example, in *New York v. Ferber*,[24] the Supreme Court ruled that states can prohibit distribution of child pornography. The Court wrote that states have a compelling interest in protecting the physical and psychological well-being of children, and that criminalizing distribution of child pornography is a permissible exercise of that interest. In its 1990 decision in *Osborne v. Ohio*,[25] the Court went a step further and held that the Constitution permits states to punish possession of child pornography. Thus, under the *parens patriae* and police powers, states have ample authority to protect children from abuse, neglect, and exploitation.

E. Children's Rights

In addition to the rights of parents and the state, it is clear that children possess legal rights. The United States Supreme Court wrote in *In re Gault*[26] that "neither the Fourteenth Amendment nor the Bill of Rights is for adults alone."[27] And in *Bellotti v. Baird*,[28] the Court stated that "[a] child, merely on account of his minority, is not beyond the protection of the Constitution."[29] Although every one agrees that children have rights, there is little consensus on the scope of children's rights. Professor Wald observes that "[t]o date, neither legislatures nor courts have developed a coherent philosophy or approach when addressing questions relating to children's rights."[30]

Decisions from the United States Supreme Court recognize "three reasons justifying the conclusion that the constitutional rights of children cannot be equated with those of adults."[31] First, children are particularly vulnerable to exploitation and maltreatment. To afford children the special protection that is their due, children's rights must be limited in some, although not all, respects. Second, children are unable to make certain decisions in a rational and mature manner. Finally, the role of parents in child rearing dictates that children's desires must sometimes be subordinated to parental judgment and control.

Although children's rights are not coterminous with the rights of adults, American law protects the rights mentioned in the Convention. By way of example, American constitutional and statutory law prohibit discrimination against children on the basis of race, color, sex, language, religion, political or other opinion, national, ethnic or social origin, property, disability, birth or other status (article 2). The child's right to life is protected by the fourteenth amendment to the United States Constitution and by state constitutions (article 6). American law provides for registration of infants at birth, and birth in the United States automatically makes the child a U.S. citizen (article 7). The first amendment of the Constitution affords children the right to freedom of expression (article 13).[32] American law respects the right of children to freedom of thought, conscience, religion, and association (articles 14 and 15). Children have a right to freedom from arbitrary or unlawful interference with their privacy, family, home, and correspondence (article 16). Disabled children have a right to be free from discrimination, and to receive special care and protection (article 23).[33] American child labor laws strive to protect children from economic exploitation (article 32). The United States, like other nations, has not done all in its power to protect children. Nevertheless, American law has accomplished a great deal on behalf of the Nation's youngest citizens.

F. The Rights of Native American Children

The rights of Native Americans have too often been ignored and violated in American history. In particular, many Indian children have been improperly removed from their parents and extended families. In 1978, Congress enacted the Indian Child Welfare Act (ICWA)[34] "to remedy discriminatory state treatment of Indian children and their families."[35] Congress found:

> *[T]hat there is no resource that is more vital to the continued existence and integrity of Indian tribes than their children and that the United States has a direct interest, as trustee, in protecting Indian children who are members of or are eligible for membership in an Indian tribe;*
>
> *[T]hat an alarmingly high percentage of Indian families are broken up by the removal, often unwarranted, of their children from them by nontribal public and private agencies and that an alarmingly high percentage of such children are placed in non-Indian foster and adoptive homes and institutions; and*
>
> *[T]hat the States, exercising their recognized jurisdiction over Indian child custody proceedings through administrative and judicial bodies, have often failed to recognize the essential tribal relations of Indian people and the cultural and social standards prevailing in Indian communities and families.*[36]

With these findings in mind, Congress declared that the policy of the United States is "to protect the best interests of Indian children and to promote the stability and security of Indian tribes and families by the establishment of minimum Federal standards for the removal of Indian children from their families and the placement of such children in foster or adoptive homes which will reflect the unique values of Indian culture . . . ."[37]

ICWA applies to proceedings concerning foster care, institutional placement, guardianship, termination of parental rights, and adoption of Indian children. Generally speaking, tribal courts are the preferred forum for litigation concerning Indian children, and when litigation takes place in state court, the tribe has the right to intervene.

An Indian child, who is placed in foster care or a pre-adoptive placement, must normally be placed within reasonable proximity to the child's home. Absent good cause to the contrary, a preference must be given to placement with a member of the child's extended family, a foster home licensed, approved, or specified by the child's tribe, an Indian foster home, or an institution approved or operated by the child's tribe.

When a child is placed for adoption under state law, a preference must normally be given for placement with a member of the child's extended family, other members of the Indian child's tribe, or other Indian families. The Indian Child Welfare Act protects the welfare and rich cultural heritage of Indian children. The Act also protects the parents, extended families, and tribes of Indian children. Overall, the Act furthers the requirement of article 5 of the Convention that "States Parties respect the responsibilities, rights, and duties of parents, or where applicable, the members of the extended family or community as provided for by local custom . . . ."

■ STATE ASSISTANCE TO CHILDREN AND FAMILIES

Article 18 requires States Parties to guarantee and support the rights of children and families by rendering "appropriate assistance to parents and legal guardians in the performance of their child-rearing responsibilities". article 18 also requires States Parties to develop "institutions, facilities and services for the care of children." Finally, the article mandates government to "take all appropriate measures to ensure that children of working parents have the right to benefit from child care services and facilities for which they are eligible." Although much remains to be done to improve services and facilities supporting children and families, enough has been accomplished to conclude that the United States is making progress toward fulfilling the important goals set forth in article 18 of the Convention.

A. Education

Every state provides a public education system available to all children. (For detailed discussion of education, see chapter 9.) State and local education funding is supplemented by federal expenditures. The United States Department of Education administers federal education funds and provides technical assistance to the states. In 1975, Congress passed the Education for All Handicapped Children Act (P.L. 94-142), which requires states receiving funds under the Act to guarantee all handicapped children a free and appropriate public education. During the quarter century since passage of 94-142, the educational opportunities provided America's disabled students improved significantly. The Head Start Program provides high quality preschool programming for low-income children.

B. Health Care

The American health care system is among the most advanced in the world, and the majority of America's children enjoy access to primary and tertiary medical care. (For detailed discussion of health care, see chapter 11.) Tragically, many American children live in poverty, and too many poor children lack adequate medical care. Medicaid is the primary government program designed to provide medical care for low-income children and families. Medicaid is administered by the states, and is funded through a combination of state and federal funds. Children's health care needs are also supported under Title V of the Social Security Act, which creates the Maternal and Child Health Block Grant Act.[38] Under Title V, states provide a range of health-related services to women and children. In particular, Title V funds are employed to support services for handicapped children and children with chronic medical conditions. The immunization needs of America's children are met in several ways, including publicly-funded immunizations funded through the Childhood Immunization Program.[39] Mental health services for children and families are available from professionals in private practice and through several publicly-supported programs, including community mental health centers.

C. Nutrition

The nutritional needs of America's children are supported by an array of state and federal programs. The federal Food Stamp Program was established in 1964 to provide low-income people with coupons that are used to purchase food. The federally funded Special Supplemental Food Program for Women, Infants, and Children provides nutrition education and food for low-income pregnant women and mothers of young children who are at nutritional risk.[40] The National School Lunch Program serves millions of children, including many whose nutritional needs are not met at home due to poverty.[41]

D. The Impact of Poverty

Conditions of poverty undermine the ability of parents to raise their children, and much remains to be done to reduce the large number of American children living in poverty. Although existing programs of financial support for the poor do not eliminate poverty, they nevertheless provide essential funds that enable millions of parents to provide at least minimally-adequate shelter, nutrition, and clothing for their children.

E. Child Care Services

Article 18 requires States Parties to "take all appropriate measures to ensure that children of working parents have the right to benefit from child care services and facilities for which they are eligible." It is estimated that there are 19.9 million American children under age six. There are approximately 10.2 million preschool children whose mothers are employed. By 1995, as many as two-thirds of mothers of preschool children will be in the work force. Of children under age five with working mothers, approximately 31% are cared for in the home, primarily by relatives. Another 37% are cared for in another home, primarily by non-relatives. Approximately 23% attend some form of organized child care facility.

It is very difficult to determine the unmet need for day care in the United States. There is general consensus, however, that the need is great and growing. There is also agreement that many children receive inadequate supervision and care. Steps are now underway in the private sector and in government to improve the quality of day care in the United States, and to make it available to parents of modest means.

■ PROTECTING CHILDREN FROM ABUSE AND NEGLECT

The major human rights documents of the United Nations and other international organizations state clearly that society owes children protection.[42] The Universal Declaration of Human Rights states that children "are entitled to special care and assistance."[43] The United Nations Declaration of the Rights of the Child states that "the child, by reason of his physical and mental immaturity, needs special safeguards and care, including appropriate legal protection, before as well as after birth."[44] The International Covenant on Economic, Social and Cultural Rights echoes this theme by stating that "[s]pecial measures of protection and assistance should be taken on behalf of all children . . . ."[45] The International Covenant on Civil and Political Rights states that "[e]very child shall have . . . such measures of protection as are required by his status as a minor . . . ."[46] The Preamble of the United Nations Convention on the Rights of the Child states that children are entitled to grow up "in an atmosphere of happiness, love and understanding." Finally, article 3 of the Convention states that "States Parties [shall] undertake to ensure the child such protection and care as is necessary for his or her well-being." Thus, the protection of children is a pervading principle of international human rights law.

Four articles of the Convention give direct effect to the broad goals of providing children safe, nurturing environments in which to develop. article 19 requires states to protect children from physical abuse, psychological abuse, sexual abuse, neglect, and exploitation. Article 34 reiterates the obligation of States Parties to protect children from "all forms of sexual exploitation and sexual abuse." Article 36 enjoins States Parties to protect children from all forms of harmful exploitation not otherwise specified in the Convention. Article 9 recognizes that children must sometimes be removed from the custody of their parents to protect them from abuse or neglect.

Child maltreatment is a serious problem in the United States, as it is elsewhere in the world. The Federal Government and the states devote considerable resources to preventing child abuse and neglect, and to protecting children who have been maltreated from further abuse or neglect. Although the child protection system in the United States is far from perfect, the United States can act with a clear conscience in ratifying the portions of the Convention dealing with child protection.

A. History of the American Child Protection Movement

The child protection movement in the United States got underway in the late nineteenth century. In 1899, the first juvenile court was established, and within a relatively short time, juvenile or family courts were operating in every state. The juvenile courts remain one of the vital components of the child protection system. The early years of this century also witnessed the growth and professionalism of social work.

In 1962, Dr. C. Henry Kempe and his associates published their seminal article describing the battered child syndrome.[47] Kempe's description of physical abuse focused professional and public attention on child abuse. Also in 1962, progress was made toward model legislation to require professionals working with children to report suspected child abuse and neglect to designated law enforcement or child protection authorities. The first reporting statute was enacted in 1963, and within four years, every state had a reporting law. States continue refining and improving their reporting statutes. The reporting laws disclosed that child abuse and neglect are widespread problems. As the magnitude of child maltreatment became apparent, child protective services agencies (CPS) grew to meet the needs of families and children. In most locations, CPS agencies are seriously overworked, understaffed, and underfunded. Nevertheless, despite chronic problems, CPS agencies continue to provide essential investigative and case work services to millions of children and families.

The Federal Government has long been involved in the effort to protect children and support families. In 1912, the Children's Bureau was created by Congress to report on the welfare of children. The Bureau is now part of the Department of Health and Human Services. In 1935, the Social Security Act was passed. Among other programs, the Act created what is now Aid to Families with Dependent Children (AFDC). In 1974, Congress enacted the Child Abuse and Neglect Prevention and Treatment Act to assist states in developing programs to prevent and respond to child maltreatment. And in 1980, Congress passed the Adoption Assistance and Child Welfare Act, which assists states in preventing unnecessary foster care, reuniting foster children with their biological parents, and providing permanent adoptive families for children who cannot return home.

B. Reporting and Investigation of Child Maltreatment

Article 19 of the Convention requires States Parties to establish laws and procedures to detect, report, and investigate child maltreatment. As discussed above, the reporting statutes in force in every state require relevant professionals to report suspected abuse and neglect. Thus, America possesses the detection and reporting system contemplated by the Convention. Article 19 also requires States Parties to establish mechanisms to investigate reports of child abuse and to make referrals for appropriate support and services, including treatment and follow-up. CPS and law enforcement agencies routinely investigate suspected maltreatment. Following investigation, professionals select among a range of alternative dispositions, including those set forth in article 19. In appropriate circumstances, law enforcement and CPS workers refer cases to the judicial system for action. Articles 9 and 19 require States Parties to provide judicial involvement in child maltreatment cases, and, here again, the United States complies with the requirements of the Convention.

C. Emergency Protective Custody

Article 9 specifies that a child may not be removed from her or his parents unless removal is required to protect the child's best interests. (For detailed discussion of the "best interests" principle, see Chapter 1). American law recognizes the danger of inappropriate removal of children from their parents. At the same time, however, the law recognizes the need to allow appropriate authorities to take children into emergency protective custody. Emergency custody is short-lived, and, when children must remain in protective custody pending resolution of their case, professionals must seek judicial approval.

D. The Juvenile Court and Reasonable Efforts to Reunify Families

The juvenile or family court is available in every American state to protect abused and neglected children. Proceedings are commenced in the juvenile court by filing a petition alleging that a child has been maltreated and is in need of protection. Petitions are usually filed by a social worker or the district attorney's office. As required by article 9 of the Convention, all interested parties are provided notice of hearings in the juvenile court, and are permitted to participate and to make their views known to the court. At the adjudicatory stage of proceedings, the court considers the evidence offered by the parties and determines whether the child was abused or neglected. If a judgment is made that maltreatment occurred, the court proceeds to the dispositional phase of proceedings, during which the judge selects from a wide array of dispositional alternatives. American law recognizes the importance of the parent-child relationship, and, in many cases, juvenile court judges permit maltreating parents to retain custody of their child on condition the parents avail themselves of services to enable them to improve their parenting ability. In some cases it is unsafe to leave children at home, however, and alternative living arrangements, such as foster care, are ordered by the court.

When children are removed from parental custody, parents are generally encouraged to visit their children, and to maintain the parent-child relationship. American law requires courts and social service agencies to make efforts to reunify the family. The law also mandates periodic review of the appropriateness of children's placements and treatment. The requirements of periodic review and efforts to reunify families fulfill the mandate of article 9 that "States Parties shall respect the right of the child who is separated from one or both parents to maintain personal relations and direct contact with both parents on a regular basis, except if it is contrary to the child's best interest," and the requirement of article 25 that "States Parties recognize the right of a child who has been placed by the competent authorities for the purposes of care, protection, or treatment of his or her physical or mental health, to a periodic review of the treatment provided to the child and all other circumstances relevant to his or her placement."

■ COMBATING ILLICIT TRANSFER AND NON-RETURN OF CHILDREN

International child abduction by parents struggling over custody has become a serious problem. Article 11 of the Convention requires States Parties to "take measures to combat the illicit transfer and non-return of children abroad." Among the measures required of States Parties is the promotion and conclusion of bilateral or multilateral agreements or accession to existing agreements relating to international child abduction.

A. Hague Convention on the Civil Aspects of International Child Abduction

Several international agreements exist to combat parental child abduction.[48] Of immediate relevance to the United States is the Hague Convention on the Civil Aspects of International Child Abduction, adopted unanimously by the Hague Conference on Private International Law on October 24, 1980. "The specific objectives of the Hague Convention are two-fold: to secure the prompt return of wrongfully removed or retained children to the country of their habitual residence, and to ensure that visitation rights are respected between the Contracting States."[49] In an effort "to spare children the detrimental emotional effects associated with transnational parental kidnapping,"[50] the United States ratified the Hague Convention on July 1, 1988, after Congress enacted enabling legislation.[51]

B. Uniform Child Custody Jurisdiction Act

The Hague Convention is not the only law designed to deter and remedy international child abduction by parents. Every American state has adopted a version of the Uniform Child Custody Jurisdiction Act (UCCJA).[52] Section 23 of the UCCJA provides:

> The general policies of this Act extend to the international area. The provisions of this Act relating to the recognition and enforcement of custody decrees of other states apply to custody decrees and decrees involving legal institutions similar in nature to custody institutions rendered by appropriate authorities of other nations if

reasonable notice and opportunity to be heard were given to all affected persons.

Section 23 requires American states to recognize and enforce foreign country child custody decrees provided they are based on principles and procedures that are consistent with the UCCJA. The United States has taken important steps to fulfill the mandate of article 11 of the Convention on the Rights of the Child to combat illicit transfer and non-return of children abroad.

■ IMMIGRATION AND FAMILY REUNIFICATION

Article 10 of the Convention concerns the right of children and parents "to enter or leave a State Party for the purpose of family reunification." Family reunification lies at the heart of American immigration law and policy. Professors Aleinikoff and Martin write that "[t]he dominant feature of current arrangements for permanent immigration to the United States is family reunification."[53]

American immigration law allows admission of two groups of aliens: immigrants and nonimmigrants. A nonimmigrant is an alien who seeks temporary admission to the United States for a specific purpose. Immigrants are those seeking to make the United States their permanent home. Since 1921, numerical limits have been imposed on permanent immigration to the United States. In 1965, Congress established a preference system for immigration. "Currently, the preference provisions of the law allow the immigration of 270,000 individuals annually, with these numbers allocated among six basic categories. Eighty percent of these numbers are reserved for family reunification preference categories, and twenty percent are granted to persons based on the employment needs of the United States."[54] Professors Gordon and Mailman describe the preference system as follows:

> [T]he high priority given to the principle of family unity in the scheme of the immigrant selection system is reflected by the allocation of 80 percent of the 270,000 preference numbers to certain relatives of American citizens and lawful permanent residents . . . :

- First preference: unmarried sons and daughters [*over* 21 years of age] of American citizens—20 percent.

- Second preference: spouses and unmarried sons and daughters of lawful permanent residents—26 percent.

- Fourth preference: married sons and daughters of American citizens—10 percent.

- Fifth preference: brothers and sisters of American citizens who are at least twenty-one—24 percent.[55]

In addition to annual immigration under the preference system, which is limited to 270,000 visas worldwide (20,000 visas per nation), United States law allows unlimited immigration of certain immediate relatives of United States citizens, including spouses and unmarried children *under* 21 years of age. Thus, unmarried minor children of American citizens are admitted without regard to the numerical limits of the preference system.

For purposes of family reunification, American immigration law generally treats adopted and "illegitimate" children the same as it treats "legitimate" children. Mothers have long been able to seek reunification with their "illegitimate" child. It was not until 1986, however, that fathers of "illegitimate" children were accorded similar treatment. Under current law, natural fathers who demonstrate a bona fide parental relationship with their "illegitimate" child may seek reunification.

One aspect of United States family reunification policy that comes in for criticism relates to the different treatment afforded immediate family members of resident aliens and immediate family members of American citizens. Immediate family members of citizens are admitted without reference to the preference system and its numerical limits on immigration. By contrast, spouses and children of resident aliens are admitted under the preference system. Calling this difference a "major inequity," Professor Guendelsberger writes:

> The only preference category including families of permanent resident aliens is the second, which limits the preference to spouses

and unmarried sons or daughters. This difference creates serious disparities between residents and citizens, especially resident aliens from countries of high immigration demand. The wait for second-preference visas for Mexican applicants, for instance, has been estimated at approximately eight years. While these spouses and children wait, the law reserves 24% of the total visas for the siblings of citizens. As the Select Commission on Immigration and Refuge Policy (SCIRP) concluded in its Final Report in 1981: "There is something wrong with a law that keeps out—for as long as eight years—the small child of a mother or father who has settled in the United States while a nonrelative or less close relative from another country can come in immediately."[56]

The law does not place a numerical ceiling on nonimmigrant admissions to the United States, and thousands of children enter the country every year to visit noncustodial parents and to accompany parents who are studying or working temporarily in the United States.

American citizens, including children, enjoy the right to enter[57] and leave[58] the United States. Professors Gordon and Mailman note that "[a]n American citizen's liberty to travel freely in foreign countries cannot be arbitrarily restricted."[59] Richard Plender adds that "[t]he right to travel abroad is protected under the fifth amendment to the Constitution of the United States as an aspect of the 'liberty' of which an individual cannot be deprived save by due process of law."[60]

Despite remaining inequities, United States immigration law has come very far indeed since the discriminatory days of the Chinese Restriction and Exclusion Act of the late nineteenth century. The spirit and letter of modern immigration law are largely consistent with the requirement of article 10 of the Convention that States Parties respond to applications for family reunification "in a positive, humane and expeditious manner."

Conclusion

The relationship between children, their parents, and the State is complex. On the one hand, the State is available to support families and protect children from maltreatment. On the other hand, American law and tradition carve out broad areas of family privacy and parental autonomy which the state may not infringe. The challenge is to find the proper balance. Adoption of the United Nations Convention on the Rights of the Child will materially assist in the effort to strike the proper balance.

Footnotes

1. International Covenant on Economic, Social, and Cultural Rights, G.A. Res. 2200 (XIX), 21 U.S. GAOR Supp. (No. 16) at 49, U.N. Doc A/6316 (1966), article 10(1).
2. International Covenant on Civil and Political Rights, (U.N.T.S. 171, G.A. Res. 2200 (XIX), U.N. GAOR Supp. (No. 16) at 52, U.N. Doc. A/16316 (1966), article 23(1).
3. Maynard v. Hill, 125 U.S. 190, 205, 211 (1888).
4. Loving v. Virginia, 388 U.S. 1, 12 (1967).
5. 405 U.S. 645 (1972).
6. *Id.* at 651.
7. 431 U.S.494 (1977).
8. *Id.* at 503-04.
9. Lehr v. Robertson, 463 U.S. 248, 261 (1983).
10. Skinner v. Oklahoma, 316 U.S. 535 (1942).
11. 262 U.S. 390 (1923).
12. *Id.* at 399.
13. 268 U.S. 510 (1925).
14. *Id.* at 535.
15. 390 U.S. 629 (1968).
16. *Id.* at 639.
17. 406 U.S. 205 (1972).
18. *Id.* at 232.
19. 321 U.S. 158 (1944).

[20] *Id.* at 166. American constitutional law is consistent with the requirement of Article 14 of the Convention, which states that "States parties shall respect the rights and duties of the parents and, when applicable, legal guardians, to provide direction to the child in the exercise of his or her right in a manner consistent with the evolving capacities of the child."

[21] 321 U.S. at 166.

[22] *Id.* at 167.

[23] *Id.* at 166.

[24] 458 U.S. 747 (1982).

[25] 110 S. Ct. 1691 (1990).

[26] 387 U.S. 1 (1967).

[27] *Id.* at 13.

[28] 443 U.S. 622 (1979).

[29] *Id.* at 633.

[30] Wald, *Children's Rights: A Framework for Analysis*, 12 U. CAL. DAVIS L. REV. 255, 258 (1979). See also, Cohen, *Relationships Between the Child, the Family and the State: The United Nations' Convention on the Rights of the Child*, in PERSPECTIVES ON THE FAMILY (M. Bayles, R. Moffat & J. Grcic eds. 1990).

[31] 443 U.S. 634 (1979).

[32] Hazelwood School District v. Kuhlmeier, 108 S. Ct. 562 (1988).

[33] *See, e.g.*, Education for All Handicapped Children Act, 20 U.S.C. §§1400-1461 and Section 504 of the Rehabilitation Act of 1973, 29 U.S.C.A. § 794 (1988).

[34] 25 U.S.C.A. § 1901 et seq. (1983).

[35] A. HARALAMBIE, HANDLING CHILD CUSTODY CASES § 16.01, at 246 (1983).

[36] 25 U.S.C.A. § 1901.

[37] 25 U.S.C.A. § 1902.

[38] 42 U.S.C. § 701.

[39] 42 U.S.C. § 247b.

[40] 42 U.S.C § 1786(a).

[41] 42 U.S.C. § 1751.

[42] In addition to the documents cited in the text see also, American Declaration of the Rights and Duties of Man, article VII ("All women, during pregnancy and the nursing period, and all children have the right to special protection, care and aid"); American Convention on Human Rights, article 19 ("Every minor has the right to the measures of protection required by his condition as a minor on the part of his family, society, and the state"); European Social Charter, Part I, subpart (7) ("Children and young persons have the right to a special protection against the physical and moral hazards to which they are exposed").

[43] Universal Declaration of Human Rights, article 25(2). G.A. Res. 217A (ICC), U.N. DOC. A/810, (1948).

[44] Declaration of the Rights of the Child, 14 U.N. GAOR Supp. 2 (No. 16); U.N. DOC. A/4054 (1959).

[45] International Covenant on Economic, Social and Cultural Rights, *supra* note 1, article 10(3).

[46] International Covenant on Civil and Political Rights, *supra* note 2, article 24(1).

[47] Kempe, Silverman, Steele, Droegmuller & Silver, *The Battered-Child Syndrome*, 181 J.A.M.A. 17 (1962).

[48] *See* Rivers, *The Hague International Child Abduction Convention and The International Child Abduction Remedies Act: Closing Doors To The Parent Abductor*, 2 TRANSNAT'L LAW 589 (1989).

[49] *Id.* at 616-17.

[50] Letter of Submittal from Secretary of State George P. Schultz to President Ronald Reagan (Oct. 4, 1985), *reprinted in* 51 Fed. Reg. 10,495 (1986).

[51] 42 U.C.S.A. §§ 11601-11610 (1988). *See also* 22 C.F.R. Part 94 and Legal Analysis of the Hague Convention on the Civil Aspects of International Child Abduction, 51 Fed. Reg. 10503 (March 26, 1988).

[52] Uniform Child Custody Jurisdiction Act, 9 U.L.A. 115 (1968).

[53] T. ALEINIKOFF & D. MARTIN, IMMIGRATION: PROCESS AND POLICY 125 (1985).

[54] *Id.* at 101. For discussion of the preferences see Guendelsberger, *The Right to Family Reunification in French and United States Immigration Law*, 21 CORNELL INT'L L.J. 1, 19-22 (1988).

[55] C. GORDON & S. MAILMAN, IMMIGRATION LAW AND PROCEDURE §1.03[2][e], at 1-20 (1989).

[56] Guendelsberger, *The Right to Family Unification in French and United States Immigration Law*, 21 CORNELL INT'L L.J. 1, 21 (1988)(footnotes omitted).

[57] *See* R. PLENDER, INTERNATIONAL MIGRATION LAW at 133 (rev. 2d ed. 1988)("The principle that every State must admit its own nationals to its territory is accepted so widely that its existence as a rule of law is virtually beyond dispute").

[58] The right to travel abroad finds expression in Article 13(2) of the Universal Declaration of Human Rights, Article 12(2) of the International Covenant on Civil and Political Rights, and Article 5(d)(ii) of the International Convention on the Elimination of All Forms of Racial Discrimination. See also, the Final Act of the Conference on Security and Cooperation in Europe—Basket III.

[59] 4 GORDON AND MAILMAN, *supra* note 54 at § 11.14c, at 11-37.

[60] PLENDER, *supra* note 56 at 102.

CHAPTER 6

Anti-Discrimination and Identity Rights of the Child
Articles 2, 7, 8, 22, and 30

Daniel L. Skoler

Introduction

The United Nations has done its work well in fostering development and adoption of the Convention on the Rights of the Child. The instrument became a binding treaty on September 2, 1990. However, the real value and contribution of this instrument to the interests and well-being of the world's children will lie in its tangible impact within States which become Parties. As Eleanor Roosevelt observed over thirty years ago:

> Where, after all, do universal human rights begin? In small places, close to home—so close and so small that they cannot be seen on any map of the world. Yet, they are the world of the individual person: the neighborhood he lives in; the school or college he attends; the factory, farm or office where he works. Such are the places where every man, woman and child seeks equal justice, equal opportunity, equal dignity without discrimination.[1]

This chapter will explore and speculate on areas where the new Convention's anti-discrimination and identity mandates can help bring a greater measure of realization to children in the "small places" of the United States. The role is one typically to be played out through changes in legal formulations and their implementation, a task rendered especially difficult by the multiple lawmakers, law interpreters, and law implementers in our federal nation.

The Convention contains two articles protecting children against discrimination (articles 2 and 30), two which protect their identity (articles 7 and 8) and yet another which seeks to foster comparable benefits for refugee children (article 22). The first subject would be immediately recognized as an arena of struggle, pain and legal evolution in America. The other would hardly be viewed as a present battleground of civil rights on the one hand, or hurtful abuse of children on the other.

On both counts, federal and state law does not offer significant conflict with the Convention's formulations. The United States Government, as it analyzes the Convention's obligations, should find little change or challenge to current domestic law and social policies mandated by the discrimination and identity articles. On the other hand, finding the resources to fully meet many of the Convention's standards, especially in child health and welfare matters, and to avoid *de facto* discrimination in implementing laws which embody such standards, may prove to be a different story.

■ ANTI-DISCRIMINATION GUARANTEES

It is inconceivable that any new international human rights treaty would not feature a broad and strong mandate against discrimination. This has been the pattern, both with the comprehensive and the more narrowly-focused instruments that have been brought into being within the past three decades. Indeed, a number of these specifically focus on discrimination, e.g., the Conventions on Elimination of All Forms of Discrimination Against Women (1981), Elimination of All Forms of Racial Discrimination (1969), Discrimination in Education (1962) and Discrimination in Respect of Employment and Occupation (1960).

The specific formulation adopted for the Convention on the Rights of the Child is broad, proclaiming a duty on the part of all adopting nations to "respect and ensure" to each child within its jurisdiction all of the substantive rights set forth in the Convention:

> ... *without discrimination of any kind, irrespective of the child's or his or her parent's or legal guardian's race, colour, sex, language, religion, political or other opinion, national, ethnic, or social origin, property, disability, birth, or other status (Article 2).*

An additional subsection calls for appropriate measures to assure protection from discrimination on the basis of parental or family member status, activities and beliefs, and two other articles protect, by implication, discrimination against refugee children in enjoyment of rights afforded by the Convention (article 22) and against minorities and indigenous children in enjoyment of cultural, religious and language heritages (article 30).

It is interesting that the new Convention's basic anti-discrimination provisions track very closely those of the Universal Declaration of Human Rights, the International Covenant on Civil and Political Rights, the International Covenant on Economic, Social and Cultural Rights, the American Convention on Human Rights, and the European Convention on Human Rights.[2] There are semantic differences (e.g., the use in two of these instruments of "distinction" in lieu of "discrimination" and of the weaker terminology "undertake to" rather than "shall ensure" or "is entitled to"). However, these broad human rights documents are notably similar in their application of anti-discrimination strictures to all rights enumerated in the instruments and in their rather detailed listing of personal and group attributes which may not form the basis of discriminatory treatment.

■ IMPACT FOR UNITED STATES LAW—CONSTITUTIONAL GUARANTEES

By positioning its discrimination protections so as to apply to all rights set forth in the Convention, the new treaty offers a real challenge to the anti-discrimination law and jurisprudence of the United States. However, this nation's basic anti-discrimination charter, the "equal protection" (and, in lesser degree, the "due process" and "privileges and immunities") guarantees of our Constitution's fourteenth amendment, although constructed differently than the new Convention's formulations, are equally sweeping in breadth and need take no back seat to the Convention's broad anti-discrimination coverage.

The fourteenth amendment to the U. S. Constitution forbids any state "to deny to persons within its jurisdiction the equal protection of the laws". It was enacted in the post-Civil War period, but soon abandoned and not really activated as an anti-discrimination tool for the better part of a century.[3] Then, beginning in the late 1940's and supplemented by a growing body of anti-discrimination legislation and "friendly" judicial interpretation, the notion took hold that discrimination in administration of any protection or

Anti-Discrimination

benefit afforded by law to American citizens was illegal and impermissable, whether in a code of children's rights or any other substantive cluster of legal entitlements. The struggle was not easy nor was the pace of change an even one (many states achieved a large measure of "equal rights" justice early on while others lagged), but general acceptance of the concept, in some quarters still hesitantly, is now well engraved in the American ethos.

It is remarkable to note that what may be the most seminal case in our history on the illegitimacy of unreasoned distinctions in treatment of American citizens because of religious belief, political persuasion, skin color, or similar characteristics was one relating to children. When our Supreme Court decided in *Brown v. Board of Education* (1954)[4] that segregation by race in access to public school education was impermissable under the "equal treatment" mandates of our Constitution, an egalitarian revolution began, first in the realization of racial equality in education; but soon, under its sweeping momentum, that revolution encompassed other kinds of governmental functions, benefits, and protected activities and a wide variety of classifications beyond race, that has not abated until this very day.

Race was not the only discriminatory classification to feel the weight and disapproval of the fourteenth amendment's equal protection clause, unreinforced by any specific legislative standard. "Illegitimacy" as a state law bar to a child's recovery of damages for the wrongful death of a parent or to enforcement of parental support rights was struck down in *Levy v. Louisiana* (1968) and *Gomez v. Perez* (1973)[,5] and local government exclusion of alien children from public school attendance or from educational assistance benefits was also determined to be constitutionally impermissible discrimination in *Plyler v. Doe* (1982) and *Nyquist v. Mauclet* (1977).[6] Thus, Constitutional guarantees, by themselves, have validated and are in harmony with the Convention's anti-discrimination mandates. Yet, the uncertainties of Constitutional interpretation, including the varying levels of scrutiny applied to statutory enactments or to other governmental practices which treat different groups of citizens differently, have left direct Constitutional enforcement of discriminatory treatment a less than optimal and often quite uncertain instrumentality. Indeed, our Supreme Court has declined to consistently accord either illegitimacy or alien status the "strict scrutiny" standard of review applied to racial distinctions in assessing whether legislation which unfavorably impacts on those groups is, under a particular set of circumstances or in a specific governmental activity or service setting, an impermissable discrimination.[7]

■ IMPACT FOR UNITED STATES LAW—LEGISLATIVE GUARANTEES

Fortunately, the United States, at both federal and state levels, has a broad network of anti-discrimination legislation to lend particularity to the concept of equal treatment and equal participation in the "privileges and immunities" of citizenship.[8] Most notable, but often focussed in greater degree on interests of adults than children, are our present Civil Rights Act protections (some going back to the Reconstruction Amendments and their original cluster of implementing civil rights legislation). These protect such basic personal rights as access to and treatment with respect to voting, contracting, property ownership, public accommodations, employment, housing, and participation in federally-supported benefit and service programs, from discrimination on the basis of race, color, religion, national origin and, more recently, sex.[9]

In effect, statutory anti-discrimination bars have been a frontline mechanism for outlawing discriminatory treatment against children "where it counts". They permit a targeting that can be adapted to a particular emergency or need confronting children and then can provide the specificity as to right, remedy and detail that permits meaningful and fair enforcement in that particular context.

Four recent examples in federal law are:

> (i) the Fair Housing Amendments Act of 1988 which prohibits discrimination against children, (i.e., families with children) in the sale or rental of housing,

> (ii) enactment of the McKinney Homeless Assistance Act which, in effect, prohibits states and their local school districts from discriminating against homeless children in school enrollment (i.e., by ensuring enrollment in either their prior school district or the district in which their temporary shelter is located),

(iii) provisions under federal law, i.e., our Rehabilitation Act of 1973 and the Education for All Handicapped Children Act, protecting children with disabilities, among other things, against discrimination in access to normal classroom participation and attendance, and

(iv) last year's Social Security amendments to eliminate discrimination between adopted and natural children in eligibility criteria for child's insurance benefits. All of those were enacted and are now being used to prevent discrimination against children in enjoyment of rights, i.e., education, housing, and social insurance benefits, to which they should be entitled.[10]

How will the Convention advance or impact upon United States anti-discrimination law? Well, the Convention, once it becomes a binding treaty (and therefore a legal obligation of the United States), could impact upon us in several ways:

(a) The Convention's anti-discrimination obligations are broad and not necessarily satisfied by merely enacting appropriate laws. The legal obligation that ratifying nations undertake is to "ensure the rights" set forth in the Convention. This places a burden on government to agressively implement and enforce anti-discrimination law, an area in which performance has often been hesitant. Ensuring rights requires more than just enacting law.

(b) There are certain areas of rights enumerated in the Convention where even facially neutral laws may impact more harshly on certain groups. For example, the Convention binds ratifying nations to take measures to reduce child and infant mortality, to provide pre-natal and post-natal health care for expectant mothers, and to ensure that children receive necessary medical assistance and health care, all in terms of "enjoyment of the highest attainable standard of health" (article 24). Today, there are millions of children without medical insurance and millions of expectant mothers in the United States without pre-natal care. Moreover, the absence of such services impacts much more adversely on minority racial groups than on the population at large. That is, our health care system, as currently operated, has a disparate impact on minority children and may well discriminate against them in terms of the mandate of article 2 of the Convention.

■ DISCRIMINATION IN EDUCATIONAL RIGHTS—A CASE STUDY

As indicated, the reach of the Convention's basic anti-discrimination mandate extends to all the rights set forth in the Convention. Thus, analysis of the extent of the Convention's conformity to and potential impact on American law requires a broad-ranging inquiry, complicated by our federal system and its several sources of binding law in this area. A good way to illustrate "impact"—or lack of it—might be to play through a few major areas of Convention rights and examine their current status under United States law, gaps in protection, and other issues and uncertainties in terms of discrimination protections. Educational rights are critically important to the well-being of children and present an excellent arena for this kind of analysis. Within the United States, problems of discrimination in education have been numerous, varied, and highly visible. They have touched virtually every protected status enumerated in article 2 (race, color, sex, language, religion, political affiliation, disability, birth, etc.).

The education articles of the Convention (articles 28 and 29) are basic and modest in their substantive thrust, seemingly offering little challenge to the affluent and education-oriented society that exists in the United States. Article 28 recites the general "right of children to education", recognizes it as a requirement to be achieved "progressively and on the basis of equal opportunity" (the latter phrase itself constituting a form of anti-discrimination standard) and then enumerates a group of specific steps for implementation. These include (i) free and compulsory primary education, (ii) development of different forms of secondary education accessible to all, (iii) accessibility of higher education "on the basis of capacity", (iv) availability of educational and vocational information and guidance, and (v) steps to encourage regular attendance at schools and reduced dropout rates. Further injunctions call for humanely administered school discipline and international cooperation in matters relating to education (with focus on illiteracy reduction, access to scientific and technical knowledge, and modern teaching methods).

Anti-Discrimination

Finally, as a kind of broad definition of policy objectives for ratifying nations, article 29 recites the agreement of each party to the Convention that education is to be directed to development of children's personality and abilities "to their fullest potential", to development of respect for parents, for the natural environment, and for human rights, fundamental freedoms, cultural identity and national values, and to preparation for responsible life in a free, tolerant, and peaceful society.

These substantive standards, apparently geared to world conditions and realities, and not necessarily those of more technologically-advanced nations with well-established educational systems, will be reviewed elsewhere (Chapter 9). However, they would seem, in the main, to be consistent with current United States practice, standards, and values (although we have been surprised recently by the extent to which even basic literacy remains an unrealized goal for many in our population). However, discrimination in access to and administration of our educational apparatus has been a matter of contention and considerable legal conflict and definition for the past fifty years.

Brown v. Board of Education, as has been observed, was the landmark decision enshrining in our fundamental law the principle of equal education in general and the unacceptability (and unconstitutionality) of racially-segregated public education in particular. Since that decision, hundreds of cases have gone to the courts to further define the meaning of integrated education in our nation, e.g., with respect to student population imbalances, busing of students, choices of schools, testing and classification of students, administration of discipline, etc. Generally, these have clarified and extended rights to racially-fair educational practices and programs.

However, other important issues of educational discrimination have been contested and dealt with in this nation. These relate to virtually every impermissable status classification specified in the Convention's basic antidiscrimination article. Thus, determinations have been made, through litigation, legislation, or regulatory issuances (and at federal or state levels, or both) that, in important aspects of educational access and services, schools may not discriminate against children because of non-citizen status (i.e., withdrawal of state funds and barring of public school enrollment to undocumented aliens);[11] because of language status (e.g., refusal to provide

Anti-Discrimination

instruction or bilingual education to non-English speaking children);[12] because of economic or property status (e.g., denial of free public education and instructional credits to children of migrant workers);[13] because of marital, parental, or pregnancy status (e.g., denial or restriction of school attendance);[14] because of religious orientation (e.g., prohibition of high school clubs because of religious content)[15] or because of handicap or disability (e.g., misplacing minority groups in special education programs and denial of regular classroom attendance to children with handicapping conditions such as AIDS infection).[16]

Sex discrimination in education is prohibited by specific federal legislation (commonly known as Title IX) and by Constitutional interpretation in a number of areas.[17] Prohibitions apply to such practices as maintenance of enrollment quotas on the basis of sex, use of higher admission standards for female than male applicants, restriction of courses which may be taken by girls, and, with some qualifications, provision of athletic services.[18]

Most of the foregoing educational discrimination protections apply to public education. The article 28 mandate of the Convention has no such limitation and refers to education generally. Even here, the pattern of strong governmental protections is evident in the United States. Our Supreme Court has construed the Civil Rights Act of 1866, implementing the thirteenth amendment's abolition of slavery, to prohibit private school discrimination on the basis of race in its provisions guaranteeing "full and equal benefit of all laws and proceedings for the security of persons and property as is enjoyed by white citizens".[19] Moreover, discrimination on the basis of race, color, national origin, sex or handicap in any school program or activity receiving federal funds is prohibited by civil rights legislation and impacts on private as well as public schools.[20]

As can be seen, an intricate and quite comprehensive network of constitutional, legislative, and regulatory enactment stands ready to ensure the Convention's antidiscrimination guarantees as applied to children's educational rights and entitlements. There remain, however, a number of open areas in school anti-discrimination obligations. These include the permissability of "separate but equal" schools for males and females, the extent to which schools may be obliged to provide programs for handicapped students which not only reasonably meet educational requirements but maximize

Anti-Discrimination

their learning potential, and the extent of private school student "due process" rights (notice, hearings, etc.) in disciplinary matters and other major decisions affecting educational careers and interests.[21] Such issues are not specifically covered by the Convention nor would its broad substantive guarantees, while offering some implied support for strict equal treatment interpretation, be readily seen as obligations "forcing the hand" of U.S. legal interpretation in such matters.

■ DISCRIMINATION IN HEALTH CARE AND BENEFITS—ANOTHER CASE STUDY

Article 24 of the Convention binds nations which become Parties to:

> ... *recognize the right of the child to the enjoyment of the highest attainable standard of health and to facilities for the treatment of illness and rehabilitation of health*

Ratifying nations agree to "pursue full implementation" of the basic right, with particular focus on measures to (a) diminish infant and child mortality, (b) emphasize primary health care, (c) combat disease and malnutrition, (d) ensure pre- and post-natal health care to pregnant women, (e) provide access to education and support in the use of knowledge of good health, hygiene and sanitation practices, and (f) develop preventive health care, parental guidance and family planning services, including international cooperation in achieving the full realization of children's medical and health rights.

Problems of discrimination in health care services have not received the attention accorded educational services. The body of antidiscrimination law and legislation is sparse in this area, and yet, all the indicators are that health care systems in the United States, whether by design or not, operate to discriminate against minorities. Moreover, court challenges of discriminatory treatment (i.e., "equal protection" claims) in the content or administration of health and welfare programs associated with children (Medicaid, Food Stamps, Aid to Families with Dependent Children, Social Security Disability and Dependency Benefits) have, in contrast to educational program claims, been generally unsuccessful.[22] This may relate to the fact that "strict scrutiny" review is rare in such situations, and program standards and

Anti-Discrimination

criteria focus on "poverty" status with its facially neutral eligibility impact on citizens and persons asserting benefit and service entitlements. Nevertheless, even for disparities not reached by our anti-discrimination laws, correction can be achieved by new legislation. Thus, after court constitutional challenges failed in virtually every federal judicial circuit on disparate treatment of adopted and biological children in qualifying for Social Security dependents benefits, the U.S. Congress recently corrected the discrimination by special legislative enactment.[23]

Progress in achieving article 24 standards has been slow in the United States. Indeed, in recent years we have seen an alarming backslide in important indicators of child health, such as extent of infant mortality, low-birthweight babies, inadequate pre-natal care for expectant mothers, child immunization, and primary health care for pregnant women and infants. As bad as this slippage has been for the population in general, it has been worse for black and non-white mothers and children—virtually twice as bad on every indicator as for the majority white population. Thus, in accordance with recent data and reports, black infant mortality at 18 deaths per 1,000 children doubles the 8.9 rates for whites, black mothers receiving inadequate prenatal care at 15.3% more than double the rate of white women in this category (6.3%), and the low birth-weight rate for black babies at 12.5% is more than twice that for white babies (5.6%).[24]

This kind of disparate impact suggests that black and other non-white children are being discriminated against *in fact*, if not in terms of the intendment of our positive law. Such disparities may well amount to discrimination in access to the health and medical rights of minority children guaranteed by the Convention. The case becomes persuasive, even for a nation like the United States with its vaunted medical technology and high health care standards, when one takes into account our current halt in progress. The black/white infant mortality gap in the mid-eighties reached its greatest disparity since 1940, when such data first began to be recorded by race. Indeed, several of the Surgeon General's announced 1990 goals on immunization of infants, low-birthweight baby and infant mortality reductions, and early pre-natal care will have to be postponed for decades, or even the better part of a century, unless the present pace of progress is improved. That hardly seems to comply with Convention obligations, especially as to minority groups, to ensure "enjoyment of highest attainable standards" and "pursue full implementation of rights" under article 24.

There seem to be few ways for the United States to eliminate this discrimination in health care other than through allocation of additional resources to government health and dependant care programs for poor and near poor citizens since the white/non-white disparity seems to relate primarily to the fact that proportionately more non-whites are in poverty status—and markedly so.[25] Progress in fighting this kind of discrimination through allocation of increased resources to meet health needs has not been insubstantial. In the past five years, for example, there have been significant increases in Medicaid coverage for pregnant women and infants among our poverty level and working poor populations in which minority children are so heavily over-represented. Just last year, the Congress increased mandatory Medicaid coverage for pregnant women and infants to provide eligibility to those with family income up to 133% of poverty levels (and several states have raised eligibility to households earning up to 185% of poverty levels).[26]

■ OTHER DISCRIMINATION CONCERNS

Although comprehensive treatment of child discrimination issues is difficult within the contours of a single chapter, some reflections on disparate treatment in other areas of rights protected by the Convention is in order. This would include matters of child custody, child employment, operation of the criminal/juvenile justice system, and child inheritance and dependency benefit rights.

A. Child Custody and Reunification

The Convention establishes a preference for natural parent care and custody (articles 7 and 9) and its anti-discrimination provision (article 2) makes it clear that discrimination on the basis of parental, as well as child status is proscribed. In harmony with this, racial classifications in the consideration of custody awards have been disapproved by our Supreme Court as a violative of the Constitution's fourteenth amendment equal protection guaranties.[27] On the other hand, our Supreme Court has upheld discrimination between illegitimate children of natural mothers and natural fathers in access to special preference immigration status under our Immigration and Nationality Laws as a justified exercise of largely unreviewable Federal powers to expel or exclude aliens.[28] This distinction on the basis of parental gender, however, would seem to run afoul of article 2 in its tendency to impinge on full enjoyment by alien children of family reunification rights (article 9) and family care rights (article 7) recognized by the Convention.

B. Child Labor

The Convention has little to say about the child's right to work. Instead, it focuses on protection from exploitation in work activities (minimum ages for employment, regulation of hours and conditions of employment, etc.). The measuring standards are non-quantitative, i.e., hazardous character of work, interference with education, and harmfulness to health or development.

Discrimination among different groups in child labor regulation in the United States would appear to be largely a non-issue (although child exploitation may be a different question). The network of federal and state child labor laws is well established in this country and seems solidly in line with Convention's principles.[29] On the other hand, American employment discrimination law protects children as well as adults. This is true of our basic protective legislation in this area, Title VII of the Civil Rights Act of 1964, a number of comparable state statutes, and other special-focus federal enactments such as the Equal Pay Act (which prohibits wage discrimination on the basis of sex).

C. Criminal Violations

The Convention's criminal justice standards (article 40) offer a sound set of protections for children accused of crime, including due process guarantees (presumption of innocence, notice of charges, legal representation, fair hearing proceedings, privilege against self-incrimination, appeals rights, etc.), a preference for establishment of special juvenile codes, tribunals, and procedures, minimum ages for criminal accountability, options for non-judicial dispositions and appropriate alternatives to institutional care. Discriminatory treatment is not dealt with explicitly, and yet juvenile justice administration in the United States has not been without issues in this area, most related to classifications on the basis of sex, i.e., different treatment and penalities for male and female offenders. In the United States, it has been held constitutionally permissable to punish only a male for statutory rape even though the male and female actors are both children and to punish only male adult perpetrators of such conduct and not female perpetrators.[30] As for sex-related crimes other than rape (e.g., molestation), discrimination in criminal liability and punishment based on sex has been disapproved.[31]

In a somewhat related area, our Supreme Court has ruled that prohibitions on the purchase of alcoholic beverages by children must impact equally on males and females[32] but has approved legislation which requires only males and not females to register for draft military service[33]. While some of the broad mandates of the Convention's juvenile crimes article (treatment in a manner which reinforces respect for "human rights" and "fundamental freedoms") might be read to disapprove discriminatory treatment in sex-related crimes, the connection is at best a tenuous one and, to the extent still unsettled, will probably continue to turn on U.S. anti-discrimination doctrine unaffected by the new treaty.

D. Intestacy and Survivor Benefit Rights

The Convention incorporates a strong guarantee (a "shall recognize" right) for every child to enjoy the benefits of social security and social insurance programs (article 26) and affirms the "primary responsibility" of parents for support of children (article 27). Yet, in application of American equal protection doctrine, a checkered record of protection from discrimination has been forged for illegitimate children. Both with respect to inheritance rights and social security survivor benefits, the Supreme Court has approved illegitimacy distinctions in legislative eligibility requirements. Thus, parental support or residence requirements at time of death have been imposed on certain illegitimate children, but not other children, in determining entitlement to social security survivor benefits and, on two occasions, the Supreme Court has rejected "equal protection" challenges to state laws denying inheritance rights to some classes of illegitimate children.[34]

There are Constitutional interpretations which go the other way in the intestacy/survivor benefits area and in assuring equal treatment of illegitimate children in other governmental benefit programs.[35] However, at best, the current state of American law is uncertain as to the extent of governmental authority to treat illegitimate children differently, particularly with regard to male parent relationships, in decedent-related entitlements.

■ NAME, NATIONALITY AND IDENTITY

Article 7 of the Convention assures registration immediately after birth, the right, from birth, to a name, the right to acquire a nationality and, as far as possible, the right for a child to be cared for by parents. Article 8 adds a child's right to preserve his or her identity, including nationality, name and family relations.

Generally, children in the United States have a common law right to take any name they may choose, and generally parents have a right to give their child any name they wish. Common law presumptions that a child will bear the surname of a father and that the father has a primary or vested right that this will occur are giving way to the concept of equal parental rights in such matters and the absence of any legal impediment to prevent married parents from giving their child the mother's surname.[36]

Although the birth registration, name and nationality rights of article 7 are common features in comprehensive human rights treaties, there is little history on what the drafters of the Convention had in mind with article 8 and its new right of "preservation of identity"[37]. Preservation of identity is illustratively defined as including "name" and "nationality" (already covered under article 7) and "family relations". The family relations nexus might well support the kind of "constitutionally protected liberty interest to live with family members" that recently led to invalidation in our courts of state laws discriminating between relatives and non-relatives in entitlement to state funded foster care benefits and medical assistance.[38]

Since the foregoing Convention provisions are quite general and not controversial, there seems little possibility that they will affect American law, including legal requirements relating to acquisition of nationality. Actually, American law on nationality is quite broad. Children of U.S. parents are citizens of the United States regardless of where born; children of aliens, whether resident in the United States or otherwise, are citizens of the United States if born here; and children whose parents are naturalized take derivative U.S. citizenship as a result of such naturalization.[39]

One area where the name and identity articles may guarantee rights not fully recognized in many local U.S. jurisdictions involves article 7's articulation of a "right to know . . . parents." In a majority of American states, statutory provisions restrict access by adopted children to their birth records, and these have withstood constitutional challenges.[40] A number of these laws permit records to be opened, but only by court order upon a showing of "good cause," variously defined to require more than curiosity about parentage (i.e., "psychological necessity," establishment of inheritance rights, etc.). Thus, the effect of these prohibitions, absent voluntary disclosure by adoptive parents, is to bar, or significantly burden, an adopted child's attempt to know natural parentage or natural family identity. This is a deprivation that, joined with the child's article 8 right to "preserve his or her identity," could be viewed as in conflict with the terms of the Convention, should the latter become a binding treaty obligation in this country. There does appear to be some rethinking (and relaxation) occurring in the United States, at least in terms of the adoptive child's access to these birth-related data restrictions and their underlying policy premises.[41] The Convention could be an additional force in that direction.

Indigenous children, along with ethnic, religious and linguistic minorities, are accorded a supplemental "identity" guarantee under article 30's announced right for any child in these categories:

> . . . to enjoy his or her own culture, to profess and practice his or her own religion or, to use his or her own language.

In this nation, existing anti-discrimination and substantive civil rights laws applicable to all citizens provide extensive protection to this nation's indigenous groups, i.e., American Indians. These are reinforced in one enormously important area for Indian children by the Indian Child Welfare Act of 1978.[42] The emphasis in the Act on vesting tribal governments with authority to determine child custody matters, intervene in state child welfare proceedings, qualify for family assistance and training funds and provide for tribal court disposition of appropriate disputes, should go far toward realization and maximization of the Indian child's right to full enjoyment of his or her cultural practices and heritages.

■ THE SPECIAL CASE OF REFUGEE CHILDREN

The drafters of the Convention created a special article obligating nations which become parties to take appropriate action to ensure the enjoyment of the document's substantive rights, by refugee children, whether already in or seeking such status, and whether accompanied or unaccompanied by parents or other caretakers (article 22). The protection is cautious and qualified, referring to this group's right to

> ... receive appropriate protection and humanitarian assistance in the enjoyment of applicable rights set forth in the present Convention and in other international human rights or humanitarian instruments.

Where parents or family members cannot be found, a refugee child is to be "accorded the same protection as any other child permanently or temporarily deprived of his or her family environment for any reason."

Alien children enjoy a significant amount of civil rights protection under American law, it being well established that fourteenth amendment "equal protection" and "due process" guarantees (which run to "persons" and not "citizens") apply to them.[43] Presumably, refugee children would fall within this group. Also, United States law is liberal in granting to children refugee admission status. There are preferences for refugee admission and children can be readily assimilated, by and large, to the parent's status when the latter obtains lawful admission or citizenship rights. American law also provides flexibility for admission of refugees for "humanitarian considerations" and in "emergency situations."[44]

On the other hand, both adults and children seeking asylum and refugee status have often been denied constitutional due process protections in the very processes by which entitlement to such protection is evaluated. Under our increasingly criticized immigration law "entry doctrine," refugees presenting themselves openly and honestly but deemed not to have

Anti-Discrimination

"entered" the United States, may be subjected to physical detention and to exclusion proceedings not measured or constrained by due process guarantees and substantive rights available even for illegal aliens who have successfully penetrated our borders by evasion of authorities.[45] This would seem, as regards children, to be in potential conflict with the new Convention's guarantees of means to challenge deprivations of liberty before appropriate tribunals (article 30), as well as other international instruments to which the United States is presently a party, such as the U.N. Protocol Relating to the Status of Refugees (1907).[46]

For refugee children whose parents can not be located (and literally tens of thousands of "unaccompanied children" have been admitted to the United States since World War II), the Convention speaks in strong and unqualified terms of their right to the same Convention protections as are available to all children deprived of a family environment. This would seem to call forth observance of Convention obligations as to adequate standards of living and provision of housing, nutrition and clothing assistance to children in need (article 27), provision of special protection or assistance, including foster care and other alternative care for those deprived of a family environment (article 20), benefit rights under social insurance (article 25), and other rights to health care, educational services, and protection from exploitation and abuse that necessarily become governmental responsibilities where parental guidance and support is absent. Federal legislation (the Refugee Act of 1980) specifically provides for reimbursement to states and non-profit agencies to meet many of these economic and child welfare obligations to refugee children, including foster care and health benefits.[47]

In terms of the foregoing social and economic rights, it should be noted that deprivations or curtailments for refugee children below benefits afforded other children would quite often be subject to "strict scrutiny" review under established American constitutional law principles.[48] Thus, where the question has been raised, alien children have generally been held to be entitled to participation on a normal basis in needs-tested welfare and public assistance programs.

Conclusion

The anti-discrimination and identity protection guarantees of the Convention on the Rights of the Child appear to be quite consistent with present law in the United States. Hesitancy about ratification on this score would not be warranted. Indeed, with our relative affluence and longstanding dedication to principles of individual rights and human freedom and dignity, we are probably ahead of most nations in records of observance as the world community begins to "sign up" and bring the new treaty into force.

On the other hand, living up to our nation's obligation and full potential for achievement, even on a progressive basis, of the social and economic rights and benefits guaranteed by the Convention, but presently denied to various groups and classes of minority children in much greater degree than other children (and possibly in discriminatory proportions), should be the banner and real challenge under which we embrace the Convention and get to work to confirm the full accessibility of its prescribed rights and intended benefits to all of America's children.

Footnotes

[1] Remarks to United Nations Commission on Human Rights at New York City (March 27, 1958).

[2] *See* article 2 (antidiscrimination) and article 7 (equal protection), Universal Declaration of Human Rights (signed Dec. 10, 1948); articles 1 (antidiscrimination) and 26 (equal protection), International Covenant on Civil and Political Rights (adopted Dec. 16, 1966, entered into force Mar. 23, 1976); article 2, International Covenant on Economic Social and Cultural Rights (adopted Dec. 16, 1966, entered into force on Jan. 3, 1976); article 1 (antidiscrimination) and article 24 (equal protection), American Convention on Human Rights (signed Nov. 22, 1969, entered into force July 18, 1978); Article 14, European Convention on Human Rights, signed Nov. 4, 1950, entered into force, Sept. 8, 1953. None of these treaties have yet been ratified by the United States. On antecedents and rationale for the antidiscrimination provisions of the new Convention, see generally Hitch, *Non-Discrimination and the Rights of the Child: Article 2*, 7 N.Y.L. SCH. J.HUM. RTS. 47 (1989).

Anti-Discrimination

3   As Supreme Court Justice Harry Blackmun observed in describing the rapid neutralization of the new federal citizenship and antidiscrimination rights created by the Reconstruction Amendments and Civil Rights Acts enacted between 1866 and 1875, "The story of how this edifice crumbled during the succeeding half-century might be characterized as a somber one in American legal history . . . Thus, as the 20th Century dawned, the Nation's commitment to civil rights lay in remnants. It was our Dark Age of Civil Rights. For the first 40 years of this century, the only judicial relief available was in suits involving official action denying negroes the right to vote". Blackmun, *Section 1983 and Federal Protection of Civil Rights*, 60 N.Y.U.L. REV. 1, 8 & 11 (1985).

4   Brown v. Board of Education of Topeka, Kansas, 347 U.S. 483 (1954). *See also* Bolling v. Sharpe, 347 U.S. 497 (1954) (companion case to Brown challenging school segregation in the District of Columbia and interpreting the fifth amendment due process clause to guarantee equal protection against federal government denial) and Runyon v. McCrary, 427 U.S. 160 (1976) (prohibiting racial discrimination by private schools).

5   Levy v. Louisiana, 391 U.S. 73 (1968) and Gomez v. Perez, 409 U.S. 535 (1973); see also Weber v. Aetna Casualty and Surety Co., 406 U.S. 164 (1972) (discrimination in eligibility for residual benefits under state workman's compensation law) and New Jersey Welfare Rights Commission v. Cahill, 414 U.S. 619 (1973) (discrimination in eligibility for state public assistance benefits).

6   Plyler v. Doe, 457 U.S. 202 (1982) [confirming that 14th Amendment's guarantee of equal protection of the laws "to any person" applies both to aliens lawfully admitted for residence and illegal (undocumented) aliens].

7   *See* LEVY, KARST, AND MAHONEY, ENCYCLOPEDIA OF THE AMERICAN CONSTITUTION, 947-948 (illegitimacy) and 41-43 (aliens) (1986). While the Court has announced that discrimination against aliens should be viewed as involving a suspect classification, that position has been erratic and large exceptions exist, especially with respect to federally imposed restrictions and activities related to governmental functions.

8   For instances of state antidiscrimination legislative initiatives stronger than federal protections, see AMERICAN CIVIL LIBERTIES UNION, THE RIGHTS OF YOUNG PEOPLE (1985) at 263 (housing rights) and THE

Anti-Discrimination

RIGHTS OF STUDENTS (1988) at 111 (handicapped rights) and 125 (sports participation rights).

9 See 42 U.S.C. §§ 1971 & 1973 (voting); 42 U.S.C. § 1981 (making contracts and access to courts); 42 U.S.C. § 1982 (property rights); 42 U.S.C. § 2000(a) (public accommodations); 42 U.S.C. § 2000(e) (employment - Title VII); 42 U.S.C. §§ 3603, 3604 (sale or rental of housing); and 42 U.S.C. § 2000(d) (participation in and receipt of benefits under federally assisted programs - Title VI). See also Americans with Disabilities Act of 1990, Pub. L. 101-336 (1990) (discrimination in employment, public services and public accommodations).

10 42 U.S.C. §§ 3601 et seq. & 24 C.F.R. 100.31 et seq. (housing discrimination prohibiting not only exclusion from access but practices of restricting families with children to certain buildings, floors, or units of a housing complex or denying or curtailing child access to common or recreational areas and facilities); 42 U.S.C. § 11432 (educational access discrimination against homeless children—protected through mandated state plans); 29 U.S.C. § 794 and 20 U.S.C. §§ 1401 et seq. (discrimination against handicapped children); 1989 Omnibus Budget Reconciliation Act amendments to 42 U.S.C. § 402(d)(8) (equal benefit eligibility for social security dependents benefits to adopted and natural children).

11 See, Plyler v. Doe, 457 U.S. 202 (1982) (disapproving state exclusion of undocumented alien children from public schools) and Nyquist v. Mauclet, 432 U.S. 1 (1977) (rejecting state statutory bars on educational assistance for resident aliens).

12 See Lau v. Nichols, 414 U.S. 563 (1974); Aspira of New York, Inc. v. New York City Board of Education, 58 F.R.D. 62 (S.D.N.Y. 1973); Sema v. Portales Municipal Schools, 499 F.2d 1147 (10th Cir. 1974). See also Educational Opportunity Act of 1974, 20 U.S.C. § 1703(f) (educational non-discrimination statute specifically citing failure "to take appropriate action to overcome language barriers that impede equal education" as a violation).

13 Zavala v. Contreras, 581 F. Supp. 704 (S.D. Tex. 1984). 20 U.S.C. § 2762(a)(1) and 3803(a).

14 See, e.g., Kentucky Board of Education of Harrodsberg v. Bentley, 383 S.W. 2d 677 (Ky. 1964) (married students); Ordway v. Hargraves, 323

F. Supp. 1155 (D. Mass 1971) (pregnant students); Shull v. Columbus Municipal Separate District, 338 F. Supp. 1376 (N.D. Ala. 1972) (unmarried mothers). *See generally* AMERICAN CIVIL LIBERTIES UNION, THE RIGHTS OF STUDENTS, ch. 10 (1988).

[15] *See, e.g.*, Board of Education at Westside Community Schools v. Mergens, 58 L.W. 4720 (Sup. Ct., June 5, 1990) (finding violation of Equal Access Act, 20 U.S.C. § 4071).

[16] *See, e.g.*, Lora v. Board of Education, 587 F. Supp. 1572 (E.D.N.Y. 1984) (discriminatory ethnic and racial placements in programs for the emotionally disturbed); Thomas v. Atascadero Unified School District, 662 F. Supp. 376 (C.D. Cal. 1987) (exclusion of AIDS-infected child from kindergarten classes); Robertson v. Granite City Community School District, 684 F. Supp. 1988 (S.D. Ill. 1988) (right to normal classroom setting for AIDS-infected hemophiliac children).

[17] Title IX of Education Amendments of 1972, 20 U.S.C. § 1681.

[18] *See, e.g.*, Bray v. Lee, 337 F. Supp. 934 (D. Mass. 1972) (enrollment quotas); Berkelman v. San Francisco United School District, 501 F.2d 1264 (9th Cir. 1974) (higher admission standards for girls); Brendan v. Independent School District 742, 477 F.2d 1292 (8th Cir. 1973) (right of girls to compete on boys teams where no alternative competitive programs are provided); Darrin v. Gould, 540 P.2d 882 (Wash. 1975) (absolute right of girls to compete on boys teams).

[19] *See* Runyon v. McCrary, *supra* n.4, and 42 U.S.C. § 1981.

[20] 42 U.S.C. § 2000(d) (race, color or national origin); 20 U.S.C. § 1681 (sex); 29 U.S.C. § 784 (handicapped).

[21] *See, e.g.*, Vorchaimer v. School District of Philadelphia, 532 F.2d 880 (3d Cir. 1976), *aff'd* by equally divided court, 430 U.S. 703 (1977) (maintenance of two academically superior single-sex schools in district not unlawful discrimination); Mississippi University v. Hogan, 458 U.S. 718 (1982) (exclusion of male student from all female nursing school held unlawful, even where state system included coed schools); Board of Education v. Rowley, 458 U.S. 176 (1982) (in providing "appropriate public education" under Education for All Handicapped Children Act, state not obliged to maximize potential of each handicapped child); Milonas v. Williams, 691 F.2d 931 (10th Cir. 1982), *cert. denied*, 460 U.S. 1069 (1983) and Powe v. Miles 407 F.2d 73 (2d Cir. 1968) (find-

Anti-Discrimination

ing, respectively, state action and no state action requiring due process protections in disciplinary action taken by private educational institutions).

22   *See, e.g.,* Jefferson v. Hackney, 406 U.S. 535 (1972) (lower benefit scale for Aid to Families with Dependent Children program than for other needy groups not an impermissable racial discrimination although AFDC minority composition is greater); and Sullivan v. Stroop, 58 LAW WEEK 4790 (June 2, 1990) (stressing "rational basis" test in upholding eligibility distinction between children of absent parents and custodial parents in determining family minimums for AFDC purposes). Goodman v. Wyman, 330 F. Supp. 1038 (1971), aff'd 406 U.S. 964 (1972). *But see* Sullivan v. Zebley, 110 S. Ct. 885 (Feb. 1990) where the Supreme Court overturned, as a matter of Social Security Act interpretation, discriminatory treatment between children and adults in eligibility tests for disability benefits.

23   P.L. 101-239, Title X, sec. 10301.

24   CHILDREN'S DEFENSE FUND, THE HEALTH OF AMERICA'S CHILDREN, pp. ix-xiii (1989) (1986 statistics, National Center for Health Statistics). Under current Constitutional doctrine, disparities in access to important governmental services such as basic education (and presumably basic health care) do not violate "fundamental rights" or the Equal Protection Clause when based generally on wealthy vs. poor classifications or outcomes. San Antonio School District v. Rodriguez, 411 U.S. 1 (1973); Kadrmas v. Dickinson Public Schools, 108 S. Ct. 2481 (1988); *but see* the more generous protection provided under some state constitutions *e.g.,* Robinson v. Cahill, 303 A.2d 273 (N.J. 1973).

25   The present poverty rate, while about 20% for all children, is nearly 50% for black children and 33% for Hispanic children (1988 statistics). Moreover, lack of health insurance among the working poor is alarmingly high and, as with other health indicators, the burden falls much more heavily on black children than white children (about 70% greater). *See* Select Committee on Children, Youth and Families, *Children and Families:Key Trends in the 1990's* at 11 & 37 (GPO 1989).

26   Omnibus Budget Reconciliation Act of 1989, P.L. 101-239 (Dec. 1989), amending 42 U.S.C. § 1396a(l)(2)(A).

27 Palmore v. Sidoti, 466 U.S. 429 (1984) (disapproving custody award against natural mother on basis of residence in a racially mixed household).

28 Fiallo v. Bell, 430 U.S. 787 (1977).

29 *See* AMERICAN CIVIL LIBERTIES UNION, THE RIGHTS OF YOUNG PEOPLE, Ch. 9 at pp. 218,225 (1985).

30 Michael M. v. Superior Court of Sonoma County, 450 U.S. 469 (1981)

31 Matter of D.H.W., 614 P.2d 81 (Okla. Crim. App. 1980)

32 Craig v. Boren, 429 U.S. 190 (1976)

33 Rostker v. Goldberg, 453 U.S. 853 (1982).

34 Matthews v. Lucas, 427 U.S. 495 (1976); Lalli v. Lalli, 439 U.S. 259 (1978) (no Equal Protection violation in law permitting intestate inheritance rights for illegitimate children only where father entered court declaration of paternity during lifetime); Labine v. Vincent, 401 U.S. 332 (1971) (upholding denial of intestate inheritance rights for father's publicly acknowledged child).

35 *See* Trimble v. Gordon, 430 U.S. 702 (1977) (disapproving state law which allowed inheritance by intestate succession only from mothers and not fathers of illegitimate children) and Jiminez v. Weinberger, 417 U.S. 728 (1974) (equal protection violation to deny Social Security disability benefits to illegitimate child born after parent's onset of disability although other groups of illegitimate children were not barred); *cf.* cases cited at f.n. 5.

36 *See* 57 Am. Jur. 2d, *Name*, secs. 14-15 (1988)

37 As to background and motivations for the new "identity" right, see Cerda, *The Draft Convention on the Rights of the Child: New Rights*, 12 HUM. RTS. Q. 115 (1990).

38 Lipscomb v. Simmons, 884 F.2d 1242 (9th Cir. 1989) (due process denial found in making foster parents ineligible for state cash assistance and medical benefits coverage solely on basis of status as relatives of the foster child).

39 *See* 3A AM. JUR. 2d, *Aliens and Citizens*, secs. 189-219 & 1553-1566 (1986).

[40] Alma Society v. Mellon, 459 F. Supp. 912 (S.D.N.Y. 1978), aff'd. 601 F.2d 1225 (2d Cir. 1979), *cert. denied*, 444 U.S. 995 (1979); Schecter v. Boren, 535 F. Supp. 1 (W.D. Okla. 1980).

[41] *See* RIGHTS OF YOUNG PEOPLE, *supra* n. 8 at 154-155.

[42] 25 U.S.C. §§ 1901-1963. See Myers, *Dealing with the Indian Child Welfare Act of 1978*, in PROTECTING CHILDREN THROUGH THE LEGAL SYSTEM at pp. 824-832 (ABA 1982).

[43] *See* Plyler v. Doe and Nyquist v. Mauclet, *supra* n. 11.

[44] 8 U.S.C. 1157(c)(2).

[45] *See* Landon v. Plasencia 459 U.S. 21, 25-28 (1982) and Klingsberg, *Penetrating the Entry Doctrine: Excludable Aliens' Constitutional Rights in Immigration Processes*, 98 YALE L. J. 639 (1989).

[46] *See, e.g.*, Articles 31(2) of the Protocol (prohibiting unnecessary restriction of refugee movement) and article 31(1) (no penalties for illegally present refugees who present themselves promptly to proper authorities and show cause for their illegal entry or presence).

[47] Public Law 96-212, 94 S. Ct. 102 (1980). See Steinbock, *The Admission of Unaccompanied Children in the United States*, 7 YALE L. & POL. REV. 137, 154-57 (1989).

[48] *See* LEVY, KARST AND MAHONEY, *supra* note 7 (strict standard applicable generally to deprivations based on alien status with some exceptions for federally imposed alienage classifications); *cf.*, Perry, *Modern Equal Protection: A Conceptualization and Appraisal*, 79 COLUM. L. REV. 1023, 1060-65 (1979) (section on "alienage").

CHAPTER 7

Civil Rights of the Child
Articles 13, 14, 15 and 16

Robert E. Shepherd, Jr.

Introduction

When the United Nations adopted its Declaration of the Rights of the Child in 1959, that articulation of the universal rights of children was one of the earliest and broadest statements of children's rights yet promulgated.[1] It was still to be eight years before the Supreme Court of the United States was to recognize the due process rights of children in the juvenile delinquency context in *In re Gault*,[2] and ten years before the *Tinker*[3] case clearly stated that children were "persons" under the United States Constitution. That United Nations Declaration embodied what Lee Teitelbaum has described as an "integrative" view of rights, one "that emphasizes needs rather than choice" and thus "places its primary emphasis upon the integration of persons into society."[4]

The recently-adopted United Nations Convention on the Right of the Child takes a quantum leap beyond the more hortatory pronouncements of the earlier Declaration, and other similar, single-document, expressions of children's rights.[5] The Convention expresses an "autonomous" view of the rights of children, one which is more based on choice than needs and which focuses primarily on "providing a sphere of autonomy and freedom from control" rather than integration into society.[6] The Convention, thus, is more consistent with the concept of "individual rights" as developed in twentieth century constitutional law in the United States.

Nowhere in the Convention is this acceptance of the "autonomous" view of rights more evident than in articles 13 through 16, defining, in a very broad sense, what may be described as the "civil rights" of the world's children. These four articles provide a very basic framework for choice or liberty interests or individual rights of children by articulating freedoms of "expression. . . either orally, in writing or in print, in the form of art, or through any other media,"[7] "thought, conscience and religion,"[8] "association and . . .

Civil Rights

peaceful assembly,"[9] and freedoms from "arbitrary or unlawful interference with his or her privacy, family, home or correspondence" and from "unlawful attacks on his or her honour and reputation."[10]

Although several of these rights are quite familiar to observers of the American constitutional landscape—especially the freedoms of expression, religion, association, to peaceful assembly, and, by implication, to privacy—the others are less well-known to students of the United States Constitution. And even those rights that correspond most closely to the American idea of individual rights are generally described and delineated more broadly than contemporary constitutional case law has done.

■ FREEDOM OF EXPRESSION: ARTICLE 13

In Section 1. of article 13 the Convention says:

> *The child shall have the right to freedom of expression; this right shall include freedom to seek, receive and impart information and ideas of all kinds, regardless of frontiers, either orally, in writing or in print, in the form of art, or through any other media of the child's choice.*

This is a very broad definition of freedom of expression, as it includes not only free speech, oral and written, and press, as protected by the first amendment to the United States Constitution, but also expression through art and "any other media of the child's choice," and it specifically includes the rights to "seek" and "receive" information and ideas as well as to "impart" them. Art and "other media" might include anything from finger paintings to film, from rhymes and riddles to sound recordings, from letters to an editor and an article in a school newspaper to multi-media presentations, from a poster in a classroom to graffiti on a wall, and from a slogan on a button to, perhaps, one's attire and personal appearance.[11] The breadth of the Convention's delineation of freedom of expression is very much reminiscent of the United States Supreme Court's language in *Tinker*. Justice Fortas, in that case, wrote grandly of the fact that neither "students [n]or teachers shed their constitutional rights to freedom of speech or expression at the school house gate" and that students ranging from 8 years old to 15 years old were "entitled to freedom of expression of their views. . . .," although the Court concluded that this freedom of expression was not unlimited, since conduct "which for any reason—whether it stems from time, place, or type of behavior—materially disrupts classwork or involves substantial disorder or invasion of the rights of other is, of course, not immunized by the constitutional guarantee of freedom of speech. . . ." So too the second section of article 13 allows "restrictions . . . as are provided by law and are necessary . . . for the protection . . . of public order (*ordre public*). . . ."

However, the resonances of *Tinker* in article 13 also remind us that the United States Supreme Court has more recently narrowed the application of the quoted grand language in *Bethel v. Fraser*[12] to political speech, so as to permit the punishment of a student for an offensively indecent nominating speech for a fellow student at a school assembly, and in *Hazelwood School District v. Kuhlmeier*,[13] where the Court upheld the censorship of articles in a school-sponsored student newspaper because its publication was not a "public forum." In both cases, the Court emphasized the significant interest of school authorities in inculcating appropriate values, "so long as their actions are reasonably related to legitimate pedagogical concerns."

The Supreme Court, thus, defines the first amendment expression rights of school children as being significantly narrower than those of adults. Even in *Board of Education, Island Trees Union Free School District No. 26 v. Pico*,[14] where the plurality decision for the Court stated that "the First Amendment rights of students may be directly and sharply implicated by the removal of books from the shelves of a school library," the dissent argued that the inculcation of "fundamental values necessary to the maintenance of a democratic political system" was an obligation of school officials, and it could only be pursued "by having school boards make content-based decisions about the appropriateness of retaining materials in the school library and curriculum." Note that in *Fraser*, *Kuhlmeier* and *Pico* there is a strong view on the Court that treats transmitted expression rights and received expression rights similarly, as in article 13, but with a much narrower focus.

Article 13 is far more consistent with *Tinker* than the later Supreme Court cases described above, even with the expressed limitations on the rights defined in the first section articulated in Section 2:

> *The exercise of this right may be subject to certain restrictions, but these shall only be such as are provided by law and are necessary:*
>
> *(a) For respect of the rights or reputations of others; or*
>
> *(b) For the protection of national security or of public order (ordre public), or of public health or morals.*

The child's expression rights thus must be weighed in the balance against respect for the rights of others, a common consideration in American constitutional law, but also against respect for the reputations of others, a less recognized consideration except in the rules governing libel and slander. Also, expression rights are limited by the need for protecting national security and for preserving public order, the latter a clear consideration in both *Tinker* and *Fraser*, as well as in cases involving the wearing of buttons to school where the courts frequently focus on the creation of disorder and disturbance by the expression of views thereon.[15]

A more troublesome issue is presented by the qualification permitting a restriction of expression rights for the protection of public health or morals. This may be where the freedom of expression represented by certain forms of symbolic speech, such as long hair, collide with arguments that regulations governing hair length and other forms of grooming are for health and safety purposes.[16] The morals consideration raises all the difficult problems presented by the restriction of youth access to indecent materials not legally obscene.[17] The current debate over limiting juvenile access to recordings or audiotapes with explicit lyrics or to indecent videotapes obviously implicates the protections of article 13, even though constitutional protections are slight under current American case law. Articles 17 and 34 both address the need of the child to be protected from "material injurious to his or her well-being" and from "exploitative use . . . in pornographic performances and materials," so the Convention preserves the balance articulated in Supreme Court and other cases.

■ FREEDOM OF THOUGHT, CONSCIENCE AND RELIGION: ARTICLE 14

Article 14 of the Convention protects the child's right to freedom of thought, conscience and religion, which it defines in the following fashion:

> *1. States Parties shall respect the right of the child to freedom of thought, conscience and religion.*
>
> *2. States Parties shall respect the rights and duties of the parents and, when applicable, legal guardians, to provide direction to the child in the exercise of his or her right in a manner consistent with the evolving capacities of the child.*
>
> *3. Freedom to manifest one's religion or beliefs may be subject only to such limitations as are prescribed by law and are necessary to protect public safety, order, health, or morals or the fundamental rights and freedoms of others.*

The right, and it is described in the singular, thus seems to encompass a coherent whole of "thought, conscience and religion." It is probably the child's civil right described by the Convention that owes most to the United States Constitution and its Bill of Rights as it goes beyond the right to toleration described in most earlier governmental documents. The right described in article 14 is thus consistent with the post-World War II development of freedom of religion and conscience in this country, a right which includes the choice to embrace a particular religion or no religion at all. It also recognizes the reality that the world is becoming more pluralistic, a reality which the United States has had to address since the nineteenth century.

Despite the Supreme Court's refusal in *Minersville School District v. Gobitis*[18] to recognize the right of Jehovah's Witnesses to refuse to participate in saluting the flag on the eve of the second world war, the Court quickly reversed itself and protected the religious rights of schoolchildren to refuse to participate in a ceremony inconsistent with their religious beliefs in the wartime case of *West Virginia State Board of Education v. Barnette*.[19] The protection of the right of school children to freedom of thought, conscience and religion has continued in the *Engel*,[20] *Schempp*,[21] *Stone*,[22] and *Wallace*[23] cases. Less clear has been the concomitant "right" of students to participate in religious activities on school grounds without the assistance or involvement of the state. During the 1989 term of the U. S. Supreme Court, however, the Court upheld the constitutionality of the federal "Equal Access Act,"[24] and determined that school recognition of a student religious organization did not violate the Establishment Clause of the first amendment where other "noncurriculum related student groups" similarly were recognized and met on school premises during non-instructional time.[25]

Article 14 is somewhat less clear about balancing the "right of the child to freedom of thought, conscience and religion" when "public safety, order, health or morals" are implicated, but the balance is probably illustrated by the Supreme Court's decisions in *Prince v. Massachusetts*,[26] holding that the state's interest in protecting children through child labor laws outweighs the religious rights of the child and her guardian, and in the classic dilemma case of *Wisconsin v. Yoder*,[27] overturning the convictions of Old Order Amish parents under the state compulsory school attendance law where their religious views conflicted with the statute.

Justice Douglas' dissent in *Yoder*, arguing that the children's rights to freedom of thought and conscience must be weighed against the parents' views, was challenged by the majority's assertions that the children testified that they shared the religious perspec-tives of their parents. No case has yet been presented to the Court posing the pure conflict between the child's religious or conscience views and the parents' views. Section 2 of article 14 recognizes the role of parents in providing "direction to the child in the exercise of his or her right," but it moderates that delegation to the parents by limiting it to "a manner consistent with the evolving capacities of the child." Thus, when Justice Douglas referred in a footnote to the works of Piaget, Elkind, Kohlberg, Kay, Gesell and Ilg, and Goodman in describing the moral and intellectual maturity of adolescents, he was laying the groundwork for the Convention's explicit recognition that children's civil rights are not static but must be considered in light of the developmental milestones, especially where moral and cognitive abilities are concerned. There is also the dilemma that may be presented if the child articulates religious, or anti-religious, views repugnant to the parents, and they do not wish the child to remain in their home while engaging in practices consistent with his or her views, such as while attending a secular school beyond the compulsory school age.

Section 2 of the article also gives some support to those state laws that require public agencies to take account of the child's and parents' religion in making placements in families or institutions out of the home, especially on a temporary basis and when the child is quite young and still largely subject to the direction of the parents on religious matters.

The public safety and health qualifiers would also address the thorny medical treatment issues where life-preserving intervention is contrary to the religious views of the parents or the child.[28] The Convention thus attempts to expressly balance competing interests, although no easy formulas are attempted to resolve the dilemmas recognized.

■ THE RIGHTS TO FREEDOM OF ASSOCIATION AND PEACEFUL ASSEMBLY: ARTICLE 15

Although the United States Constitution recognizes the right to peaceful assembly explicitly, and freedom of association implicitly, in the first amendment, there are few cases applying these rights to children. Consequently, article 15's exposition of these rights is quite important, and this may be one area in which the Convention stretches current constitutional doctrine. The article says:

1. States Parties recognize the rights of the child to freedom of association and to freedom of peaceful assembly.

2. No restriction may be placed on the exercise of these rights other than those imposed in conformity with the law and which are necessary in a democratic society in the interests of national security or public safety, public order (ordre public), the protection of public health or morals or the protection of the rights and freedoms of others.

The rights articulated in article 15 have been asserted most often in this country in connection with disputes over the constitutionality of curfew ordinances. The cases are numerous, but the results are diverse.

Associational rights, as mentioned above, are lodged in the first amendment and are defined most precisely in Justice Brennan's opinion in *Roberts v. United States Jaycees*,[29] stating:

> that certain kinds of personal bonds have played a critical role in the culture and ideals of the Nation by cultivating and transmitting shared ideas and beliefs; they thereby foster diversity and act as buffers between the individual and the power of the State. . . . Moreover, the constitutional shelter afforded such relationships reflects the realization that individuals draw much of their emotional enrichment from close ties with others . . . [and further advances the] ability to define [their] identity that is central to any concept of liberty.

Although defined in an adult context, the rationale for protection of associational rights may be even greater for youths because of their need for a supportive peer group, especially during adolescence, in order to develop naturally.

In *City of Dallas v. Stanglin*,[30] the Supreme Court denigrated the associational rights of 14-to-17-year-old patrons of a dance hall to mix with persons outside that age bracket contrary to a city ordinance, because the right to "social association" exemplified by "chance encounters in dance halls" were not the types of intimate or expressive associations contemplated in *Roberts*. However, in the recent district court opinion in *Waters v. Barry*,[31] striking down a newly-enacted curfew ordinance for the District of Columbia, the court defined the association and expression rights of the first amendment and the concept of substantive due process within the fifth amendment in the following manner:

> the right to walk the streets, or to meet publicly with one's friends for a noble purpose or for no purpose at all—and to do so when one pleases—is an integral component of life in a free and ordered society.

Civil Rights

This would appear to be the sort of "freedom of association" contemplated by article 15.

There are even fewer cases alluding to freedom of peaceful assembly for children, but the Convention's explicit reference to this right would seem consistent with the idea that children have important expression rights that may be asserted in groups as well as individually. This right will also contribute to the capacity of children to participate fully in the democratic process both as children and later as adults, by giving them the opportunity to acquire experience in political decision-making by a group process.[32]

■ FREEDOM FROM ARBITRARY OR UNLAWFUL INTERFERENCE WITH PRIVACY, FAMILY, HOME OR CORRESPONDENCEAND FROM UNLAWFUL ATTACKS ON HONOUR AND REPUTATION: ARTICLE 16

The United States Constitution does not explicitly recognize a right to privacy, but much of the most controversial and politically volatile of the Supreme Court's work of the past two decades has dealt with its sources and its parameters. For it is out of the right to privacy that the constitutional protections for procreation and abortion decision-making has come. Article 16 is explicit in defining a right to privacy, among other rights not precisely mentioned in the Constitution:

> *1. No child shall be subjected to arbitrary or unlawful interference with his or her privacy, family, home or correspondence, nor to unlawful attacks on his or her honour and reputation.*
>
> *2. The child has the right to the protection of the law against such interference or attacks.*

The right to privacy includes to some degree the protection of the right to personhood defined by the other articulated in other articles of the Convention, but it further includes what Justice Brandeis called "the right to be let alone—the most comprehensive of rights and the right most valued by civilized men."[33] This is the concept that has given rise to the constitutional protection of choice in matters of procreation and abortion.

The right of the adult woman to make choices regarding abortion in consultation with her physician was extended to minors in *Planned Parenthood of Central Missouri v. Danforth*,[34] *Bellotti v. Baird*,[35] *Bellotti v. Baird*,[36] *Planned Parenthood of Central Missouri v. Ashcroft*,[37] *Akron v. Akron Center for Reproductive Health*,[38] *Thornburgh v. American College of Obstetricians & Gynecologists*,[39] and *Hartigan v. Zbaraz*.[40] These cases concluded that a mature minor had the right to choose an abortion, unfettered by a legislative requirement that she have the consent of her parents. If a minor is immature, the state may require parental involvement, but there must be a confidential and expeditious procedure for judicial bypass in order to enable the minor to demonstrate whether she is mature or that an abortion would be in her best interests. A statute requiring a physician to "notify, if possible" the parents or guardian of an immature minor is constitutional,[41] as are statutes that require notice to one or both parents of a girl under eighteen, so long as a judicial bypass procedure is afforded to enable the minor to secure an abortion without parental notification.[42] Article 16 would seem to preserve these rights, although with somewhat greater protection for the privacy rights of the child as distinguished from the family's privacy rights. The right to privacy also protects other procreational choices, and the Supreme Court in *Carey v. Population Services International*[43] invalidated a New York statute prohibiting the sale or distribution of contraceptives to minors under the age of sixteen.

The Convention also explicitly recognizes a right to protection of the law against "arbitrary or unlawful interference with his or her . . . family . . [or] . . . home. . . ." Although subsequent articles more specifically address the rights of the child who is abused or neglected and who is subject to removal, or has been removed, from the home, article 16 seems to acknowledge the existence of a right to "family privacy" or "family autonomy" that is entitled to protection by the state.[44]

Article 16 similarly protects the child against interference with his or her correspondence and against "unlawful attacks on his or her honour and reputation." These seem to be related to the privacy interests addressed above. Protecting a child's correspondence against arbitrary and unlawful interference is a natural extension of the rights to privacy and freedom of expression. Indeed, Standard 4.9 of the *IJA-ABA Juvenile Justice Standards Relating to Corrections Administration* addresses the adjudicated juvenile's

Civil Rights

right to uncensored mail in the context of the juvenile's right to "enjoy privacy." Professor Laurence Tribe also addresses the individual's right to protection of his or her "reputation" in the setting of his discussion of the right to privacy.[45] Tribe points to the case of *Doe v. McMillan*[46] as one where parents were permitted to sue the printer and Superintendent of Documents for disseminating the names of their children acquired during a congressional investigation of the District of Columbia public schools, even though congressional committee members and their staffs were protected by the speech and debate clause of the Constitution. This provision would also seem to afford protection to children suffering from diseases like AIDS from disclosure of their identities unless there was some overriding interest in doing so.

Conclusion

It is difficult to deal with such a vast volume of constitutional material protecting individual rights in such a summary fashion, and to similarly address the important protections of the articles protecting the civil rights of children in a seemingly cursory fashion, but this chapter, like the others, is intended as an introduction to the Convention and not as an exhaustive treatise on all the implications of its approval in the United States.

Some general observations regarding articles 13 through 16 are in order. As noted earlier, the Convention takes an "autonomous" view of children's rights rather than an "integrative" view, thus focusing on those choice and liberty interests that are more generally protected for adults. These articles are also highly demonstrative of a more American view of rights than traditionally have been found in other international documents, with a focus on the rights of individuals rather than groups.

Also, the concepts incorporated in these articles addressing children's civil rights are reflective of the Convention's emphasis on the "dignity" of the child as a person.[47] The Preamble to the Convention, for example, mentions the term "dignity" in three different clauses. The term is not utilized in the United States Constitution but Tremper has conclusively argued that it inheres in the articulations of constitutional theory over the years.

Civil Rights

Although the Convention emphasizes individual rights for children to a greater extent than other documents, it also recognizes and emphasizes the importance of the family for insuring those rights and for the complete development of the child. Two consecutive clauses of the Preamble explicitly state this principle:

> CONVINCED *that the family, as the fundamental group of society and the natural environment for the growth and well-being of all its members and particularly children, should be afforded the necessary protection and assistance so that it can fully assume its responsibilities within the community,*
>
> RECOGNIZING *that the child, for the full and harmonious development of his or her personality, should grow up in a family environment, in an atmosphere of happiness, love and understanding.*

Thus, there is a balance between protecting the individual rights of the child and the need to protect and preserve the family and the home to insure the normal development of the child.

Finally, the Convention recognizes that the ability of the child to exercise his or her individual rights is often dependent on the child's capacity in light of his or her age and maturity. Thus, choices, while protected by the Convention, are to be exercised by children in keeping with their cognitive and developmental capacity.

Articles 13 through 16 of the Convention are significantly the products of decades of efforts to define the rights of children in American law. Most of the concepts imbedded in those articles are derived from case law in this country. The Convention clearly does a much better job than case law in articulating a coherent and consistent body of law defining the rights of children. This country should take the lead among the nations by recognizing the ideological child it conceived and largely nourished to birth and through infancy.

Footnotes

1. United Nations, General Assembly Resolution 1386 (XIV), November 20, 1959, published in the Official Records of the General Assembly, Fourteenth Session, Supplement No. 16, 1960, p. 19. The Declaration acknowledged its debt to the Declaration of the Rights of the Child which was stated in 1923 by the International Union for Child Welfare, and adopted in 1924 by the League of Nations.
2. 387 U.S. 1 (1967).
3. Tinker v. Des Moines Independent School District, 393 U.S. 503, 511 (1969).
4. Teitelbaum, *Forword: The Meanings of Rights of Children*, 10 N. M.L. REV. 235, 238 (1980).
5. *See, e.g.*, Foster & Freed, *A Bill of Rights for Children*, 6 FAM L. Q. 343 (1972); Report of the Joint Commission on Mental Health of Children, *Crisis in Child Mental Health: Challenge for the 1970's* 3-5 (1970).
6. Teitelbaum, *supra* note 4, 10 N.M.L. REV. at pp. 242-243.
7. Article 13.
8. Article 14.
9. Article 15.
10. Article 16.
11. *See* the recent, and very insightful, discussion of children's freedom of expression rights in D. MOSHMAN, CHILDREN, EDUCATION, AND THE FIRST AMENDMENT: A PSYCHOLEGAL ANALYSIS (1989).
12. 478 U.S. 675 (1986).
13. 108 S.Ct. 562 (1988).
14. 457 U.S. 853 (1982).
15. *Compare* Burnside v. Byars, 363 F.2d 744 (5th Cir. 1966) *with* Blackwell v. Issaquena County Board of Education, 363 F.2d 749 (5th Cir. 1966), both decided by the same panel of the United States Court of Appeals for the Fifth Circuit on the same day reaching contrary conclusions based on the factual settings. The phrase *ordre public* inserted parenthetically in Section 2.(b) is similar to the concept of public order but is a somewhat narrower limitation on rights from the civil law.

[16] The difficulty in addressing hairstyle regulation issues in the constitutional context is epitomized by the fact that six federal circuit courts have upheld school regulations while five circuits have decided that grooming choices are protected by the constitution.

[17] *See, e.g.*, Ginsberg v. New York, 390 U.S. 629 (1968); Interstate Circuit v. City of Dallas, 390 U.S. 676 (1968); Eznoznik v. City of Jacksonville, 422 U.S. 747 (1975); F.C.C. v. Pacifica Foundation, 438 U.S. 726 (1978); New York v. Ferber, 458 U.S. 747 (1982).

[18] 310 U.S. 586 (1940).

[19] 319 U.S. 624 (1943).

[20] Engel v. Vitale, 370 U.S. 39 (1962), prohibiting use of a state-composed prayer in school religious exercises.

[21] School District of Abington Township v. Schempp, 374 U.S. 203 (1963), along with the companion *Murray* case striking down the practice of Bible reading in the schools.

[22] Stone v. Graham, 449 U.S. 39 (1980), holding the posting of the Ten Commandments in classrooms to be unconstitutional.

[23] Wallace v. Jaffree, 472 U.S. 38 (1985), invalidating a state statute providing for a period of silent prayer or meditation.

[24] 20 U.S.C. §§ 4071-4074.

[25] Board of Education of the Westside Community Schools v. Mergens, 110 S.Ct. 2356 (1990).

[26] 321 U.S. 158 (1944).

[27] 406 U.S. 205 (1972).

[28] *See In re* Green, 448 Pa. 338, 292 A.2d 387 (1972), where the Pennsylvania Supreme Court ordered that the views of the sixteen-year-old patient be ascertained before performing serious elective surgery rather than simply relying on or overriding the mother's religious objections to the surgery. *Compare In re* Sampson, 29 N.Y.2d 900, 278 N.E.2d 918 (1972).

[29] 468 U.S. 609 (1984).

[30] 109 S.Ct. 1591 (1989).

[31] 711 F.Supp. 1125 (D.D.C. 1989).

[32] Professor Franklin Zimring has advocated the expansion of such rights for youths as a means for acquiring experience through a "learner's permit" approach. F. ZIMRING, THE CHANGING LEGAL WORLD OF ADOLESCENCE 89-98 (1982).

[33] Olmstead v. United States, 277 U.S. 438, 478 (1928)(dissenting opinion).

[34] 428 U.S. 52 (1976).

[35] 428 U.S. 132 (1976)(*Bellotti* I).

[36] 443 U.S. 622 (1979)(*Bellotti* II).

[37] 462 U.S. 476 (1983).

[38] 462 U.S. 416 (1983).

[39] 106 S.Ct. 2169 (1986).

[40] 108 S.Ct. 479 (1987)(equally divided court).

[41] H.L. v. Matheson, 450 U.S. 398 (1981).

[42] Hodgson v. Minnesota, 110 S.Ct. 2926 (1990); Ohio v. Akron Center for Reproductive Health, 110 S.Ct. 2972 (1990). These decisions do tip the balance more against the minor in abortion decision-making than had previously been the case.

[43] 431 U.S. 678 (1977).

[44] *See, e.g.*, Stanley v. Illinois, 405 U.S. 645 (1971) and Alsager v. District Court of Polk County, Iowa (Juvenile Division), 406 F.Supp. 10 (S.D. Iowa 1975).

[45] L. TRIBE, AMERICAN CONSTITUTIONAL LAW § 15-16 (2d ed. 1988).

[46] 412 U.S. 306 (1973).

[47] Professor Charles Tremper has creatively examined the concept of human dignity as applied to children in Tremper, *Respect For The Human Dignity Of Minors: What The Constitution Requires*, 39 SYRACUSE L. REV. 1293 (1988).

CHAPTER 8

The Child's Right to Be Heard and Represented
Article 12

Howard A. Davidson

Introduction

Article 12 of the United Nations Convention on the Rights of the Child addresses the need for children to have their voices heard, with the assistance of effective legal counsel, in all judicial or administrative hearings affecting them. This essay explores the laws and practices in the United States that relate to this important provision of the Convention.

There are a wide variety of legal matters affecting children that commonly result in a court or administrative body taking actions that can have a significant impact on them. The most frequent legal proceedings affecting children will be analyzed herein, including:

(a) Proceedings brought against a juvenile for the alleged commission of an offense, or because the child is allegedly ungovernable by a parent and thus requires court supervision;

(b) Proceedings affecting a child's custodial or parental visitation status (including parental divorce or separation, child abuse and neglect, and termination of parental rights legal actions);

(c) Proceedings to establish a child's paternity or to establish or modify a parent's support obligation;

(d) Proceedings to have a child adopted;

(e) Proceedings related to the commitment of a minor child to a psychiatric facility; and

(f) Proceedings related to public school actions affecting a child, such as expulsion or suspension and the entitlement of a disabled child to certain special education programs and services.

There are, of course, other legal actions related to the status of children, such as immigration and deportation proceedings that affect unaccompanied minors from another country. Since this is being written as part of an examination of how U.S. federal and state law relates to the Convention, the limited space allotted to this essay has necessitated that such matters [affecting many fewer children than in (a)-(f)] be covered elsewhere. The right of a child to be adequately represented in a judicial action brought on his or her behalf for the general enforcement of federal and state constitutional rights or statutory entitlements will be discussed at the outset. The problems in assuring that a child has *access* to competent representation for the judicial enforcement of rights are pervasive to all the categories listed above.

■ REPRESENTATION OF THE CHILD IN GENERAL LITIGATION

A. When the Child is a Party

The most significant procedural difference between the child and adult litigant in American courts involves the issue of representation. Because of their legal incapacity, minor children cannot initiate or defend lawsuits without adult assistance.[1] Traditionally, the minor plaintiff has been required to bring a lawsuit through a "next friend," while a minor who is sued must be represented by a "guardian ad litem." Today, these terms are used interchangeably (guardian ad litem will be used herein).[2]

Most states now model their rules related to the representation of children in litigation on Rule 17(c) of the Federal Rules of Civil Procedure which states:

> Whenever an infant (minor child) has a representative, such as a general guardian, committee, conservator, or other like fiduciary the representative may sue or defend on behalf of the infant....If an infant...does not have a duly appointed representative he may sue by his next friend or by a guardian ad litem. The court shall appoint

a guardian ad litem for an infant...not otherwise represented in an action or shall make such other order as it deems proper for the protection of the infant.

Normally, of course, a minor child affected by civil litigation will not initially come before the court with a "duly appointed representative," and thus the court will have to address at the outset the question of who should perform that function. Usually, parents of the child will serve in this capacity, and they generally can do so without formal appointment by the court.[3] But what about where the interests of the parents may conflict with that of the child? Some examples of such actions include:

(a) Where a child is suing his parents, something that is becoming more common as the traditional legal doctrine of parental immunity has eroded;[4]

(b) Where children seek an order from the court under laws related to judicially authorized abortions without parental notification or consent;[5]

(c) Where a parent is seeking a court order to have their mentally retarded child sterilized;[6] and

(d) Where a child seeks to challenge some administrative action (e.g., a school suspension) against the parent's wishes.

In such situations, any person with an interest in the welfare of the child may generally serve as the guardian ad litem. Some states will permit the child to nominate his or her own representative. In addition, some courts will even permit litigation affecting the child to proceed without such an appointment where the child is an older, "mature" minor who is able to participate in the legal action and is represented by legal counsel.

Guardians ad litem for minor children in civil actions affecting the child are usually considered "officers of the court," and although they are not a party to the action, they are responsible for representing and protecting the best interests of the child until the litigation is concluded (or until the child reaches the age of majority). The powers of the guardian ad litem include the authority to engage legal counsel on behalf of the child and to facilitate settlement or other methods of speedy resolution of the case. Their conduct will be subject to the scrutiny of the court, and if their actions adversely affect the child, they can be removed.

B. When the Child is Not a Party, But Has an Interest in the Outcome of the Litigation

In cases where the child may be affected by some form of on-going civil lawsuit, American courts have clear authority to appoint a guardian ad litem to protect the interests of the child. The judge in such cases may even add the child as a party to the litigation. Some examples of where the child may need to be represented and heard in litigation affecting his or her rights include:

(a) Actions involving insurance policy claims where the child has a potential monetary interest in such policy;

(b) Probate/inheritance proceedings in which the child may have a financial stake in the outcome;

(c) Claims for certain benefits to which an adult, and their child, may be entitled, such as workers' compensation, social security, public assistance, etc.; and

(d) Suits to determine ownership of certain assets, the resolution of which may affect children as the later beneficiaries of such property.

Although the above suggests that the child's interest in existing litigation must always be monetary in order for him or her to be added as a party, this is not true. Courts have been given wide discretion to add children as parties and provide them with the assistance of guardian ad litem representation when critical to the protection of their interests.[7]

■ SOURCES OF, AND STANDARDS FOR, LAWYERS FOR CHILDREN

A. Resources for Child Representation

Given the broad authority of American courts to protect the rights and interests of children through appointment of a guardian ad litem, it is disconcerting that the ranks of specially qualified *attorneys for children* are so thin. Unlike jurisdictions, such as Canada's Ontario Province, which maintains an "Official Guardian" child representation program, there are no federal or state agencies in this country which are established specifically to protect children's interests in all forms of civil litigation. In order to address these concerns, in 1978 the American Bar Association founded the ABA Center on Children and the Law as its primary vehicle for responding to the legal needs of the nation's children.[8] There is also a National Association of Counsel for Children, a membership organization that is a vehicle for training and information-dissemination for attorneys who specialize in what its founder, Donald Bross, has dubbed "pediatric law."[9]

There are a minuscule number of small law offices in America that specialize in representation of children (e.g., San Francisco's Legal Services for Children; Charlotte, North Carolina's Children's Legal Center; and in suburban Boston, the North Shore Children's Law Project). Although public defender agencies, legal services or legal aid offices, and even a few special county guardian ad litem programs are available to provide representation of children, their assistance is generally obtainable only in the special proceedings described below (and typically only in one or two types of these). The most common source of representation for children is the ranks of the private bar, whose members are regularly appointed by the courts in cases involving indigent parties or minors (but usually without any prerequisite education on the special knowledge and talents needed by those who represent children).

In a few states (e.g., Florida and North Carolina), legislatures have created statewide guardian ad litem programs that involve the use of trained lay volunteers to represent children in court (but limited to civil child protection-related cases and, in rare instances, representation of children in abuse-related child custody disputes). In recent years, a nationwide movement to utilize such lay volunteers, in place of court-appointed lawyers for children, has become widespread. Such volunteers are commonly called Court-Appointed Special Advocates (C.A.S.A.).[10]

B. Improving the Quality of Child Representation

In 1979, the American Bar Association's House of Delegates approved a set of *Juvenile Justice Standards* developed by a joint commission of the ABA and the Institute of Judicial Administration. One volume, *Standards Relating to Counsel for Private Parties*, over a decade after its approval by the ABA, remains one of the few comprehensive sets of guidelines available to court-appointed lawyers for children (another is available from the National Association of Counsel for Children).

These ABA *Standards* address such subjects as the lawyer's:

(a) time of entry into a case and duration of representation;

(b) relationship with social workers involved with the child;

(c) need to have available adequate investigative and case planning support services;

(d) means of determining what is in the child client's interests;

(e) ability to maintain the confidentiality of the child's communications to the attorney;

(f) role in advising and counseling the child; and

(g) protection of the child's right to treatment.

These *Standards* reject the use of attorneys as merely guardians ad litem, but rather suggest the preference that lawyers exercise their professional responsibility as they would in representing an adult. The *Standards* are therefore oriented toward assuring that the child's own views concerning the case will be effectively heard in court through a lawyer-advocate.

THE CHILD'S RIGHT TO COUNSEL IN SPECIFIC PROCEEDINGS

A. Juvenile Delinquency and Status Offender Cases

Two important United States Supreme Court cases of the 1960's, *United States v. Kent* and *In re Gault*, established the right of minor children to be represented by counsel at all critical stages of delinquency proceedings where they are subject to deprivation of liberty.[11] Such "critical" stages have been construed to include, but are not limited to, preadjudication interrogations, identifications, responses to charges in the court petition, and adjudication and disposition hearings. This right is, however, generally waivable by the juvenile—although state laws and court decisions have placed some limits on the child's ability to do so.

Neither *Kent* and *Gault*, nor any other Supreme Court decision, has addressed the issue of the child's right to representation in cases brought by parents or others alleging the child's incorrigibility, runaway behavior, or school truancy (referred to as "status offender" cases). Even when a child may be locked up in a secure correctional or treatment institution as a result of a status offender proceeding, a child may not have the right to legal counsel under state law. Many states, by legislation, have provided such a right, although appellate courts have varied on their view of whether counsel should be required in such cases.

In cases where an allegedly recalcitrant youth has defied a juvenile court's order in a status offender proceeding, the federal Juvenile Justice and Delinquency Prevention Act has given states an exception to the Act's general prohibition of secure detention for status offenders. In 1980, Congress amended the Act to permit states participating in federal financial assistance under that Act to grant judges the authority to order children who had defied prior treatment and placement related "valid court orders" into secure residential settings. The federal agency administering the Act has, however, issued regulations that require that the child have a judicial hearing, with representation by counsel, before such a youth can be securely incarcerated under this exception to the Act.[12]

B. Child Custody and Visitation-Related Cases

In almost every state, by statutory law, children in civil child protective proceedings initiated by the state or county (commonly called child abuse and neglect cases) have the right to have a representative appointed by the court to independently protect their interests in the litigation. A primary impetus for such laws was not a Supreme Court decision, but rather, the 1974 federal Child Abuse Prevention and Treatment Act.[13] This Act tied certain federal financial assistance for state child protective services agencies to a requirement that states have laws that, among other things, assure that every child involved in a civil child protective proceeding has a court-appointed guardian ad litem.

Today, in most civil child protective proceedings, a legal counsel, lawyer serving as guardian ad litem, or C.A.S.A. (or some combination of these) must by law be appointed for the child at some point in time after the child protection petition is filed in court. These representatives typically are involved with the case through adjudication and disposition. After that, in post-dispositional case review and separate termination of parental rights proceedings, state statutes and appellate courts have rarely required—and thus children are much less likely to have—court-appointed legal representation in these judicial hearings.

The Convention, in article 25, specifically provides all children who have been removed from their homes with the right to a "periodic review" that would be most meaningful if the child was represented during the review process. Furthermore, given the provision in article 9 for the child to participate in the judicial review of all cases where he or she has been involuntarily separated from a parent, it seems odd that all state laws would not clearly mandate appointment of counsel for the child in termination of parental rights hearings. Clearly, the long-term consequences for the child of the court's actions are greatest in these cases.[14]

In intra-family custody or visitation disputes related to parental separation or divorce, the child's right to independent legal representation is even less established than in termination of parental rights proceedings. Only a few states provide, by law, that a court must appoint a counsel or guardian ad litem for a child who is the subject of a parent (or grandparent) custody or visitation conflict case.[15] However, it is clear that judges always have discretion to appoint such a representative, even when not mandated.

Although it is not routine for courts to appoint a legal representative for the child in intra-family conflict cases, courts have given varying degrees of consideration to the child's stated custodial preferences, with increased weight given to the views of children nearing the age of majority. Approximately half of the states have statutes listing the child's custodial wishes as one factor that the court must consider when making a custodial determination. A few states make the child's custodial wishes generally binding on the court, so long as the parent is fit. These include Ohio (children 12 and over) and Georgia (children 14 and over).

Even in the absence of such special laws, judges who fail to elicit, or totally ignore, children's custodial preferences are increasingly likely to do so at the peril of having their custody orders reversed by appellate courts. The views of the affected children are also increasingly likely to be heard in special custodial situations, such as when one or both parents seeks a change from sole to joint custody, or where a custodial parent seeks the court's permission to move to another state (or the non-custodial parent seeks to block such a move).

C. Paternity and Support Cases

It is generally accepted that a child, acting through either the mother, a guardian, or the state may bring a paternity action. Under the Uniform Parentage Act (UPA), which has only been adopted in a few states, a child must be made a party to any paternity action. The UPA also requires that if the child is a minor, then he or she must be represented by a guardian or guardian ad litem, but neither the child's mother nor father may serve in either of those capacities due to the potential of conflict of interest. However, in states that have not adopted the UPA, the prevailing view is that a guardian ad litem is not required where the state views the mother and child's interests as not being sufficiently different.

If paternity is contested, some states—regardless of whether they have adopted the UPA—will appoint a guardian ad litem for the child. The reason for both making the child a party, and providing a guardian ad litem, is that if a court fails to do so, the paternity action may later be subject to relitigation by the child. Courts have also spoken clearly about the child's interests in these cases. For example, in the case of *Ford v. Ford* the Supreme Court of Nebraska stated that:

> ...a decision as to legitimacy is one in which the two children, independent of the dispute between the parents, have a vital and enduring interest affecting their own life, which requires that it be independently protected by the court and the representation of counsel. The children's interests may be adverse to both parents in the case.[16]

That view, however, still only applies in a minority of states that have mandatory counsel or guardian ad litem appointment laws for children in paternity cases, or where court decisions have so mandated (as in the *Ford* case).

In a concurring opinion in the United States Supreme Court case of *Mills v. Habluetzel*, 456 U.S. 91, 100 (1982), Justice O'Connor gave support to the concept of making the child a party to paternity actions and providing that child with independent representation. She noted that motives, unrelated to the child's best interests, such as the mother's desire to maintain cordial relationships with the father, may stop the mother from bringing a paternity action.

When the issue is one of establishing or modifying a child support obligation, rather than paternity, the law is clear that the duty of support is owed to the child, not to the custodial parent. However, the usual initiators of court actions related to child support are custodial mothers or state/county welfare agencies that have provided them with public assistance. Only when children reach the age of majority, or are otherwise emancipated, have courts permitted them to pursue enforcement actions on their own behalf.

D. Adoption Cases

State laws generally designate a minimum age above which children who are the subject of adoption actions must give consent to an adoption before it can become effective. This age typically ranges from ten to fourteen. The preferences of younger children may also be considered by the court, but they are not binding.

In uncontested step-parent adoptions, or adoptions arranged through licensed adoption agencies, it would be unusual to find a court appointing independent representation for the child. Even in uncontested privately-arranged adoptions, few state laws require the appointment of a lawyer or guardian ad litem for the child. Appointments are more common, although still at the discretion of most courts, when a private adoption proceeding becomes contested (e.g., when fraud, duress, or coercion in connection with the adoption is alleged by the biological parent, where such parent seeks to revoke their prior consent, or where there is a controversy over whether a non-custodial parent's consent is required).

At present, there are two proposed "model" state laws on adoption in various stages of development. The more complete and refined product is the American Bar Association Model State Adoption Act. Although this Act has been approved by the ABA Family Law Section, it has not been approved by the Association's House of Delegates and thus does not constitute official ABA policy. In section 21, that Act provides only for discretionary appointment of independent representation for children subject to adoption proceedings. In a recently-developed "discussion draft" of a proposed new Uniform Adoption Act to be considered by the National Conference of Commissioners on Uniform State Laws, section 60 (as it read prior to July 1990) also makes appointment of an attorney or guardian ad litem for the child discretionary, both in "agency placement" (licensed) adoptions as well as "direct placement" (independent) adoptions.

E. Psychiatric Commitment Cases

Historically, almost all states have permitted parents to commit their minor children to mental institutions without any form of due process of law or a judicial hearing. The first major challenges to the "voluntary" juvenile commitment process were the parallel U.S. Supreme Court cases of *Bartley v. Kremens* and *J.L. v. Parham*.[17] In both of these cases, federal courts had nullified state statutory civil commitment laws that failed to adequately protect the due process rights of minors.

In the *Parham* case, however, the Supreme Court reversed a federal court decree that had granted children a right to prompt hearings related to their psychiatric hospitalization and to the appointment of counsel to represent them at all significant stages of the commitment process. The Court merely required that children subject to mental commitments be afforded an independent inquiry by an informal, non-judicial "neutral factfinder," who would simply evaluate whether the legal psychiatric admission standards were met.

One major impact of this decision was the determination that minor children, subject to psychiatric commitment actions initiated by their parents, do not have a constitutional "right to be heard" in such actions through the mandatory appointment of a legal representative. The Court even extended the scope of its ruling to include those children who were in the custody of the state or county, rather than their parents, at the time of their commitment.

Few Supreme Court cases have been as criticized by child advocates and those who deal with the rights of the mentally disabled as has the *Parham* case. However, the majority of state laws still permit parents to commit their child to a mental health facility, against the child's own wishes, without the requirement of a judicial or administrative hearing or the appointment of a legal representative for the child. Even where state laws or court decrees have given children the "right to be heard" in cases involving commitment to public psychiatric facilities, these safeguards may not have been extended to minors who are committed by their parents to private psychiatric hospitals, actions which in recent years have become more prevalent. Critics have charged that parents are using such private facilities as placements for a troublesome or rebellious child, particularly since state status offender laws no longer afford the easy institutionalization of such young people.[18]

F. Administrative and Judicial Actions Related to Public Education

In a number of U.S. Supreme Court cases, children and their parents have been clearly vested with certain due process rights related to the child's attendance at school, the child's educational program, and the exercise of disciplinary sanctions against the child by the school. Although under the *Goss v. Lopez* case, schools are not required to give children suspended for ten days or less a full panoply of due process protections,[19] longer suspensions, expulsions, and transfers to another school for disciplinary reasons have been considered by courts to be major sanctions warranting full due process procedures. It is by no means clear, however, that states will require children subject to such sanctions to be afforded a full hearing with the right to representation by counsel.

The Court's *Ingraham v. Wright* case, the leading case on the use of corporal punishment by schools, not only held that such punishment was not "cruel and unusual punishment," but also that it could be administered without the child being afforded any prior hearing whatsoever.[20] Although a rapidly growing number of states have, by legislation, prohibited the use of corporal punishment in the schools, the large number of states still permitting its use do not provide the child with a right to be heard about whether his or her misbehavior justifies the use of such sanctions.

It is the area of special education services for handicapped children that has generated the most specific federal policy concerning the child's right to hearings and representation. Under the federal Education for All Handicapped Children Act,[21] parents have the right to challenge in both administrative and judicial hearings the school system's educational placement or services provided to their child. Parents can initially request an "impartial due process hearing" to resolve such differences with school administrators.

The federal regulations governing such hearings require that parents be given notice of any free or low-cost legal services that might be available to help secure an appropriate educational program for the child, and that the parents have the right to be represented by counsel at such a hearing.[22] In 1986, this Act was amended to authorize courts to award attorney fees to parents of handicapped children for successful legal work in connection with any administrative or judicial hearings related to the securing of legally-required special education services for a child.[23]

Conclusion

From the above brief overview, it should be clear that the child's right to be heard and represented in judicial proceedings and other legal matters affecting his or her welfare is extremely varied in its application. Certainly, the state legislatures and courts of this nation have advanced these rights considerably during the past two decades. Areas in which independent representation for children may have been lacking are receiving new consideration. Many legal scholars concerned with the American family and the rights of the child have studied this issue, and policymakers have begun to appreciate the need to have clear laws, agency regulations, and court rules addressing the child's need to be adequately heard and represented. Clearly, much remains to be done to ensure that children, and their attorneys, are given a real—not merely symbolic—role in administrative and judicial hearings that affect the interests of children.

Footnotes

[1] Federal Rule of Civil Procedure 17(c), which addresses the capacity of parties, treats minor children and incompetent persons identically.

[2] *See* 42 AM. JUR. 2D *Infants* sec. 158 (1969).

[3] *See* Annot., 118 A.L.R. 401 (1939).

[4] *See* Horowitz and Goodman, *The Child Litigant*, in LEGAL RIGHTS OF CHILDREN (HOROWITZ AND DAVIDSON, eds., 1984), sec. 3.08.

[5] *See* Dodson, *Legal Rights of Adolescents*, in LEGAL RIGHTS OF CHILDREN (HOROWITZ AND DAVIDSON, eds.), SEC. 4.16.

[6] *See, e.g., In re* AW, 637 P.2d 366 (Colo. 1981); *In re* Grady, 426 A.2d 467 (N.J. 1981).

[7] Indeed, some federal courts have held it to be reversible error for a trial court to fail to determine whether a guardian ad litem for a child is necessary. *See, e.g.*, Noe v. True, 507 F.2d 9, 11-12 (6th Cir. 1974).

[8] The ABA Center on Children and the Law can be contacted by writing to it at 1800 M Street, N.W., Washington, DC 20036.

[9] The National Association of Counsel for Children can be contacted by writing to it at 1205 Oneida St., Denver, CO. 80220.

[10] The National Court Appointed Special Advocate Association can be contacted by writing to it at 2722 Eastlake Avenue East, Suite 220, Seattle, WA. 98102.

[11] *In re* Gault, 387 U.S. 1 (1967); Kent v. U.S., 383 U.S. 541 (1966).

Right to Be Heard

[12] Juvenile Justice Amendments of 1980, Pub. L. 96-509; 28 C.F.R. sec. 31.03.

[13] 42 U.S.C. sec. 5101 *et seq.*

[14] Some states have legislatively provided for mandatory appointment of counsel for the child, and some state courts have found a constitutional basis for the required appointment of counsel. However, although the U.S. Supreme Court has never ruled on this issue, in a somewhat analogous situation the Court held, in the case of *Smith v. Organization of Foster Families for Equality and Reform*, 432 U.S. 816 (1977), that a child facing removal from a long-term foster home may not always be entitled to independent counsel.

[15] The most prominent state laws to require appointment of a guardian ad litem for a child in all contested custody cases are WISC. STAT. ANN. SEC. 767.045 and N. H. REV. STAT. ANN. SEC. 458-17-a.

[16] 216 N.W.2d 176, 177 (1974).

[17] Bartley v. Kremens, 402 F. Supp. 1039 (E.D. Pa. 1975), *vacated*, 431 U.S. 119 (1977), *on remand sub nom.* Institutionalized Juveniles v. Secretary, Public Welfare, 459 F. Supp 30 (E.D. Pa. 1978), *rev'd*, 442 U.S. 640 (1979). J.L. v. Parham, 412 F. Supp. 112 (M.D. Ga. 1976), *rev'd sub nom.* Parham v. J.R., 442 U.S. 584 (1979).

[18] *See* Lambert, *Growing Numbers of Youth Committed to Psychiatric Hospitals*, YOUTH LAW NEWS, March-April 1990, 12.

[19] 419 U.S. 565 (1967).

[20] 430 U.S. 651 (1977).

[21] 20 U.S.C. sec. 1400 *et seq.*

[22] 34 C.F.R. sec. 300.506(c),.508(a)(1)(1986).

[23] The Handicapped Children's Protection Act, Pub. L. 99-372.

CHAPTER 9

Educating the Child for a Productive Life
Articles 28 and 29

Susan H. Bitensky[1]

Introduction

The education provisions of the Convention on the Rights of the Child should be of particular interest to Americans these days since, for some time now, this country has found itself in the grips of a continuing national crisis in public elementary and secondary education.[2]

In fact, the 1980's saw an avalanche of newspaper articles and other publications documenting the evolving crisis.[3] What they reveal is that the nation's children are emerging from the public schools uneducated in droves. American children consistently rate at or near the bottom in most international comparisons of mathematics performance.[4] They are frequently "culturally illiterate"[5]—unfamiliar with that basic core of factual information comprising society's shared heritage and convention wisdom.[6] Vast numbers of these children are not acquiring the reading and writing skills that will enable them to successfully pursue post-secondary education[7] or hold even low-level jobs upon graduation.[8] Things have become so grave that U.S. Secretary of Education Lauro F. Cavazos was prompted to admit that, "frankly, this situation scares me. . .," and to warn that "[w]e must do better or perish as the nation we know today."[9]

It is my view that the impact of the Convention's education provisions on U.S. law cannot responsibly be considered without taking into account this factual context. I say this because the direction which domestic education law takes may have a significant bearing on the nation's ability to overcome the education crisis.

Were the United States to become a party to the Convention, the effects in this regard would be twofold. First, the Convention would bring heightened prestige to American education and education laws, thereby enhancing the salutary impact of the law on the crisis. Second, the Convention would engender the public perception that this is a nation fully-committed to educating its children—a perception which may be key to turning the crisis around.[10]

■ THE CHILD'S RIGHT TO EDUCATION: ARTICLE 28

Article 28.1 posits that the "States Parties recognize the right of the child to education," and that they must achieve this right "progressively" and "on the basis of equal opportunity." Article 28.1 then goes on to list in subsections (a) through (e) the particular measures which States Parties must undertake in order to attain these ends.

A. The Duty to Provide Elementary and Secondary Education: Article 28.1 (a) and (b)

As a practical matter, the United States already is in compliance with subsections (a) and (b). Article 28.1(a) provides that States Parties shall "[m]ake primary education compulsory and available free to all." Article 28.1(b) provides that States Parties shall "[e]ncourage the development of different forms of secondary education, including general and vocational education, make them available and accessible to every child, and take appropriate measures such as the introduction of free education and offering financial assistance in case of need." The United States, through the laws of each state, has achieved universal, free, public elementary and secondary education. Each state requires that children within certain age ranges (typically, 7 to 16 years old) must attend primary and secondary school pursuant to either compulsory education or compulsory attendance statutes.[11] All state constitutions contain provisions supportive of education as well.[12] The net effect is that each child residing in the United States currently receives the benefits of article 28.1(a) and (b)[13] primarily through the operation of state laws.

B. The Child's Right to Education: Introductory Language of Article 28.1

However, the introductory language of article 28.1 provides that it is the "States Parties", not merely their governmental subdivisions, which must

Education

recognize the child's right to education. The question thus arises as to whether children residing in the United States also have a right to education as against the federal government. Although neither the U.S. Constitution nor any federal statutes expressly address whether such a general right exists, the Supreme Court has considered the status of the right under the Constitution as a function of equal protection analysis.

The first case in which the issue arose is *San Antonio Independent School District v. Rodriguez*.[14] The gravamen of the *Rodriguez* plaintiffs' complaint was that Texas statutes, which caused funding disparities among school districts, violated the fourteenth amendment's equal protection clause. Plaintiffs urged the Supreme Court to review the challenged legislation under the strict scrutiny standard, the most stringent and, therefore, most favorable standard of review available to them. However, in order to successfully invoke strict scrutiny, plaintiffs were required to meet one of two criteria. Either the challenged law must adversely affect a suspect class or infringe upon a fundamental right under the U.S. Constitution.[15] It is in considering the second criterion that the Court confronted the question of whether there is a right to education under the federal Constitution. The Court's analysis on this point is strikingly inconsistent. On the one hand, the *Rodriguez* opinion concludes in unequivocal language that education is not a right under the U.S. Constitution.[16] On the other hand, the *Rodriguez* Court also concludes that, in an appropriate case, it might find that there is a right in the child to "some identifiable quantum of education" sufficient to provide the child with the "basic minimal skills" necessary for the enjoyment of the rights of speech and of full participation in the political process.[17] Although this projection of a future right to education is *dicta*, the language is significant in two respects. First, it signifies that the *Rodriguez* decision can not be read to foreclose the Court from finding a constitutional right to education, i.e., the status of education under the federal Constitution remains an open question. Second, the language represents a tacit acknowledgement by the Court that the Constitution may be interpreted to support a positive right to education, i.e., a right to have government provide education (in contrast to a negative right to be free of governmental impediments to the acquisition of education).[18] In equal protection cases, subsequent to *Rodriguez*, which have involved the claim that education is a fundamental right, the Court has continued to shy from closure on the issue,[19] and, on one occasion, expressly stated that the question remains unsettled.[20]

Article 28.1 of the Convention conceives of a positive right to education, requiring States Parties to take measures aimed at substantively providing education. *Rodriguez* and its progeny demonstrate that the United States Supreme Court considers recognition of such a right a real possibility within the strictures of acceptable constitutional interpretation.

C. The Duty to Provide Equal Educational Opportunity: Introductory Language of Article 28.1

A second guarantee of article 28.1 is that the right of the child to education must be achieved on the "basis of equal opportunity". Domestic laws concerning the various aspects of equal educational opportunity are numerous and complex. However, even a cursory survey of the pertinent statutes and cases indicates that the equal opportunity provision of article 28.1 should require no change in U.S. laws on the subject. In fact, the American legal system fairly abounds with prohibitions on discrimination in education on the basis of race, skin color, national origin, sex, and handicapping conditions.

For example, Title VI of the Civil Rights Act of 1964 provides that no person shall, on the ground of race, color, or national origin, be subjected to discrimination in relation to any program or activity receiving federal financial assistance.[21] Since virtually all public schools receive some form of federal assistance, they are governed by Title VI's prohibition. Another example is Title IV of the Civil Rights Act of 1964 which empowers the Attorney General to bring suit upon the complaint of any parent that his or her children, as members of a class of persons similarly situated, are being denied equal protection of the laws by a school board.[22] In addition, the fourteenth amendment's equal protection clause[23] has been interpreted by the Supreme Court to require that the public schools provide equal educational opportunities to children from various minority groups.[24]

In the area of sex discrimination, Title IX of the Education Amendments of 1972 requires, with certain limited exceptions, that no person shall, on the basis of sex, be subjected to discrimination in relation to any educational program or activity receiving federal financial assistance.[25] Again, since most educational institutions receive federal funding, they are subject to the prohibitions of Title IX. The Women's Educational Equity Act mandates that measures be taken promoting education equity for women and girls at all levels of education.[26] There is also precedent for invoking the equal protection clause to prevent the denial of equal educational opportunity on the basis of sex.[27]

Handicapped children's education interests are protected by U.S. law as well. Congress has enacted two major pieces of legislation to protect such children from discrimination by educational institutions: Section 504 of the Rehabilitation Act of 1973[28] and the Education of the Handicapped Act.[29] Section 504 of the Rehabilitation Act provides that no otherwise qualified handicapped person shall, solely because of his or her handicap, be subjected to discrimination under any program or activity receiving federal financial assistance. The Education of the Handicapped Act is designed to ensure that there is made available to all handicapped children a free, appropriate public education which includes special education and related services.[30]

Finally, it should be pointed out that there is federal law which is directed at minimizing disparities in educational opportunity related to wealth. For example, Congress has enacted the Hawkins-Stafford Elementary and Secondary School Improvement Amendments of 1988 which, in part, are directed at improving the educational opportunities of educationally-deprived children from low-income families.[31] In addition, the Supreme Court has held that discrimination in educational opportunities caused solely by disparate funding of school districts may contravene the equal protection clause if the disparity is not rationally related to a legitimate state objective.[32]

The recitation of this impressive array of laws protecting children's equal educational opportunities is not meant to suggest that equal educational opportunity has been fully achieved in the United States or that these laws have been fully adequate to the task. However, the equal opportunity language of article 28.1 does not require perfection. Rather, it appears to prescribe the nature of the process by which States Parties must achieve the right of the child to education. In this context, and given the thrust of domestic statutes and cases discussed above, it is evident that U.S. law on equal educational opportunity fulfills the equal opportunity provision of article 28.1.

Education

D. The Duty to Provide Higher Education: Article 28.1(c)

Article 28.1(c) of the Convention provides that States Parties shall "[m]ake higher education accessible to all on the basis of capacity by every appropriate means." The U.S. Congress has enacted an extensive matrix of statutes which furthers this goal by furnishing eligible students, directly or indirectly, with financial assistance to help meet the costs of higher education. The Pell Grant program is a major component of this legislation.[33] The stated purpose of the program is, among other things, to assist in making available the benefits of post-secondary education to eligible students in institutions of higher learning. Besides Pell Grants, other federal programs enacted to assist students in obtaining higher education include the Supplemental Educational Opportunity Program;[34] the State Student Incentive Grant Program;[35] programs providing direct loans to students in institutions of higher learning, such as the Perkins Loan Program;[36] and the PLUS Program providing parent loans for undergraduate students.[37]

Even this sampling of federal initiatives shows that the U.S. government unquestionably has committed itself to making higher education accessible to needy students on the basis of capacity. However, article 28.1(c) specifies that accessibility to higher education must be for "all" who are capable. Taken by itself, the use of the word "all" would seem to present compliance problems for the United States, since not everyone in this country who has the capability to pursue a higher education is able to do so.[38] As a matter of fact, during the 1980's, college tuition rose dramatically, often at more than twice the inflation rate,[39] while the Reagan administration actually contracted the amount of federal funds available to assist students seeking postsecondary education.[40]

A solution to this potential compliance problem may rest in the fact that article 28.1(c) qualifies the word "all" by adding that such accessibility is to be achieved "by every appropriate means." This phrase does not lend itself to definitive interpretation. What may constitute "every appropriate means" in one nation may not in another. And, within a particular nation, "every appropriate means" might well fluctuate in relation to the size of the national budget and the competing demands placed on that budget. Thus, "all", as used in article 28.1(c), may not actually mean "all" if "every appropriate means" in a given country at a given time does not make it possible to provide accessibility to everyone who has the capacity. Given such a sliding scale for measuring compliance, and given the array of federal legislation discussed above, a strong argument can be made that the United States meets the requirements of article 28.1(c). This is particularly true in light of the fact that in 1985, 5% of the United States population was enrolled in some form of higher education—at least twice the percent of any other industrialized nation except Canada.[41]

E. The Duty to Provide Educational and Vocational Information: Article 28.1(d)

Article 28.1(d) requires that States Parties "[m]ake educational and vocational information and guidance available and accessible to all children." While there is no one over-arching statute making such information and guidance available to American children, there are numerous provisions scattered throughout various federal statutes which, taken together, bring the United States into full compliance with article 28.1(d).[42]

F. The Duty to Encourage School Attendance: Article 28.1(e)

Article 28.1(e) mandates that States Parties shall "[t]ake measures to encourage regular attendance at schools and the reduction of drop-out rates." As mentioned earlier, the fifty states all have enacted compulsory attendance or compulsory education statutes.[43] The federal government also has assumed a role in promoting regular school attendance. For example, the Secondary Schools Basic Skills Demonstration Assistance Act of 1988[44] provides that funding under the Act may be used to develop innovative approaches to making secondary school attendance easier for certain students.[45] The federal government has appropriated funds to provide special child care services so that disadvantaged parents, including those who have not reached adulthood, are able to attend institutions of higher learning.[46] And, the federal government has undertaken programs, such as the School Lunch Programs,[47] which may have the effect of inducing poorer children to attend school, even though that is not the primary purpose of the program.

The federal government recently has taken measures to reduce dropout rates, too. Congress enacted the School Dropout Demonstration Assistance Act of 1988,[48] the basic purpose of which is to reduce the number of children who do not complete their elementary and secondary education. The Act specifies that this goal is to be achieved by, among other things, providing grants to local educational agencies to establish programs that will identify potential student dropouts and prevent them from dropping out, and that will identify and encourage children who have already dropped out to complete their elementary and secondary education.[49] Furthermore, the United States' commitment to reducing the dropout rate has become a priority for the executive branches of both the federal and state governments. In his State of the Union speech, President Bush set a goal of graduating 90% of the nation's high school students by the year 2000,[50] an objective subsequently adopted by the governors as well.[51] It is plain, then, that the direction and tenor of United States law and policy is fully consistent with the provisions of article 28.1(e).

■ CONSTRAINTS ON SCHOOL DISCIPLINE: ARTICLE 28.2

Article 28.2 sets the parameters for permissible school discipline by placing on States Parties the obligation to "take all appropriate measures to ensure that school discipline is administered in a manner consistent with the child's human dignity and in conformity with the present Convention." Articles 19.1 and 37(a) reveal what sort of discipline would not be "in conformity" with the Convention. Article 19.1 requires that States Parties take all appropriate measures "to protect the child from all forms of physical or mental violence, injury or abuse,...[or] maltreatment...while in the care of...any...person who has the care of the child." Article 37(a) declares that States Parties must ensure that "[n]o child shall be subjected to torture or other cruel, inhuman or degrading treatment or punishment."

At the very least, these provisions of the Convention require that States Parties outlaw corporal punishment as a means of effectuating school discipline. For, corporal punishment is indisputably "physical violence", and arguably may be characterized as "mental violence", "injury", "abuse", "maltreatment", "cruel, inhuman or degrading treatment", as well as an affront to the "child's human dignity". Although the majority of American parents have come to oppose corporal punishment in the schools,[52] their sentiments are not yet reflected in federal or most state law on the subject.

Education

The leading federal case on the constitutionality of corporal punishment of students is *Ingraham v. Wright*.[53] In *Ingraham*, the U.S. Supreme Court, in a five to four decision, held that the eighth amendment's prohibition against cruel and unusual punishment does not apply to corporal punishment in the public schools.[54] The Court also held that although corporal punishment in the public schools implicates a constitutionally protected liberty interest under the due process clause of the fourteenth amendment, that clause does not require notice and hearing prior to the imposition of such punishment where traditional common law remedies are available.[55] Thus, *Ingraham v. Wright* makes corporal punishment of children in public school constitutional in jurisdictions where state law and local school board policy permit.[56]

As it turns out, most states do permit corporal punishment of students in the public schools.[57] It is noteworthy, though, that a growing minority of states, such as California,[58] Wisconsin,[59] Michigan,[60] Minnesota,[61] Nebraska,[62] New Jersey,[63] Oregon[64] and Virginia,[65] now prohibit corporal punishment in the public school setting to one degree or another.[66]

What this means in relation to the Convention is that insofar as state and federal laws allow corporal punishment of children in the schools, the United States will be unable to fulfill the standards of article 28.2. Ratification of the Convention would require the U.S. to reconsider and reform this area of law. While the precedent set by *Ingraham* is daunting, the fact that four Justices dissented from the holding is perhaps grounds for some optimism that reform is possible.

Nor should it be overlooked that with respect to school discipline by suspensions and expulsions, United States law is in full accord with article 28.2. In relation to suspensions from school of 10 days or less, the Supreme Court held in *Goss v. Lopez*[67] that the due process clause requires that the student be given "oral or written notice of the charges against him and, if he denies them, an explanation of the evidence the authorities have and an opportunity to present his side of the story."[68] The Court further admonished that longer suspensions or expulsions from school may require more formal procedures in order to satisfy the due process clause.[69] These procedural safeguards for students are in keeping with the stipulation of article 28.2 that school discipline be administered so as to preserve the child's human dignity and are compatible with the rest of the Convention. They satisfy article 12.2's charge that the child must be afforded the opportunity to be heard in any administrative proceedings affecting him or her. And, they fulfill the rule of article 16.1 that "[n]o child shall be subjected to arbitrary or unlawful interference with his or her privacy,....nor to unlawful attacks on his or her honor and reputation."

■ EDUCATION PURPOSE: ARTICLE 29

The other provision of the Convention dealing directly with the education of the child is article 29. Subsection 1 concerns the quality and content of school curricula, while subsection 2 recognizes the right to establish non-public schools and stipulates the conditions for their operation.

A. The Duty to Educate to the Child's Fullest Potential: Article 29.1(a)

Article 29.1(a) posits that the States Parties shall direct the education of the child to the "development of the child's personality, talents and mental and physical abilities to their fullest potential". In the United States, education experts and government officials alike probably would agree with this goal.[70] However, the Convention poses this standard for the child's development not as an aspiration, but, rather, as a legal commitment. Making this legal commitment is problematic for the United States under existing federal law. In *Rodriguez v. San Antonio Independent School District*, the U.S. Supreme Court disclosed that the future right to education which it envisioned would be a right to the "basic minimal skills" necessary for the exercise of free speech and voting rights.[71] This conception of the right was essentially reiterated in subsequent Supreme Court cases.[72]

Of course, the *Rodriguez* conception of the right may actually translate into a very high level of education in this "information age" of increasingly complex political and technological challenges.[73] But, even accepting that interpretation, the fact remains that the proposed U.S. standard is described as "basic minimal skills" while the article 29.1(a) standard is phrased in terms of the child's maximum potential. In view of this discrepancy, full compliance with the Convention would require that the United States government recognize a right to education that encompasses the "fullest potential" standard of article 29.1(a).

B. The Duty to Teach Certain Values: Article 29.1(b), (c), (d) and (e)

Subsections (b), (c), (d) and (e) of article 29.1 prescribe certain values which the States Parties agree to transmit to children through education. At first glance, these subsections seem to be of doubtful constitutionality under the first and tenth amendments. The concern under the tenth amendment is that the federal government, by requiring such curricular content, would be usurping the states' authority over education.[74] The concern under the first amendment is that such federally-prescribed curriculum content would constitute indoctrination violating students' free speech rights.[75]

Closer analysis shows, however, that neither the tenth nor first amendment need preclude the federal government from fulfilling the obligations set forth in article 29.1(b), (c), (d) and (e). First, it should be noted that in *Missouri v. Holland*,[76] the U.S. Supreme Court ruled that the tenth amendment does not prevent the federal government from entering into treaties endowing the federal government with powers reserved to the states. Hence, were the United States to become a party to the Convention on the Rights of the Child, article 29.1 would empower the federal government to prescribe the curricular content set forth in subsections (b), (c), (d) and (e) without violating the tenth amendment.

Second, the federal government is and has been involved for quite a long time in promoting certain types of curricula, apparently without running afoul of the first or tenth amendments.[77] Article 29.1 would merely represent a continuation of this federal role.

Third, the values which would be taught pursuant to article 29.1 are the very same values already embodied in current United States legal obligations and moral commitments. Therefore, article 29.1 mandates nothing more controversial than teaching students their country's value system. The Supreme Court has indicated that although the first amendment does not permit the public schools to indoctrinate children in a particular orthodoxy,[78] the free speech clause does allow schools to convey a message[79] educating youth to "the shared values of a civilized social order"[80] and the "fundamental values necessary to the maintenance of a democratic political system."[81] The public schools are "a principle instrument in awakening the child to cultural values, in preparing him for later professional training, and in helping him to adjust normally to his environment."[82] As one commentator has observed, "[m]ost educators accept the general view that schools cannot avoid dealing with values and should not try to do so."[83] Consequently, an examination of the American sources of article 29.1 values is in order.

Article 29.1(b) provides that States Parties agree that the child's education shall be directed to the "development of respect for human rights and fundamental freedoms, and for the principles enshrined in the Charter of the United Nations." The United States has signed and ratified the Charter,[84] signifying agreement with its principles. Moreover, one of the principles enshrined in the Charter is that the United Nations will encourage respect for human rights and fundamental freedoms[85] —a principle which Member States pledge themselves to achieve.[86] Even more on point, the Universal Declaration of Human Rights,[87] recognized by leading international law scholars as customary international law binding on all countries,[88] declares that "[e]ducation shall be directed to...the strengthening of respect for human rights and fundamental freedoms."[89] Likewise, the mandate of article 29.1(d), that the child's education be directed to "the spirit of understanding, peace, tolerance, equality of sexes, and friendship among all peoples," also mirrors values enunciated in the Charter[90] and the Universal Declaration of Human Rights.[91]

While the enforceability in domestic courts of the Charter's human rights clauses and the Universal Declaration of Human Rights has proven controversial,[92] the fact remains that the United States has indicated its approval of the norms set forth in these documents.[93] Indeed, there is authority that as customary international law, the Universal Declaration of Human Rights constitutes binding federal law by virtue of the U.S. Constitution's supremacy clause.[94] In any event, the point is that the provisions of article 29.1(b) and (d) do not represent the imposition of any orthodoxy upon the nation's children, but, rather, merely require that children in the United States be awakened to the shared values which their countrymen embrace in order to maintain a democratic society.

Education

The values prescribed by article 29.1(c), (d) and (e) also are embodied in congressional enactments and/or rulings of the federal judiciary. Indeed, the language in subsection (d) on tolerance and equality is paralleled by the panoply of domestic civil rights statutes and cases discussed above.[95]

Article 29.1(c) is paralleled by domestic law as well. Article 29.1(c) requires that education be directed to development of respect for the child's "own identity, language and values," including respect for the values of the country in which he or she is living and the country from which he or she may originate. The Bilingual Education Act[96] is designed to enable children of limited English proficiency to learn English while using their native tongue in the process. The idea behind the statute is to build upon the child's self-esteem by instructional use of his or her native language and cultural heritage, so as to increase the child's mastery of English and enable him or her to participate fully in national life.[97] The American Folklife Preservation Act[98] enhances children's respect for the values of the country in which they are living by funding exhibitions, projects, presentations and materials specially designed for classroom use and illustrating some aspect of American folklife.[99] The Hawkins-Stafford Elementary and Secondary School Improvement Amendments of 1988 provide native Hawaiians with educational programs responsive to "the unique cultural and historical circumstances of Native Hawaiians".[100] For native Hawaiians identified as gifted and talented, the statute authorizes the funding of demonstration projects exploring the use of the native Hawaiian language and providing exposure to native Hawaiian cultural traditions.[101] Article 29.1(c) further stipulates that the education of the child must foster respect "for civilizations different from his or her own." To this end, Congress has enacted legislation to stimulate, in undergraduate students, the attainment of foreign language acquisition[102] and to provide a full understanding of areas or countries in which the language is used.[103]

Finally, article 29.1(c) directs that education must develop respect in the child for his or her parents. The laws of the United States are basically compatible with this provision. Congress has repeatedly enacted legislation designed to involve parents in their children's education,[104] and the Supreme Court has manifested longstanding deference to parent preferences with respect to the education and upbringing of their children.[105] While none of these statutes or cases expressly require that education serve the purpose of developing the child's respect for his or her parents, these laws do have the effect of enhancing parental prestige and authority by making parents more knowledgeable and powerful in relation to their children's education and general development.

Article 29.1(e) mandates that education of the child shall be directed to the "development of respect for the natural environment." The United States has many environmental protection statutes demonstrating that respect for the natural environment is a shared value among Americans.[106] On a smaller scale, Congress has commanded the Secretary of Agriculture to establish and maintain a national arboretum for purposes of research and education concerning tree and plant life.[107]

To summarize, each of the values enumerated in article 29.1(b), (c), (d) and (e) reflect the norms underlying United States domestic law and international commitments. As such, the directive of article 29.1, that these values be taught to public school children, does not offend the free speech clause of the first amendment. Rather, article 29.1, by encouraging tolerance and respect for different groups and by stressing fundamental freedoms and human rights, furthers the very diversity of opinion that the first amendment protects.[108] Indeed, such values could comfortably be integrated into the national core curriculum which many experts are recommending as a palliative to the education crisis.[109]

C. Nonpublic Schools: Article 29.2

Article 29.2 essentially establishes two principles. First, it posits that articles 28 and 29 may not be construed to preclude "individuals and bodies" from founding and directing educational institutions. Second, article 29.2 states that all such institutions must conform to certain standards, specifically those enumerated in article 29.1 and such minimum standards as may be laid down by the State.[110]

United States education law fully comports with the first principle by permitting individuals and institutions to establish and maintain their own schools. This right was indisputably established by *Pierce v. Society of Sisters*, in which the U.S. Supreme Court held that the due process liberty right of parents to direct the upbringing and education of their children encompasses the right to have their children educated at private schools rather than public ones.[111] Periodically, this principle has been reaffirmed, as in *Wisconsin v. Yoder*, where the Supreme Court relied, in part,[112] on the *Pierce* reasoning to uphold the right of Amish parents to substitute hands-on, informal vocational educational experiences for public school education beyond the eighth grade. In fact, in the United States today there is a vast system of religious and secular private schools,[113] as well as provision under a number of state laws for home schooling.[114]

The second principle set forth in article 29.2 is more troublesome, presenting, as it does, the issue of whether the federal government has the power to compel private schools to abide by the curriculum requirements of article 29.1(b), (c), (d) and (e).[115] Perhaps the most enlightening case on the subject is *Runyon v. McCrary*.[116] In the context of striking down private schools' racially-discriminatory admissions practices under section 1981, the Supreme Court took the occasion to announce, in *dictum*, that parents have a first amendment right to send their children to private schools which teach the belief that racial segregation is desirable. According to the Court, the parental right is a variant of the right of association for the advancement of beliefs and ideas,[117] regardless of whether those beliefs and ideas run counter to national policy.[118] The *Runyon* Court's message, then, appears to be that the first amendment gives private schools a very free hand with respect to the values conveyed by their curricula.[119]

The *Runyon* case involved nonsectarian private schools, but the *dictum* concerning curriculum applies to all private schools.[120] However, the issue of state control over curricular values content in sectarian private schools implicates not only the right of association, but rights under the free exercise clause of the first amendment as well.[121] Although the Supreme Court has indicated that the states are authorized to assure the minimal academic competence of religious schools,[122] case law suggests that any attempt by government to impose curricular content conflicting with the schools' religiously grounded values will probably encounter difficulty under the clause.[123]

In view of this body of law, the U.S. could find it problematic to compel private schools to observe the principles of article 29.1. It is inevitable that certain article 29.1 principles will clash with principles taught at one or another of the private schools dotting the United States. For example, the best-known curriculum used in fundamentalist private schools is Accelerated Christian Education which, as part of the tenth-grade American history course, teaches that "[t]he United Nations was created by Communists and has always been used by Communists to further Communist goals," and that "Satan is the real force behind man's efforts to achieve world government."[124] Obviously, this concept is hostile to the United Nations and at odds with the precepts of article 29.1(b). Or, consider the values taught at Bethany Baptist Academy in Illinois that "[t]his is not a place where there are alternative world views....[W]e put ourselves in a position of being the first and only among the religious of the world".[125] Such lessons fly in the face of article 29.1(b), (c) and (d). And, it appears that there is little the federal government can do, without violating the first amendment and the due process clause, to require that such private school values give way to article 29.1 values.

Yet, there is a growing concern in this country over the values children are being taught. It is indicative that the Supreme Court has become increasingly protective of the public schools' role in promoting important national values linked to the promotion of democracy and a civilized society.[126] It is conceivable that the Court could someday move towards prescribing some values content in private school curriculum. In fact, the Court already has insinuated itself into the private school milieu by holding that the Constitution tolerates private school liability for discriminatory admissions practices,[127] and by sanctioning the withdrawal of tax-exempt status from private schools which engage in such practices.[128]

Conclusion

As the foregoing analysis demonstrates, U.S. law is, in the main, consistent with the provisions of articles 28 and 29. There are only four provisions that raise potential legal obstacles for the United States: recognition of a right to education; adoption of a standard requiring that education develop children's abilities to their fullest potential; repudiation of corporal punishment as a form of school discipline; and imposition of article 29.1 values on nonpublic school curricula. But, with respect to each of these issues, it is possible that domestic law will develop so as to come more into conformance with the Convention. For example, the changing attitudes of

Education

Americans towards corporal punishment and of the Court towards curricular values content may be harbingers of legal developments that are more harmonious with articles 28 and 29. In a similar dynamic, the social and political pressures arising from the education crisis may generate "new thinking"[129] (to steal a phrase) on the need for a federally recognized right to education and for a standard of education pitched to developing the child's fullest potential.

From a policy perspective, the Convention's education provisions could well be instrumental in the national effort to overcome the education crisis. Were the United States to become a party to the Convention, articles 28 and 29 would make clear, before the world community and the American people, that this country has made a wholehearted commitment to educating its young. This commitment, in turn, would hopefully provide the inspiration and means enabling policy makers, lawmakers, educators and parents to attack the crisis with renewed vigor and effectiveness. More, the Convention would send a powerful message to the children that their education is a concern of the first order and that this society looks forward to, and, indeed, counts upon their intellectual and spiritual development.

Footnotes

1 I would like to thank law students Michael Behan, Patrice Villani and William Asimakis for their assistance in researching various issues covered in this chapter.

2 W. BENNETT, AMERICAN EDUCATION: MAKING IT WORK (April 26, 1988)[hereinafter W. BENNETT]; NAT'L COMM'N ON EXCELLENCE IN EDUCATION, A NATION AT RISK: THE IMPERATIVE FOR EDUCATIONAL REFORM (April 26, 1983)[hereinafter NAT'L COMM'N ON EXCELLENCE IN EDUCATION].

3 For a sampling of newspaper articles, see *Companies Step in Where the Schools Fail*, N.Y. Times, September 26, 1989, at 1, col. 2; *Impending U.S. Jobs "Disaster": Work Force Unqualified to Work*, N.Y. Times, September 25, 1989, at 1, col. 1; *Education Crisis: Bush Can Lead Us in Doing Three Things*, Chicago Tribune, April 30, 1989; *System Failure: Businesses Say Schools Are Producing Graduates Unqualified to Hold Jobs*, Wall Street Journal Reports, March 31, 1989. Other publi-

cations detailing the crisis include W. BENNETT, *supra* note 2; E. BOYER, HIGH SCHOOL: A REPORT ON SECONDARY EDUCATION IN AMERICA (1983); D. DOYLE & D. KEARNS, WINNING THE BRAIN RACE: A BOLD PLAN TO MAKE OUR SCHOOLS COMPETITIVE (1988); J. KOZOL, ILLITERATE AMERICA (1985); NAT'L COMM'N ON EXCELLENCE IN EDUCATION, *supra* note 2; D. RAVITCH & C. FINN, JR., WHAT DO OUR 17-YEAR-OLDS KNOW? A REPORT ON THE FIRST NATIONAL ASSESSMENT OF HISTORY AND LITERATURE (1987); S. SCHLOSSSTEIN, THE END OF THE AMERICAN CENTURY 217-300 (1989).

[4] W. BENNETT, *supra* note 2, at 12; NAT'L COMM'N ON EXCELLENCE IN EDUCATION, *supra* note 2, at 8.

[5] The term "culturally literate" is defined by E.D. Hirsch, Jr.:

> To be culturally literate is to possess the basic information needed to thrive in the modern world. The breadth of that information is great, extending over the major domains of human activity from sports to science. It is by no means confined to 'culture' narrowly understood as an acquaintance with the arts.

E. HIRSCH, JR., CULTURAL LITERACY: WHAT EVERY AMERICAN NEEDS TO KNOW xiii (1987).

[6] W. BENNETT, *supra* note 2, at 10-14.

[7] *Id.* at 10-12.

[8] *Companies Step in Where the Schools Fail*, *supra* note 3; *Impending U.S. Jobs "Disaster": Work Force Unqualified to Work*, *supra* note 3; *Trying to Coax a Work Force from the Schools of New York*, N.Y. Times, July 30, 1989, §4, at 5, col. 1; *System Failure: Businesses Say Schools Are Producing Graduates Unqualified to Hold Jobs*, *supra* note 3.

[9] L. Cavazos, Remarks Prepared for Delivery at Press Conference on 1989 State Education Performance Chart (May 3, 1989).

[10] Diane Ravitch comments that, "For everyone involved, the critical factor that must change is the attitude toward the importance of good education." D. RAVITCH, THE SCHOOLS WE DESERVE: REFLECTIONS ON THE EDUCATIONAL CRISES OF OUR TIME 155 (1985). In a similar vein, John Brademas observes that the federal government's commitment to public education will be critical to establishing the importance of educa-

tion in the public mind and, ultimately, to improving public education. J. BRADEMAS, THE POLITICS OF EDUCATION: CONFLICT AND CONSENSUS ON CAPITOL HILL 62 (1987).

[11] G. GEE & S. GOLDSTEIN, LAW AND PUBLIC EDUCATION 11 (2nd ed. 1980). Taken literally, only the statutes requiring compulsory "education" require the schools to educate children once they enter the schoolhouse door. The statutes requiring compulsory "attendance" do not impose an obligation on the states to do any educating once the child is in attendance. W. AIKMAN & L. KOTIN, LEGAL FOUNDATIONS OF COMPULSORY SCHOOL ATTENDANCE 71, 74, 86-87 (1980). Be that as it may, no state with a compulsory attendance law has refused to educate children compelled to attend school.

[12] Ala. Const. §256, amend. no. 111; Alaska Const. art. VII, §1; Ariz. Const. art. XI, §1; Ark. Const. art. XIV, §1; Cal. Const. art. IX, §5; Colo. Const. art. IX, §2; Conn. Const. art. VIII, §1; Del. Const. art. X, §1; Fla. Const. art. IX, §1; Ga. Const. art. VIII, §1; Haw. Const. art. X, §1; Idaho Const. art. IX, §1; Ill. Const. art. X, §1; Ind. Const. art. VIII, §1; Iowa Const. art. IX, §12; Kan. Const. art. VI, §1; Ky. Const. §183; La. Const. art. VIII; Me. Const. art. VIII, §1; Md. Const. art. VIII, §1; Mass. Const. pt. 2, Ch. 5, §2; Mich. Const. art. VIII, §2; Minn. Const. art. XIII, §1; Miss. Const. art. VIII, §201; Mo. Const. art. 9, §1(a); Mont. Const. art. X, §1; Neb. Const. art. VII, §1; Nev. Const. art. XI, §§1 and 2; N.H. Const. pt. 2, art. 83; N.J. Const. art. VIII, §4; N.M. Const. art. XII, §1; N.Y. Const. art. XI, §1; N.C. Const. art. IX, §§1 and 2; N.D. Const. art. VIII, §1; Ohio Const. art. I, §7, art. VI §§2 and 3; Okla. Const. art. XIII, §1; Or. Const. art. VIII, §3; Pa. Const. art. III, §14; R.I. Const. art. XII, §1; S.C. Const. art. XI §3; S.D. Const. art. VIII, §1; Tenn. Const. art. XI, §12; Tex. Const. art. VII, §1; Utah Const. art. X, §1; Vt. Const. ch. 2, §68; Va. Const. art. VIII, §1; Wash. Const. art. IX, §1; W. Va. Const. art. XII, §1; Wis. Const. art. X, §3; Wyo. Const. art. VII, §1.

[13] Article 29.1(b) requires that States Parties encourage the development of vocational education in particular. The U.S. Congress has, in fact, enacted legislation which implements this purpose. See, for example, the Carl D. Perkins Vocational Education Act, 20 U.S.C.A. §§2301-2471 (West Supp. 1990).

[14] 411 U.S. 1 (1973).

Education

[15] *Id.* at 16, 17, 28.

[16] *Id.* at 35.

[17] *Id.* at 36-37.

[18] There are a considerable number of commentators who share this analysis of the *Rodriguez* case. Dimond, *The Constitutional Right to Education: The Quiet Revolution*, 24 HASTINGS L.J. 1087, 1103 (1973); Gard, *San Antonio Indep. School Dist. v. Rodriguez: On Our Way to Where?*, 8 VAL. U.L. REV. 1, 27-29 (1973); Lupu, *Untangling the Strands of the Fourteenth Amendment*, 77 MICH. L. REV. 981, 1045 (1979); Preovolos, *Rodriguez Revisited: Federalism, Meaningful Access, and the Right to Adequate Education*, 20 SANTA CLARA L. REV. 75, 83 (1980); Ratner, *A New Legal Duty for Urban Schools: Effective Education in Basic Skills*, 63 TEX. L. REV. 777, 850 (1985); Wright, *The Place of Public School Education in the Constitutional Scheme*, 13 S. ILL. U. L. REV. 53, 56-57 (1988). However, it should be noted that, in general, constitutional rights are commonly considered to be negative rights. Currie, *Positive and Negative Constitutional Rights*, 53 U. CHI. L. REV. 864 (1986).

[19] In Plyler v. Doe, 457 U.S. 202, 221 (1982), the Court refuses to treat education as "merely some governmental 'benefit'." As Justice Burger aptly notes in his dissent, the Court's approach is tantamount to a "quasi-fundamental-rights analysis." 457 U.S. at 244 (Burger, J., dissenting). In Papasan v. Allain, 478 U.S. 265, 285 (1986), the Court states that it is an open question whether education is a fundamental right under the Constitution. In Kadrmas v. Dickinson Pub. Schools, 487 U.S. 450, 458 (1988), the Court states, without discussion, that it has not yet "accepted the proposition that education is a 'fundamental right'." It is difficult to believe that in her *Kadrmas* opinion, Justice O'Connor meant to close the question left open in *Rodriguez*, *Plyler* and *Papasan* with such a cryptic and conclusory statement. Indeed, in his dissent, Justice Marshall comments that the open question remains open after the *Kadrmas* decision, especially since *Kadrmas* focuses more on a claim to transportation services than to education. 487 U.S. at 466, n. 1 (Marshall, J., dissenting).

[20] Papasan v. Allain, 478 U.S. at 285.

[21] 42 U.S.C.A. §2000d (West 1981).

Education

[22] 42 U.S.C.A. §2000c-6 (West 1981).

[23] "No State shall...deny to any person within its jurisdiction the equal protection of the laws." U.S. CONST. amend. XIV, §1.

[24] For example, see Plyler v. Doe, 457 U.S. 202 (1982)(equal protection clause requires state to provide free, public education to illegal alien children); Brown v. Bd. of Educ., 347 U.S. 483 (1954)(equal protection clause requires abandonment of segregated schooling for black children).

[25] 20 U.S.C.A. §1681 (West 1978 & Supp. 1990).

[26] 20 U.S.C.A. §§3041-3047 (West Supp. 1990).

[27] Miss. Univ. for Women v. Hogan, 458 U.S. 718 (1982).

[28] 29 U.S.C.A. §794 (West Supp. 1990).

[29] 20 U.S.C.A. §§1400-1485 (West 1990).

[30] 20 U.S.C.A. §1400(c) (West 1990).

[31] For example, see U.S.C.A. §§2701-2731 (West Supp. 1990).

[32] Papasan v. Allain, 478 U.S. 265, 289 (1986) (remanded for a determination under the equal protection clause as to whether funding disparities are rationally related to a legitimate state interest); *but cf.* Rodriguez v. San Antonio Indep. School Dist., 411 U.S. 1 (1973)(under equal protection clause, state financing scheme is rationally related to a legitimate state interest even though scheme resulted in funding disparities).

[33] 20 U.S.C.A. §§1070a-1070a-6 (West Supp. 1990).

[34] 20 U.S.C.A. §§1070b-1070b-3 (West Supp. 1990).

[35] 20 U.S.C.A. §§1070c-1070c-4 (West Supp. 1990).

[36] 20 U.S.C.A. §§1087aa-1087hh (West Supp. 1990).

[37] 20 U.S.C.A. §1078-2 (West Supp. 1990).

[38] *Lessons: Are Colleges Winning—or Even Fighting—the Battle to Recruit More Minority Students?*, N.Y. Times, Apr. 25, 1990, at B6, col. 1.

[39] *About Education: Why Is College Tuition So High? Families Want Answers, Not Excuses,* N.Y. Times, Apr. 25, 1990, at B7, col. 1.

[40] J. BRADEMAS, *supra* note 10, at 95-97.

Education

[41] *Flashcard*, N.Y. Times, Apr. 8, 1990, §4A, at 7, col. 5.
[42] Such statutes include: 20 U.S.C.A. §1070d-1c(a)(1) (West Supp. 1990)(establishing "educational opportunity centers" designed to provide information with respect to financial and academic assistance available for individuals wishing to pursue postsecondary education); 20 U.S.C.A. §1070d-2(b)-(c) (West Supp. 1990)(making certain information and guidance available to students who are members of families engaged in migrant and seasonal farmwork and who are desirous of obtaining a high school equivalency degree or postsecondary education); 20 U.S.C.A. §1090(e)(West Supp. 1990) (establishing a toll-free number in order to give the public timely information in connection with financial assistance for postsecondary education); 20 U.S.C.A. §1417(a)(1)(C) (West 1978) (disseminating information in relation to the education of handicapped children); 20 U.S.C.A. §1431c(5)(E) (West Supp. 1990) (assisting parents in obtaining information about the programs and resources available to further the education of their handicapped children); 20 U.S.C.A. §2382(a)(6) (West Supp. 1990) (assisting individuals to obtain and use information on job training and on financial assistance for postsecondary and vocational education); 20 U.S.C.A. §2534 (West 1978) (providing programs to enhance guidance qualifications of teachers and counselors, including programs to expose students to workplace environments); 20 U.S.C.A. §3245(b)(4)(C) (West Supp. 1990) (disseminating information to students and parents in connection with the dropout problem); 20 U.S.C.A. §3291(d)(1)(D) (West Supp. 1990) (with respect to those students identified for enrollment in bilingual education programs, informing their parents of the nature of the bilingual education program and of instructional alternatives); 20 U.S.C.A. §5065(a)(7) (West Supp. 1990) (providing guidance, and exploration of postsecondary educational opportunities). Some of the cited statutory provisions directed at providing parents with information or guidance have been included because such provisions generally are aimed at benefiting children.
[43] *See supra* notes 11-12 and accompanying text.
[44] 20 U.S.C.A. §§5061-5066 (West Supp. 1990).
[45] *Id.* at §5065(a)(2)(A).
[46] 20 U.S.C.A. §1070f (West Supp. 1990).

47 42 U.S.C.A. §§1753-1769 (West 1978 & Supp. 1990).
48 20 U.S.C.A. §§3241-3247 (West Supp. 1990).
49 *Id.* at §3242.
50 *Cutting the Dropout Rate: High Goal But Low Hopes*, N.Y. Times, Feb. 17, 1990, at 26, col. 4.
51 *Governors' Group and Bush Envision Stronger Schools*, N.Y. Times, Feb. 26, 1990, at 12, col. 1.
52 *Parents and Teachers Split on Spanking*, N.Y. Times, Aug. 16, 1989, at B10, col. 2.
53 430 U.S. 651 (1977).
54 *Id.* at 664-671.
55 *Id.* at 672-682.
56 The *Ingraham* Court did not review the question of whether *severe* corporal punishment could constitute a substantive due process violation, leaving that question unresolved. *Id.* at 679, n. 47.
57 *Parents and Teachers Split on Spanking*, *supra* note 52. According to the National Coalition to Abolish Corporal Punishment in the Schools, the latest statistics show that 30 states still permit school-administered corporal punishment and 20 states forbid it. *Debate Over School Paddling Grows Amid Rising Concerns*, N.Y. Times, Aug. 16, 1990, at A1, col. 1.
58 CAL. EDUC. CODE §49001(b) (Deering 1990).
59 WIS. STAT. ANN. §118.31(2) (West Supp. 1989).
60 MICH. COMP. LAWS. ANN. §380.1312 (West Supp. 1989).
61 MINN. STAT. §127.45 (1989).
62 NEB. REV. STAT. §79-4, 140 (1988).
63 N.J. STAT. ANN. §18A:6-1 (West 1987).
64 OR. REV. STAT. §339.250 (1989).
65 VA. CODE ANN. §21.1-279.1 (1989).
66 Some statutes contain limited exceptions. For example, the New Jersey statute allows the use of force to quell a disturbance that threatens physical injury to others, to obtain possession of a weapon within the

Education

control of a pupil, for the purpose of self-defense, and for the protection of persons or property. N.J. STAT. ANN. §18A:6-1 (West 1987).

[67] 419 U.S. 565 (1975).

[68] *Id.* at 581.

[69] *Id.* at 584.

[70] The National Commission on Excellence in Education observed that "[o]ur goal must be to develop the talents of all to their fullest" and that "[w]e should expect schools to have genuinely high standards." NAT'L COMM'N ON EXCELLENCE IN EDUCATION, *supra* note 2, at 13. Similarly, at the education "summit meeting" convened by President Bush with the nation's governors, the President proposed "[e]xploiting the potential of every student, not only those who are gifted, but also the 'average students' and the disadvantaged." *Bush and the Governors Set Education Goals*, N.Y. Times, Sept. 28, 1989.

[71] 411 U.S. at 37.

[72] Plyler v. Doe, 457 U.S. 202, 222, 226 (1982); Papasan v. Allain, 478 U.S. 265, 286 (1986).

[73] NAT'L COMM'N ON EXCELLENCE IN EDUCATION, *supra* note 2, at 7.

[74] The tenth amendment provides that the "powers not delegated to the United States by the Constitution, nor prohibited by it to the States, are reserved to the States respectively or to the people". U.S. CONST. amend. X. The tenth amendment commonly is understood to make education the primary responsibility of state governments. 1 J. RAPP, EDUCATION LAW §3.02[2] (1989). As such, curricular decisions have been regarded mainly as a matter within the purview of state and local governments. 3 J. RAPP, EDUCATION LAW §11.02[2][a]-[b] (1989).

[75] The free speech clause of the first amendment provides that "Congress shall make no law...abridging the freedom of speech." U.S. CONST. amend. I. The Supreme Court has applied the first amendment to invalidate curricular decisions that impede students' free speech. W. Va. State Bd. of Educ. v. Barnette, 319 U.S. 624 (1943) (compulsory flag salute violates first amendment); *but cf.* Hazelwood School Dist. v. Kuhlmeier, 484 U.S. 260 (1988) (first amendment does not preclude school from restricting student speech that is inconsistent with educational mission).

Education

76 252 U.S. 416 (1920).

77 The involvement of the federal government in curriculum increased dramatically after the Soviet Union launched Sputnik. J. BRADEMAS, *supra* note 10, at 8-9, 61, 110. One of the results of Sputnik was the National Defense Education Act, 20 U.S.C.A. §511(a) (West 1974) (repealed 1980), which promoted the teaching of modern foreign languages, among other things. Statutes currently authorizing the federal government to promote certain types of curricula include the following: Dwight D. Eisenhower Mathematics and Science Education Act, 20 U.S.C.A. §2986(b)(1)(D) (West Supp. 1990) (providing that local educational agencies must use federal funding under the Act for integrating higher order analytical and problem-solving skills into the mathematics and science curricula); Foreign Language Assistance Act of 1988, 20 U.S.C.A. §3003(a) (West Supp. 1990) (funding the commencement or improvement of foreign language study in elementary and secondary schools); Drug-Free Schools and Communities Act of 1986, 20 U.S.C.A. §3173 (West Supp. 1990) (establishing drug abuse education in elementary and secondary schools).

78 *Barnette*, 319 U.S. at 642.

79 Bd. of Educ., Island Trees Union Free School Dist. No. 26 v. Pico, 457 U.S. 853, 869 (1982). In *dictum*, the Court stated that the school district "might well defend their claim of absolute discretion in matters of *curriculum* by reliance upon their duty to inculcate community values." *Id.* at 869.

80 Bethel School Dist. No. 403 v. Fraser, 478 U.S. 675, 683 (1986).

81 Ambach v. Norwick, 441 U.S. 68, 76-77 (1979).

82 Brown v. Bd. of Educ., 347 U.S. 483, 493 (1954).

83 D. MOSHMAN, CHILDREN, EDUCATION, AND THE FIRST AMENDMENT: A PSYCHOLEGAL ANALYSIS 160 (1989).

83 The Charter entered into force for the United States on October 24, 1945. A. D'AMATO, R. FALK & B. WESTON, BASIC DOCUMENTS IN INTERNATIONAL LAW AND WORLD ORDER 6 (1980).

85 U.N. CHARTER art. 1, para. 3, and art. 55(c).

86 U.N. CHARTER art. 56.

[87] G.A. Res. 217A (III), U.N. Doc. A/810, at 71 (1948) [hereinafter Universal Declaration].

[88] M. McDOUGAL, H. LASSWELL & L. CHEN, HUMAN RIGHTS AND WORLD PUBLIC ORDER 325, 338 (1980); Greenberg, *Race, Sex and Religious Discrimination in International Law*, in HUMAN RIGHTS INTERNATIONAL LAW: LEGAL AND POLICY ISSUES 314 (T. Meron ed. 1984).

[89] Universal Declaration, *supra* note 87, at art. 26, para. 2.

[90] The Charter commits the U.N. to the maintenance of peace. U.N. CHARTER art. 1, para. 1. The Charter also commits the U.N. to encouraging rights and freedoms for all "without distinction as to race, sex, language, or religion". *Id.* at art. 1, para. 3, and art. 55(c).

[91] The Universal Declaration proclaims that all human beings "should act towards one another in a spirit of brotherhood", Universal Declaration, *supra* note 87, at art. 1; that everyone is entitled to the rights and freedoms set forth in the Declaration "without distinction of any kind, such as race, colour, sex, language, religion, political or other opinion, national or social origin, property, birth or other status", *Id.* at art. 2; and that education shall promote "understanding, tolerance, and friendship among all nations, racial or religious groups, and shall further the activities of the United Nations for the maintenance of peace", *Id.* at art. 26, para. 2.

[92] Domestic courts typically have taken the position that the human rights clauses of the U.N. Charter are non-self-executing and, consequently, unenforceable without an act of Congress. Sei Fujii v. Cal., 217 P.2d 481 (1950), *aff'd*, 38 Cal. 2d 718, 242 P.2d 617 (1952). Nevertheless, some international law scholars argue that since 1977, when President Carter addressed the U.N. General Assembly, the U.S. has effectively acknowledged the obligatory nature of the Charter's human rights clauses. Greenberg, *Race, Sex and Religious Discrimination in International Law*, in HUMAN RIGHTS IN INTERNATIONAL LAW: LEGAL AND POLICY ISSUES, *supra* note 88, at 314 (quoting Schacter, *International Law Implications of U.S. Human Rights Policies*, 24 N.Y. L. SCH. L. REV. 63, 67 (1978)).

[93] Not only has the United States signed and ratified the Charter, but it also has become an active member of the United Nations. *See supra*

notes 84 and 92. The moral commitments which the Charter imposes were eloquently described by the court in *Sei Fujii v. Cal.*:

> The humane and enlightened objectives of the United Nations Charter are, of course, entitled to respectful consideration by the courts and Legislatures of every member nation, since that document expresses the universal desire of thinking men for peace and for equality of rights and opportunities. The Charter represents a moral commitment of foremost importance, and we must not permit the spirit of our pledge to be compromised or disparaged in either domestic or foreign affairs.

38 Cal. 2d at 722-25, 242 P.2d 617, 621-22.

Although the United States was a strong supporter of the Universal Declaration at the time of its adoption, the U.S. initially refused to recognize its obligatory character. However, the federal government subsequently has had occasion to treat the Universal Declaration as binding customary international law. These developments are more fully discussed in Lillich, *Invoking International Human Rights Law in Domestic Courts*, 54 CINCINNATI L. REV. 367, 393-99 (1985).

[94] In *The Paquete Habana*, 175 U.S. 677 (1900), the Supreme Court ruled that customary international law is the supreme law of the land by virtue of article VI of the Constitution.

[95] *See supra* notes 21-32 and accompanying text.

[96] 20 U.S.C.A. §§3281-3341 (West Supp. 1990).

[97] *Id.* at §3282(a)(5)-(8).

[98] 20 U.S.C.A. §§2101-2107 (West 1978 & Supp. 1990).

[99] 20 U.S.C.A. §2104(a)(1)(D) (West 1978).

[100] 20 U.S.C.A. §4901(9) (West Supp. 1990).

[101] 20 U.S.C.A. §4906(b)(2) (West Supp. 1990).

[102] For example, see 20 U.S.C.A. §1121(b) (West Supp. 1990).

[103] 20 U.S.C.A. §1122(a)(1) (West Supp. 1990).

[104] For instance, the Even Start Program, 20 U.S.C.A. §§2741-2749 (West Supp. 1990), places a heavy emphasis on helping "parents become full

partners in the education of their children". *Id.* at §2744(a). Similarly, that portion of the Hawkins-Stafford Elementary and Secondary School Improvement Amendments of 1988 which authorizes federal support for basic programs operated by local educational agencies stresses parental involvement in order to expand the parents' capacity to improve their children's learning at home and in school. 20 U.S.C.A. §2726(a)(3), (b) (West Supp. 1990). The Fund for the Improvement and Reform of Schools and Teaching Act also contains a program for establishing a family-school partnership in the education of children, based on the finding that parental involvement is directly related to student achievement in school. 20 U.S.C.A. §§4822-4823 (West Supp. 1990).

[105] Wisconsin v. Yoder, 406 U.S. 205 (1972); Pierce v. Society of Sisters, 268 U.S. 510 (1925); Meyer v. Neb., 262 U.S. 390 (1923). For a discussion of this point, see L. TRIBE, AMERICAN CONSTITUTIONAL LAW 1299-1300 (2nd ed. 1988).

[106] Toxic Substances Control Act, 15 U.S.C.A. §§2601 *et seq.*; Clean Water Act, 33 U.S.C.A. §§1251 *et seq.*; National Environmental Policy Act, 42 U.S.C.A. §§4321 *et seq.*; Clean Air Act, 42 U.S.C.A. §§7401 *et seq.*

[107] 20 U.S.C.A. §191 (West 1974).

[108] *See* W. Va. Bd. of Educ. v. Barnette, 319 U.S. 624, 641-42 (1943).

[109] NAT'L COMM'N ON EXCELLENCE IN EDUCATION, *supra* note 2, at 24; Goodwin, *The Crisis in Public Education and a Constitutional Rationale for Federal Intervention*, 4 DET. C. L. REV. 937, 938-50 (1988).

[110] The language of Article 29.2 does not make such minimum standards mandatory. Instead, Article 29.2 simply requires that if, in its discretion, a nation has seen fit to create minimum standards for nonpublic education, then schools governed by the standards must adhere to them.

[111] 268 U.S. 510 (1925).

[112] 406 U.S. 205, 213-14 (1972). Most of the Court's analysis in *Yoder* dealt with Amish parents' rights under the free exercise clause of the first amendment.

[113] "Of an estimated 46 million students enrolled in elementary and secondary schools in fall, 1989, about 12% were at private schools." *Flashcard*, N.Y. Times, Apr. 8, 1990, §4A, at 8, col. 5 (citing information

Education

from NATIONAL CENTER FOR EDUCATION STATISTICS, KEY STATISTICS FOR PRIVATE ELEMENTARY AND SECONDARY EDUCATION: SCHOOL YEAR 1989-90 (EARLY ESTIMATES)).

[114] 2 J. RAPP, EDUCATION LAW §8.03 [3][c] (1989).

[115] I do not address the applicability of Article 29.1(a) to nonpublic schooling inasmuch as the federal government does not even currently embrace the Article 29.1(a) standard in relation to public schools. See supra notes 70-73 and accompanying text.

[116] 427 U.S. 160 (1976).

[117] Id. at 176.

[118] See supra notes 21-32 and accompanying text for a description of the laws manifesting national policy on race relations and discrimination generally.

[119] "[I]t should be noted that the state apparently cannot control the subjects taught in those [private sectarian and nonsectarian] schools beyond its assurance that children are given competent instruction in specified secular subjects and that they are in a safe and healthy environment". 3 J. NOWAK, R. ROTUNDA & J. YOUNG, TREATISE ON CONSTITUTIONAL LAW: SUBSTANCE AND PROCEDURE §21.7 (1986) [hereinafter NOWAK, ROTUNDA & YOUNG TREATISE].

[120] 427 U.S. at 176.

[121] The free exercise clause states, "Congress shall make no law...prohibiting the free exercise [of religion]". U.S. Const. amend. I.

[122] NOWAK, ROTUNDA & YOUNG TREATISE, supra note 119, at §21.7.

[123] The Supreme Court's approach to this issue is reflected in Wisconsin v. Yoder, 406 U.S. 205 (1972), in which the Court held that under the free exercise clause, the Amish have the right to give their children hands-on, vocational educational experiences in lieu of the two years of schooling beyond the eighth grade required by Wisconsin. However, Yoder deals with an informal, apprenticeship-type educational alternative to public schooling rather than the more traditional religious school. Presumably, the Court would be even more protective of curricula of the traditional religious school which challenges fewer of the state's education interests. Compare Yoder with Fellowship Baptist Church v. Benton, 815 F.2d 485 (8th Cir. 1987) (the court of appeals

held that Iowa's imposition of a human relations course on religious school teachers did not violate the free exercise clause; however, the court expressly stated that exposure to the course was not inconsistent with the training given prospective teachers by colleges run by the church.)

[124] D. MOSHMAN, *supra* note 83, at 167.

[125] *Id.* at 166-67.

[126] Hazelwood School Dist. v. Kuhlmeier, 484 U.S. 260 (1988); Bethel School Dist. v. Fraser, 478 U.S. 675 (1986). For a full discussion of this trend, see Rebell, *Values Inculcation and the Schools*, in PUBLIC VALUES, PRIVATE SCHOOLS 44-46 (N. Devins ed. 1989).

[127] Runyon v. McCrary, 427 U.S. 160 (1976).

[128] Bob Jones Univ. v. United States, 461 U.S. 574 (1983).

[129] M. GORBACHEV, PERESTROIKA: NEW THINKING FOR OUR COUNTRY AND THE WORLD (1987).

CHAPTER 10

Assuring an Adequate Standard of Living for the Child
Articles 26 and 27

James Weill

Introduction

Articles 26 and 27 of the Convention on the Rights of the Child concern a child's most basic material needs—for items such as food, clothing and shelter. Through these articles, ratifying countries recognize the right of a child to an adequate standard of living and its links to child development. The Convention then sets out the responsibilities of various sectors of the society for assuring an adequate standard of living: the parents, including a parent who is not present in the child's home, are primarily responsible; children are also to be eligible to benefit from social insurance; when these sources of assistance are insufficient, the ratifying country must assist the parents in providing for the child and must itself provide material assistance.

This arrangement of responsibilities is very much in accord with American law, tradition, and social policy. In general, in the U.S., parents are primarily responsible for the adequate support of their children and for meeting the children's material and developmental needs. Absent parents have child support obligations, the enforcement of which has been greatly stepped up since the early 1980s. The U.S. has a highly developed social insurance scheme, as well as certain methods to help parents support their children and a set of safety net programs to provide material assistance.

While the conceptual structure of the U.S. system is very much in accord with the Convention, for one-fifth of America's children the implementation falls far short of what the Convention apparently contemplates. The United States does not "within [its] means ... provide" for a standard of living adequate for many American children. With one of the highest child poverty rates among Western industrial democracies and with a labor market and public assistance structure that is leaving children in poverty at close to twice the rate of adults, the U.S. is not assuring all of its children an adequate standard of living and is not living up to its own laws or the Convention.

■ MORE THAN 12 MILLION CHILDREN IN THE UNITED STATES DO NOT HAVE A STANDARD OF LIVING ADEQUATE FOR THEIR PHYSICAL, MENTAL, SPIRITUAL, MORAL AND SOCIAL DEVELOPMENT: ARTICLE 27(1)

Under article 27(1) of the Convention, "States Parties recognize the right of every child to a standard of living adequate for the child's physical, mental, spiritual, moral and social development." More than 12 million children (one out of five) in the United States live in families that have incomes below the nation's poverty line. These children's standard of living is developmentally inadequate.

In the United States, poverty is defined as having household income below an official "poverty line" set by the federal government. The poverty line amount increases with family size and is adjusted annually to reflect changes in the cost of living. In 1988, the amount was $9,435 for a family of three and $12,092 for a family of four.

While widely accepted as one useful way to measure poverty, the official U.S. poverty line is not a wholly adequate gauge of the extent of child poverty. For one thing, some other societies define poverty as a percentage of the per capita or per family income. The poverty level is thereby adjusted for real growth as well as for inflation. The U.S. does not adjust its poverty, definition this way. As the U.S. economy and real median income have grown in recent decades, the static definition of poverty, increasingly, has lagged behind.

This means that some families should be defined as poor, but are not, and that those families defined as poor are even poorer in relative terms than comparable families a generation earlier (their incomes are a smaller share of a typical family's income). They have become further detached from the mainstream society. In the U.S. the poverty level for a family of three was

41 percent of the median three-person family income in 1960. But, the poverty level was only 28 percent of that median in 1988.

In any event, a family needs income at least above the official poverty line before its children will have, in the Convention's terms, an adequate standard of living. But in 1988, 12.6 million U.S. children lived in poverty—in families with incomes below the poverty line. That is *20 percent* of the 63 million Americans under the age of 18. The proportion of U.S. children in poverty grew by one-fifth from 1973/1974 to 1988. Children are by far the poorest group of Americans. Adult poverty rates, including rates for the elderly, are considerably lower, and have declined since the 1960's.

During the past decade, the U.S. child poverty rate has been only barely responsive to economic growth. The reduction in the number of children living in poverty from 1982 to 1988 (1.1 million) was smaller than the increase in the number in poverty just from 1981 to 1982. This means that the benefits of modest economic growth are no longer reaching many poor families. At the 1982-1988 rate, it would take until the year 2005 just to get the number of U.S. poor children back to its unacceptable 1973 level.

The child poverty rate remains far higher than that which prevailed for the entire period of 1966 to 1980. A number of factors have made the child poverty rate almost impervious to the economic growth of the 1980's: the replacement of higher-paying manufacturing jobs by lower-paying service sector jobs for young, non-college educated workers; the phenomenal growth in jobs that are only part time, temporary or both; the failure of the U.S. government from 1981 to 1990 to adjust the minimum wage to compensate for inflation (a parent working full time year-round at the minimum wage does not earn enough to raise a family of three out of poverty); the shift in family composition to more single-parent families; and the huge drop in earnings for young workers (from 1973 to 1987 the median earnings of all young family heads fell 24 percent).

The overall child poverty rate, as high as it is, obscures extraordinary concentrations of poverty among some groups of U.S. children:

> *Young children.* Among infants and toddlers younger than age three, one out of every four is poor.

Standard of Living

Minority children. Nearly one out of two black children is poor. Among black and Latino children younger than age six living in female-headed families, nearly three out of four are poor.

Children in single-parent families. More than half of all children who live in female-headed families are poor.

Children in young families. More than one-third of all children living in families headed by someone under the age of 30 are poor.

Children in rural families. Nearly one in four children living in non-metropolitan areas is poor.

Children in working families. Having one or more family members in the labor force is no insurance against poverty. Almost half of the 7 million poor families in 1987 had at least one person in the labor force for more than half of the year.

Not only the breadth of poverty is extraordinary, but so is the depth. In 1988, 43% of all poor families with children had incomes of less than half the poverty level. (For a family of three, this meant an income below $4,718.)

The U.S. child poverty rates are not even approached by those of most other comparable nations. A 1988 report comparing eight industrial democracies showed the U.S. child poverty rate two to three times that of Switzerland, Sweden, Norway, West Germany, Canada and the United Kingdom, and slightly higher than Australia's.[1]

■ THE CONVENTION PLACES PRIMARY RESPONSIBILITY ON THE PARENT TO MEET THE CHILD'S NEEDS, BUT ALSO REQUIRES THE STATE TO PURSUE PARENTAL SUPPORT FOR THE CHILD: ARTICLE 27(2) AND 27(4)

A. Parental Responsibility

Article 27(2) provides that "The parent(s) or others responsible for the child have the primary responsibility to secure, within their abilities and financial capacities, the conditions of living necessary for the child's development." This is generally consistent with U.S. law.

All states, usually by statute, require parents, at least those who are financially able, to support their children throughout the children's minority.[2] A few states put the primary responsibility for supporting the child on the father, but the constitutionality of such gender-based differences in the duty is questionable. In all states, failure to provide support for the necessities of life (e.g., adequate food, clothing, and shelter, medical care and education), or to provide parental care and supervision can lead to a neglect proceeding, and in some states it can lead to a criminal prosecution for non-support.

The duty to support applies both to biological children and to adopted children. Most states do not impose on the step-parent a duty to support step-children (unless, of course, they have been adopted as well).

Male and female children have an equal right to support. State laws that make the parents' responsibility different depending on the gender of the child have been held unconstitutional.[3]

In all these respects, U.S. law appears to accord with the Convention.[4]

The Convention's requirement that parents have the primary responsibility to secure what is necessary for the child's development should apply with equal force to the parents of children born out-of-wedlock. The Convention does not define the term "parents," but there is no suggestion that the concept excludes biological parents merely because they are not married. Furthermore, article 2 of the Convention bars discrimination based on "birth...status;" article 7 gives the child "the right from birth to a name...and, as far as possible, the right to know and be cared for by his or her parents"; and article 18 requires States Parties to "use their best efforts to ensure recognition of the principle that *both parents* have common responsibilities for the upbringing and development of the child." (Emphasis added.)

Under U.S. law, children born out-of-wedlock generally have the same rights to support as other children. State laws that do not give them an enforceable right to support violate the Equal Protection Clause of the fourteenth amendment.[5] These policies would comply with the Convention.

One possible exception lies in the realm of inheritance. Some state laws do not allow children born out-of-wedlock to inherit in intestacy from a parent dying without a will in the same way as children born in-wedlock. The U.S. Supreme Court has said that states may not wholly exclude from intestate succession children born out-of-wedlock. For example, states must allow intestate succession by those whose paternity previously has been adjudicated in court. But states can exclude from such succession other children born out-of-wedlock whose paternity is established by other means, such as acknowledgment rather than adjudication.[6] To the extent that state intestacy laws grant inheritance rights in part to provide support to minor children, state bars to intestate succession, by children who can prove paternity, might represent noncompliance with the Convention.

B. Enforcement of Child Support Obligations of Absent Parents

Twenty-five percent of American children are born out of wedlock. About 30% will see their parents divorce or separate during childhood. Overall, three in five will live with a single parent, usually the mother, at some point during their minority. More than half of all children living in female-headed families are poor.

These very high numbers of children who need support from parents outside the home, a trend of fairly recent vintage in U.S. history, underline the importance of effective enforcement of the child support obligation of absent parents. The Convention addresses this issue. Article 27(4) provides that:

> *States Parties shall take all appropriate measures to secure the recovery of maintenance for the child from the parents or other*

persons having financial responsibility for the child, both within the State Party and from abroad.

Moreover, as noted earlier, article 18 says that "States Parties shall use their best efforts to ensure recognition of the principle that both parents have common responsibilities for the upbringing and development of the child."

For many years most states in the U.S. were extremely lax in enforcing the child support obligations of absent parents, particularly obligations to children born out-of-wedlock. Congress passed laws in 1950, 1967 and 1974 successively strengthening states' obligations to seek child support from the absent parents of children receiving Aid to Families with Dependent Children, but with only minimal effect.

Congress acted twice in the 1980's to ratchet up enforcement efforts, due to rising numbers of out-of-wedlock births, a string of U.S. Supreme Court decisions giving children born out-of- wedlock new legal rights, a concern about absent fathers' poor record of supporting their children and states' poor records of pursuing support, and a perceived opportunity to reduce expenditures in public assistance programs. First, the Child Support Enforcement Amendments of 1984[7] required states to put in place several mechanisms to make sure child support is awarded and paid. Because of inadequacies in the policies and implementation of the 1984 law, Congress made further changes through the Family Support Act of 1988[8] to improve upon some of the earlier reforms. The new law will prod states to implement the 1984 requirements more quickly and effectively.

The two laws together significantly strengthen the ability of children and their custodial parents to obtain support from absent parents. They require states to provide child support enforcement services both to families receiving welfare and to other families that request assistance. States must: establish expedited processes for obtaining and enforcing support orders; permit the establishment of paternity at least up to a child's eighteenth birthday;[9] have and apply uniform guidelines for the amount of child support awards; have systems to withhold part of absent parents' paychecks; recover past-due support from absent parents' tax refunds; cooperate on interstate cases; and obtain support for medical, as well as cash, needs.

This panoply of laws would appear to satisfy the Convention, although the actual implementation sometimes leaves a good deal to be desired. Much of the available data on implementation predates the 1988 amendments, but it shows the shortcomings of enforcement efforts:

- In 1986 the majority of divorced, separated and never-married mothers were rearing their children with no financial help from the fathers. As of the spring of 1986, 8.8 million mothers were living with children younger than 21 whose fathers were absent from the home. Only 61% of the women had been awarded child support, and among them, one-quarter received nothing and one-quarter received only partial payment. The situation was even worse for those women and children living in poverty.

- Less than one-quarter of all women who have borne children out-of-wedlock have had the children's paternity adjudicated.

- The mean amount of support in 1985 for women with one child was $1,679 per year.[10]

Full implementation of the Convention can be expected to bring vast improvements. But the picture has been fairly dismal, and many state child support enforcement efforts to this date remain under-funded and under-staffed.

Even if enforcement of child support obligations were much more aggressive and more certain, the impact on child poverty would be modest. Support is a partial, but limited, answer to the child poverty problem in the U.S. As the Congressional Research Service notes, "child support payments *per se* are unlikely to lift the majority of families out of poverty or eliminate the need for welfare programs.... [However,] child support payments could help reduce the severity of poverty for many non-AFDC children even if it did not end their poverty."[11]

■ SOCIAL INSURANCE: ARTICLE 26(1)

Article 26(1) provides that "States Parties shall recognize for every child the right to benefit from social security, including social insurance, and shall take the necessary measures to achieve the full realization of this right in accordance with their national law."

It is not particularly clear what this provision means, since the drafters presumably did not mean that "every child" should *receive* social insurance. At a minimum, it would seem to mean that the country's social insurance scheme should not arbitrarily exclude children. It may suggest, as well, that every child has a right to "social security" —a right of protection and adequacy of living standards parallel to those rights expressed elsewhere in articles 26 and 27, and that social insurance is one element of this right.

In the U.S., children are beneficiaries of the social insurance system, albeit in relatively limited ways.

A. OASDI

The Old Age, Survivors, and Disability Insurance program (OASDI—commonly known as Social Security)[12] is the nation's largest insurance program. The federal government makes monthly payments to insured retired and disabled workers and to the spouses, minor children, and (infrequently) grandchildren or parents of insured workers upon the workers' retirement, disability, or death. Generally, the length and level of the worker's past contributions to government trust funds, rather than the family's current need, determine eligibility and benefit levels.

OASDI is a huge program. In 1987, for example, there were payments of over $204 billion to 38 million beneficiaries. Roughly 2.6 million of the beneficiaries are minor children.[13] Millions of other children, while not direct beneficiaries, live with parents, grandparents, or other relatives in households substantially supported by Social Security. The program is thus a very important source of social insurance for many children. Social Security payment levels to families with children are significantly higher than public assistance payments in virtually all states.

Nevertheless, children have been getting less and less of the OASDI system's benefits because of demographic change and because of alterations in program rules. In 1940, one out of four OASDI program beneficiaries was a child; by 1960 this number had fallen to one out of seven; and by 1987, only one in 12. In 1950, 15% of OASDI dollars went to children, but in 1987 children's share was only 5%.

Generally, each child of a retired, disabled, or deceased insured wage earner gets benefits through the age of 18 (19 if the child is still a full-time student in secondary school). Benefits for each child are reduced when there are so many entitled dependents in the family that aggregate payment would exceed a statutory family maximum.[14]

In order to obtain benefits, a child must meet the definition of child under the act and, in certain circumstances, also must have been dependent on the insured worker.[15] All the worker's biological children born in-wedlock and adopted children are eligible. A step-child is eligible, however, only if he or she was the step-child of the insured worker for a certain amount of time before application and lived with or received one-half of his or her support from the step-parent (the dependency test).

A child born out-of-wedlock, to be eligible, must show that: the insured wage earner has acknowledged the child in writing; or has been decreed by a court to be the parent; or has been ordered by a court to provide child support; or was his or her parent and was living with or contributing to the child's support at the time of the child's application (or, in a survivor's case, at the time of the worker's death). Alternatively, the child is eligible if he or she can inherit from the parent under state law determining the devolution of intestate personal property.[16] Other children born out-of-wedlock are not eligible.

There may be some inconsistency between the Convention and the OASDI program's exclusion of children born out-of-wedlock, whose paternity is proven, but who do not meet these various tests. They are ineligible for Social Security insurance even though their status as the worker's "child" is unquestioned. This may violate article 26(1) of the Convention.[17]

B. Unemployment Insurance

Another key form of social insurance is unemployment insurance. Many Americans assume that unemployment insurance provides a temporary lifeline for all jobless workers and their families. But fewer than one-third of all unemployed workers received unemployment benefits in 1988, down from the one-half of all unemployed workers who received such benefits as recently as 1980. Due to the adoption of more restrictive federal and state eligibility rules during the 1980s and changes in the labor market that have made insured status less common among workers, particularly young workers, unemployment insurance now rescues far fewer jobless workers than it misses. The structure and amount of unemployment benefits generally depend on state law. Only fourteen states make provision for dependents' allowances—raising the amount paid to an unemployed worker if minor dependent children are present in the household. Even in these states, moreover, a typical dependent's allowance is only in the $5-$10/week range.[18]

C. Other Social Insurance Programs[19]

State workmen's compensation, the temporary disability programs that some states operate, and a variety of other public insurance programs (e.g., for public workers who retire or become disabled) are useful social insurance programs that are beyond the scope of this paper. Many of these laws include archaic disqualifications of children born out-of-wedlock, and the Supreme Court has held such exclusions unconstitutional.[20] The Convention might require the scrutiny of such laws for residual arbitrary exclusions of such children or other categories of children.

One form of social insurance, that is very common among other Western democracies but is rare in the United States and whose absence is noteworthy, is protected job security during parental leave after a child is born or adopted or when a child is ill. The United States and South Africa are the only major industrialized nations which do not guarantee some form of job-protected maternity leave, paid or unpaid. Of 135 countries providing leave, 125 mandate paid leave, including all European nations and most nations in Central America, the Caribbean and South America.[21]

■ HELPING PARENTS MEET THE CHILD'S MATERIAL NEEDS: ARTICLE 27(3)

Article 27(3) provides that "States Parties in accordance with national conditions and within their means shall take appropriate measures to assist parents and others responsible for the child to implement this right [to an adequate standard of living]...."

These clauses seem to provide that the nation must have income maintenance or employment programs that assist low-income working or able-bodied parents to meet the basic needs of their children. U.S. policy falls far short of this goal.

In recent years, the federal government has failed to address the changing economic and social conditions that have weakened the ability of American families to support children, and in some cases actually has retreated from its previous, already inadequate commitments to aid low-income or unemployed parents. It has cut back on its investments in education and training. And the supplements for incomes of workers who are employed at wages inadequate to support a family fall far short of what is needed.

First, the government has come close to abandoning trying to maintain the minimum wage at a level that will let parents working full-time maintain their families at an adequate standard of living. In 1979, earnings from full-time, year-round work at the minimum wage were sufficient to lift a family of three above the poverty line. But failure to compensate for inflation will leave the wage only slightly more than 80% of the poverty line even after scheduled increases in 1990 and 1991. And only about a dozen states and the District of Columbia mandate minimum wages higher than the federal wage floor.

Inadequate wages or hours of work for parents leave millions of children in poverty. Research on heads of poor households in the mid-1980's showed that roughly two-thirds of those who were not disabled, elderly or single parents of very young children were employed either full- or part-time.

Even if the federal government fails to keep the wage floor at adequate levels, there are other ways to supplement the wages of low-income workers so as to raise out of poverty those families that remain poor despite the parents' best efforts. One is a children's allowance. Sixty-seven industrialized nations, excluding the U.S., provide a monthly or weekly cash benefit to families for every child, regardless of income and work status of parents. In Europe such family allowance benefits typically range between 5 and 10% of the median wage and may be higher for larger families. Single mothers often receive extra assistance.[22] There is no general children's allowance in the U.S. to help parents provide for their children.

The closest the U.S. has to such a children's allowance, or to a negative income tax for families with children, is the Earned Income Credit (EIC). This federal credit is designed to offset Social Security taxes and supplement wages for poor families with children. It is a major source of direct federal assistance to low-income working families. More than 11 million families were eligible for the EIC in 1988; most families with incomes between $5,000 and $11,000 qualified for a credit of at least $700. Since the EIC is refundable, eligible low-income families can benefit even if they owe no federal income tax.

This wage supplement is very effective, but has some serious weaknesses. The size of the maximum annual credit—a little over $900 per family in 1990—remains too small to lift many families out of poverty. And because the EIC does not increase as family size increases, it is particularly inadequate for larger families.

As to job creation and training for low-income adults, the federal government has cut back on its already inadequate efforts. For example, the major job training program—the Job Training Partnership Act (JTPA)—represents only a modest investment in improving the basic academic and vocational skills of disadvantaged youths and parents. Current funding is adequate to serve only about five percent of the eligible population. Moreover, program rules basically prohibit use of the money for wages for parents.

Although the federal Job Corps has a strong record of success in training young high school dropouts with poor employment prospects, it does not come close to meeting the need. The program serves roughly 40,000 young adults, which is only one in seven of the 290,000 poor high school dropouts who are unemployed or not in the labor force at any given time.

The new federal welfare reform law—the Family Support Act of 1988 — will provide additional federal support for state education, training, and employment efforts for families receiving welfare payments through the Aid to Families with Dependent Children (AFDC) program. The scope, quality and effectiveness of the new Act's Job Opportunities and Basic Skills (JOBS) program will depend primarily on the willingness of each state to invest its own matching funds in intensive programs that realistically address recipients' employment and training needs. In depressed areas, where private sector employment is scarce, however, even the most ambitious state JOBS programs are likely to have little impact. And the reductions passed by Congress in the 1980s in the amount of earned income an AFDC family can retain as a work incentive, without AFDC benefits being reduced, demonstrate further the shortcomings in policies and programs to support low-income parents in providing for their children's needs.

■ MEETING THE NEEDS OF CHILDREN WHEN OTHER SUPPORTS FAIL: ARTICLES 27(1) AND 27(3)

Article 27(3) of the Convention requires that "States Parties in accordance with national conditions and within their means shall take appropriate measures to assist parents... to implement this right [to an adequate standard of living] and *shall in case of need provide material assistance and support programmes*, particularly with regard to nutrition, clothing and housing." (Emphasis added.) In other words, when parental support, enforcement of support from the absent parent, social insurance, and efforts to assist parents fall short, the ratifying nation, in the end, must act to assure that the child gets adequate food, clothing, shelter, and other basic necessities. The State Party's obligation to help is limited by the condition that it must be "in accordance with national conditions and within [its] means."

The U.S., with one in five children living in poverty, in part due to terribly inadequate safety net programs, has the means to do far better. The United States is a nation of extraordinary wealth. It has the world's largest GNP and one of the highest per capita GNPs. While its rate of economic growth slowed in the 1980's compared to the 1950's and 1960's, the United States' abundance is still increasing. From 1976 to 1989, U.S. GNP in real terms (after adjusting for inflation) grew 47 percent. Per capita income rose 27 percent.

Many U.S. children are beneficiaries of this affluence. They are part of well-to-do families, live in comfortable homes, never know hunger, go to good schools and receive some of the best health care in the world. Millions of others, however, live in poverty even though the U.S. has the means to lift them out of destitution.

In 1988, the cost of eliminating poverty in families with children would have been $26.1 billion. This is a considerable amount of money, but very affordable in context—it is equivalent to only 1/2 of 1 percent of our gross national product. It is about one-eighth of what is spent on OASDI. Eliminating poverty in families with children would cost about 1.5 cents of every dollar that federal, state, and local governments spend. And that $26.1 billion is less than half of the income actually redistributed in this nation from 1978 to 1988, when economic change and changes in social and tax policy shifted $61 billion a year from the poor and middle class to the rich.

Our history also shows that the nation has the means to eliminate poverty, when it has the will. From 1964 to 1969, the U.S. pulled more than 6 million children out of poverty. From 1967 to 1974, we reduced poverty among the elderly by one-half. But waiting for economic growth to do the job does not work. It requires government assistance as well:

- From 1964 to 1969, when we had economic growth and the government was committed to fighting poverty, 1.25 million children each year were pulled out of poverty;

- From 1982 to 1988, when we had economic growth but the government did not act to reduce poverty, we did only one-seventh as well— about 180,000 children each year were removed from poverty.

And since so many children (3.6 million) became poor from 1969 to 1982, because of recessions and program cuts, the child poverty rate is pretty much back to where it was in 1965.

Standard of Living

Despite the basic responsibilities of the government to provide a safety net for those who cannot work because of illness, disability, family responsibilities, or spells of unemployment, the existing federal-state structure for meeting the most basic income needs of poor families is a tattered and increasingly inadequate patchwork. While in 1979 this social safety net pulled nearly one in five otherwise poor families out of poverty, by 1987 this number was down to one in ten.[23] The programs are simply inadequate to give families enough to live on.

A variety of assistance programs provide crucial help to the poor and near-poor, but both separately and together their complex eligibility rules and inadequate levels of funding leave millions of children mired in poverty.

- One of the few direct income supports available to both the working and non-working poor, food stamps provide an essential non-cash supplement to assist low-income families. However, the program fails to reach between one-third and one-half of those eligible. Moreover, food stamp benefits are too low to ensure an adequate diet. Even though, according to the House Select Committee on Hunger, "low-income families spend their food budget dollars more efficiently than higher-income households," the federal Food and Nutrition Service has found that only one in 10 low-income households can meet the recommended dietary requirements when spending only the maximum food stamp benefit.[24]

- The Low Income Home Energy Assistance program, designed to help poor households pay their home energy bills, was slashed from $2.1 billion in funding in FY 1985 to $1.4 billion in FY 1990 and now provides such modest help that low-income families participating in the program still must spend between 14 and 20% of their annual incomes on energy bills.

- Rising housing costs and declining incomes, especially for young families, have squeezed families' ability to pay for housing, causing more doubling up, more homelessness, and rents that are a huge share of young and poor families' incomes. Yet, federal housing assistance dropped by 80% from 1980 to 1989.

Standard of Living

Aid to Families with Dependent Children (AFDC) is the main federal-state income support program for poor families, the last strands in the safety net. But it is reaching a dwindling proportion of poor children and providing those it does reach with less and less assistance. Rigid categorical restrictions on the types of families that are eligible and unduly burdensome verification requirements often disqualify even the neediest families.[25] Federal budget cuts have narrowed AFDC eligibility further. In 1973, AFDC benefits were provided to 83.6 children for every 100 poor children; by 1987, AFDC benefits reached only 59.8 children for every 100 poor children.

AFDC benefit levels are set by the states and have fallen dramatically, virtually everywhere. In constant dollars, the median state's benefit for a family of four fell by 38% between 1970 and 1989. By 1989, the median state's benefit was less than half the poverty line. In 37 states, just the fair market rent (as determined by the U.S. Department of Housing and Urban Development) for a modest two-bedroom apartment in the metropolitan area with the lowest housing costs in the state is more than the state's entire AFDC grant to a three-person family for food, clothing, shelter and other basic needs. Increasingly, AFDC families are doubled up, homeless, or in housing far below minimum standards of safety and decency.

While the U.S. is very far in practice from adequately meeting the needs set out in article 27(3), the gap between U.S. law and the Convention is far narrower. The U.S. Supreme Court has ruled that there is no fundamental federal constitutional right to such goods as food, shelter, or education,[26] but the rights to the basics of life are frequently set out in federal or state statutes or state constitutions. For example, federal housing law has had the explicit goal, since 1949, of ensuring "a decent home and a suitable living environment for every American family...."[27] The AFDC statute gives federal matching funds to states "to furnish financial assistance... to help maintain and strengthen family life."[28] And state welfare statutes frequently require that payments be adequate to meet basic needs. While such requirements are often ignored in practice, their existence in federal and state law demonstrates that many of the principles and rights embedded in article 27(3), already are to be found in a significant part in U.S. law.

Conclusion

The recognition in international law that a society owes its children the basics for their development is not new. In 1924 the Geneva Declaration of the Rights of the Child recognized that "mankind owes to the Child the best that it has to give" and that "The child must be given the means requisite for its normal development, both materially and spiritually. The child that is hungry must be fed.... The child must be the first to receive relief in times of distress." The 1959 United Nations Declaration of the Rights of the Child gives the child the right to "enjoy the benefits of social security" and "the right to adequate nutrition, housing, recreation and medical services," with public authorities given a "duty to extend particular care to children...without adequate means of support."

The Convention is one further large step in the progression toward requiring that nations, at least to the extent of their national abilities and means, assure that children obtain what they need. The United States has not been doing this. U.S. child poverty rates are directly at odds with the resources the U.S. has to combat child poverty. The Convention should be read as requiring the U.S. to move progressively[29] toward child support, social insurance, parental support and income maintenance policies and practices that assure that every child in the U.S. has, in the words of article 27, "a standard of living adequate for the child's physical, mental, spiritual, moral and social development." The U.S. Congress and the President must, in this decade, attack the problem of child poverty with the same vigor that their predecessors attacked the problem of elderly poverty. State and local officials must join in the attack. Improvements in the minimum wage, the availability and amount of tax credits, education, job training and job creation efforts, social insurance programs and benefits in safety net programs are all necessary.

Footnotes

[1] Smeeding, Torrey & Rein, *Patterns of Income and Poverty: The Economic Status of Children and The Elderly in Eight Countries*, in THE VULNERABLE (J. Palmer, T. Smeeding and B. Torrey, eds, 1988).

[2] In some states the obligation ends if and when the child becomes emancipated. There has also arisen some tension between the longer periods

of education (often through college) that are becoming more typical in society and the recent decline (typically from 21 to 18) in the states' legal age of majority. This has created a variety of legislative and judicial responses as to the extent of the parents' support obligation to a young adult in college. These issues are beyond the scope of this paper. The Convention refers to support of the "child," defined by article 1 as a human being below the age of 18 or an earlier age of majority.

3   Stanton v. Stanton, 421 U.S. 7 (1975).

4   One possible exception is the absence of a broader stepparent responsibility, but the Convention does not define "parent."

5   Gomez v. Perez, 409 U.S. 535 (1973).

6   *Compare*, Trimble v. Gordon, 430 U.S. 762 (1977), *with* Lalli v. Lalli, 439 U.S. 259 (1978). One rationale for *Lalli* (upholding the constitutionality of excluding nonadjudicated children) was the prevention of spurious claims by children whose paternity had not been adjudicated in court, so it might be argued that *Lalli* merely controls the definition of "child." But *Lalli* allows states to exclude from intestate succession children whose proof of paternity is sufficient to require the fathers to pay child support or to entitle the children to public benefits, including Social Security.

7   Pub.L. 98-378.

8   Pub.L. 100-485.

9   Prior to this amendment many states had very short statutes of limitation for children born out of wedlock, their mothers or state officials to bring paternity and child support actions. Shortly before Congress preempted these laws with the 18-year minimum, the Supreme Court had held that states violated the equal protection clause by having one year and two year statutes of limitation on paternity actions. Mills v. Habluetzel, 456 U.S. 91 (1982); Pickett v. Brown, 462 U.S. 1 (1983). After Congress passed the legislation, the Court still used equal protection to invalidate a six-year statute of limitations. Clark v. Jeter, 108 S. Ct. 1910 (1988).

10 *See* CHILDREN'S DEFENSE FUND, A VISION FOR AMERICA'S FUTURE 19-20 (1989).

[11] CONGRESSIONAL RESEARCH SERVICE, THE CHILD SUPPORT ENFORCEMENT PROGRAM: POLICY AND PRACTICE 84 (1989).

[12] Title II of the Social Security Act, 42 U.S.C. § 401 *et seq.*

[13] U.S. Department of Health and Human Services, Social Security Bulletin, Annual Statistical Supplement 124, 170, 205 (1988).

[14] 42 U.S.C. § 403(a). A provision wholly denying benefits to children born out of wedlock when other dependents exhaust the family maximum was found unconstitutional and is no longer applied. Griffin v. Richardson, 346 F. Supp 1226 (D. Md.), *affd. mem.*, 409 U.S. 1069 (1972); Davis v. Richardson, 342 F. Supp 588 (D. Conn.), *affd. mem.* 409 U.S. 1069 (1972).

[15] The provisions discussed herein appear in 42 U.S.C. § 402(d) and 416(e).

[16] 42 U.S.C. § 402(d), 416(h). *See*, Matthews v. Lucas, 427 U.S. 495 (1976).

[17] This exclusion has been upheld against attack based on the U.S. Constitution. Matthews v. Lucas, 427 U.S. 495 (1976).

[18] United States Department of Labor, Employment and Training Administration, *Comparison of State Unemployment Insurance Laws*, Comparison Revision #4 at 3-10, 3-11, 3-44 (1/7/90).

[19] Some other major social insurance as well as assistance programs provide health insurance. Health care access rights are covered separately in the Convention (e.g., article 24) and separately in this book.

[20] Weber v. Aetna Casualty and Surety Co., 406 U.S. 164 (1972).

[21] U.S. House of Representatives, Select Committee on Children, Youth and Families, *Children and Families: Public Policies and Outcomes—A Fact Sheet of International Comparisons* 2 (June, 1988).

[22] *Id.*

[23] CENTER ON BUDGET AND POLICY PRIORITIES, THE DECREASING ANTI-POVERTY EFFECTIVENESS OF GOVERNMENT PROGRAMS: 1979-1987 (September, 1988).

[24] Food Research and Action Center, "Fact Sheet on Food Stamp Program," 1990.

25 Some states or localities have very modest and patchy "home relief" or "general assistance" programs for the poorest individuals or families who are not reached by federal programs.

26 *See* San Antonio Independent School Dist. v. Rodriguez, 411 U.S. 1, 29-39 (1973); Jefferson v. Hackney, 406 U.S. 535, 549-51 (1972); Lindsey v. Normet, 405 U.S. 56, 73-74 (1972); James v. Valtierra, 402 U.S. 137, 141-43 (1971); Dandridge v. Williams, 397 U.S. 471, 487 (1970). *But see,* Edelman, *The Next Century Of Our Constitution: Rethinking Our Duty To The Poor,* 39 HASTINGS L. J. 1 (1987).

27 42 U.S.C. § 1441.

28 42 U.S.C. § 601.

29 It is beyond the scope of this chapter to discuss the speed at which such progressive implementation should occur. Both the language of articles 26 and 27 themselves and that of article 4 of the Convention recognize possible resource constraints and contemplate phased implementation. (Article 4 says: "States Parties shall undertake all appropriate legislative, administrative, and other measures for the implementation of the rights recognized in this Convention. In regard to economic, social and cultural rights, States Parties shall undertake such measures to the maximum extent of their available resources....") The U.S. was a primary proponent of amendments seeking to soften the duty to implement economic rights. It succeeded in amending the social insurance article to make it more of "a goal or objective whose realization would be sought progressively rather than a legal right requiring immediate implementation." RADDA BARNEN INTERNATIONAL, COMPILATION OF THE ON-GOING WORK OF THE DRAFTING OF THE UNITED NATIONS CONVENTION ON THE RIGHTS OF THE CHILD, 1978-1987, FIRST DRAFT, 166 I 87 (1987). But a similar effort to weaken the basic guarantee in article 27(1) was rebuffed. *Id,* 170, I 42, 43.

CHAPTER 11

Assuring Adequate Health and Rehabilitative Care for the Child
Articles 6, 23, 24 and 25

Kay A. Johnson and Molly McNulty

Introduction

Protecting children's health is essential to ensuring child survival. Article 6 of the Convention on the Rights of the Child recognizes each child's inherent right to life and the responsibility of ratifying countries to "ensure to the maximum extent possible the survival and development of the child." Through articles 23, 24, and 25, the Convention recognizes the right of each child to "enjoyment of the highest attainable standard of health" and to access to health care services needed for maintenance of health, treatment of illness, and rehabilitation of disability.

For many children, U.S. law and policy demonstrate a commitment to these principles. In part, due to the U.S.' wealth and the large share of its Gross National Product spent on health care, the majority of children in the U.S. have adequate access to health care and, compared to millions of children in many other countries around the world, especially developing countries, live relatively free from disease and disability.

On the other hand, approximately twelve million children in the U.S. have no health insurance, public or private.[1] Despite attempts to establish public health programs to assist uninsured children, disabled children, and other children with access problems or special health care needs, too often funding and implementation fall far short of what is needed. Despite its enormous wealth, the United States has failed to ensure universal access—or anything approaching such access—to health care for all children. This failure has led to unnecessary illness, disability and death, particularly among those children born to or living in the poorest families.

Health and Rehabilitation

Approximately 80% of the 63 million U.S. children younger than 18 have some contact with a physician during a year.[2] However, low-income children are less likely than more affluent children to have access to physician services. One in four children is born to a mother who does not receive timely prenatal care.[3]

As a result, U.S. practice has not yet fulfilled the promise to either its own laws or the assurance of optimal health status for children, as called for by the Convention. Although the United States ranks first in the world in gross national product, it does not even rank in the top 10 on key child health indicators.

- In 1988, the U.S. infant mortality rate was 10 deaths per 1,000 live births. At this rate, the United States ranked 19th world-wide in infant mortality—behind nations such as Hong Kong, Spain, and Ireland. Mortality for children from birth to age five stood at 13 deaths for every 1,000 live births. This rate ranks us 22nd, behind a list of countries that includes Japan, Singapore, New Zealand, and East Germany.

- Birth-weight is a significant predictor of infant health. Low birth-weight (babies weighing less than 2500 grams or 5.5 pounds at birth) is a leading cause of infant death and of childhood disability. In 1988, 7% of infants born in the United States had a low birth-weight. Twenty-eight countries, including Hong Kong, Czechoslovakia, and Australia, did better.

- Immunization is the most effective form of preventive health care for children. The proportion of one-year-olds immunized against polio in the United States is estimated to be 95%. However, the U.S. rate lags behind 14 other nations, including Chile, Jordan, Poland, and China.[4]

■ STRUCTURE OF THE UNITED STATES HEALTH CARE SYSTEM

A. Primacy of Private Providers and Insurance

The health care delivery system in the U.S. is based primarily upon services from privately-owned hospitals and private physicians and other practitioners. In order to have access to this mostly private system, individuals are expected to pay for care, which they generally do through insurance coverage. Insurance often but decreasingly is available through a person's place of employment as an employee benefit. If an individual's private health insurance does not include certain medical services, or if a person is uninsured, the individual is expected to purchase these services with cash.

Most children have health insurance coverage, if at all, through a parent's insurance plan. This number is dwindling as employers increasingly refuse to provide dependent coverage, or charge premiums for dependent coverage that employees cannot afford. For example, between 1980 and 1988, the proportion of medium and large firms fully subsidizing employees' health insurance costs for dependents dropped from 72 to 51%.[5] Smaller businesses are even less likely to provide or pay for dependent coverage.

Employer-based private health insurance dominates the health care financing system and determines access to health care for the vast majority of children. In 1986, 61.4% of all children were covered by private employer-based health insurance.[6] In 1984, American businesses spent about $90 billion on employee health insurance premiums, an amount equal to 38% of their pre-tax profits.[7] Excluding employer-paid health insurance benefits from taxable income is a subsidy to the system that cost the United States Treasury about $27 billion in foregone tax revenues in 1985. When all federal tax subsidies for health expenditures are considered, the total cost was an estimated $50 billion in 1985.[8]

Private insurance is barely regulated by the federal government. The Internal Revenue Code has some anti-discrimination provisions in return for the tax break on employer-provided insurance. The enactment in 1974 of the Employer Retirement and Income Security Act (ERISA) reduced states' ability to regulate health insurance.[9] Virtually all of the authority to regulate private insurance, such as life insurance, rests with the states, but ERISA severely curtailed states' powers. Under ERISA, employers can establish so-called "self-funded" health insurance plans that are not subject to state regulation.[10]

By 1986, over 40% of employees covered by employer- provided insurance plans were insured under self-funded plans. These limitations have already affected children's coverage. For example, ERISA makes inapplicable, to children of workers in self-funded plans, state mandates that an employer's insurance cover a basic package of preventive services for children or home health benefits for children with disabilities.

Other failings of the private insurance system result in the denial of health care coverage to many children. In general, private insurance plans do not pay for preventive care, such as well-child care. As a result, many moderate-income families must pay for these services out-of-pocket, which many cannot afford to do. Furthermore, it is a common insurance practice to refuse coverage for "pre-existing conditions," health problems which existed before that particular insurance coverage began. Such pre-existing condition clauses in insurance policies exclude many children with disabilities, whose chronic health care needs may have arisen before private insurance was purchased.[11]

B. U.S. Governmental Commitment to Public Health

The U.S. does have public insurance and other public programs for some of the people who cannot obtain insurance through employment. But, instead of the approach adopted by many other countries designed to attain universal coverage, U.S. health care programs cover only some of the uninsured (except for the elderly, almost all of whom are covered by Medicare). Thus, the United States is not one of 70 nations worldwide that provide medical care and financial assistance to all pregnant women. Nor is it one of 61 nations that insure or provide basic medical care to all workers and their dependents.[12]

The absence of a health coverage system for all pregnant women and children, combined with the increasing weakness of our employer-based health insurance system in providing dependent coverage, leaves these vulnerable groups among those most likely to lack basic health care insurance. As a result, in 1987, children younger than 18 and young adults between 18 and 24 years old made up 37% of the total U.S. population but 50% of the uninsured.[13] Among families without insurance are not just the very poor, but also employed families whose employers may not provide insurance as an employee benefit, and whose incomes are not sufficient to pay the large cost of medical care out-of-pocket. In 1986, 19% of children in employed families were uninsured.[14]

Anticipating the commitment expressed by articles 6 and 24 of the Convention, which call upon ratifying States to ensure a child's survival and development and to recognize the child's right to the highest attainable standard of health, for fifty years the United States has developed public health programs designed to ensure that needy children without insurance or resources receive health care.

For low-income children, the nation's main health care financing mechanism is the Medicaid insurance program.[15] Medicaid is a federal-state program designed to provide health care coverage for some, but not all, low-income pregnant women, children, caretaker relatives of children, and elderly, blind, or disabled persons. Created in 1965, the program is operated by states under broad federal guidelines. In order to control growth in the total cost of Medicaid, and limit the entitlement to a selected number of the poorest or most severely disabled persons, a complex web of federal and state laws and regulations has been developed during the program's 25-year history.

As a result, Medicaid does not provide protection to all low-income children left outside of the private insurance system. In 1988, approximately 11 million children younger than 21 used services paid for by Medicaid, at an average cost of $619 per child per year. In that year, children were approximately 50% of all program recipients, but because children's average health care costs are relatively low, they accounted for only 15% of Medicaid payments to providers.[16]

In recent years, Congress has passed significant expansions of Medicaid's eligibility for children and pregnant women.[17] Congress has mandated that all states extend coverage to pregnant women and children younger than age six so long as their families have incomes below 133% of the federal poverty guidelines (an amount equal to approximately $13,500 per year for a family of three in 1990) and to children between ages six and nineteen whose families are below 100% of the federal poverty guidelines ($10,560 for a family of three in 1990).[18] Unless and until these recent program expansions are implemented fully, Medicaid will continue to serve only about half of poor children older than six.

Thus, unlike those in many other countries, the health care delivery system in the U.S. is characterized by a combination of public and private responsibility, as well as federal and state governmental programs. For a majority of children, this system has fulfilled the Convention's recognition of children's right to a very high standard of health and to facilities for the treatment of illness and rehabilitation. For a very large minority, however, it has not.

■ PREVENTIVE AND PRIMARY HEALTH SERVICES

Article 24 of the Convention calls upon States Parties to pursue full implementation of a series of measures related to preventive and primary care. These include measures to: diminish infant and child mortality; ensure the provision of necessary care with emphasis on primary care; combat disease and malnutrition; ensure appropriate prenatal care; and develop family planning and parent education services. These provisions emphasize preventive and primary care that combat disease and malnutrition through regular health status checks and simple therapeutic interventions.

Preventive and primary services are provided through private physicians' offices and freestanding public and private health clinics across the United States. However, because low-income children are less likely than their more affluent counterparts to have the means or the insurance to pay for such visits, only one in six of low-income U.S. children sees a health provider annually for routine preventive care.[19] Therefore, the federal government has created certain public health programs to ensure greater access to preventive and primary care.

These programs, most of them created since 1965, led to a dramatic increase in the utilization of health services by low- income children. Average use of health care by poor children increased from 2.3 physician contacts per year in 1964 to 4.4 contacts per year in 1988.[20] These gains have been linked to the creation and expansion of programs such as Medicaid, the Title V Maternal and Child Health Block Grant, Community Health Centers and the Childhood Immunization Program.

A. Medicaid

Medicaid provides broad insurance for many poor and near-poor children, and it has some special emphasis on primary and preventive care services for children. In fact, young, low- income children with Medicaid coverage have been found to be more likely than privately insured low income children to have a preventive care visit in a year.[21]

The key preventive component of Medicaid is the Early and Periodic Screening, Diagnosis and Treatment program (EPSDT), under which federal law requires states to provide a package of preventive, screening, diagnostic and follow-up services to children. However, throughout the 1980s, only three out of 10 EPSDT-eligible children received an annual preventive exam. Recent statutory changes in the EPSDT program are intended to raise children's participation levels in EPSDT. According to state performance standards established by the federal government, eight out of ten eligible children must receive medical screening exams by 1995.[22]

Medicaid's EPSDT program reflects many of the principles called for by the Convention's health-related articles. The early identification of potentially life- or health-threatening illnesses or conditions reflects article 6's concern with the survival and development of each child. The program's emphasis on preventive health through regular check-ups, and its recognition of the role of health education for parents parallel article 24's concerns.

The Medicaid program also has been the vehicle for a variety of initiatives designed to boost pre-natal care and reduce infant mortality. Recognizing that access to pre-natal care is an essential factor in the reduction of infant mortality, and reducing low birth-weight and disability, Congress, in 1984, began a series of expansions of Medicaid eligibility for pregnant women that has continued through 1989. Pregnant women also are entitled to a minimum benefit package under Medicaid, which includes prenatal care and other pregnancy-related medical services.

B. Service Delivery Programs

Ensuring the provision of necessary medical assistance requires not only health care financing but development of an accessible service system as well. Three programs form the core of a limited U.S. public service delivery system for preventive and primary care services for children.

Through the Title V Maternal and Child Health Block Grant program, federal funds are made available to states to "provide and to assure mothers and children (in particular those with low income or with limited availability of health services) access to quality maternal and child health services."[23] The promotion of the health of mothers and children through provision of preventive and primary care services is a stated purpose of the program.

Most states combine federal block grant dollars with some state general revenues to deliver services at the local level. However, funding for the program is inadequate to meet the need for pediatric care. No state is able to offer comprehensive primary pediatric services on a statewide basis to those poor and near-poor uninsured or underinsured children who need them.[24]

Despite funding shortfalls, the Title V program reflects U.S. commitment to providing primary care, free of charge when necessary, to its children. Indeed, 1989 amendments to federal law established that 30% of Title V funds should be set aside for the delivery of pediatric care. This emphasis comports with article 24(4)(b)'s call to deliver primary care services to children.

Title V also has been the focus of recent initiatives to improve access to prenatal care and to reduce infant mortality. 1989 amendments clarified that Title V dollars are intended to reduce infant mortality, and to increase the availability of prenatal, delivery, and postpartum care to low-income women. The amended law now also authorizes four categories of infant mortality initiatives: (1) maternal and infant health home visiting programs, (2) integrated maternal and infant health service delivery systems, (3) maternal and child health centers operated under the direction of not-for-profit hospitals, and (4) projects designed to increase the participation of obstetricians and pediatricians in the Title V and Medicaid programs.[25]

A second statutorily-established federal health program that provides primary health care is the Community and Migrant Health Center programs.[26] The nearly 600 federally-funded community health centers, operating in medically underserved communities, serve 5 million patients each year. Two-thirds of health center patients are women of childbearing age and children.[27]

Research has demonstrated the effectiveness of delivering comprehensive primary care through health centers. Patients who receive care from these centers have reduced infant mortality rates, improved birth-weights, and more adequate rates of immunization. At the same time, due to funding shortfalls for health centers and a general maldistribution of providers, 30 million individuals live in communities with an inadequate number of primary care providers and no health center.

The community health centers serve many of the functions called for by the Convention. The health centers deliver free care, thus helping to assure that "no child [be] deprived of ...access" as required by article 24(1).

A third program vital to the public health system is the National Health Service Corps.[28] The purpose of the Corps is to deploy physicians and mid-level practitioners to health personnel shortage areas, primarily rural and inner-city regions. The Corps offers medical school scholarships or loan repayment in exchange for service in a designated area. Members of the Corps must be providers of primary health care, such as pediatricians, obstetrician/gynecologists, or family practitioners. Unfortunately, funding for the Corps has been virtually eliminated over the past decade due to mistaken beliefs about oversupply of physicians. As a result, fewer than 50 physicians received Corps scholarships in 1989.

Other federal programs which deliver critical maternal and child health services, such as the Title X Family Planning program and the Supplemental Food Program for Women, Infants, and Children (WIC), operate at levels adequate to reach only about half of those in need of and eligible for services. These shortfalls create further gaps in the public maternal and child health delivery system.

C. Immunization

Immunization is one of the most basic preventive health services. The use of vaccines to prevent once common childhood diseases, such as polio, measles, and pertussis (whooping cough) is a major success story in U.S. public health and modern medicine. Generally about one-half of all childhood vaccines are financed through the private sector—primarily through out-of-pocket payments by families. The remaining half are financed publicly through a combination of federal and state program dollars, with federal funding channelled through the Childhood Immunization Program at the Centers for Disease Control.[29] Through this blended system, an adequate supply of vaccine has been made available in the United States.

Despite these efforts, hundreds of thousands of young children are not adequately immunized, and thus are unprotected from exposure to preventable illness and disability. Between 1980 and 1985 there was a significant decrease in the proportion of two-year-olds who were fully immunized. Moreover, only approximately half of poor preschool-age children living in inner-city areas are fully protected.[30] These children are not adequately immunized because of flaws in the U.S. health care delivery system, such as the high cost of vaccines in the private sector; overburdened or non-existent public health clinics; and physical or cultural isolation from the health care system.

Measles epidemics currently are sweeping the nation, signalling the failure of the U.S. to assure that all its children receive basic preventive health care. Measles cases, concentrated among low-income urban children, have risen from approximately 1,500 in 1983 to over 17,000 in 1989, a more than tenfold increase.[31]

D. Measuring U.S. Commitment to Child Health

Despite the establishment of these public health programs, designed to ensure that every child has access to health care, U.S. efforts to date have been insufficient. A number of factors posing barriers to access still remain: difficulty in recruiting physicians willing to treat low-income pregnant women and children; grossly under-funded public health clinics and hospitals; rising poverty among children; and the growing number of uninsured children. The inadequacy of U.S. investment in the health of its poorest children is evidenced by measurements of child health status:

- Infant mortality remains very high in the United States, even in the "best" states. In 1987, the lowest state infant mortality rate, 7.2 per 1000 live births in Massachusetts, was higher than the infant mortality rate in Japan;

- Between 1986 and 1987, the proportion of infants born at low birthweight increased nationally from 6.8% to 6.9%. The 1987 rate represents a return to 1979 levels;

- During 1987, the nation's late or no prenatal care record worsened or failed to improve for the eighth consecutive year. Between 1980 and 1987, the proportion of births to women receiving late or no care increased 20%.

Although U.S. law and policy reflect principles acknowledging the importance of assuring health care to its most vulnerable children, actual commitment of resources to fulfilling this promise has fallen short.

■ SERVICES FOR DISABLED CHILDREN

Article 23 of the Convention concerns the special needs of mentally or physically disabled children. This article calls upon ratifying countries to recognize a disabled child's right to "a full and decent life, in conditions which ensure dignity, promote self-reliance, and facilitate the child's active participation" in community life. Ratifying countries then acknowledge the right of the disabled child to special care and to extend resources and assistance, free of charge where possible, to the child's family. In particular, State Parties' assistance to disabled children should ensure effective access to education, training, health care and rehabilitative services.

Through a variety of legislative and judicial actions, U.S. children with physical or mental disabilities have seen vast expansions of their rights during the past two decades. At the same time their numbers have grown. For example, between 1960 and 1981 the number of children with chronic conditions, that result in a limitation of daily activity, doubled. In part, this increase was a result of increased awareness of such conditions, and their impact on children's lives that led to better identification and reporting. However, a substantial proportion of the increase was found to be real growth in the number of chronically disabled children, rather than better identification.[32] Much of this growth can be attributed to the development of medical technology which permitted the more frequent survival of children with serious chronic illnesses and disabling conditions. The United States has the world's greatest capacity to save infants born prematurely or at very-low birth- weight. But many such children suffer from life-long disability as a result of being born too small or too soon.

For children with disabilities, four existing programs are central to our national efforts for protecting their rights to a decent life and special care. These include the Title V Maternal and Child Health Block Grant, Medicaid, Supplemental Security Income and the Education for Handicapped Children Act programs. The latter three reflect increasingly broad entitlements under federal law for children with special health needs.

In addition, two laws, Section 504 of the Rehabilitation Act of 1973 and the Americans with Disabilities Act, protect children from discrimination on the basis of disability and help to ensure their right to health care. These antidiscrimination laws move the U.S. toward the recognition required by Article 23 of the disabled child's right to dignity, self-reliance, active participation, and effective access to education, health and training services.

A. Title V Maternal and Child Health Block Grant

Throughout its history, the Title V program has addressed not only the primary and preventive health care needs of children, but their rehabilitation needs as well. State Title V programs are a relatively small but essential set of programs providing care for children with disabilities and chronic illnesses. Under Title V programs for Children with Special Health Care Needs (formerly known as Crippled Children's Services programs), states

Health and Rehabilitation

arrange and pay for a range of specialized health services. Current law requires that a minimum of 30 percent of the federal funds in the Title V program be used for services for children with special health care needs. Consistent with the provisions of article 23 of the Convention, these services must be provided without charge to poor families.

From their early days, these programs tended to focus more on orthopedically-related disabilities or on a dozen common chronic illnesses leading to disability. Today, in response to recent trends in disability, more state programs have broadened their scope to include children with AIDS or HIV infection, mental retardation, and speech-language-hearing disorders. However, despite statutory protections, limited resources often lead to state-level decisions which result in the arbitrary exclusion of some poor children by age or by diagnosis. Despite article 23's requirement that ratifying countries "ensure the extension, subject to available resources" of special care to disabled children, the U.S. clearly has not committed the necessary resources to assist this population.

B. Medicaid

Under Medicaid, disabled children, like other poor children, are entitled not only to primary and preventive services, but also to a broad range of treatment services. The Early and Periodic Screening, Diagnosis and Treatment component also has the purpose to discover, as early as possible, the ills that handicap children and to provide continuing follow-up and treatment so that handicaps do not go neglected.

The right of eligible children to special treatment services was made even more extensive by 1989 amendments to the EPSDT program.[33] The law now requires that children be provided a very broad range of diagnostic and treatment services when medically necessary. Previously, states often left certain classes of services, such as rehabilitation, completely uncovered or set arbitrary limits on the amount, scope and duration of services. Under current law, benefits must be related to the condition of the individual child. Full implementation of these provisions will entitle millions of low-income children—many of them disabled —to previously uncovered services such as physical, occupational, or speech therapy and other rehabilitation services.

C. Supplemental Security Income

Another important federal program related to article 23 is the Supplemental Security Income (SSI) program.[34] Congress enacted the SSI program in 1972 to assist low-income "individuals who have attained age 65 or are blind or disabled" by providing a federal cash income payment for such persons. Children are among those eligible if they are disabled, and if their family income falls below a certain level. Some states supplement federal aid with state payments. In addition to cash assistance, virtually all children served under SSI are entitled to health care coverage through Medicaid. In February 1990, the United States Supreme Court substantially broadened disabled children's legal entitlement to SSI support by invalidating overly strict regulations as to how disabled a child must be before being determined eligible.[35]

Approximately 250,000 children, most with severe disabilities, receive SSI monthly cash payments.[36] A child receiving SSI may receive up to $386 per month from the federal government, a crucial amount for a family facing the many costs associated with having a child with a disability. The SSI cash payments, in combination with Medicaid coverage, are basic steps toward fulfilling article 23's requirements for assistance that is free of charge to ensure a disabled child's access to health care.

D. Education of Handicapped Children Act

Enacted in 1975,[37] and substantially amended in 1986,[38] the Education of Handicapped Children Act is intended to make it possible for all children with disabilities to receive a free and appropriate public education. While primarily focused on assisting families and children to secure access to public education in the "least restrictive setting," the act also requires that children with disabilities be entitled to so-called "related services," which may include therapies and health services needed to benefit from the educational services. Needed services are to be provided without cost to a family.

Approximately four million preschool and school age children are served each year by the program. Congress amended the Act in 1986 to provide early intervention services to millions of infants and toddlers from birth to age three, including necessary health and educational services. The Act is explicit recognition of the need for a full range of services to assist a child with a disability in achieving "the fullest possible social integration and individual development...," according to article 23.

E. Section 504

Section 504 of the Rehabilitation Act of 1973 prohibits discrimination in federally-funded programs on the basis of disability or perceived disability. Section 504 provides that no otherwise qualified handicapped individual shall be excluded from participation in, or be denied the benefits of, any program receiving federal financial assistance.[39] For example, many health care providers are reluctant to treat people with AIDS, particularly those who are also poor. Under Section 504, hospitals that receive federal funds are prohibited from denying medical care to such persons solely on the basis of their illness.

F. Americans with Disabilities Act

In 1990, Congress passed landmark legislation entitled the "Americans with Disabilities Act."[40] The ADA is a sweeping expansion of legal protections and rights for the disabled, accomplished by expanding the Civil Rights Act of 1964 (which prohibits certain types of discrimination against women and racial minorities) to millions of Americans with physical and mental handicaps. The law will provide persons with disabilities with broadened employment opportunities and greater access to public accommodations, transit systems, and communications networks. Congress' passage of the ADA reflects the acknowledgment of the fact that "a severe, lifelong disability may be handicapping, but more handicapping has been the practice of congregating services for persons with disabilities in settings different or separate from those in which the rest of us are provided those services."[41] ADA will bring the United States closer to full recognition that a disabled child should enjoy a full and decent life, in conditions which ensure dignity, promote self-reliance and facilitate the child's active participation in the community.

Disabled children will benefit particularly from the new entitlements to access to public accommodations, which include recreational facilities, restaurants, retail facilities, and transportation. The ADA reflects a firm national commitment to ensure that a child with a disability will have, in the words of article 23, "effective access to and receives education, training, health care services, rehabilitation services, preparation for employment and recreation opportunities in a manner conducive to the child's achieving the fullest possible social integration and individual development."

Conclusion

Medicaid and other public health programs are bona fide efforts to fill in some of the vast gaps in the private health insurance system, but fall short of fulfilling the Convention's call that ratifying countries "strive to ensure that no child is deprived of his or her right of access to such health care services" as are necessary for children to enjoy the highest attainable standard of health. Most U.S. children enjoy access to high-quality health care, particularly compared to their counterparts in other countries, but millions of poor and near-poor children who are uninsured or live in medically underserved areas do not have such access.

The child health status of U.S. children is, thus, far worse than one would expect, given the vast wealth of the United States. The signs are widespread that the U. S. has failed, to date, to assure that the most vulnerable children have their basic health care needs met. Indicators such as the stagnating infant mortality and low birth-weight rates, outbreaks of preventable disease and the growing number of uninsured children call for a stronger U.S. commitment to the health of children, involving a full commitment of its resources.

Both the federal and state governments have taken some steps to heed this call. Congress has taken a number of actions to expand Medicaid, especially for younger children, and legislation is now pending that would provide Medicaid for all children younger than 19 living below the federal poverty level. Several states have moved ahead and are providing state-based insurance to all poor children (Minnesota) or all poor residents (Maine) whom Medicaid does not cover. These changes indicate a growing trend toward complying more fully with the Convention's call to "ensure to the maximum extent possible the survival and development of the child."

Footnotes

1. HUGHES, JOHNSON, ROSENBAUM, & LIU, THE HEALTH OF AMERICA'S CHILDREN: MATERNAL AND CHILD HEALTH DATA, BOOK 44 (1989).
2. P.F. ADAMS, A.M. HARDY, CURRENT ESTIMATES FROM THE NATIONAL HEALTH INTERVIEW SURVEY: UNITED STATES, 1988 10(173) (1989).
3. CHILDREN'S DEFENSE FUND, MATERNAL AND INFANT HEALTH: KEY DATA, SPECIAL REPORT ONE (1990).
4. CHILDREN'S DEFENSE FUND, S.O.S. AMERICA! A CHILDREN'S DEFENSE BUDGET 57-65 (1990).
5. HAY MANAGEMENT CONSULTANTS, THE 1988 HAY/HUGGINS BENEFITS REPORT (1988).
6. *See supra* note 1.
7. CALIFANO, J., AMERICA'S HEALTH CARE REVOLUTION: WHO LIVES? WHO DIES? WHO PAYS? (1986).
8. *Tax Expenditures: Current Issues and Five Year Budget Projections for Fiscal Years 1984 - 1988*, Government Printing Office (1983).
9. Pub.L. 93-406, 88 Stat. 829 (1974), codified at 29 U.S.C. Section 1001, et seq.
10. Rosenbaum, *Children and Private Health Insurance*, in CHILDREN IN A CHANGING HEALTH SYSTEM: ASSESSMENTS AND PROPOSALS FOR REFORM, (1990).
11. Intergovernmental Health Policy Project, *Focus on ERISA and the States* (March 1986).
12. SIVARD, RUTH LEGER, WORLD MILITARY AND SOCIAL EXPENDITURES, (1989).
13. *See supra* note 1.
14. *See supra* note 1.
15. 42 U.S.C. § 1396 et seq. (1982 & Supp. 1989).
16. Health Care Financing Administration. Published and unpublished statistics.
17. Deficit Reduction Act of 1984, Pub.L. 98-369; Consolidated Omnibus Reconciliation Act, Pub.L. 99-272; Omnibus Budget Reconciliation Act

of 1986, Pub.L. 99-509; Omnibus Budget Reconciliation Act of 1987, Pub.L. 100-203; Medicare Catastrophic Coverage Act of 1988, Pub.L. 100-360; Family Support Act of 1988, Pub.L. 100-85; Omnibus Reconciliation Act of 1989, Pub.L. 101-329; Omnibus Budget Reconciliation Act of 1990, Pub. L. 101-508.

[18] 1990 Federal Poverty Income Guidelines, 55 Federal Register 5664, Feb. 16, 1990.

[19] Rosenbach, M., *Insurance Coverage and Ambulatory Medical Care of Low-Income Children: United States, 1980*, National Medical Care Utilization and Expenditure Survey, Series C, Analytical Report No. 1, DHHS Publication No. 85-20401, Government Printing Office (1985).

[20] *Id.*

[21] *Id.*

[22] U.S. Health Care Financing Administration, *Expected Improvement in State EPSDT Participation*, unpublished memorandum (1990).

[23] Pub.L. 97-35, Title XXI, 95 Stat. 818 (1981), codified at 42 U.S.C. 701-716 (1982).

[24] Rosenbaum, Hughes & Johnson, *Maternal and Child Health Services for Medically Indigent Children and Pregnant Women,* in 26 MED. CARE 316 (1988).

[25] Omnibus Budget Reconciliation Act of 1989, Pub.L. 101-329.

[26] 42 U.S.C. §§ 329, 330 (1982 & Supp. 1989).

[27] NAT'L ASS'N OF COMMUNITY HEALTH CENTERS, TWO DECADES OF ACHIEVEMENT (1986).

[28] 42 U.S.C. § 2541 - q (1982 & Supp. 1989).

[29] 42 U.S.C. § 300aa-2 (1982 & Supp. 1989).

[30] JOHNSON, K., WHO IS WATCHING OUR CHILDREN'S HEALTH? THE IMMUNIZATION STATUS OF AMERICAN CHILDREN, 1987.

[31] Centers for Disease Control, "Measles - U.S., 1989 and First 20 Weeks 1990," in *MORBIDITY AND MORTALITY WEEKLY REPORT*, Vol, 39, No. 21, June 1, 1990, p. 353-363.

[32] Newacheck, P.N, Budetti, P.P., and Halfon, N., *Trends in Activity-Limiting Chronic Conditions Among Children,* 76 AM J. PUB. HEALTH 178 (1986).

[33] Omnibus Reconciliation Act of 1989, Pub.L. 101-329.

[34] 42 U.S.C. § 1382 et. seq. (1982 & Supp. 1989).

[35] Sullivan v. Zebley, 58 U.S.L.W. 4177, Feb. 20, 1990.

[36] Committee on Ways and Means, U.S. House of Representatives, Background Material and Data on Programs Within The Jurisdiction of the Committee on Ways and Means, 1988, p. 533.

[37] Education for All Handicapped Children Act, Pub.L. 94-142.

[38] Education for the Handicapped Amendments of 1986, Pub.L. 99-457.

[39] Rehabilitation Act of 1973, 29 U.S.C. § 794 (1982).

[40] Americans with Disabilities Act, Pub.L. 101-336.

[41] Floor Statement of Congressman Dellums, Cong. Record H2639, May 22, 1990.

CHAPTER 12

Promoting the Dignity of the Child Through Mental Health Services[1]
Articles 23, 25 and 39

Gary B. Melton

Introduction

To a large extent, the separation of child mental health policy from children's policy as a whole is arbitrary, for three reasons. First, the lines between the various children's service systems have become increasingly diffuse. Programs historically in the child welfare and juvenile justice systems have shifted their primary purpose from custody to treatment, as all of the public children's service systems have increased their reliance on contracting with private treatment programs. Private programs, in turn, have become sophisticated in attracting funds from all of the major public systems.

It is not unusual to find that a single program describes itself as a residential treatment center for the purpose of receiving insurance payments (as a mental health program), but that it also is a group care facility (licensed and funded under the auspices of the state child welfare agency), a residential school (licensed and funded under the auspices of the state special education agency), and a juvenile justice facility (approved by the state youth service agency and funded by that agency or the juvenile court). The diffuseness of boundaries is intensified by the facts that the various children's service systems have essentially the same purpose (the provision of treatment), that they have a common heritage, and that the population that they serve is largely coextensive.[2] Policy-making that proceeds on a system-by-system basis is inevitably doomed to failure, as caseworkers follow the path of least resistance, regardless of its congruence with overarching policy goals of protection of minors' privacy and liberty, promotion of family integrity, and facilitation of healthy socialization through provision of effective treatment.[3]

Second, not only are the lines between *systems* of service often blurred, but the *types* of services that now commonly are labeled as child mental health

239

services bear close resemblance to, or are the same as, those that historically have been provided in other service systems. Recognizing that traditional unit-based services (e.g., hospitalization, billed by the day, and psychotherapy, billed by the hour) seldom match the diverse needs of the behavior-disordered youth who fill the child mental health system (as well as the other children's service systems), mental health planners recently have emphasized the need for more intensive and flexible treatments for children and adolescents.[4] Many of these services could be delivered as easily in other systems, and dual-agency, "coordinated" administration has become increasingly common.[5] For example, a therapeutic day school, a commonly recognized but seldom provided form of special education, is magically transformed into a day treatment or partial hospitalization program in the mental health system.

Increasingly, public schools and community mental health programs share in the costs of such programs. Similarly, intensive home-based services have many features in common with older neighborhood-based approaches to child welfare. Intensive home-based services can be based in child welfare, juvenile justice, mental health, or a combination of service systems.[6] Thus, specialized services delivered by mental health professionals in the specialty mental health system often could be delivered, whether by mental health specialists, other professionals, or even paraprofessionals and volunteers, in other service systems, even if part of an overall child mental health plan.

Third, insofar as it affects children's mental health, all children's policy can be said to be encompassed in child mental health policy. For example, protection of minors' privacy and liberty can be justified on the basis of their salutary effects on mental health, especially among adolescents grappling with the task of individuation.[7] Although the mental health consequences of some areas of juvenile and family law (e.g., procedures and standards for resolution of child custody in divorce) are obvious, many of the legal rules that affect the socialization of children are in areas of law that at first glance appear unrelated to child development.[8]

In short, an attempt to catalogue all of the "mental health" aspects of the United Nations Convention on the Rights of the Child clearly would encompass a scope that is not appropriate for a single chapter in an anthology. On the other hand, it is equally clear that reference simply to those sections of

Mental Health Services

the Convention that specifically mention mental health would provide a starkly attenuated picture of the Convention's significance for child mental health policy, even when relatively narrowly defined. Such a myopic approach also would trivialize the Convention's significance as a "constitutional" document to guide policymakers and practitioners in children's services—a conceptualization that will be discussed later in this chapter.

■ FAILURES IN CHILD MENTAL HEALTH POLICY

Amid the complexity of the child mental health system (if indeed the term *system* is appropriate at all) and the pervasiveness and persistence of problems experienced by seriously emotionally disturbed youth, their families, and their communities, it perhaps should come as no surprise to find a cacophony of voices of commissions, individual scholarly commentators, and mental health administrators declaring that the system is badly deficient.[9] Indeed, it may be fairly stated that the conclusion that child mental health policy has been replete with failures is itself now official policy.[10] I count myself among the commentators who have called for a radical restructuring of the child mental health system and associated models of professional service delivery.[11]

The criticisms that have been leveled at the child mental health system cover virtually every aspect of its functioning. Critics have charged—and research supports—a litany of fundamental problems in child mental health:

- vast numbers of seriously emotionally disturbed children are underserved;

- those children who are served typically do not receive services of documented efficacy;

- service models that have been shown to be effective often are unreimbursable within conventional mental health financing systems;

- many children are served in needlessly restrictive settings;

- the use of institutional settings is steadily increasing;

241

- the research base for services is largely undeveloped;
- the system is largely unplanned and uncoordinated;
- preventive services (despite documented efficacy in many instances) are virtually nonexistent in most states;
- there is a serious shortage of specialists in child mental health;
- when specialists are available, their training commonly is limited to traditional, often ineffective, treatment models;
- mental health providers typically have failed to make parents partners in service planning and implementation;
- child mental health services often have not been culturally sensitive, and minority youth commonly have been treated in more restrictive settings than white youth with similar problems;
- children and adolescents themselves rarely have had direct access to mental health services when they have perceived a need for help.

These criticisms are not unique to child mental health policy. Commentators have noted the enormous gap between *de jure* and *de facto* policy in adult mental health services,[12] and similarly sweeping criticisms have been applied, usually justifiably, to some other children's service systems.[13]

■ NEW DIRECTIONS IN CHILD MENTAL HEALTH POLICY

On the other hand, child mental health policy is unusual in the nearly uniform acceptance of the criticisms (they now are part of the conventional wisdom), the absolute vacuum in planning that has existed in the past (until the mid-1980's, most states lacked a single person charged with responsibility for planning and supervising child mental health services[14]), and the near-consensus about the goals that should be applied to the development of the child mental health system. Although child mental health services have been especially poorly developed relative to other parts of the children's service system, "fixing" the child mental health system appears to be a manageable task when compared with other service systems (e.g., foster care[15]) that appear to be deteriorating and for which a consensus about appropriate goals is lacking. Few ascribe responsibility to the mental health system for resolving the terrible economic and social conditions in which increasing numbers of children find themselves,[16] even if the child mental health system is left to try to ameliorate the effects of those conditions. Moreover, although few states have begun even to approach a comprehensive child mental health system, most state plans are similar in their aspirations.

Much of the consensus about the nature of an adequate child mental health system can be traced to the federal Child and Adolescent Services System Program [CASSP], a small program to stimulate child mental health planning and to enhance states' and communities' capacity to deliver an appropriate range of services to seriously emotionally disturbed children and adolescents.[17] Most states have participated in the CASSP, and many also have been nudged by parallel efforts of private foundations.[18] Whether as a direct result of those incentives or as a consequence of their own concern, several state legislatures in recent years have mandated expansion[19] or coordination[20] of child mental health services, and others have adopted broad policy frameworks in which to develop child mental health policy.[21] Most states recently have adopted child mental health plans,[22] and some have been led into expansive service systems by court order.[23]

■ A "CONSTITUTIONAL" APPROACH TO CHILD MENTAL HEALTH POLICY

A. The U.N. Convention as a "Constitutional" Document

In such a climate of change, the Convention offers guideposts to mental health policymakers about the values and principles that should guide the development of the child mental health system. Indeed, the Convention is also a potential source of guidance to individual clinicians about the ethical conduct of their practice with children and adolescents.

Like many human rights treaties,[24] the Convention is "constitutional" in scope. Although there are few specific requirements with which American jurisdictions are not already in compliance, if the language is read narrowly, however, the Convention also was crafted in a manner that offers noble principles for policy development and implementation.[25] In that respect, the Convention is as meaningful for economically developed, democratic nations as it is for those that have been unable to provide for the basic needs of many of their children or that have been reluctant to recognize civil liberties for their adult citizens.[26] The Convention offers moral lessons even for rights-conscious nations about the personhood of their youngest citizens, but it does so in a "mainstream" manner. Notably, the Convention is consistent with the highest ideals of American constitutional law and with the principles underlying the codes of ethics of American mental health professionals.[27]

Although the subjects expressly addressed by the Convention are wide-ranging, it is a remarkably coherent document. The Convention is unified by an emphasis on the moral and legal personhood of children and the corollary duty to respect their *dignity*—a word that appears expressly seven times in the Convention and that is implicit throughout. Consistent with that theme, the Convention embodies six principles for the development and delivery of child mental health services.[28]

B. Entitlement to Mental Health Services

First, *the provision of high-quality services for children should be a matter of the highest priority for public mental health authorities.* Whether children's dependency is *de facto* or *de jure*, the state enforces a moratorium on their self-determination so that they may acquire the skills necessary for full and meaningful autonomy in the community. In such a context, justice demands that the state prevent a *de facto* punishment for dependency, when children in need of services are not able to seek them on their own.

Conceptualized somewhat differently, respect for human dignity requires treating children in a manner that will maximize their ultimate autonomy as persons. Therefore, society owes its children not only a period of protection in which their development is largely unfettered by adult responsibilities but also an entitlement to those services that will permit their healthy socialization. Otherwise, the period of protection is oppressive rather than enabling and, therefore, disrespectful of children's dignity. Such a theory is especially applicable to a right to mental health services, because such services may be critical to development and preservation of the self in some children and hence necessary to their integrity as persons.

Accordingly, the Convention appears to establish a principle of *children first* in the allocation of mental health services. Starting from the long-standing doctrine that children are "entitled to special care and assistance,"[29] the drafters of the Convention recognized "the right of the child to the enjoyment of the highest attainable standard of health."[30] Children with disabilities, presumably including mental and emotional disabilities, have a special entitlement to a wide range of services "conducive to the child's achieving the fullest possible social integration and individual development, including his or her cultural and spiritual development."[31] Such services should include assistance to the child's parents and should be delivered free of charge or with due consideration for the family's means.[32] Consistent with the underlying principle of respect for human dignity, the guidepost to the adequacy of services is their sufficiency in ensuring that children with mental disabilities "enjoy a full and decent life, in conditions which ensure dignity, promote self-reliance and facilitate the child's active participation in the community."[33]

Although *some* child mental health services are available in most communities, the paltry share of public mental health budgets that remains available for children suggests that most states have a substantial distance to travel before they comply fully with children's right to mental health services when needed. As suggested earlier, full compliance will require not only that the level of investment in such services is increased but also that the financing structure is altered so that the services that are purchased are effective. Nonetheless, the direction in which most states are headed is the correct one, and recognition of a moral and legal commitment to fulfill such an entitlement may be the most important step toward such a goal.

C. Respect for Autonomy and Privacy

Second, children should be viewed as active partners in child mental health services, with heavy weight placed on protection of their liberty and privacy.

As illustrated by the Convention's injunction that services be delivered in a manner that ensures children with disabilities "a full and decent life,"[34] paternalism, even if benevolent, is insufficient as a show of respect for dignity. The Convention supersedes the all-or-nothing view of self-determination that is common in Anglo-American law,[35] by providing that "any child who is capable of forming his or her own views [has] the right to express those views freely in all matters affecting the child, the views of the child being given due weight in accordance with the age and maturity of the child."[36] Research shows that virtually all children in the mental health system are capable of expressing their views,[37] that the liberty and privacy interests that are implicated in mental health interventions are important to children,[38] and that the opportunity to participate in treatment planning increases the efficacy of services.[39] In that regard, the implicit duty that the Convention places on mental health professionals to involve child-clients in treatment decision- making is consistent with both sound practice and professional ethics.[40]

Not only should children's right to participate in decision making about personal matters be respected, but mental health professionals also have a duty to avoid assaults on children's personal integrity through unjustified restrictions on their liberty or intrusions on their privacy. The Convention expressly bars degrading practices in the name of treatment.[41] Although such practices fortunately are well outside the standards of practice in the mental health professions, it also is true that most of the outrageous state-sanctioned behavior that has been committed against American children in recent years has occurred for purportedly therapeutic reasons.[42] In that regard, the Convention bolsters the ethical duty of mental health professionals to respect their clients'—including child-clients'—dignity and civil rights.[43]

D. Support for Family Integrity

Third, *mental health services for children should be respectful of parents and supportive of family integrity*. The drafters of the Convention apparently rejected the assumptions both that children's interests and those of their parents are necessarily congruent and that they are typically in conflict. Although children have their own perspective to apply to personal decisions, both their own interests and the need to accommodate the interests of other family members—itself consonant with the child's interest in a "family environment"[44]—suggests the wisdom of a model of shared decision-making in which parents provide "appropriate direction and guidance in the exercise by the child of the rights" provided by the Convention.[45] Supporting that general approach, parental autonomy is limited under the Convention in a manner "consistent with the evolving capacities of the child."[46] Thus, the partnership between clinician and child-client extends to the child's parents.

As I have discussed in detail elsewhere,[47] the child's interests in preservation of liberty and privacy and access to effective treatment typically are consonant with the parents' interest in preservation of parental autonomy and family integrity. This is because all of those interests should be met by availability of intensive home-based services and other alternatives to residential treatment.[48] Accordingly, the Convention implicitly presumes that parents and children have compatible interests against the state. Thus, the Convention recognizes parents' "primary responsibility for the upbringing and development of their child,"[49] but also invokes a societal responsibility to provide assistance to parents as they fulfill their duty to care for their children, especially when the children have disabilities.[50]

E. Community-Based Alternatives

Fourth, *states should apply a strong presumption against residential placement of children for the purpose of treatment, with due procedural care in decision making about treatment and with provision of community-based alternatives. When out-of-home placement is necessary for the protection or treatment of the child, it should be in the most family-like setting consistent with those objectives.* The drafters of the Convention stated a strong preference for children's developing in a "family environment,"[51] language that implies both that deference ordinarily should be given to parents' and children's wishes and that residential treatment, when it occurs, typically should be in family-like settings, such as therapeutic foster care and small group homes, with due effort made to strengthen and reunite the biological family.[52] Consistent with the seriousness of the interests at stake, whenever the State seeks to separate a child from his or her family, the Convention requires judicial review of a State's plan for out-of-home placement for the purpose of treatment.[53] When placement does occur, the Convention establishes a right to "periodic review of the treatment provided to the child and all other circumstances relevant to his or her placement,"[54] surely including the need for continuing out-of-home care.

As a matter of practice, such procedural rights probably will assume their greatest importance as a means of vindicating children's substantive right to access to community-based alternatives for treatment of disabilities[55] and juvenile delinquency.[56] Available research on treatment efficacy suggests that full enforcement of that right will obviate the need for out-of-home placement in most or all cases where placement is proposed for the purpose of treatment.[57]

F. Protection of Institutionalized Children

Fifth, *when the state does undertake the care and custody of emotionally disturbed children, it also assumes an especially weighty obligation to protect them from harm.* Although the Supreme Court has been reluctant to recognize constitutional rights to services, it has concluded that, at a minimum, the State owes protection of personal integrity to those children for whom it assumes care.[58]

The Convention extends that right beyond protection from harm to promotion of the child's development.[59] Each child in residential treatment has a right to "such protection and care as is necessary for his or her wellbeing,"[60] in conformance with professional standards, including an adequate number and training of staff.[61]

G. Prevention

Sixth, *prevention should be the cornerstone of child mental health policy.* If respect for human dignity is the foundation for the right to mental health services when children are in need of them, then it follows that the State should not permit preventable mental health problems to occur at all, in that effective prevention obviously provides greater protection of children's personal security than does treatment after such security is jeopardized. Accordingly, the drafters of the Convention recognized that the right to the "highest attainable standard of health"[62] subsumes a right to preventive services.[63] The drafters further recognized that promotion of mental health cannot be accomplished simply through mental health education and other narrowly tailored prevention programs. Rather, broad "social programmes"[64] are necessary to enable children to enjoy "a standard of living adequate for the child's physical, mental, spiritual, moral and social development."[65] It is noteworthy in that regard that evaluation studies of carefully developed prevention services generally have shown quite positive effects.[66]

The Convention also establishes an express duty of the State to prevent exposure to psychologically noxious environments—"mental violence"[67]—and to remediate the effects when such exposure does occur,[68] with care taken to ensure "the health, self-respect and dignity of the child."[69] Such rights extend to cases involving all forms of child maltreatment[70] and thus go well beyond the existing practice in most American communities, where child-welfare prevention services commonly are underdeveloped and treatment for maltreated children typically is not provided.[71]

Conclusion

Consideration of the implications of the Convention for child mental health policy illustrates both the conceptual power of the Convention and its potential to inform child policy development in numerous spheres. A commitment to respect the dignity of children would confirm the directions in which most states are already headed in their efforts to reform their child mental health systems, but it would show the moral necessity of those efforts and provide the foundation for a comprehensive system that is duly respectful of the interests of children and their families.

Full implementation of the Convention would substantially diminish the assaults to personal integrity that lead to serious emotional disturbance in children. Moreover, it would minimize the likelihood that such disturbance, when it does occur, results in lasting impairment of the child's ability to "live an individual life in society...in the spirit of peace, dignity, tolerance, equality and solidarity."[72] Ultimately, child mental health services should be planned and administered in a manner that recognizes the critical significance of psychological well-being for personal dignity and community life. The Convention provides a guidepost to reach such goals, which are fully consistent with the most fundamental values in American law and culture as well as the purposes of the mental health professions.

Footnotes

[1] Some of the ideas presented in this chapter also appear in Melton, *Socialization in the Global Community: Respect for the Dignity of Children*, 46 AM. PSYCHOLOGIST _____ (1991)(in press).

[2] G. MELTON & D. HARGROVE, PLANNING MENTAL HEALTH SERVICES FOR CHILDREN AND YOUTH ch. 2 (forthcoming) (the characteristics of youth are largely the same across service systems); G. MELTON & W. SPAULDING, NO PLACE TO GO: CIVIL COMMITMENT OF MINORS ch. 4 (forthcoming) (the children's service systems are heavily intertwined); Levine, Ewing, & Hager, *Juvenile and Family Mental Health Law in Sociohistorical Context*, 10 INT'L J. L. & PSYCHIATRY 91 (1987).

[3] *See generally* FOLLOWING THE MONEY: FINANCING AND REGULATION OF CHILDREN'S SERVICES (G. Melton ed. forthcoming); G. Melton & W. Spaulding, *supra* note 2; Melton, *Law and Random Events: The State of Child Mental Health Policy*, 10 INT'L J. L. & PSYCHIATRY 81 (1987).

[4] *See generally* G. MELTON & D. HARGROVE, *supra* note 2, ch. 3. For an example of a carefully evaluated flexible, intensive approach to child mental health services, *see* S. HENGGELER & C. BORDUIN, FAMILY THERAPY AND BEYOND: A MULTISYSTEMIC APPROACH TO TREATING BEHAVIOR PROBLEMS OF CHILDREN AND ADOLESCENTS (1990). Useful reviews of the literature on alternative service models in child mental health are published regularly in UPDATE: IMPROVING SERVICES FOR EMOTIONALLY DISTURBED CHILDREN, a newsletter distributed nationally by the CASSP, *see infra* note 10, technical assistance center at the Florida Mental Health Institute, associated with the University of South Florida.

[5] *See generally* Soler & Shauffer, *Fighting Fragmentation: Coordination of Services for Children and Families*, __ NEB. L. REV. __ (forthcoming).

[6] *See generally* FAMILY- AND HOME-BASED SERVICES (I. Schwartz ed. forthcoming).

[7] Tremper & Kelly, *The Mental Health Rationale for Policies Fostering Minors' Autonomy*, 10 INT'L J. L. & PSYCHIATRY 111 (1987).

⁸ Because of the contributions of ecological theory, experts in child development now commonly recognize the complex relationships between social events and developmental processes, including downstream effects of policies that were not intended to have any effect on children. Such a perspective is contrary to the univariate, unidirectional theories that formerly dominated developmental psychology. *See generally* U. BRONFENBRENNER, THE ECOLOGY OF HUMAN DEVELOPMENT: EXPERIMENTS BY NATURE AND MAN (1979). I have noted the diverse areas of law that affect child development and family life and the multitude of effects of law that can be observed. Melton, *The Significance of Law in the Everyday Lives of Children and Families*, 22 GA. L. REV. 851 (1988).

⁹ Examples of influential statements on child mental health policy include: INSTITUTE OF MEDICINE, RESEARCH ON CHILDREN AND ADOLESCENTS WITH MENTAL, BEHAVIORAL, AND DEVELOPMENTAL DISORDERS: MOBILIZING A NATIONAL INITIATIVE (1989); J. KNITZER, UNCLAIMED CHILDREN: THE FAILURE OF PUBLIC RESPONSIBILITY TO CHILDREN AND ADOLESCENTS IN NEED OF MENTAL HEALTH SERVICES (1982) (report of the Children's Defense Fund); JOINT COMMISSION ON THE MENTAL HEALTH OF CHILDREN, CRISIS IN CHILD MENTAL HEALTH: CHALLENGES FOR THE 1970s (1969); OFFICE OF TECHNOLOGY ASSESSMENT, CHILDREN'S MENTAL HEALTH: PROBLEMS AND SERVICES—A BACKGROUND PAPER (1986). Similar statements by state commissions and task forces are legion. *See, e.g.*, N. Spanos, Pay Now...Or Pay Later: A Look at Mental Health Services for Children in New York (Nov. 1987) (report of N.Y. Senate Comm. on Ment. Hygiene).

¹⁰ Congress has joined in this conclusion. The Child and Adolescent Service System Program (CASSP), *see* 42 U.S.C.A. § 290cc-13 (1990), is a small federal program to induce states to approach child mental health policy more planfully. CASSP has started from the premise that states not only need to do more in child mental health, but that they should provide qualitatively different services from those traditionally available in the specialty mental health system. *See* Meyers, *Federal Efforts to Improve Mental Health Services for Children: Breaking a Cycle of Failure*, 14 J. CLIN. CHILD PSYCHOLOGY 182 (1985); Lourie, Stroul, Katz-Levy, Magrab, Friedman, & Friesen, *Advances in Children's Mental Health*, 45 AM. PSYCHOLOGIST 407 (1990). Congress currently

is giving serious consideration to a new, large-scale initiative to expand child mental health services. *Congress Considers Children's MH Services Bill*, 6(1) UPDATE: IMPROVING SERVICES FOR EMOTIONALLY DISTURBED CHILDREN 1 (1990).

11 *See, e.g.*, Melton, *The Jericho Principle: Lessons from Epidemiological Research*, in SOCIAL WORK EDUCATION FOR WORKING WITH SERIOUSLY EMOTIONALLY DISTURBED CHILDREN AND ADOLESCENTS (L. Abramczyk ed. 1989).

12 *See, e.g.*, Kiesler, *Mental Health Policy as a Field of Inquiry for Psychology*, 35 AM. PSYCHOLOGIST 1066 (1980). Congress attempted to increase planning in the mental health system as a whole through the State Comprehensive Mental Health Services Plan Act of 1986, 42 U.S.C.A. §§ 300x, 300x-3, 300x-4, and 300x-10 to 300x-13 (Supp. 1990).

13 *See, e.g.*, U.S. Advisory Board on Child Abuse and Neglect, Child Abuse and Neglect: Critical First Steps in Response to a National Emergency (June 1990).

14 J. KNITZER, *supra* note 9, at 51.

15 *See generally* House Select Comm. on Children, Youth, & Families, No Place to Call Home: Discarded Children in America (1989).

16 *See, e.g.*, D. MOYNIHAN, FAMILY AND NATION (Harvest/HBJ edition 1987).

17 *See supra* note 10. One monograph developed by faculty of two federally funded technical assistance projects has been particularly influential in defining a desirable "balance" in child mental health services. B. STROUL & R. FRIEDMAN, A SYSTEM OF CARE FOR SEVERELY EMOTIONALLY DISTURBED CHILDREN AND YOUTH (1986).

18 The Robert Wood Johnson Foundation has worked closely with CASSP (*supra* note 10) in providing grants to states for further system development. Complementary efforts have been undertaken by the Annie E. Casey Foundation in juvenile justice and child welfare and the Edna McConnell Clark Foundation in child welfare, sometimes with positive spillover to the mental health system. *See generally* Jacobs, *Child Mental Health: Service System and Policy Issues*, 4(2) SOC'Y FOR RESEARCH IN CHILD DEV. SOC. POL. RPT. 1 (1990).

[19] *See, e.g.,* MINN. STAT. ANN. §§ 245.487 to 245.4887 (Cum. Supp. 1990).

[20] *See, e.g.,* OHIO REV. CODE ANN. § 3(a)10.02 (Baldwin 1989).

[21] *See, e.g.,* NEB. REV. STAT. § 43-532 (Supp. 1989).

[22] *See, e.g.,* Del. Div. of Child Ment. Health Servs., FY 90 Plan (1989); S.C. Dep't of Ment. Health, State Plan: Children and Adolescents (July 1989). Such plans are an outgrowth in part of the State Comprehensive Mental Health Services Plan Act of 1986, *see supra* note 12.

[23] *See, e.g., Willie M. v. Hunt,* No. 79-0294, slip op. (W.D.N.C. Feb. 20, 1981). Although the decree in *Willie M.* was limited to violent youth, it laid the foundation for more widespread reform of child mental health services in North Carolina. *See* Behar, *Changing Patterns of State Responsibility: A Case Study of North Carolina,* 14 J. CLIN. CHILD PSYCHOLOGY 188 (1985); Behar, *Fort Bragg Demonstration Project: Community Mental Health Services for Children/Adolescents,* 13(2) CHILD, YOUTH, & FAM. SERVS. Q. 3 (1990); Larkins, *In Support of Saxe, Cross, and Silverman,* 45 AM. PSYCHOLOGIST 408 (1990).

[24] *See* Sundberg, *Human Rights as Comparative Constitutional Law,* 20 AKRON L. REV. 593 (1987).

[25] An example of the variable ways that the Convention on the Rights of the Child (*hereafter Convention*) can be read is found in the right to health care "of the highest attainable standard." Convention, *infra* note 29, art. 24, § 1. Read most literally, the provision is vacuous: that which has been attained is that which is attainable. Read more broadly, the right could be framed as the highest-quality health care that the society can afford. That interpretation obviously leaves open questions of allocation to various classes not only of health care but also of other benefits. Read most broadly, the Convention provides that children have an entitlement to state-of-the-art health care. The last alternative is the one most consistent with the moral theory underlying the Convention. *See infra* notes 29-33 and accompanying text.

[26] I have previously explored this point in regard to Norway, a country that often is regarded as having a substantially more developed child welfare system than does the United States. Melton, *Respect for Dignity: Blueprint for Children's Law in the Welfare State,* 1989(4) BARN [CHILDREN] 73. Besides providing overarching policies on virtually

every children's issue currently on the Norwegian national agenda, the Convention may suggest problems with the Scandinavian administrative system of juvenile justice and child welfare. *See* Convention, *infra* note 29, art. 40, § 1 (requiring States Parties to "recognize the right of every child...[in juvenile justice proceedings] to be treated in a manner consistent with the promotion of the child's sense of dignity and worth, which reinforces the child's respect for the human rights and fundamental freeedoms of others...."). In practice if not in law, American juvenile courts often also may fall short of compliance with the spirit of this provision, which might guide the development of juvenile courts more in keeping with American constitutional values. *See* Melton, *Taking Gault Seriously: Toward a New Juvenile Court*, 68 NEB. L. REV. 146 (1989).

[27] *See, e.g.,* American Psychological Association, *Ethical Principles of Psychologists*, 45 AM. PSYCHOLOGIST 390, 390 (1990) ("Psychologists respect the dignity and worth of the individual and strive for the preservation and protection of fundamental human rights").

[28] Respect for personal dignity has been said to be the core value underlying the American Constitution and other national constitutions that have been based on it. Fletcher, *Human Dignity as a Constitutional Value*, 22 U. W. ONT. L. REV. 171 (1984); Murphy, *An Ordering of Constitutional Values*, 53 S. CAL. L. REV. 703 (1980). In an important conceptualization of American children's law, Tremper has argued that a lack of consistent concern with the dignity of children has led to unprincipled, seemingly chaotic legal decision making that often has failed to give due respect to children's personhood. Tremper, *Respect for the Human Dignity of Minors: What the Constitution Requires*, 39 SYRACUSE L. REV. 1293 (1988).

[29] United Nations Convention on the Rights of the Child, U.N. Doc. A/Res/44/25 (1989), at preamble, para. 4 [hereinafter Convention].

[30] *Id.*, art. 24, § 1. Given their reference elsewhere to "physical or mental health," *e.g., id.*, art. 25, the drafters apparently intended "health" to be inclusive of mental health.

[31] *Id.*, art. 23, § 3.

[32] *Id.*, art. 23, §§ 2 and 3.

[33] *Id.*, art. 23, § 1.

34 *Id.*, art. 23, § 1.
35 *See* F. ZIMRING, THE CHANGING LEGAL WORLD OF ADOLESCENCE (1982); Melton, *The Clashing of Symbols: Prelude to Child and Family Policy*, 42 AM. PSYCHOLOGIST 345 (1987). In law, the concept of *infancy* generally is as applicable to a 17-year-old as it is to a 17-day-old.
36 Convention, *supra* note 29, art. 12, § 1. *See also id.*, art. 16 (right to privacy).
37 *See, e.g.*, Kaser-Boyd, Adelman, Taylor, & Nelson, *Children's Understanding of Risks and Benefits of Psychotherapy*, 15 J. CLIN. CHILD PSYCHOLOGY 165 (1986); Weithorn & Campbell, *The Competency of Children and Adolescents to Make Informed Treatment Decisions*, 53 CHILD DEV. 1589 (1982).
38 *See, e.g.*, L. RIVLIN & M. WOLFE, INSTITUTIONAL SETTINGS IN CHILDREN'S LIVES (1985); Bush, *Institutions for Dependent and Neglected Children: Therapeutic Option of Choice or Last Resort?*, 50 AM. J. ORTHOPSYCHIATRY 239 (1980); E. Roth & L. Roth, Children's Feelings about Psychiatric Hospitalization: Legal and Ethical Implications (Apr. 1984) (paper presented at the meeting of the American Orthopsychiatric Association, Toronto). *See generally* Melton, *Children, Politics, and Morality: The Ethics of Child Advocacy*, 16 J. CLIN. CHILD PSYCHOLOGY 357 (1987).
39 *See, e.g.*, Bastien & Adelman, *Noncompulsory Versus Legally Mandated Placement, Perceived Choice, and Response to Treatment Among Adolescents*, 52 J. CONSULTING & CLIN. PSYCHOLOGY 171 (1984); Holmes & Urie, *Effects of Preparing Children for Psychotherapy*, 43 J. CONSULTING & CLIN. PSYCHOLOGY 311 (1975).
40 *See* Melton, *supra* note 38; Taylor & Adelman, *Facilitating Children's Participation in Decisions that Affect Them: From Concept to Practice*, 15 J. CLIN. CHILD PSYCHOLOGY 346 (1986); Weithorn, *Involving Children in Decisions Affecting their Own Welfare: Guidelines for Professionals*, in CHILDREN'S COMPETENCE TO CONSENT (G. Melton, G. Koocher, & M. Saks eds. 1983).
41 Convention, *supra* note 29, art. 37(a). Presumably, the prohibition of degrading treatment would subsume humiliation rituals (e.g., forcing children to wear self-debasing signs) and intense, attacking confrontation. Other disrespectful practices that are less reprehensible but also

may be common in private adolescent inpatient facilities are barred by other provisions of the Convention. *See, e.g., id.,* art. 16 (prohibiting interference with correspondence and requiring protection of "honour and reputation").

[42] For discussion of relevant cases, see G. MELTON & W. SPAULDING, *supra* note 2, ch. 5; Melton & Davidson, *Child Protection and Society: When Should the State Intervene?*, 42 AM. PSYCHOLOGIST 172 (1987).

[43] *See, e.g.,* American Psychological Association, *supra* note 27, at Preamble and Principle 3c.

[44] Convention, *supra* note 29, preamble.

[45] *Id.,* art. 5. For a thoughtful exposition of such an approach to decision making about treatment, see Weithorn, *supra* note 40. The only place where such a model is expressly established in American law is in decision making about minors' participation in research. *Additional Protections for Children Involved as Subjects in Research*, 45 CFR pt. 46(D) (1990). *See* Melton & Stanley, *Research Involving Special Populations*, in PSYCHOLOGY AND RESEARCH ETHICS __, __ (forthcoming).

[46] U.N. Convention, *supra* note 29, art. 5.

[47] G. MELTON & W. SPAULDING, *supra* note 2.

[48] In that regard, the much-discussed question of allocation of decision making about psychiatric hospitalization of minors, *see, e.g.,* Parham v. J. R., 442 U.S. 584 (1979), deflects attention from more central problems of ensuring availability of less restrictive alternatives. *See* G. MELTON & W. SPAULDING, *supra* note 2.

[49] Convention, *supra* note 29, art. 18, § 1.

[50] *See, e.g., id.,* art. 18, § 2, and art. 23, § 2.

[51] *Id.,* Preamble, para. 6.

[52] *See id.,* art 9, § 1.

[53] *Id.,* art. 9, § 1. This provision applies only when placement is contrary to the *parents'* will. *Id.* The Convention is silent on the question whether judicial review is required when parents "volunteer" their children for admission to mental hospitals. At a minimum, though, some procedure is necessary to ensure that the child's wishes are heard

and considered. *Id.*, art. 12. Whether the constitutionally minimum procedure under American law—consideration of the need for inpatient treatment by a mental health professional acting as neutral fact finder, *Parham v. J. R.*, 442 U.S. 584 (1979)—is sufficient to meet the requirements of Articles 9 and 12 probably would turn on the empirical validity of the Supreme Court's dubious assumption that such a procedure provides an adequate opportunity for the child to be heard and for an unbiased assessment of the availability of less restrictive alternatives to occur. *See* Perry & Melton, *Precedential Value of Judicial Notice of Social Fact:* Parham *as an Example*, 22 J. FAM. L. 633 (1984). Regardless, enforcement of the substantive entitlements under the Convention probably would obviate parents' desire to hospitalize their children in most instances. *See infra* notes 55-56 and accompanying text.

54 Convention, *supra* note 29, art. 25.
55 *Id.*, art 23., § 3.
56 *Id.*, art. 40, § 4.
57 G. MELTON & D. HARGROVE, *supra* note 2, at ch. 3.
58 Youngberg v. Romeo, 457 U.S. 307 (1982). Such a right does not apply under the Constitution when the child remains in the custody of his or her parents, even when the state has invoked child protective jurisdiction. DeShaney v. Winnebago Co. Dep't of Soc. Serv., 109 S.Ct. 998 (1989). Article 19 of the Convention appears to go beyond the U. S. Convention in that regard.
59 Such an extension may follow necessarily from the logic of the right to protection from harm. Youngberg v. Romeo, 457 U.S. 307, 327-29 (Blackmun, J., concurring); Halderman v. Pennhurst State School & Hosp., 610 F. Supp. 1221 (E.D.Pa. 1985); N.Y.S. Ass'n for Retarded Children v. Carey (Willowbrook), 393 F. Supp. 715 (E.D.N.Y. 1975); G. MELTON, CHILD ADVOCACY: PSYCHOLOGICAL ISSUES AND INTERVENTIONS 177-85 (1983). In decisions involving state schools for people with mental retardation, the *Pennhurst* and *Willowbrook* courts found not only that institutionalized persons are owed services necessary for the enhancement of their development but also that institutional settings are inherently incompatible with that purpose. That finding is consistent with the Convention's strong presumption in favor of community-based services.

[60] Convention, *supra* at 29. art. 3, § 2.
[61] *Id.*, art. 3, § 3.
[62] *Id.*, art. 24, § 1.
[63] *Id.*, art. 24, § 2(f).
[64] *Id.*, art. 19, § 2.
[65] *Id.*, art. 27, § 1.
[66] 14 OUNCES OF PREVENTION (R. Price, E. Cowen, R. Lorion, & J. Ramos-Kay eds. 1988) (report of a task force of the American Psychological Association); G. MELTON & D. HARGROVE, *supra* note 2, at __-__.
[67] Convention, *supra* note 29, art. 19, § 1.
[68] *Id.*, art. 39.
[69] *Id.*
[70] *Id.*
[71] *See generally* U.S. Advisory Board on Child Abuse and Neglect, *supra* note 13.
[72] Convention, *supra* note 29, preamble.

CHAPTER 13

The Child's Rights in Adoption and Foster Care
Articles 20 and 21

Joan Heifetz Hollinger and Alice Bussiere

Introduction

In recognition that children "should grow up in a family environment" (preamble to the United Nations Convention on the Rights of the Child) and recalling the provisions of the U.N. Declaration with "Special Reference to Foster Placement and Adoption" (preamble), this Chapter assesses United States compliance with the goals and guidelines of the United Nations Convention on the Rights of the Child [Convention] as they apply specifically to foster placement and adoption. Part I provides an overview of American adoption law and practice, analyzes the diverse functions served by contemporary adoption, and, with the Convention as backdrop, explores the tensions between traditional views of what adoption means and our present understanding of the needs and rights of children. Part II focuses on the American foster care system: how this system addresses the multiple needs of children who have been abused, or otherwise mistreated or abandoned by their parents, and how it often, but not always, functions as a prelude to permanent adoptive placements. Lack of resources, rather than the inadequacy of the laws governing foster care, are noted as the primary reason for America's failure to fulfill completely the goals of the Convention.

PART I. ADOPTION

■ UNITED STATES COMES WITHIN PURVIEW OF ARTICLE 21

Article 21 of the Convention applies to countries "which recognize and/or permit the system of adoption." Because the United States has permitted formal adoption since the enactment of the first state adoption statute in Massachusetts in 1851, and prior to that, recognized informal adoptions, article 21 is clearly applicable to this country.[1]

Adoption in the United States is a legal process which creates the status of parent and child between individuals who are not each other's biological parent or child. In accord with article 21(1)(a), only "competent authorities"—state court judges, and in some instances, Indian tribal court judges—are authorized to grant adoptions. Upon issuance of a judicial decree of adoption, the legal relationship between children being adopted and their birth parents and other members of their original family is completely severed and these children become, for all purposes, the children of their new adoptive parents.[2]

Consistent with article 21(1), the guiding principle of adoption in America is to promote the welfare of children, and particularly, to facilitate the placement of children, whose biological parents cannot raise them, in stable homes with adoptive parents who are willing to assume all the rights and responsibilities of parents with respect to these children. Although ensuring the best interests of children is "the paramount consideration," it is not, as article 21 recognizes, the sole or exclusive one—*see* articles 20, 21(1)(b). American adoption laws and practices are premised on a belief that adoption offers significant legal, economic, social and psychological benefits not only for children who might otherwise be homeless, but also for parents who are unable to care for their biological children, childless adults who want children to nurture and support, and state governments ultimately responsible for the well-being of children.

Adoption is not just a bundle of legal rules and regulations that create new legal and economic ties. It is also a social process intended to encourage affectional bonds within adoptive families. Despite evidence that some adoptions are problematic, research on the long-term consequences of adoption generally substantiates the belief in the benefits of adoption.[3]

A. Numbers and Types of Adoption in United States

As many as five or more million adoptees now live in America, including children who are still under the age of eighteen and who were born in this or other countries, adults who were adopted while minors, and, to a much lesser extent, adults who were adopted as adults.[4] At least 100,000, and perhaps as many as 150-160,000 adoptions, are now granted each year.

B. Adoptions by Stepparents and Other Close Relatives

Perhaps the most striking characteristic of these adoptions is how many different kinds of people they involve. Half or more are adoptions by close relatives, especially by stepparents. This continues the pattern of the past thirty years whereby intrafamily adoptions have increased, both proportionately and in absolute numbers, more than any other kind of adoption. Because intrafamily adoptions often give legal recognition to a *de facto* custodial family that has existed for some time, they provide "continuity in the child's upbringing" (article 20(3)) and are conducive to respecting the child's right "to preserve his or her identity, including nationality, name and family relations" (article 8(1)). Intra-family adoptions are generally the least regulated type of adoption, yet they lead to some of the most hotly contested proceedings, as when a non-custodial parent, typically a father, objects to a proposed adoption by a step-parent married to the child's custodial parent, or when grandparents seek to maintain contact with a child over the objection of an adoptive step-parent or other relative.

C. Adoptions of Unrelated Infant Children

While intrafamily adoptions have increased, the number and proportion of all adoptions that are of infants adopted by unrelated adults has decreased sharply. From the 1930's until the late 1960's, well over half of all adoptions were thought to involve infants born out-of-wedlock who were adopted by childless married couples. At present, however, even when adjustments are made for under-reporting, adoptions of infants born in this country by non-relatives probably do not exceed 30,000 to 50,000 per year, or no more than 20 to 30% of all adoptions. It is estimated that most of these are the result of direct private placements in which a birth parent personally selects adoptive parents for a child, with or without the assistance of a third party intermediary.

The decline in the number and rate of adoptions of infants by unrelated adults is not due to any lack of interest in finding adoptable newborns. Many

Adoption and Foster Care

of our one million or more involuntarily childless couples[5] would like to adopt a healthy newborn. They soon discover, however, that few such children are available for adoption, not simply because abortion remains safe and legal, nor because of any reduction in out-of-wedlock births, but more importantly, because of: (1) the substantial drop in the percentage of the children born out of wedlock who are voluntarily relinquished for adoption, and (2) the recent growth in the number of abandoned infants who suffer from prenatally acquired drug addiction or fetal alcohol syndrome, or who are at high risk of developing AIDS or other sexually-transmitted diseases.

The numbers of out-of-wedlock births and the ratio of out-of-wedlock births to the total number of births have gone up sharply since the 1960's among women aged 15-29, and especially among teenagers.[6] These increases have occurred despite the accompanying rise in the use of contraceptives to avoid pregnancy and in abortions to terminate unwanted pregnancies. Nonetheless, of the more than 700,000 children born out-of-wedlock each year, fewer than 8% are placed for adoption.[7] It remains to be seen whether more American-born children will become available for adoption as funds for contraceptive research virtually disappear and as we assess the burdens imposed on teenage and adult women and their children by state legislatures in the wake of recent U.S. Supreme Court decisions constraining women's reproductive freedom.[8]

D. Adoption of Foreign-Born Children

By contrast to the decline in adoptions of healthy American newborns by unrelated adults as a proportion of all adoptions, the number and proportion of adoptions by American citizens of foreign-born children, many of whom are under the age of one, are increasing more rapidly than any other type of adoption of unrelated children. In 1988, nearly 10,000 such adoptions took place, about 2,000 of them completed in the country of origin, and the remainder finalized in the U.S.. Although still only 6 to 7% of all adoptions, intercountry adoptions are sought by childless unmarried and married adults as well as by many who have biological offspring. Believing it is easier to locate an adoptable young child in other countries, these prospective adopters may have been discouraged by marital, age or religious criteria imposed by some American child-placing agencies, or rebuffed in their efforts to adopt an American Black or mixed-race child by child welfare workers opposed to transracial adoption. Most of those who pursue intercountry adoption are idealistically committed to adoption as a far better alternative for the millions of abandoned children in other countries than homelessness or institutionalization.[9]

Many who attempt an intercountry adoption are frustrated to discover that procedures in sending countries as well as in the United States, as primarily a receiving country, often impede, rather than facilitate, adoptions and do not serve the basic principles of the Convention. Intercountry rivalries and suspicions lead to unpredictable "openings" and "closings" of countries.[10] The language of article 21(1)(c), calling for "safeguards and standards equivalent to those...in national adoption" may even encourage the accretion of bureaucratic layers and the perpetuation of archaic immigration rules—for example, the U.S. definition of who is an "orphan"—that increase costs, take time, and operate to the detriment of the very children intercountry placements are intended to serve.

E. Adoption of Older Children by Unrelated Adults

Many thousands of children other than American or foreign-born infants are adopted by unrelated adults. Approximately 10 to 12% of all adoptions are of children over the age of two or three by unrelated adults, many of whom have been with these children's foster parents for a year or more. The biological parents of a majority of these children have had their parental rights terminated for abusing, neglecting or otherwise mistreating their children. Many of the parents relinquished their children to state agencies only after being threatened with an involuntary termination action, or after being convinced that their own mental or physical problems rendered them incapable of providing adequate child care.

Before they are legally freed for adoption, many older adoptees spend years in one foster placement after another, sometimes interspersed with brief returns to the custody of their own parents. Not surprisingly, these children have difficulty forming permanent attachments to adoptive parents. Some qualify for the financial subsidies authorized by the federal and state programs for children with "special needs" discussed in Part II of this chapter. Others who do not qualify for subsidies may nonetheless come to their adoptive parents with unresolved problems from their earlier years which may be exacerbated, rather than resolved, over time. Unlike healthy infants, who are eagerly sought by prospective adopters, these older children are not likely to be adopted unless prospective adoptive parents are actively recruited for them (See articles 19 and 20).[11]

F. Adoption of Indian Children

Finally, as many as 1,000 to 3,000 Indian children are adopted each year by non-Indian adopters. Whether adoption is a viable legal status for Indian children, who have been born into or raised in an Indian community, is a highly contested socio- cultural issue, analogous to concerns about the wisdom of certain intercountry placements. Even when adoption is considered acceptable, controversy persists: (1) should a child not raised in or near a reservation nonetheless be placed on one; (2) should non-Indians ever be permitted to adopt Indian children; (3) should a birth parent's desire to place a child outside of a tribal community prevail over the statutory preferences for a tribal placement?

Because of the unique and historic relationship between the federal government and Indian tribes, the U.S. Congress is empowered to legislate with regard to family law matters affecting tribal members. The Indian Child Welfare Act of 1978 (ICWA) governs many of the jurisdictional, procedural and substantive aspects of adoptions of Indian children, superceding state laws usually applicable to adoptions.[12] In their current intepretations of ICWA's mandate to preserve tribal integrity and promote the welfare of Indian children by, for example, following strict tribal placement preferences, our state and federal courts are attempting to strike a balance among the potentially conflicting principles of tribal survival, child welfare, and parental autonomy. These are not unlike the potentially conflicting principles that underlie articles 7, 8(1), 20(3), and 21(1)(b) of the Convention.[13]

■ COMPLEXITY OF AMERICAN ADOPTION LAWS AND PRACTICES

Adoption affects all aspects of the lives of the many different kinds of persons who become adoptees, as well as the lives of their biological and adoptive relatives. Adoption laws and practices are therefore among the most interesting and complex manifestations of government regulation of the lives of private citizens. For the most part, adoption, like other family relationships, is the product of and subject to state laws, not federal ones. Nonetheless, federal statutory and constitutional laws increasingly pertain to adoptions. As indicated above, the Indian Child Welfare Act (ICWA) governs the adoptive placement of Indian children and, analogously to articles 7, 8 and 20(3), presumes that the best way to serve the needs of Indian children is to preserve ties to their tribal and ethnic heritage. In accord with article 21(1)(c), immigration and naturalization laws regulate the entry into this country of adoptees who are born in other countries.[14] The federal Adoption Assistance and Child Welfare Acts provide guidelines and reimbursements to states for financial and other assistance given to families adopting children with "special needs."[15] Other provisions in federal welfare, social security and tax laws also affect adoptive relationships. Finally, many recent U.S. Supreme Court rulings on family law and individual rights have important ramifications for adoption law and practice.

Despite their common themes and similar provisions, the various state adoption statutes are not and never have been uniform, nor have they been subject to consistent judicial interpretations. Moreover, local rules and customary practices vary substantially and may conflict with each other, especially with regard to the handling of voluntary consents and relinquishments and the preferred method of placement—direct or agency.

Jurisdiction over adoption proceedings is deceptively straitforward. State courts have original jurisdiction over consensual as well as contested adoptions; but federal courts are increasingly called upon to consider the constitutional due process and equal protection aspects of adoption proceedings, most notably, the status of unmarried parents and the involuntary termination of the relationship between birth parents and a child. Moreover, federally-recognized Indian tribal courts have exclusive jurisdiction over adoption proceedings involving Indian children who are domiciliaries of an Indian reservation and concurrent jurisdiction with state courts over adoption proceedings involving children of Indian lineage who are not reservation domiciliaries. The adoptive parents of a child born in another country may have to complete two adoption proceedings —one in the child's country of origin and another in the state where the adoptive parents reside —and also fulfill the requirements for immigration and naturalization of the child.

■ IS MORE UNIFORMITY AND CONSISTENCY FEASIBLE OR DESIRABLE?

To date, efforts to achieve more uniformity in adoption laws and practice have faltered. Only eight states enacted a version of the original NCCUSL Uniform Adoption Act of 1953 or its 1969 and 1971 revisions.[16] Fewer than twenty states have enacted the Uniform Parentage Act,[17] which is not a general adoption code, but attempts to clarify when married and unmarried parents have a legal right to withhold consent to their child's adoption; and only a few states have considered the NCCUSL Putative and Unknown Fathers Act (1988) or the Status of Children of Assisted Conception Act (1988), both of which would affect adoption proceedings. Although every state and the District of Columbia have now joined the Interstate Compact on the Placement of Children (ICPC), its lack of uniform administration is notorious, except for its uniform ability to slow-down interstate adoptions. At least thirty states have enacted procedures for the consensual disclosure of the identities of adult adoptees and birth parents, but these procedures vary from one state to another, few people are aware of their existence, and Congressional attempts to enact a national mutual consent registry have stalled.[18]

In the 1970's, efforts by the federal government to produce comprehensive model adoption legislation for enactment by the states were unsuccessful and eventually produced a more modest "Model Act for the Adoption of Children with Special Needs."[19] The Family Law Section of the American Bar Association spent the 1980's working on a Model State Adoption Act, but it never won ABA approval, perhaps because it failed to strike a satisfactory balance between permissible and impermissible adoption placement activities.

Despite our inability to achieve more uniformity, interest in doing so remains high. A NCCUSL committee is drafting an entirely new proposed Uniform Adoption Act that presumably will establish general guidelines for handling adoptions without stifling reasonable local customs or innovations.[20] The U.S. State Department is participating in a three year project of the Hague Conference on Private International Law to develop an international convention on intercountry adoption that presumably will adhere to the principles of the Convention and attempt to alleviate the frustrations, referred to above, of those eager to adopt children from other countries. The U.S. Congress has acted to end discrimination against adopted children as social security recipients, and will again consider proposals for a national repository to facilitate the consensual exchange of information about adoptees and their families of origin as well as proposals for tax deductions for adoption expenses, coverage for adoptees in adoptive parents' health insurance plans, and more extensive recruitment of adoptive parents for children with special needs.

■ ESSENTIAL SIMILARITY OF LEGAL AND SOCIAL ISSUES AFFECTED BY ADOPTION: THE SEVEN PRINCIPAL ATTRIBUTES

Despite the striking lack of uniformity among our adoption statutes and procedures, the individual and social issues reflected in and shaped by them are essentially the same in every jurisdiction. As a consequence, the apparent differences among the states often mask important similarities in practice and basic principles. Indeed, adoptions generally share seven principal attributes: each pertains to some of the concerns of the Convention and each is being scrutinized and reinterpreted in this country in light of the diverse functions contemporary adoptions serve.

A. First Attribute: Parental Consent or Appropriate Grounds for Waiver

The first and most essential attribute of adoptive relation- ships is that they will not be created at all unless a court is confident that voluntary and informed consents have been obtained from the birth parents (See article 21 (1)(a)). Alternatively, a court has to be convinced that appropriate grounds exist to waive the right of a parent to consent to the child's adoption or that parental rights have been otherwise legally terminated (See articles 9, 18(1) & 19). Parental consent, or a legitimate basis for dispensing with parental consent, is thus a jurisdictional prerequisite to the granting of an adoption.

The requirement of parental consent to adoption derives in this country from the principle of parental autonomy which, in turn, is a product of natural rights, delegation of rights, and cultural traditions that endow biological parents with superior rights to the possession and control of their offspring. Both common law and constitutional precedents incorporate elements of these traditions into what has come to be called the doctrine of family privacy or parental autonomy.[21] Central to this doctrine is the presumption that parents are fit to determine where and how to raise their children, and should be permitted to make these determinations without interference by the State. Absent a voluntary or provable forfeiture of parental status, the State has no license to remove children from their parents in order to seek a "better" placement.[22] The presumption of parental fitness is not easy to overcome. From common law decisions comes the insistence that an actual intent to abandon or forfeit parental rights must be proven: mere "loans" or informal transfers of children to unrelated adults are not sufficient.[23] From recent constitutional decisions comes the recognition that a biological connection to one's child is not, by itself, sufficient to give a person the benefit of the presumption of parental fitness. Nonetheless, a person with this connection has an incomparable opportunity to develop a full-fledged parental relationship with the child.[24] Once established, this relationship cannot be terminated without proof of unfitness on the basis of clear and convincing evidence.[25]

Our courts and legislatures are now struggling to determine precisely which mothers and fathers have earned a right to consent to—or to veto—their child's adoption, what procedural protections are most conducive to ensuring that consents are voluntary and informed, what the most appropriate grounds are for waiving the right to consent, and whether a consent, once executed, should ever be revocable, and if so, for how long and for what reasons. Underlying these struggles is an attempt to balance respect for parental autonomy against the child's interest in being placed expeditiously in a stable family environment.

B. Second Attribute: Serving the Child's Interests by Placement with Suitable Adoptive Parents

If the requisite consents or waivers of consent exist, the creation of adoptive relationships further depends on a judicial finding that the prospective adopters are suitable parents and, above all, that the adoption will serve the best interests of the child. Pre-placement background investigations of prospective adoptive parents, as well as probationary placement periods, have traditionally been required in adoptive placements made by public or private agencies that have derived their legal authority to place a child from a voluntary relinquishment or an involuntary termination of parental rights. Consistent with articles 8, 14(3), 20(3) & 30, in many American states, agencies are required or permitted to place a child "when practicable" with adoptive parents of the same religious belief as that of the child, or to establish priorities for placement "which reflect consideration of the racial background, ethnic heritage, religion, and cultural heritage" of the child.[26]

Post-placement assessments of prospective adoptive parents are also routine in direct private placements in which a child's birth parent personally selects the individuals who will adopt the child; but only in the past decade have some states begun to require pre-placement assessments for direct private adoptions.[27] It remains to be seen whether more "fitness" scrutiny will actually weed out unsuitable people from the pool of prospective adopters or merely discourage potentially excellent parents from submitting to elaborate assessments that may have only questionable relevance to their skills as parents.

The legal conclusion that an adoption is warranted ultimately rests on a judicial evaluation of the personal and psychological dynamics of the relationship between the child and the adoptive parents. Successful development of this relationship depends to a large extent on how much the adoptive parents know about the medical, social and genetic history of the child, including pre-natal care. One of the most important changes in contemporary adoption practice is the abandonment of the once-fashionable emphasis on characterizing adoptees as "blank slates" whose lives and personalities can be shaped entirely by the personal and social environment offered by adoptive parents. As our understanding of the nexus between hereditary and environmental factors in personality development becomes more sophisticated, the demands of adoptive parents for more information about a child's background are being heard. Most states now require that all non-identifying information that is "reasonably available" about a child and the biological family be shared with adoptive parents prior to placement, as well as during and after, the adoption proceeding.[28] Moreover, state courts are ruling that agencies and other professionals who assist in adoptive placements may be liable in tort for intentional or negligent failures to disclose information about a child's mental or physical condition to adoptive parents.[29] Although the commitment to learning about a child's background is one of the most encouraging developments in American adoption practice, it would be sad, indeed, if prospective adoptive parents felt they could not face the inevitable mysteries and risks of any kind of parenting without having a veritable DNA profile of a child.[30]

C. Third Attribute: Adoption is Not a Bargained-for Exchange

A third attribute of adoption is the fiction that it is a judicially-approved unilateral or gratuitous transfer, analogous to a testamentary disposition or the donative deeding over of real property. Most adoptions are, in fact, consensual, but they are not thought of as the product of a bargained-for-exchange. In direct placements, the birth parent simply "bestows" the child upon the adoptive parents. In agency placements, the agency acquires the child through the voluntary or involuntary forfeiture of parental rights, then transfers the child "gratuitously" to the adoptive parents. In accord with articles 21(1)(d) and 35, these transfers should "not result in improper financial gain for those involved," and all forms of "trafficking" in children should be outlawed. No money or other valuable consideration is to be paid in exchange for the child or for the birth parent's consent to the adoption. By statute or case law, all American states decry "baby-selling" and most bar "finders' fees" to unlicensed intermediaries or any reimbursement to prospective adopters of expenses they have paid on behalf of a birth parent who has withdrawn her consent to the adoption.[31]

The fiction that adoption is not contractual is so powerful that it denies the elements of bargain intrinsic to a transfer of a child by a birth parent in exchange for a promise by adoptive parents to support and care for the child and thereby relieve the birth parent of these legal duties. This bargain element often plays a role in step-parent adoptions, and is especially manifest in direct placements of children by unwed mothers who seek payments from prospective adoptive parents for their pregnancy and birth-related expenses, and for legal and counseling fees. Indeed, most states now recognize that adoptive parents may pay, and agencies and other professionals may charge, for certain adoption-related expenses, subject to court approval.

Bound by the non-contractual fiction, our courts and legislatures struggle to determine which placement activities and payments by or on behalf of individuals and agencies are legitimate and to devise appropriate sanctions for those deemed unlawful. For example: if otherwise in the best interests of the child, should an adoption be denied because adoptive parents paid "excessive" living expenses for the birth mother, or because an agency charged the adoptive parents an "exorbitant" placement fee, or because an unlicensed third party brought the birth parent and the adoptive parent together, or because the parties failed to submit an itemized accounting? Or should the adoption be granted, but the perpetrators fined or otherwise punished? The issue of how many contractual elements should be allowed to tarnish the fiction that adoption is a donative transfer thus remains in this, as in other countries, a problematic one.

D. Fourth Attribute: Adoptive Relationships as Complete Substitute for Biological Relationships

The creation of an adoptive parent-child relationship is said to displace completely the child's prior ties to the biological family and to replicate within the adoptive family the characteristics of an original parent-child relationship "in all respects." Adoptive parents have exclusive responsibility for the child, including the right to determine when and how to disclose to the child his or her adoptive status. The adoptive parents acquire the same rights to parental autonomy and family privacy that the birth parents previously had. For purposes of inheritance and other property claims made from and through the adoptive parents, the adopted child is treated as equivalent to biological offspring. This complete absorption of the child into the legal and economic web of the adoptive family presumably encourages the emergence of a lasting personal and psychological bond between the child and the adoptive parents.

In contemporary adoption practice, the notion that adoptive relationships substitute completely for biological ones is being challenged by: (1) concerns about preserving children's ethnic, racial, religious and cultural heritage that are similar to the concerns expressed in articles 5, 8(1) & 20(3) and (2) the recognition that, in fact, adoptive relationships are not identical to biological ones except in the formal legal sense of equivalence. For older children, intercountry adoptees, and children adopted by relatives, the notion of complete substitution makes the least sense; these adoptees apparently do best over time when their adoptive parents acknowledge their children's different heritages and accept these differences not as indicia of second class status but of a welcome and prized diversity.[32]

E. Fifth Attribute: Confidentiality and Anonymity of Adoption

For a half century or more, adoptions in this country have been confidential. Judicial or administrative proceedings are closed to the public. In agency placements, the biological and adoptive parents typically do not know each other's identities. Even in direct placements where the birth parents meet or learn about the adoptive parents, they often do not learn each other's names nor agree to have further contact with each other once the adoption is complete. The records of the adoption proceeding are sealed to prevent unwanted intrusions upon the privacy of all parties to the adoption. These records may not be opened except upon a judicial finding of "good cause," or, in a majority of states, upon the mutual consent of those seeking disclosure. The child's original birth certificate is sealed, and a new one issued which contains only the child's adoptive name.

Confidentiality is said to serve the interests of the birth parents by providing closure on the experience of having an unwanted child, and enabling them to go on with their lives secure in the belief that their child will not return to invade their privacy. It is said to serve the interests of the adoptive parents by allowing them to get a "fresh start" with their new child without being concerned about unwanted interference by the birth parents or other members of the child's original family. Confidentiality is also said to serve the interests of the child by diminishing the likelihood of the psychological confusion that is allegedly a consequence of maintaining any contact with biological relatives once an adoption is final. In sum, confidentiality is consistent with the view that adoptive relationships should exist exclusive of, and be a complete substitution for, the prior biological family.

Recent research and considerable anecdotal evidence challenge the wisdom of maintaining a permanent veil of secrecy between adoptive and biological families, particularly with respect to intrafamily, intercountry, and older children adoptions. Even with respect to adoptions of infants, the jury is out on the consequences of more "openness" in the relationship between birth and adoptive families. Many birth mothers who gave up infants in the past report that they have never come to terms with the emotional consequences of that decision and regret not having had a greater role in selecting their child's adoptive parents. Many adoptees suffer "genealogical bewilderment" and, while not doubting the benefits of their adoptive relationships, nonetheless want to know more about their own roots. Many adoptive parents, and particularly those who adopt children from other countries, support their adoptee's desire for more genealogical and cultural history. Moreover, a number of adoption agencies are rethinking and departing from their traditional opposition to allowing any communication between birth and adoptive families during or after the adoption procedure.[33]

F. Sixth Attribute: Success of Adoption Correlates with Child's Age when Adopted

From a psychosocial perspective, adoptions that occur when a child is a newborn or an infant under the age of two are consistently found to be more successful over time than adoptions of older children.[34] Mutually-sustaining emotional bonds between the child and the adoptive parents are allegedly easier to form when the child has had only minimal contact with the birth parents.[35]

Although no recent research challenges the basic finding that the long-term success of adoption correlates with the age of the child at placement, this correlation is in several respects misleading. First, although adoptions of older children may pose greater risks for a child and adoptive parents, they are not doomed to fail. They may call, however, for different kinds of parenting skills, more financial and other state assistance, and an acknowledgment that the child has a post-birth as well as pre-birth history that renders obsolete most traditional views about the anonymity and exclusivity of adoptive relationships. Second, recent experiences with the adoption of drug- or alochol- addicted infants are teaching us that optimistic forecasts about the success of infant adoptions should not be exaggerated.[36] Finally, the "younger is better" research is at odds with the message that adoption is a "last resort" that is implicit in article 21 and in American "permanency planning" procedures that consider adoption a viable option but, as suggested in Part II, *infra*, are likely to enmesh a child in years of foster care and bureaucratic limbo.

G. Seventh Attribute: Permanence of Adoptive Relationships

Adoptive relationships are permanent. They are not subject to revocation because of incompatibility between the adoptive parents and the child, or because the birth parents desire to have the child returned to them. Adoptive parents, like biological parents, may, of course, relinquish their child voluntarily for adoption by others. They may also jeopardize their rights as adoptive parents if they abandon or mistreat the child. In other words, adoptive parents have no more, and no fewer rights than biological parents typically have with respect to shedding their parental roles. Nonetheless, adoptive parenting, like biological parenting, is generally regarded as "for keeps." In the absence of fraud or some other fundamental irregularity, adoption decrees are final and irrevocable, and affect future generations as well as the present one. In the rare instances in which adoptive parents are permitted to set aside an adoption, the consent of all parties involved and a judicial proceeding are required, just as these are essential prerequisites to the creation of the adoptive relationship in the first place.

Recent media attention to the allegedly widespread number of "disrupted" adoptions may be raising doubts about the notion that adoption is a permanent status.[37] Because of the increases, as described above, of the number of older and special-needs children who are being adopted, it should come as no surprise that some of these placements prove so problematic that even the most dedicated adoptive parents find they cannot meet these children's multiple needs. In addition to statutory provisions in a few states for setting aside an adoption for a developmental or mental "deficiency" existing or unknown at the time of the adoption,[38] other states and many agencies recognize the importance of having some procedure whereby an adoptive family relationship can be unwound, not for the sake of relieving adoptive parents of an unanticipated burden, but in the interests of finding a more appropriate placement for a child.[39]

Conclusion: Consistent with U.N. Convention and Contemporary American Adoption Issues, Seven Attributes Questioned and Gradually Revised

The seven principal attributes of adoption outlined above are most frequently associated with adoptions of infants by unrelated childless couples. Because most adoptions are no longer of this type, the relevance of these attributes to the functions served by contemporary adoption is less clear. The first and second attributes are being questioned as the commitment to promoting the welfare of children comes into conflict in an increasing number of cases with deference to the constitutional "rights" of fathers and mothers to maintain custody and control of their children and with concerns about ethnic or national survival. Similarly, the extent of public regulation of adoption proceedings is being challenged as potentially interfering with the "rights" of individuals to enter into families and acquire children.[40] The traditional notions of exclusivity, confidentiality, and secrecy are at odds with the desire of adoptees to know more about their own heritage and with the principles of the Convention that encourage maintaining ties between children and their original country and culture, even when a successful adoption by unrelated adopters has taken place and the children are raised in another country. Finally, the fiction that adoption is a gratuitous transfer is giving way to the recognition that to facilitate adoptions, certain expenses should be compensable, subject to judicial approval.

In accord with the goals of the Convention, Americans involved in adoption practice will continue to explore ways to reshape the essential attributes of adoption in order to respond to the needs of children throughout the world.

PART II. FOSTER CARE

Introduction

For children who cannot live in their natural environment, state and federal laws in the United States generally provide the benefits and protections required by article 20. However, far too many children still do not receive the assistance that they need. The failure to live up to the mandates of article 20 is more often caused by a lack of resources or a failure to comply with the law than by flaws in the laws themselves.

■ THE CHILD WELFARE SYSTEM

Recent reports call attention to a crisis in the child welfare system in the United States, with one report referring to the situation as a national emergency.[41] As a result of deteriorating economic conditions, increased abuse of drugs and alcohol, and diminishing resources, the child welfare system is overwhelmed.[42] In 1988, there were 2.2 million reports of child abuse or neglect, up 82% from 1981. In 1988, over 1200 children died as a result of abuse. At present, an estimated 500,000 children are being cared for out of their homes; of these, over 340,000 are in foster care. Following a decrease in the number of children in out of home care by 9% from 1980 to 1985, that figure rose again by an estimated 23% between 1985 and 1988. In addition, more children are experiencing repeat placements, although the length of stay has remained steady at about 2 years. Disturbing trends are emerging in the types of children in out-of-home care. The age of children in foster care is getting lower: in 1988, 42% of these children were under 6 years of age, up from 37% in 1985. Also, children of color are disproportionately represented and the percentage is growing. In 1988, approximately 46% of the children in foster care were children of color, up from 41% in 1985. The 1988 figure is more than twice the percentage that children of color represent when compared to the population as a whole, and the length of stay for black children is one third longer than the national median.[43]

■ PROTECTION OF CHILDREN AT RISK OF HARM

These disturbing data are appearing despite the basic framework provided by federal and state laws for the care of children who cannot live in their original family environment. Child abuse reporting requirements and child protective services agencies often provide special protection and assistance to children who cannot remain safely at home. Although the United States Supreme Court has held that children do not have a constitutional right to protection from harm in their own homes,[44] state and federal laws provide for the protection of children who are at risk of harm.

All states have child abuse reporting laws that require professionals who work with children to report suspected abuse or neglect and permit other people to make good faith reports without fear of liability.[45] All states also

Adoption and Foster Care

have child protective services and permit the removal of children who are at risk of harm because of abuse or neglect.[46] The federal Child Abuse Prevention and Treatment Act bolsters these laws by requiring states to have child abuse reporting laws as a condition of receiving federal child abuse prevention and treatment funds.[47] The Act also requires states receiving federal funds to investigate child abuse reports promptly; to have in place appropriate resources and personnel to deal effectively with the reports that are received; and to provide protections for children, such as confidentiality of records and the appointment of a guardian ad litem to represent the child in judicial proceedings involving abuse or neglect.[48]

A. Alternative Temporary Care

When children are or must be temporarily deprived of their family environment, states provide care and assistance through the foster care system.[49] Many children enter the system through involuntary removal by the child protective services workers. However, in many states, parents who need assistance may voluntarily place their children in foster care for short periods of time. Most children in foster care are placed in family foster homes or group homes where foster parents or group home staff act as surrogate caregivers under the supervision of the local or state child welfare agency. Children are also sometimes placed in institutions, but the use of institutional care for children is limited by state and federal law,[50] and institutional care is generally regarded as not serving children's emotional needs for love and affection.

States pay for out-of-home care by providing foster care benefits for the support of each child.[51] In addition, the federal Adoption Assistance and Child Welfare Act, provides federal support for foster care benefits that are paid on behalf of children who meet the federal eligibility criteria.[52] The Act sets forth basic requirements to ensure that children are provided with adequate care when they cannot remain in their own homes. These requirements include case plans, regular case reviews, minimum standards for foster homes, mandated reporting of abuse in out of home care, and procedural protections for parent-child visitation and changes in placement. The federal law also provides additional funding for child welfare services to promote the welfare of children and their families.[53] However, because of the growing number of children in care and because their problems are growing more serious, current resources fall short of meeting the need.[54]

B. Permanency Planning

When children are permanently deprived of their family environment, state and federal laws provide for alternative care through adoption, guardianship, and long term foster care. The requirements of the Adoption Assistance and Child Welfare Act and state permanency planning requirements[55] are designed to ensure that children who cannot return home are placed in a permanent home as soon as possible. Adoption is the preferred placement unless the child's special needs or circumstances dictate otherwise.[56] In order to expedite permanency in suitable cases, some states have an expedited procedure for terminating parent rights when reunification of the family is clearly inappropriate.[57]

To encourage adoption, all states and the federal government provide adoption assistance to families who adopt children with special needs.[58] Financial assistance programs also help to ensure the stability of adoptive placements by enabling parents to provide necessary care and services for adopted children. In spite of these efforts, many children remain in foster care too long. Some commentators suggest that cumbersome child welfare procedures and the failure to recruit adoptive parents for special needs children are largely responsible for the delays in making permanent placements.[59]

C. Continuity

Continuity in a child's upbringing is addressed in part through the concept of permanency planning. One goal of the Adoption Assistance and Child Welfare Act of 1980 was to end foster care drift, in which children moved from placement to placement and were never provided with a stable home environment. The Act addresses this problem by requiring states to make reasonable efforts to keep families together; by requiring them to make reasonable efforts to reunify families when children are removed; by requiring procedural protections when there is a change in a child's placement; by requiring regular case reviews; and by mandating that states hold a disposi-

Adoption and Foster Care

tional hearing within 18 months after placement to establish a permanent plan for the child. Many states impose similar safeguards by state statute.[60]

Due regard to the child's ethnic, religious cultural and linguistic background is sometimes more difficult to address in the law. The most comprehensive example is the Indian Child Welfare Act[61], which provides specific protections for children who are enrolled members of a tribe or who are the children of enrolled members. These protections include the exclusive jurisdiction of tribal courts over many of the child welfare cases, participation of the tribe in child welfare proceedings held in state courts, a preference for placement of a child with extended family members or with tribe members, and a heightened standard of proof for terminating parental rights.

Continuity for children with other cultural heritages is less specifically defined. Federal law requires a case plan designed to achieve placement in the least restrictive, most family-like setting available in close proximity to the parents' home, consistent with the best interests and the special needs of the child.[62] The law also requires case reviews to determine the continuing appropriateness of the placement.[63] These requirements clearly encompass the consideration of ethnic, religious, cultural, and linguistic continuity.

However, it is often difficult for states to develop placements that meet the cultural and linguistic needs of all children in foster care. This situation creates a dilemma for placement workers. If they use the placements available, children may not be placed in culturally compatible homes; but, if they wait for a cultural match, the children may spend weeks or months in shelter care. Many states address this problem through policies that require social workers to consider cultural factors when placing a child, without imposing strict statutory criteria that may be impossible to fulfill. For example, the California Department of Social Services Manual of Policies and Procedures lists the child's age, sex, and cultural background, including ethnic and religious identification, as criteria to be considered in selecting a placement,[64] but state policy does not prohibit transcultural placement. The obvious long term answers to this dilemma are the recruitment of additional foster families with diverse cultural backgrounds and increased efforts to maintain children in their own homes.

D. Suggestions for Reform

Although the state and federal laws described above provide a structure to deliver alternative care for children, the child welfare system often falls short of the provisions of Article 20 in practice.[65] For example, the goals of the Adoption Assistance and Child Welfare Act have not been fully achieved.[66] Stronger federal leadership and additional funding are necessary to improve the child welfare system nationwide.[67] Experts have also recommended the redesign of programs to target preventive services, better co-ordination of available services, and the extension of federal foster care benefits and protections to all children in state care.[68] Additional resources for courts and the legal system are necessary as well.[69]

Some problems have proved to be particularly intractable. The increase in teen pregnancy, the disproportionate representation of minority children in foster care, the increased abuse of drugs and alcohol, and the rapid rise of AIDS among infants present special challenges. The system must also improve services to categories of children who are now underserved, including older children who are abused or cast out of their family environments, children who are homeless, and foreign born children who are in the United States without official immigration status. These problems require a renewed commitment by child welfare experts and policy makers to finding solutions that will meet the goals as well as the specific requirements of article 20.

CONCLUSION TO CHAPTER

As indicated throughout this Chapter, the goals of foster care and adoption in the United States are fully consistent with those of the Convention on the Rights of the Child, and especially of articles 20 and 21: to provide alternative familial care for children whose best interests cannot be served by remaining with their original families. Although resource limitations and conflicting laws and policies make it difficult to attain these goals, a great many people in this country are striving to enhance the psychosocial as well as the legal benefits of the transition that some children must make from one familial setting to another.

Footnotes

[1] For an overview of the legal and social history of adoption in America, see Hollinger, *Introduction to Adoption Law and Practice* in ADOPTION LAW AND PRACTICE ch. 1 (J.H. HOLLINGER, ed., 1988) [hereinafter cited as ADOPTION LAW AND PRACTICE].

[2] *See, e.g.*, N.Y. DOM. REL. LAW § 110: "Adoption is the legal proceeding whereby a person takes another person into the relation of child and thereby acquires the rights and incurs the responsibilities of parent in respect of such other person." Similar definitions are found in the adoption codes of all states. *See also*, the proposed definition in § 1(2) of the preliminary 1990 draft of a Uniform Adoption Act by a committee of the National Conference of Commissioners on Uniform State Laws (NCCUSL): "Adoption means the creation, under this [Act] of the relationship of parent and child between two individuals. The individual who adopts acquires the rights and incurs the responsibilities of a parent with respect to the individual who becomes the adoptee."

[3] As two researchers put it twenty years ago: "No other form of substitute care offers children—or adults seeking children—the quality of legal, psychological, and familial belonging that adoption creates," B.JAFFEE & D. FANSHEL, HOW THEY FARED IN ADOPTION p. v (1970); Feigelman & Silverman, *The Longterm Effects of Transracial Adoption*, 58 SOC. SERV. REV. 588 (1984) (six years after adoption, Columbian, Korean and Black adoptees doing as well in predominantly Caucasion adoptive homes as their Caucasian adoptee counterparts). Indeed, a comparison of the percentage of marriages that end in divorce with the percentage of adoptions that are problematic suggests that adoption is a remarkably successful legal and social institution! Research on the psychosocial consequences of adoption is summarized in Hollinger, *The Aftermath of Adoption* in ADOPTION LAW AND PRACTICE, *supra* note 1, ch. 13. *See also*, Brodzinsky, *Adjustment to Adoption: A Psychosocial Perspective*, 7 CLINICAL PSYCH. REV. 25 (1987); Scarr & Weinberg, *The Minnesota Adoption Studies: Genetic Differences and Malleability*, 54 CHILD DEVELOPMENT 260 (1983).

[4] Because neither the U.S. Census Bureau nor any other federal agency has kept track since the mid-1970's of the number of adoptees now residing in America, these numbers can only be estimated. The figure of

five or more million assumes that at least 125,000 adoptions have occurred annually since 1950 and that most of the children or adults adopted during the past 38 years are still alive. If to this figure is added the number of persons adopted since the early years of this century who are still alive, and the approximately 10,000 annual adoptions of foreign born children, as counted by the U.S. Immigration Service, the total is well over five million. The U.S. Congressional Research Service has come up with a similar estimate, as reported in 134 Cong. Rec. Jan. 26, 1988 (Statement by Sen. Levin and others).

5 As many as 1 out of every 6 married couples may be involuntarily childless, unable to achieve a viable pregnancy after at least a year of trying to conceive a child. In addition, an indeterminate number of unmarried adults would like to conceive or raise a child.

6 The number of out-of-wedlock births rose from 403,200 in 1972 to 715,227 in 1982. The percentage of all live births that are out of wedlock has risen from over 10% to slightly under 20%. Although the overall rate of adolescent childbearing has been declining since it reached a peak in the 1950's, the childbearing rate among adolescents age 15 and younger is increasing and the total number of teenage pregnancies has been fairly steady since the late 1970's at about 1,000,000 per year. Of these million pregnancies, about 400,000 terminate in abortions, and about 500,000 result in live births, over half of which occur out of wedlock. Teenage mothers, especially Black and Hispanic mothers, account for 35% of all out-of-wedlock births; women aged 20-29 account for most of the remaining ones; NATIONAL RESEARCH COUNCIL RISKING THE FUTURE: ADOLESCENT SEXUALITY, PREGNANCY AND CHILDBEARING, Vol. I (C.D. Hayes, ed. 1987); M.VINOVSKIS, AN "EPIDEMIC" OF ADOLESCENT PREGNANCY? (1988); ALAN GUTTMACHER INSTITUTE, vols. 18-22, FAMILY PLANNING PERSPECTIVES, *passim* (1986-90).

7 A higher percentage of white, than of Black and Hispanic, unwed mothers relinquish their children for adoption. But because the rate of non-marital childbearing is more than four times higher among Black and Hispanic women, and especially among Black teenagers, than among white women, the higher percentage of white babies available for adoption does not mean that the numbers are nearly high enough to satisfy the demands of the primarily white childless couples who want to adopt.

8 *See, e.g.*, the limits placed on Roe v. Wade, 410 U.S. 113 (1973), by Webster v. Reproductive Health Serv., Inc., ___ U.S. ___, 109 S.Ct. 3040 (1989), Ohio v. Akron Center for Reproductive Health, ___ U.S. ___, 110 S.Ct. 2972 (1990), and Hodgson v. Minn., ___ U.S. ___, 110 S.Ct. 2926 (1990). This author is dismayed by the contemporary exploitation of "the adoption option" by ultra-conservatives whose primary goal is to criminalize abortion and not to advance the welfare of children. Adoption and abortion are both acceptable expressions of reproductive self-determination. Those who believe that limiting access to abortion will lead to the successful adoption of more healthy newborns are hopelessly naive about the social and economic contexts within which pregnancy and childrearing occur in this country.

9 Bartholet, *International Adoption*, in ADOPTION LAW & PRACTICE, *supra* note 1, ch. 10.

10 *See, e.g.*, *South Korea Slows Export of Babies for Adoption*, N.Y. Times, Feb. 12, 1990, B10, col. 1.

11 *See, e.g.*, the work of the North American Council on Adoptable Children.

12 25 U.S.C.A. §§ 1901 et seq.

13 Mississippi Band of Choctaw Indians v. Holyfield, ___ U.S. ___, 109 S.Ct. 1597 (1989) (any state court ruling which would "permit individual Indian parents to defeat the ICWA's jurisdictional scheme is inconsistent" with Congressional intent to ensure tribal survival); *In re Halloway*, 732 P.2d 962 (Utah 1986) (tribal community has interest "distinct from but on a parity with the interests of the parents" of Indian children; primacy of tribal sovereignty in resolving custody and adoption disputes "cannot be minimized"). *But see*, in direct conflict with the Holyfield and Halloway rulings, the continued deference by state courts to desires of birth parents of Indian child to select non-Indian adoptive parents without regard to ICWA placement preferences, Cook Inlet Tribal Council v. Catholic Soc. Serv., 783 P.2d 1159 (Alaska 1989), cert. denied U.S.L.W. May 22, 1990 (state courts not required to notify tribe in voluntary parental placement of Indian child for adoption); Hollinger, *Beyond the Best Interests of the Tribe: The Indian Child Welfare Act and the Adoption of Indian Children*, 66 UNIV. DETROIT L. REV. 452 (1989).

[14] 8 U.S.C. § 1101, § 1151 et seq.; 8 C.F.R. § 204 et seq.

[15] 42 U.S.C. §§ 620-28 and §§ 670-76; *see also* Part II of this Chapter, *infra*.

[16] UNIF. ADOPTION ACT, 9 U.L.A. §§ 1-19 (rev. 1971).

[17] 9A U.L.A. 590 (1979).

[18] For analysis of mutual consent registries, see Ch. 13 and App. 13-A in ADOPTION LAW AND PRACTICE, *supra* note 1.

[19] 46 Fed. Reg. 50022-39 (1981).

[20] The first draft of the NCCUSL proposed Act was discussed at the NCCUSL annual meeting in Milwaukee in July 1990.

[21] Meyer v. Nebraska, 262 U.S. 390 (1923); Pierce V. Society of Sisters, 268 U.S. 510 (1925); Prince v. Mass., 321 U.S. 158 (1944); Wisconsin v. Yoder, 406 U.S. 205 (1972); Santosky v. Kramer, 455 U.S. 745 (1982).

[22] *See, e.g., In re* Corey L. v. Martin L., 45 N.Y.2d 383, 391, 380 N.E.2d 266, 270 (1978) (merely because "someone else might rear the child in a more satisfactory fashion" has never by itself been grounds for removing a child from its parents); Spence-Chapin Adoption Services v. Polk, 29 N.Y.2d 196, 274 N.E.2d 431 (1971) (child custody decisions reflect "considered social judgments in this society respecting the family and parenthood"); *Developments in the law —The Constitution and the Family*, 93 HARV. L. REV. 1156 (1980); Hafen, *The Constitutional Status of Marriage, Kinship and Sexual Privacy—Balancing the Individual and Social Interest*, 81 MICH. L. REV. 463 (1983).

[23] *See, e.g.*, the classic Cardozo opinion in *In re* Bistany, 145 N.E. 70 (N.Y. 1924) (in finding insufficient evidence to justify a finding of abandonment by immigrant parents of a child they had left for nearly five years in the custody of a well-to-do childless couple, Cardozo wrote: "We cannot say that silence and inaction were prolonged to such a point that an intention to surrender becomes an inference of law").

[24] Stanley v. Illinois, 405 U.S. 645 (1972); Quilloin v. Walcott, 434 U.S. 246 (1978); Caban v. Mohammed, 441 U.S. 380 (1979); Lehr v. Robertson, 463 U.S. 248 (1983).

[25] Santosky v. Kramer, 455 U.S. 745 (1982).

[26] *See, e.g.,* ILL. ANN. STAT. ch 40 § 1519 ("when possible," same religious belief); N.Y. DOM. REL. LAW § 113; SOC. SERV. LAW § 373(7) (in ascertaining child's religious faith, agencies shall abide by wishes of parent who relinquished child or whose rights were otherwise terminated); Cal. AB 3532 222.35 (1990) (proposed consolidation of all provisions of Cal. adoption laws includes a requirement that placement priorities reflect consideration of the racial background, ethnic heritage, religion, and cultural heritage of the child). These priorities are not to be construed as precluding placements across any of these lines, especially if parents request such placements; *but see,* ICWA, *supra* notes 12-13 and accompanying text.

[27] *See, e.g.,* ARIZ. REV. STAT. ANN. § 8-105; FLA. STAT. ANN. § 63.092; IOWA CODE ANN. § 600.8; KY. REV. STAT. ANN. § 199.473; MONT. CODE ANN. § 40-8-109; NEV. REV. STAT. § 127.280; N.M. STAT. ANN. §§ 40-70-34, -40; N.Y. DOM. REL. LAW §§ 115, 115-c, 115-d; N.D. CENT. CODE §§ 14-15.01 et seq.; WASH. REV. CODE ANN. § 26.33.180; WIS. STAT. ANN. § 48.8377; *see also,* 1990 Draft of NCCUSL Uniform Adoption Act, Art. 3 Part 2.

[28] *See, e.g.,* CAL. CIVIL CODE § 224-s; N.Y. SOC. SERV. LAW § 373-a; *see also,* 1990 Draft of NCCUSL Uniform Adoption Act § 16, § 10-e.

[29] *See, e.g.,* Burr v. Stark Co. Bd. Comms., 491 N.E.2d 1101 (Ohio 1986); Michael J. v. Los Angeles Dept. Adoptions, 201 Cal. App. 3d 859, 247 Cal. Rptr. 504 (1988); Meracle v. Children's Serv. Soc., 437 N.W.2d 532 (Wis. 1989); *Wrongful Adoption,* ABA J., April 1990, p. 22.

[30] This could have especially detrimental consequences for intercountry adoptions where individual medical, genetic or social histories are much more difficult to obtain than are general cultural or ethnic histories.

[31] *See, e.g.,* CAL. PENAL CODE § 273(a): payments on behalf of birth parents are "acts of charity"; N.Y. SOC. SERV. LAW § 374(6): 1990 Draft of NCCUSL Uniform Adoption Act, Art. 10.

[32] Feigelman & Silverman, *supra* note 3; R.SIMON & H.ALSTEIN, TRANSRACIAL ADOPTEES AND THEIR FAMILIES (1987); Marquis & Detweiler, *Does Adoption Mean Different?* 48 J. PERSONALITY & SOC. PSYCH. 1054 (1985); Brodzinsky, *Looking at Adoption through Rose-Colored Glasses,* 52 J PERSONALITY & SOC. PSYCH. 394 (1987) (critique of Marquis & Detweiler).

[33] Caplan, *Open Adoption-I & II*, NEW YORKER, May 21, 1990 at 40; May 28, 1990 at 73; L.M.STEIN & J.L.HOOPES, IDENTITY FORMATION IN THE ADOPTED ADOLESCENT (CWLA 1985) (questions extent of "searching" behavior). The many meanings of "open" adoption and the debate about access to adoption records are summarized in Hollinger, *The Aftermath of Adoption* in ADOPTION LAW AND PRACTICE, *supra* note 1, ch. 13.

[34] S.WOLFF, CHILDREN UNDER STRESS 108-08 (2d ed. 1981) (strong correlations found between adoption outcomes, age at placement and extent of early maternal deprivation); W. FEIGELMAN & A.SILVERMAN, CHOSEN CHILDREN: NEW PATTERNS OF ADOPTIVE RELATIONSHIPS (1983); R.SIMON & H.ALSTEIN, *supra* note 32; *cf.* Berry & Barth, *Behavior Problems of Children Adopted when Older*, 11 CHILD. & YOUTH SERV. REV. 221 (1989).

[35] For the capacity of adoptive parents to serve as a child's "psychological parents," see J.GOLDSTEIN, A.FREUD & A. SOLNIT, BEYOND THE BEST INTERESTS OF THE CHILD (2d ed. 1979).

[36] Blakeslee, *Parents Fight for a Future for Infants Born to Drugs: Adopting Drug Babies*, N.Y. TIMES, May 19, 1990, p. A1; M.DORRIS, THE BROKEN CORD (1989) (adoptive parents' frustrations trying to raise Native American child with severe fetal alcohol syndrome).

[37] *See, e.g.*, Sachs, *When the Lullaby Ends: Should Adoptive Parents be Able to Return Unwanted Children?* TIME, June 4, 1990 at 82.

[38] *See, e.g.*, CAL. CIVIL CODE § 227b (the action can be brought for up to five years after the adoption is final).

[39] Barth, Berry, Carson, Goodfield & Feinberg, *Contributors to Disruption and Dissolution of Older-Child Adoptions*, 65 CHILD WELFARE 359 (1986); Bass, *Matchmaker: Older Child Adoption Failures*, 54 CHILD WELFARE 505 (1975).

[40] *But see*, Griffith v. Johnston, 899 F.2d 1247 (5th Cir. 1990) (people have no constitutionally protected or "fundamental right" to become adoptive parents).

[41] *Child Abuse and Neglect: Critical First Steps in Response to a National Emergency*, Report of the U.S. Advisory Board on Child Abuse and Neglect (1990).

42   *Abused Children in America: Victims of Official Neglect*, H. Rep. No. 100-260, 100th Cong., 1st. Sess., xiv (1987); *No Place to Call Home: Discarded Children in America*, H. Rep. No. 101-395, 101st. Cong. 2nd. Sess., 8 & 9 (1990).

43   H. Rep. 101-395, *supra*, 5-7.

44   DeShaney v. Winnebago County Social Services, 109 S. Ct. 998 (1989).

45   *E.g.* CALIF. PENAL CODE §§ 11164, et. seq.

46   *E.g.* CALIF. WELF. & INSTIT. CODE §§ 305 - 309 & 16504.

47   42 U.S.C § 5106a(b)(2).

48   42 U.S.C. §§ 5106a(b)(2) - 5106a(b)(10).

49   *E.g.* CALIF. CIVIL CODE § 396.

50   *E.g.* CALIF. WELF. & INSTIT. CODE §§ 206, 207.1, 361.2; 42 U.S.C. § 672(c)(2).

51   *E.g.* CALIF. WELF. & INSTIT. CODE § 11400.

52   42 U.S.C. § 670, et seq.

53   42 U.S.C. § 620, et seq.

54   H. Rep. 101-395, *supra*, 33-79.

55   *E.g.* CAL. WELF. & INSTIT. CODE § 366.25.

56   *E.g.* 42 U.S.C. § 675(5)(C) & CALIF. WELF. & INSTIT. CODE § 366.25-366.3.

57   *E.g.* CALIF. WELF. & INSTIT. CODE § 361.5.

58   42 U.S.C. § 673.

59   H. Rep. 101-395, *supra*, 54-55.

60   *E.g.* CALIF. WELF. & INSTIT. CODE §§ 306, 309, 360, 364, 366-366.3.

61   25 U.S.C. § 1901, et seq.

62   42 U.S.C. §§ 675(5)(A).

63   42 U.S.C. §§ 675(5)(B).

64   Calif. DSS MPP 30-336.

65   H. Rep. No. 101-395, *supra*.

[66] *See Foster Care, Child Welfare, and Adoption Reforms, Joint Hearings before the Subcommittee on Public Assistance and Unemployment Compensation of the House Committee on Ways and Means and the House Select Committee on Children, Youth and Families*, Serial 100-61, 100th Cong. 2nd. Sess. (1988); H. Rep. No. 100-260, *supra*.

[67] H. Rep. No. 101-395, *supra*, 9-11.

[68] H. Rep. 101-395, *supra*, 11-12, 62-77, 79-84; Serial 100-61, *supra*, 186, 295, 411.

[69] H. Rep. 101-395, *supra*, 55-58.

CHAPTER 14

The Child's Access to Diverse Intellectual, Artistic and Recreational Resources
Articles 13, 17, 28, 31 and 32

Martin Guggenheim

Introduction

This chapter principally examines how American law comports with articles 17 and 31 of the Convention on the Rights of the Child. These articles have been combined for analysis because of their substantial overlap. Article 17 recognizes the important function performed by the mass media and seeks to ensure that children have broad access to information and material aimed at the promotion of their social, spiritual and moral well-being and physical and mental health. Article 31 recognizes the right of children to rest and leisure, to engage in play and recreational activities appropriate to the age of the child and to participate freely in cultural life and the arts. For the reasons set out in this chapter, there are no impediments to the United States' ratifying the U.N Convention on the Rights of the Child as it relates to these two articles.

■ DISCUSSION OF RELATED ARTICLES

A complete discussion of these articles and their implications for American law unavoidably requires some discussion of rights covered by other articles in the Convention. American law simply is not neatly cabined by the bounds of these articles.

Thus, article 17, which recognizes the rights of children to have access to information and material from a diversity of national and international sources, is inextricably connected with article 13, which recognizes the right of children to freedom of expression. A vital analogue of the right to freedom of expression is the freedom to obtain information.

Similarly, article 31, which recognizes the right of children to rest and leisure, is inextricably connected to article 28, which recognizes the right to an education, and to article 32, which bars economic exploitation and places employment restrictions of children on States Parties.

■ UNITED STATES LAW

Conditions in the United States are eminently well-suited to ensure compliance with these articles. In three significant ways the United States has created an environment conducive to children realizing the rights reflected in articles 17 and 31. *First*, the United States recognizes that children have constitutional rights. This is significant because, invariably, legislatures or agencies will deem it appropriate to restrict information to be made available to children. However, because children have recognized constitutional rights which may only be abridged under certain circumstances, these restrictions are challengeable in court. Of course, the fact that restrictions may be challenged does not guarantee that the restrictions will be voided. On the contrary, many restrictions based on age are upheld by courts. However, those restrictions which are upheld must survive judicial review as bearing a rational relationship to a legitimate state purpose. *Second*, through the twin devices of universal compulsory education laws and universal restrictions on child labor, the United States has placed significant restrictions on the possibility of exploiting children or depriving them of free time to play and grow without the burdens of working. *Third*, the United States is a relatively affluent nation in which it is possible for children to utilize the many material benefits which are conducive to the pursuit of leisurely and cultural activities.

Laws created to prohibit children from engaging in certain activities rest on two basic premises. Both appear to be fully consistent with the Convention. First, that it is permissible to discriminate on the basis of age. Second, that certain activities, which are permissible and safe for adults to undertake, are dangerous or unsafe for children. Although a number of restrictions on the rights of children may be considered by some to be excessive, all restrictions are subject to challenge in court. In the United States, it has long been established that children enjoy significant constitutional rights.[1] Thus, whenever children complain that a law or restriction infringes their constitutional liberty, they may pursue such a claim in court. For this reason, courts play a crucial role in protecting the rights of children in the United States.

When these challenges are made, there is no presumption that restrictions based on age are unconstitutional. The Supreme Court has been unwilling to recognize the category of age as a "suspect category"; that is, as a category which requires that discrimination based on age be justified by compelling or very strong justifications. Rather, the Court has required, instead, that restrictions based on age bear some rational relationship to a legitimate state purpose. This standard of review is considerably weaker than the compelling justification standard; but it is not a toothless standard. It requires, in effect, that restrictions be justified and rationalized in a forum other than the legislature.

■ CONSTITUTIONAL PRINCIPLES

Because courts ultimately play a vital role in developing norms in the United States, it is useful to begin with a discussion of certain constitutional principles. It is impossible to discuss the rights recognized in article 17 without at least some discussion of the constitutional rights children enjoy to free expression. The United States is committed to the free exchange of ideas for its adult citizens. The first amendment to its Constitution prohibits the government from abridging freedom of speech or of the press. At the same time, the United States has attempted to create an environment in which it is possible for adults to enjoy unlimited access to ideas, publications and films, while simultaneously respecting the standard in article 17(e) by developing appropriate guidelines for the protection of the child from material injurious to his or her well-being.

From one point of view, restrictions imposed on the freedom of children to receive information could be regarded as deprivations of liberty. From another point of view, however, they represent a sophisticated effort to guarantee as much freedom of expression as possible for adults. In a society committed to maximizing freedom of expression for adults, unless certain rules are developed which limit, to some degree, the type of material children may receive, there is a danger of censoring material for the general public. The United States has chosen a path which uses a variable standard based on age for dissemination of certain kinds of material.

A. Free Speech Rights of Children

The Supreme Court has developed several categories of speech in an effort to promote the greatest freedom of expression. First, there is political speech. This has been accorded virtually unlimited freedom.[2] So long as a speaker expresses an opinion about public matters, government may not censor the speaker nor punish him or her for what was said or written. Although the Supreme Court has never directly held that children enjoy *unlimited* freedom of political speech, the Court has made clear the children enjoy this same basic constitutional protection to engage in such speech.[3] (Of course, the right to express one's point of view is centrally connected to the right to be exposed to an unlimited range of ideas. Indeed, the United States' commitment to the widest dissemination of ideas has led some to support unfettered political speech rights for children on the ground that such openness contributes to the freedom and competition of ideas for the entire society.)

The second area of speech concerns sexually-explicit material. This material, which may or may not contain any political message, contains explicit sexual matters. The Supreme Court requires that such material not be suppressed when adults wish access to it. Unless the material, "taken as a whole, appeal[s] to the prurient interest in sex, . . . portray[s] sexual conduct in a patently offensive way, and . . . taken as a whole, do[es] not have serious literary, artistic, political, or scientific value," it may not be prohibited.[4] States may not make it a crime for adults to produce, distribute, or possess such material. However, it is lawful to prohibit children from purchasing or possessing certain sexually-explicit material which is not deemed to be obscene for adults. In order to explain this distinction, it is helpful to set out the third category of speech, which concerns obscenity.

Obscene material is sexually-explicit material which has been determined to be lacking in serious literary, artistic, political, or scientific value. States may prohibit the production and distribution of obscene material.[5] But they may not make it a crime to possess such material in the privacy of one's home.[6] Thus, all persons, including children, may be barred from purchasing obscene material.

B. Limitations on Access to Sexually-Explicit Materials

But, as already mentioned, children may also be barred from purchasing, possessing, or being exposed to sexually explicit material which would not be deemed obscene if intended for adults.[7] Not all sexually-explicit material may be barred to children. Sexually-explicit material which is not deemed to be "obscene as to youths . . . cannot be suppressed solely to protect the young from ideas or images that a legislative body thinks unsuitable for them, even when material contains nudity."[8] However, if the sexually-explicit material is deemed inappropriate for children (that is, obscene as applied to young people) then it may be kept from them. The Supreme Court has created a variable standard of obscenity based on age. Some material will be deemed obscene for all and is barred to all. Other material will be deemed non-obscene for adults and thus may not be barred to adults. This material may or may not be considered obscene for children. If it is, children will be prohibited from purchasing it. If it is not, they are permitted full access to it.

Most importantly, the *only* type of material available to adults which the Supreme Court has allowed government to prevent children from reading is sexually-explicit material. The Supreme Court has never accepted a restriction based on age for receipt of publications or ideas outside the area of sexually related materials. Thus, the contours of the political rights of adults and of children appear to be the same in the United States.

C. Access to Television and Radio Programming

Television programming for children is an important part of the entertainment industry. But the airwaves, both of television and radio, are considered public property. The federal government permits private companies to obtain licenses to air programs on certain frequencies, but these licenses are subject to strict federal regulation. Among the obligations imposed on broadcasters which own licenses is to provide public service broadcasting and programs geared for children.

Recreation

There are numerous programs aired in the United States during after-school hours which are devoted to child audiences. Many of these programs are public television productions of extraordinarily high quality. These programs include pre-school shows, such as the highly acclaimed Sesame Street program by the Children's Television Workshop; other educational programs, including science, art, mathematics, and language programs; and entertainment programs, some of which are public television productions and others of which are commercial television productions.

Radios are ubiquitous in the United States. However, there are very few programs geared to a children's audience for the radio, other than music stations, which often are principally geared to children, usually adolescents. As already indicated, material distributed over the public airwaves is subject to the greatest restriction in the United States. Some of these restrictions are designed specifically to prevent children from being exposed to inappropriate material. The controlling regulatory body, the Federal Communications Commission (F.C.C.), licenses businesses to use frequencies to air material on radio and television. The F.C.C. prohibits the use of certain language from the airwaves and the showing of parts of the human body on television. Violation of these rules may constitute a crime. In addition, violators risk loss of their license. The Supreme Court has upheld sanctions imposed on a broadcaster for violating regulations prohibiting the use of certain language because of the danger that children would be in the listening audience.[9]

In addition to creating rules which seek to ensure diversity of ideas and enriching programs for children, the United States has also made its society conducive to children having the time to enjoy leisurely pursuits. American law goes a very long way toward protecting children from economic exploitation and providing them with the time and means to enjoy leisurely pursuits, including intellectual, educational, athletic, and recreational pursuits. Of course, at some important level, the rights recognized in these articles are not realizable through law or legislation alone. They also require a standard of living and an adequate health care system which permits children the freedom to spend time during the day free from the struggle of survival.

■ RELATIONSHIP OF COMPULSORY EDUCATION AND CHILD LABOR LAWS TO LEISURE TIME

An important measure of the rights of children involves the interplay of laws relating to school, work, and play. If there are no restrictions of time, place, or age when young people may be employed, economic obligations may result in their working many hours each day under exploitative conditions. Similarly, if there are no requirements for compulsory education, young people have no commitment to be some place or to do certain things during each day which would preclude working.

In the United States, the relationship between compulsory education laws and child labor laws has long been appreciated. In every state, children between certain ages, commonly 6 to 16 years, are required to attend school. Similarly, child labor laws significantly restrict the opportunity for children under a certain age, typically 14, 15, or 16, to be employed during school hours, evening hours, and in a host of hazardous occupations.

New York law provides a good illustration. In New York, most children under the age of 14 are prohibited from working in most occupations. Exceptions are made for such jobs as farm and agricultural work, domestic chores (such as housecleaning and baby-sitting), delivering and selling newspapers, and work in the field of entertainment. Although 14- and 15-year olds are permitted to work, there are sharp restrictions placed on the time of day they may do so. Principally, they may only work limited hours after school and during vacations. Thus, 14- and 15-year-olds attending school may not work more than three hours on a school day or more than eight hours on other days. In addition, they are prohibited from working between 7:00 p.m. and 7:00 a.m. Even for 16-year-olds attending school, the limit for working is four hours on school days, eight hours on other days, with no work permitted from midnight to 6:00 a.m.[10]

The combination of education requirements and labor restrictions for children results in the following scheme: in most of the United States, children between the ages of 6 and 16 are required to attend school regularly, typically between the hours of 9:00 a.m. and 3:00 p.m. Most of these children—those under 14 years of age—are prohibited from working in any job except those jobs connected with their homes. Thus, children under the

Recreation

age of 14 have the vast number of their waking hours in which to engage in free or leisure time. Similarly, even for 14- to 16-year-olds, though permitted to work, ordinarily they would not work more than a very few hours during school days, and never in the evenings. Even on non-school days, they are permitted to work only eight hours. Simply by subtraction, laws in the United States require that children enjoy significant numbers of hours each week when they are free to engage in leisure activities.

Just as the amount of time an individual has to enjoy leisure activities is a function of the amount of time he or she is obligated to undertake other tasks, so too the capacity to engage in leisure is partly a function of the leisurely activities available in the community. By any world standard, the United States is a rich country. Though there is vast disparity of income in the United States, and though there are far too many impoverished children living in underdeveloped parts of the country and in deteriorating inner cities, most Americans, including children, enjoy material goods and a standard of living which is highly compatible with leisurely pursuits. For example, most Americans have running electricity and own a television set in their own homes. Virtually all Americans have neighbors or friends with television sets, and children generally are able to have access to television in their communities. Indeed, in many schools, television has become a regular part of the curriculum.

■ COMMUNITY-BASED LEISURE PROGRAMS

Aside from television and radio, most communities in the United States have a variety of programs and opportunities for children to engage in leisurely activities. For example, virtually every community has a YMCA, or its equivalent. These programs usually contain gymnasiums, swimming pools, and social gathering halls for people of all ages, including children, to enjoy. They are open to the public without fee, or for a very small fee. And they are open during hours convenient to school-aged children.

Similarly, communities throughout the United States have officially-sponsored leagues and programs for athletic activities, such as Police Athletic Leagues, Little Leagues, Pop Warner leagues and the like. These programs, often for a small fee, are organized by teams which compete against each

Recreation

other. All children in the community are eligible to join a team, and the activities involve instructional and competitive opportunities. Many communities also have playgrounds and parks open to the public and the children in the neighborhood. These frequently are part of the public school. Children are permitted to use these facilities during non-school hours.

The United States has an extensive national parks service and millions of acres of land developed or maintained by the public National Parks Department. These national parks are open to the public for camping, fishing, hiking, swimming and the like. Most communities have motion picture theatres and frequently offer discounted admission fares for children. Virtually every major city in the United States has a public zoo which contains a wide variety of species of animals. These facilities are open to children, and many include programs designed to educate children about animals and nature.

It is common in every major city for there to be a publicly- maintained museum, and in most cities, a cultural arts center of some kind. Finally, virtually every community maintains a public library which is supported by tax dollars. These libraries are open to children and are free to use. Such libraries contain a children's book section and a librarian able to assist children in doing research or locating a book they wish to find.

As already indicated, all children in the United States are required to attend school. Schools also maintain libraries. These libraries are subject to greater restriction, based on content, than are public libraries, but schools are not permitted to remove books from their shelves because school officials do not approve the contents of the material contained in them.[11] This chapter will not discuss curriculum content in the schools, because providing children with an adequate education is explicitly the subject of Chapter 9.

■ MISCELLANEOUS RESTRICTIONS ON CHILDREN

There are a number of laws in the United States which restrict children's freedom to enjoy leisurely pursuits outside of the area of sexually-explicit materials. However, none of these appear to cast any doubt on the United States' compliance with article 31. The restrictions placed on children,

Recreation

which limit their freedom to engage in leisurely activities, are quite scattered and eclectic. Several prominent examples will be described.

One feature of leisure is the freedom to be on the streets. Many local communities restrict children's access to the streets to daytime hours or to specified hours, usually prohibiting children being in public places from 10:00 or 11:00 p.m. until 6:00 a.m., unless accompanied by an adult. However, the purpose of these laws is not to limit leisurely pursuits; it is to protect children from harm. Although these laws have been challenged as violating children's rights to travel and to association, typically, they have been upheld as a legitimate exercise of the police power. Where local communities have concluded that children are at risk, either of being the victim of crime or the perpetrator of wrong-doing, by being out at night, courts generally have upheld these restrictions.[12]

In similar ways and for similar reasons, children are, or may be, excluded from participating in other enterprises available to adults. Thus, for example, laws in every state prohibit the sale of alcoholic beverages to children. Laws in most states also make it illegal to sell tobacco products to children. (Not every State makes it a crime for children to possess or consume alcohol or tobacco; many make it unlawful only to sell or distribute these products to children.) It is also unlawful for children under a certain age to engage in sex, even with children of the same age or older. In 1981, the Supreme Court upheld a California law that makes it a crime for a man, even one under the age of 18, to engage in sexual intercourse with a female under the age of 18.[13] These laws, known commonly as statutory rape laws, exist in most states in the country. Many states or local communities restrict, or absolutely prohibit, children's access to certain establishments thought to be injurious to their well-being. Thus, it is common to find restrictions on children's freedom to enter pool halls, bowling alleys, dance halls, pinball or electronic games parlors and the like.

As already mentioned, when federal courts review restrictions on children, they will typically be upheld merely by showing that a rational basis for the restriction can be found. Thus, in 1989, the Supreme Court upheld a city ordinance which restricted admission to certain dance halls to persons between the ages of 14 and 18.[14] This ordinance was challenged by dance hall operators who wished to admit persons over 18. The Court upheld the restriction by declaring that it was rational for the city to conclude that teenagers might be susceptible to corrupting influences if permitted, unaccompanied by their parents, to frequent a dance hall with older persons. This decision demonstrates that restrictions are challengeable as unconstitutional; but courts will uphold restrictions which appear to be sound. Thus, in Dallas, 14-to 18-year-olds may attend dance halls in which persons of no other age are allowed. This rule arguably expands, rather than contracts, on the freedom of children to engage in leisurely activities, since it permits local communities to create programs for children based on age and restrict the programs to the children for whom they were designed.

■ INFORMAL RESTRICTIONS ON CHILDREN'S FREEDOMS

Thus far, we have discussed only formal, legal rules. Many restrictions on access to leisurely pursuits have been developed outside of formal laws. Private industry plays an important role in the United States in regulating the dissemination of certain material. Certain private industries have developed standards or guidelines for use or viewing of products or materials based on age. These standards are voluntary efforts to keep legislatures or courts from limiting the distribution of material to adults.

A. Motion Picture Industry

Thus, for example, in the motion picture industry all films are rated by a screening committee created by the Motion Picture Association. Laws prevent the motion picture industry from producing or distributing obscene material. Thus, the ratings created by the industry affect only non-obscene matter. The industry uses five ratings for its films. The most restrictive category is a new *NC-17* rating which replaced the original *X* rating. Films rated *NC-17* will likely be non-obscene, but so sexually-explicit or violent that the industry has determined they should be viewed only by those who have reached their seventeenth birthday. These ratings are enforced by theatre owners who prohibit children into the theatre to view these films. Video store proprietors, who distribute films to the ever-growing home viewing market (which rents video cassettes of films and views them at home on video tape recorders), similarly enforce the code by renting tapes only to adults. (However, there is no enforcement of the code by making it illegal for adults to permit children to view these tapes in their own homes.)

Other movies are rated *R*. This rating means that theatre owners will not permit a person under 17 to view the film unless s/he is accompanied by an adult. Some films are rated *PG*. Still other films are rated *PG-13*. Finally, films may be rated *G*. Persons of any age may view these films in theatres. The ratings in these categories simply advise parents of the industry's own sense of the age-appropriateness of a film. Films rated *PG* recommend parental guidance for children under 17 years of age. Films rated *PG-13* suggest that parents may deem parts of the film to be inappropriate for children under 13 years. Films rated *G* are recommended as appropriate for audiences of all ages.

B. Music Industry

One of the most important purposes of the ratings is to advise parents of the possibility that the film contains material which they would not want their child viewing. A similar private industry ratings system is being developed for the vast music record and audio recording industry. Recently, that industry has agreed to publish warnings on the covers of records and audio tapes when material contains sexually-explicit language. These labels are merely conveniences. They do not make it unlawful for children to possess the materials. The Supreme Court has recognized the legitimacy of efforts to support parental control in rearing one's child by making it difficult or impossible to obtain certain material, which a parent may wish to prohibit, without the parent's involvement. Thus, when parents approve of their children having in their possession books of any kind or films or music or any kind, there is no barrier to children receiving them.[15]

Conclusion

Children in the United States may be prevented from engaging in activities which are lawful for adults. However, all such restrictions are subject to challenge and review. Only if they are sustainable as rationally related to a legitimate purpose will restrictions on children's liberties be permitted. From any point of view, the United States, a world leader in mass media entertainment, appears to be in compliance with articles 17 and 31. There can be little doubt that there are no restrictions whatsoever to the United States' ratification of the United Nations Convention on the Rights of the Child as it relates to these two articles.

Footnotes

1 *See, e.g., In re* Gault, 387 U.S. 1 (1967); Tinker v. Des Moines Independent Community School Dist., 393 U.S. 503 (1969).

2 Cohen v. California, 403 U.S. 15 (1971).

3 Tinker v. Des Moines Independent Community School Dist., 393 U.S. 503 (1969).

4 Miller v. California, 413 U.S. 15, 23 (1973).

5 *Id.*

6 Stanley v. Georgia, 394 U.S. 557 (1969).

7 *See* Ginsberg v. New York, 390 U.S. 629 (1968); F.C.C. v. Pacifica, 438 U.S. 726 (1978).

8 Erznoznick v. City of Jacksonville, 422 U.S. 205, 213-14 (1975).

9 F.C.C. v. Pacifica Foundation, 438 U.S. 726 (1978).

10 N.Y. ED. LAW §§ 3215-3230 (McKinney 1981 & Supp. 1990); N.Y. LABOR LAW § 130 *et seq.* (McKinney 1986).

11 Board of Education, Island Trees Union School Dist. v. Pico, 457 U.S. 853 (1982).

12 *See, e.g.,* Bykofsky v. Borough of Middletown, 535 F.2d 1245 (3rd Cir.), *cert. denied,* 429 U.S. 964 (1976); People v. Chambers, 66 Ill. 2d 36, 360 N.E.2d 55 (1976).

13 Michael M. v. Superior Court of Sonoma County, 450 U.S. 464 (1981).

14 City of Dallas v. Stanglin, 109 S. Ct. 1591 (1989).

15 *See* Ginsberg v. New York, 390 U.S. 629, 639 (1968).

CHAPTER 15

Preventing Exploitation of the Child
Articles 32, 33, 34, 35, 36 and 39

James B. Boskey

Introduction

Articles 32 through 36 of the United Nations Convention on the Rights of the Child are, on their face, amongst the least controversial articles of the Convention from the viewpoint of the United States. The fundamental goals set forth in those articles of protecting the child from exploitation in the context of employment (article 32), narcotic drug and psychotropic substance use (article 33), sexual exploitation (article 34), abduction and sale (article 35), and other forms of exploitation prejudicial to any aspect of the child's welfare (article 36), are generally consistent with American law and practice, although the implementation of those articles may lead to some controversy, as discussed below.

Article 39—providing that "States Parties shall take all appropriate measures to promote physical and psychological recovery and social reintegration of a child victim of: any form of neglect, exploitation, or abuse; torture or any other form of cruel, inhuman or degrading treatment or punishment; or armed conflicts"—seems on its face similarly noncontroversial, but may raise some serious questions about the nature and effectiveness of the social service systems which provide treatment for child abuse and neglect, and could raise substantial issues about the manner of dealing with child witnesses in civil and criminal cases arising out of such adult misconduct.

■ CHILDREN AT WORK

Article 32 of the Convention addresses "the right of the child to be protected from economic exploitation and from performing any work that is likely to be hazardous or to interfere with the child's education, or to be harmful to the child's health or physical, mental, spiritual, moral or social development." It further provides for the States Parties to the Convention to take appropriate "legislative, administrative, social and educational measures" to implement this article, and more specifically, requires the establishment of a minimum age or minimum ages for employment, appropriate regulation of hours and conditions of employment, and the provision of appropriate penalties or other sanctions for violation of this article.

The goal of providing children protection from economic exploitation is one that has been generally accepted in the United States since at least the early part of this century. The constitutionality of state and federal regulation of the conditions of employment of minors has long been resolved in the United States.[1] Every state and the federal government has child labor laws which control the type of employment that is permissible for minors, the hours of work permissible for minors of different ages, and related questions, and such statutes invariably impose penalties, often substantial, for employers who violate the provisions of such laws. The principal federal statute, the Fair Labor Standards Act,[2] includes specific provisions with regard to child labor,[3] including penalties for violation of the Act.[4] While a periodic review of such legislation and regulation is always appropriate, the provisions of the Convention in this regard are clearly met.

Recently, special attention has been increasingly paid to violations of the child labor law, with the establishment of Operation Child Watch in the United States Department of Labor.[5] That operation has uncovered about 11,000 violations of the law and it is anticipated that substantial administrative penalties will be assessed and collected against violators.[6] A recent action under that act has sought injunctive relief against Burger King, a major "fast food" franchisor, whose franchised units have, allegedly, repeatedly violated the requirements of the Act.[7] While a periodic review of such legislation and regulation is always appropriate, the provisions of the Convention in this regard are also met.

Similarly, the question of "pure" economic exploitation—failure to pay the child for his or her work or failure to pay an adequate wage—is met by the federal and state minimum wage laws, including the Fair Labor Standards Act, *supra*. Proposals for a lower minimum wage for youthful employees, including children, might, arguably, raise a question of economic exploitation in some circumstances, however, the minimum wage proposed for such employees appears to be high enough not to qualify as economic exploitation *per se*.

An interesting, but largely academic, question might be raised about the situation of the child employed in a family business or performing "employment type functions" in a family context. A child may be "employed" within the family without economic recompense, but it seems unlikely that the performance of even economically-productive activities by the child within the family would fall within the scope of the Convention. This would appear to be covered by article 5 of the Convention requiring, *inter alia*, respect for the rights of parents and other family members as provided for by local custom.

Some recent controversy has arisen in the area of minors employed in the entertainment industry, assertions being made that the peculiar nature of that industry requires special provision with regard to the eligibility of very young children for employment and the hours during which work is to be performed. It could be argued that the Convention's requirement that "a minimum age or ages for admission to employment" would be impacted by the appearance of infants and young children in movies and stage performances, but so long as special regulations are approved for that industry that meet the Convention's fundamental goal of preventing harm to the child, the provision of special "age of entry" provisions for a particular industry would seem to be consistent with the terms of this article.

■ CHILDREN AND DRUGS

Article 33 of the Convention requires that "States Parties shall take all appropriate measures, including legislative, administrative, social and educational measures, to protect children from the illicit use of narcotic drugs and psychotropic substances, as defined in the relevant international treaties, and to prevent the use of children in the illicit production and trafficking of such substances."

Unlike article 32, this article has no specific provisions as to the manner in which it is to be enforced, and it is less than clear what specific actions were contemplated by the Convention's drafters as meeting the requirements set forth.

One of the major focuses of United States criminal law in recent years, at both the federal and the state levels, has been the restriction of access to narcotic and psychotropic drugs for both adults and children. The production, use, and sale of such drugs is a major violation of the law in every United States jurisdiction, and prosecutions for violation of such laws is, far and away, the most extensive component of the criminal justice system.

Recent statutes in several states have attempted to address specifically the access of children to such drugs, i.e., by increasing the penalty for selling them in proximity to a school, but it is not clear that these provisions have been at all successful in reducing the availability of these drugs to children.

Outside of the criminal law, serious efforts have been made, on an educational level, to advise children of the risks and consequences of drug use. Most states require that all students in their public schools be provided with drug education curricula at various stages in their education, and anti-drug campaigns in the schools have been very extensive, if less than very effective. At a more general level, anti-drug campaigns addressed to the public at large have included the well-meant, though seriously inept, "Just Say No" campaign introduced by the Reagan administration, as well as smaller, more intensive programs at both the federal and state levels.

Probably the weakest aspect of the United States attempt to meet the needs of children in this regard has been in the provision of services to children who have already been exposed to and are using illegal drugs. The general reduction in the amount of social service funding that has been implemented throughout the country has prevented the creation of anything approaching an adequate supply of rehabilitative services for drug users, including children. In the absence of such services, it is unlikely that children who are already addicted will be provided meaningful assistance in efforts to cure themselves of the habits they have developed.

It is clear that the policy of the United States and the individual states is in conformity with the provisions of article 33 of the Convention. The need for more effective implementation of that policy and the development of means of reducing the use and availability of illegal drugs is clearly recognized throughout the country, and adherence to article 33 is, therefore, consistent with national policy.

■ SEXUAL EXPLOITATION OF CHILDREN

Article 34 of the Convention deals with issues of the sexual exploitation of children. It requires that States Parties to the Convention take all appropriate action at both national and international levels to prevent: "(a) The inducement or coercion of a child to engage in any unlawful sexual activity; (b) The exploitative use of children in prostitution or other unlawful sexual practices; [and] (c) The exploitative use of children in pornographic performances and materials."

The issues regarding sexual exploitation of children can be seen as falling into two separate categories. The first issue is that of sexual exploitation of children for economic gain (including prostitution and the production and distribution of child pornography), and the second is the direct sexual exploitation of children for the "pleasure" of the exploiter. Traditionally, these issues have been dealt with separately in the United States, although both forms of conduct are clearly prohibited under both federal and state laws.[8] An additional distinction needs to be drawn within the latter category between exploitation by relatives or close associates of the child and exploitation by strangers, as the response of the law and the social service system to these two phenomena has been quite distinct.

Prostitution involving children is illegal in every American state,[9] and prosecution for the offense is generally directed at the prostitute, him or herself, or any person profiting from the acts of the prostitute. The pimp and the person soliciting the prostitute, "the john," therefore are also subject to prosecution under these laws. In addition, statutory rape laws have often been applied in child prostitution settings as a means of simplifying the prosecution and increasing the penalty for the violation. Further, the federal Child Abuse Prevention and Treatment and Adoption Reform Act[10] requires that states receiving federal funds for child protection services must include "sexual exploitation" in their definitions of reportable child abuse, and a separate statute[11] makes rape or carnal knowledge of a female under age 16 a federal crime if it occurs within the special maritime or territorial jurisdiction of the United States.

The same subsection of article 34 further prohibits the exploitative use of children in other unlawful sexual activities. That provision is, in essence, self-executing, as the determination of the unlawfulness of the activity necessarily implies that there is a criminal statute making the conduct unlawful.

The exploitative use of children in pornographic performances and materials potentially poses some more serious problems. The United States Supreme Court has had substantial difficulty in defining the nature of pornography,[12] and several incidents have raised serious question as to the ability to prosecute for dealing in pornographic materials. A recent exhibit at the Contemporary Arts Center in Cincinnati, Ohio of the photographs of Robert Mapplethorpe, a highly regarded "artistic photographer," included several photographs of children which were deemed by many observers to be pornographic in nature. The Center, and its director, Dennis Barrie, were indicted under an Ohio law prohibiting pandering and illegal use of a minor, but the prosecution was resisted on the grounds that first amendment freedoms prohibit such prosecutions. However, because of an acquittal, this prosecution did nothing to clarify the issue of whether such constitutional protection might not violate the provisions of article 34 of the Convention. The general proposition established in the *Miller* case,[13] that "obscene material is unprotected by the First Amendment" would seem to meet the requirements of the Convention, although it is not certain that "obscene" and "pornographic" are synonymous.

A recent United States Supreme Court decision[14] has clarified, to some extent, the law regarding child pornography. An Ohio statute that prohibited the possession or viewing of any material or performance that shows a child, other than that of the viewer or possessor, in a state of nudity was held not to be constitutionally overbroad and barred by the first amendment in light of the Ohio Supreme Court's construction of the statute to apply only to a "lewd exhibition or ... graphic focus on the genitals" and a requirement of "scienter", knowledge, as an element of the offense. The existence of a compelling state interest in the protection of victims of child pornography was explicitly recognized by that court. The effect of this decision is likely to be

Exploitation

an increase in the state legislative activity regarding child pornography. On the parallel issue of exposure of children to pornography, Justice Brennan's statement in *New York v. Ferber*[15] speaks clearly. He stated that "Government has a strong interest in protecting children against exposure to pornographic materials that might be harmful to them."

Federal law also addresses these issues with a prohibition against the use of minors for the purpose of producing depictions of sexually explicit conduct and the transportation of minors in interstate or foreign commerce for such purposes.[16] Similarly, the distribution of child pornography in interstate or foreign commerce or through the mails is prohibited.[17] Both statutes carry substantial penalties for their violation.

The law governing the inducement or coercion of a child to engage in any unlawful sexual activity is clear by virtue of the "unlawful" classification. For the activity to be unlawful, it must be prohibited by the criminal law and therefore be subject to sanction. Where such conduct is committed by a member of the child's family, or with the implicit authorization of such family member, the State may often elect not to prosecute the violation criminally, but to use civil child abuse remedies as a means of preserving the child's family insofar as possible, but the selection of remedies is not seen as justifying the conduct, and thus the conduct is prohibited under American law.

■ TRAFFICKING IN CHILDREN AND CHILD KIDNAPPING

Article 35 deals with the abduction, sale, or trafficking in children for any purpose or in any form. This section covers two separate situations from the American viewpoint: first, issues involving slavery or trafficking in human beings, and second, abductions of a child by a parent or guardian of the child who does not have the right to physical custody of the child by reason of court order or otherwise.

The fundamental trafficking issue is dealt with in the United States under a variety of federal and state laws and Constitutions. The thirteenth amendment to the United States Constitution prohibits slavery and involuntary servitude, except as punishment for crime, and a variety of federal and state statutes implement that legislation in various forms. Probably the clearest federal statute addressing these problems is the so-called "Mann Act",[18] which prohibits the transportation, or inducement, enticement or coercion to travel in interstate or foreign commerce of any individual for purposes of "prostitution or ... any sexual activity for which any person can be charged with a criminal offense ...", and which specifically increases the level of the crime in the case of a minor.[19] Similar restrictions exist in the non-sexual area on trafficking in human beings.[20]

The issue of abduction of children by their parents or guardians is a more difficult one, and has only relatively recently been addressed by American law. All states are now parties to the Uniform Child Custody Jurisdiction Act which attempts to prevent such abductions by establishing uniform jurisdictional standards for child custody determinations, thereby discouraging a parent from removing a child from one jurisdiction in hopes of obtaining a more favorable determination as to custody issues elsewhere. At the federal level, the Parental Kidnapping Prevention Act[21] implements similar provisions and makes available the Federal Parent Locator Service to assist in locating the absconding parent, and further states that the statute entitled "Flight to Avoid Giving Testimony or to Avoid Prosecution"[22] is applicable to parental kidnapping cases. In an international context, the United States is now a party to the Hague Convention on Civil Aspects of International Child Abduction,[23] and has approved implementing legislation making the provisions of that treaty binding on both the state and federal courts.

■ OTHER ISSUES

Article 36 is more general in tone, requiring the protection of the child "against all other forms of exploitation prejudicial to any aspects of the child's welfare." As this article makes no specific provision of the type of exploitation to be avoided, it could always be argued that any particular type of conduct that might be deemed exploitative and is not prohibited might be enjoined under the terms of the Convention. More realistically, however, this provision should be seen as an invitation to signatories to expand the scope of their protection for children, rather than importing some unexpected provision or restriction into their law.

Exploitation

Finally, article 39 addresses the recovery of and reintegration into society of children who have been victims of a wide range of misconduct. It places special emphasis on the needs of children to have such reintegration take place in "an environment which fosters the health, self-respect and dignity of the child."

Generally speaking, American law makes no explicit provision for rehabilitation and reintegration of child victims, other than in areas of child abuse and neglect. As the United States has, fortunately, been spared recent exposure to internal warfare, and substantially spared exposure to political terrorism, the situations involving these causes have been dealt with on an ad hoc basis. The availability of civil remedies for mistreatment provides one source of funding for rehabilitation in these circumstances. In the absence of such funding, there can be problems in providing the required services.

In the area of child abuse and neglect, however, the picture is far more murky. Where a child has been victimized by either physical, emotional or sexual abuse, all states provide some services for the rehabilitation of the child, and federal law provides some funding for these purposes. The medicaid program, under the social security law, can be used to meet the medical requirements of abused children through public or private medical facilities, but funding has been severely limited by several states, and it is clear that it is often not adequate to provide the range of rehabilitative services that abused children need or could benefit from.

The appropriateness of non-medical provisions for the rehabilitation of victims of abuse and neglect is even more questionable. The American social service system relies heavily on removal of children from the parental home as a response to parental misconduct. This is increasingly being challenged, and other remedies (e.g., removal of perpetrators and/or provision of "home-based" services) offered, but funds have often been lacking for intensive in-home support services. The situation in removal cases is discussed elsewhere in this volume,[24] but the situation of children who are subject to abuse, but not removed from their homes, presents a continuing problem.

Under article 39 it appears that the typically limited efforts at supervision of families where abuse has occurred but removal of the child is unwarranted, at best, marginally meet the requirement to provide an environment fostering the "health, self-respect and dignity of the child." Some serious reexamination of the availability of services to such families and their children would be highly appropriate in light of the language of the Convention. Services addressing the needs of the children, including mental health, special educational and supportive services, as well as services assuring that the parents will not reinjure the children,[25] should be provided on a regular and consistent basis, and periodic review of the situation of the child should be assured to make certain that the child's needs are being met.

Similarly, where return of the child to the family in the immediate future is not a reasonable option, article 39 would appear to require the permanent placement of the child in an adoptive or permanent foster home as rapidly as feasible.[26] Much of the American law on termination of parental rights has the effect of delaying such permanent placement and leaving the child in a situation which compromises his or her dignity and self-respect from the lack of a permanent family. Serious consideration needs to be given to appropriate revision of the American law on, and practices involving, adoption, to provide the needed permanence.

One area of special concern has been the treatment of children serving as witnesses in court in child abuse and neglect investigations. It is clear that for a young child, and often for an older one, confrontation with the person charged with having committed abuse is a very traumatic one. A recent decision by the United States Supreme Court[27] allows a child victim in these cases to testify from a separate room on closed circuit television, so as to reduce the impact of the confrontation. In allowing the special procedure, the Court noted that "Maryland's interest in protecting child witnesses from the trauma of testifying in a child abuse case is sufficient ... to justify the use of [such] procedures."

Despite these caveats, it appears that generally American law will meet the fundamental requirements of article 39. The issues raised are ones that have been frequently addressed in the social service literature, and the basic goals set forth in the Convention are fundamentally similar to those of the social service system in the United States. The need for improvement of social services is broadly recognized, and efforts at its accomplishment are continuous.

Conclusion

In conclusion, the United Nations Convention on the Rights of the Child will not, in the area of exploitation of the child, require any substantial modification of American law. What it will provide is a new perspective on these problems, while encouraging the development of improved national and international solutions and resources to the issues addressed. While the questions addressed by these sections have long been matters of serious concern, the attention called to them by the Convention and the reexamination that it imposes of existing law cannot but be helpful in seeing that these issues are more fully dealt with.

Footnotes

[1] Prince v. Massachusetts, 321 U.S. 158 (1944) (establishing the right of states to regulate child labor even in the face of a claim that the employment was compelled by religious belief.)

[2] 29 U.S.C. §201 et. seq.

[3] 29 U.S.C. §212 et. seq.

[4] The penalty can be as high as $1000 per incident although the act requires consideration of factors such as the size of the business and the gravity of the violation.

[5] Prior to the establishment of that program, the Department of Labor detected, in 1989, about 22,500 illegally employed minors through its regular investigatory processes. See, United States General Accounting Office, *Child Labor: Increases in Detected Child Labor Violations Throughout the United States* (GAO/HRD-90-116)

[6] A second sweep by the Department of Labor's nationwide strike force on violations of the child labor law, called Child Watch II, took place on June 6, 1990. It identified a number of new problem areas including the garment and agriculture industries.

[7] Dole v. Burger King, AMER. BAR J. (June 1990).

[8] For a comprehensive analysis of the legal and social issues involved in both areas *see*, NATIONAL CENTER FOR MISSING & EXPLOITED

CHILDREN, CHILD PORNOGRAPHY AND PROSTITUTION: BACKGROUND AND LEGAL ANALYSIS (1987).

[9] Actually a very few states do not prohibit prostitution itself but only loitering and/or solicitation for prostitution, e.g., Alabama.

[10] 42 U.S.C. §5101 et. seq.

[11] 18 U.S.C. §2031-2032.

[12] Miller v. California, 413 U.S. 15 (1973)

[13] *Id.*

[14] Osborne v. Ohio, 109 L Ed 2d 98 (1990).

[15] 458 U.S. 747, 775 (1987)(concurring opinion).

[16] 18 U.S.C. §2251.

[17] 18 U.S.C. §2252.

[18] 18 U.S.C. §2421 et. seq.

[19] 18 U.S.C. §2423.

[20] *See* 18 U.S.C. §1583.

[21] P.L. 96-611 (1980).

[22] 18 U.S.C. 1073.

[23] 42 U.S.C. §11601, et. seq.

[24] For a more detailed discussion of these issues see Chapter 13, *infra*, discussing article 20 of the Convention.

[25] *I.e.*, self-help programs such as Parents Anonymous, Parent Effectiveness Training, and other similar programs which assist the parent in dealing with the issues that led to the injury to the child.

[26] For a more detailed discussion of the effect of the Convention on adoption law and practice see Chapter 13, *infra*, discussing articles 20 and 21.

[27] Maryland v. Craig, 111 L Ed 2d 666 (1990).

CHAPTER 16

Rights of the Child Charged With Violating the Law
Articles 37 and 40

Merril Sobie

Introduction

Articles 37 and 40 of the United Nations Convention on the Rights of the Child concern children who are accused of criminal activity (juvenile delinquents). Article 40 specifically applies only to children who are accused of violating the penal law. And, although article 37 applies to any child who is deprived of liberty, presumably for any reason, in the United States a deprivation of liberty, except in rare instances, must be predicated on a violation of the criminal law.

As outlined below, American law generally complies with each provision of articles 37 and 40. The federal government has, through Congressional Acts such as the Juvenile Justice and Delinquency Prevention Act of 1974, mandated standards with which the states must comply, including the separation of children from adults who are accused of or convicted of criminal activity, and the deinstitutionalization of children who have not committed crimes. The states have, in the past twenty years, enacted statutes to protect and rehabilitate youngsters, including diversion programs and alternatives to incarceration. Furthermore, federal and state courts have applied many due process constitutional standards to juvenile delinquency cases.

■ DEPRIVATION OF LIBERTY IN GENERAL: ARTICLE 37

A. Cruel, Inhuman or Degrading Treatment or Punishment

The Convention (article 37) proscribes the use of torture or other cruel, inhuman or degrading treatment or punishment of a child. American law fully complies with this provision. The eighth amendment to the United States Constitution, which is applicable to the states, prohibits the cruel and unusual punishment of all persons, including children. Several lawsuits have challenged specific cruel, inhuman or degrading practices within the juvenile justice system. When found, courts have entered decrees enjoining such practices.[1]

B. Capital Punishment

The Convention also proscribes the use of capital punishment or life imprisonment without the possibility of release for persons under the age of eighteen. The United States Supreme Court has held that the capital punishment of children who are under the age of sixteen when the crime in question was committed is unconstitutional and hence prohibited.[2] However, the court, in a five-to-four decision, subsequently held that the Constitution does not prohibit the capital punishment of a person who committed the crime of murder when over sixteen but less than eighteen years of age.[3] Nevertheless, twenty-six states and the District of Columbia prohibit, by statute, the execution of persons who have committed any crime, including murder, when under the age of eighteen, while an additional eighteen states do not provide a specific age, and may, through future litigation, determine that persons under the age of eighteen should not face capital punishment. Further, most states which allow such punishment specifically include age as a mitigating factor in determining its use.[4] As a result, the death penalty has only very limited applicability to children in the United States.[5]

C. Arrest and Detention

One central Convention theme is that no child be deprived of liberty unlawfully or arbitrarily, and that the arrest, detention or imprisonment of a child be used only as a measure of last resort and for the shortest appropriate period of time. In the United States, the arrest of a child is restricted generally by the same criteria applicable to adults. Arrest may only be for a crime and must be based on probable cause (one very limited exception is that in several states, children who are believed to be runaways may be detained for very brief periods).

Following arrest, American juvenile justice procedures favor the release or parole of the child, usually to his or her parent. Pre-trial preventive detention is permitted, but the juvenile is ordinarily entitled to a probable cause hearing at which legally competent evidence must be presented, as well as a speedy trial, usually within a few weeks of arrest.[6] The vast majority of children are paroled; those who are detained, based upon probable cause that a serious or violent criminal act occurred, are entitled to several due process safeguards, including counsel and a speedy trial.[7] American law accordingly complies with these provisions.

■ JUVENILE JUSTICE PROVISIONS: ARTICLES 37 AND 40

A. Minimum Age

Article 40 provides for "...a minimum age below which children shall be presumed not to have the capacity to infringe the penal law" (§3(a)). American law is in agreement, although the issue is somewhat complex.

Several states prescribe a minimum age for delinquency.[8] Children below the threshold age cannot be charged; in those states the presumption of incapacity is conclusive. Other states do not prescribe a minimum age. However, the lack of capacity, defined, generally, as the inability to participate in the proceedings or assist in one's defense, constitutes a defense to any criminal charge, whether the accused is a juvenile or an adult. Further, in most states the defense of mental illness, defined, generally, as the inability to differentiate right from wrong or to understand the consequences of the act charged, is available to children.[9] The younger the child, the more likely that capacity or the requisite mental state cannot be proven or, conversely, that it may be established by the defense. The burdens of proof and the precise definition vary by jurisdiction. But, the prosecution of young children, particularly below the age of ten, is very difficult, and is often precluded. It should be added that the filing of charges is always discretionary, and community-based alternatives to formal proceedings are available and widely used for younger offenders. Thus, the available presumptions and defenses are needed only in the relatively unlikely event that a very young child is charged.

B. Due Process Rights

The Convention lists several specific rights which should be afforded to children accused of committing criminal acts. Again, American law appears to comply. In many ways, the United States juvenile justice system pioneered in offering basic due process rights to juveniles, and many of these rights are reflected in the Convention.

The specific Convention provisions are as follows:

1. A proscription against *ex post facto* laws, i.e., proceedings involving acts which were not prohibited at the time they were committed. The United States Constitution specifically bars the *ex post facto* application of penal laws, and there is no doubt that the provision is applicable to children.[10]

2. A presumption of innocence until proven guilty. This principle is ingrained in American jurisprudence. The United States Supreme Court has also held that criminal charges against children, like adults, must be proven beyond a reasonable doubt.[11]

3. A right for the child and, where appropriate, his or her parent, to be informed promptly and directly of the charges. The right to specific and adequate notice of any charge was established by the landmark United States Supreme Court *Gault* decision.[12] Further, the child and his or her parent or guardian ordinarily must be served with adequate notice and a copy of legally-sufficient charges.[13]

4. A right to legal or other appropriate assistance. Whenever a child faces the possibility of a loss of liberty, he or she is automatically entitled to counsel; the right to legal counsel was also established by the *Gault* decision. In many states, an attorney must be assigned by the court even if the child or parent has the financial capability of retaining private counsel.

5. The right to have the matter determined without delay by a competent, independent and impartial authority or judicial body. Again, American law is in complete agreement. The United States Con-

stitution provides for the right to a speedy trial,[14] and many states have, by statute or case law, adopted speedy trial provisions which mandate a very rapid adjudication and disposition.[15] In all cases, the hearings are convened before an impartial tribunal, with a judge, a referee or a hearing officer presiding.

6. The right of the child and, where appropriate, his or her parent, to be present. Here too, American law is in agreement. Except for very limited situations where the best interests of the child precludes their presence, the child and, generally, the parents, must be present at every stage of the proceedings. And the child's attorney must also be present and participate at every stage of the proceedings.

7. The right not to be compelled to give testimony or to confess guilt and the right to examine or to cross-examine witnesses. All these rights, which emanate from the United States Constitution, are covered specifically in the *Gault* decision, which is applicable to every state and jurisdiction (the District of Columbia, for example).

8. The right to review by a higher competent, independent and impartial tribunal. Although the right to appeal is not a recognized constitutional principle in American law, a denial of appellate review to children accused of violating the penal law would raise very serious questions concerning the due process and equal protection clauses of the federal constitution. In fact, every jurisdiction provides for the appellate review of adverse decisions, including decisions rendered by the juvenile courts. If indigent, the child is entitled to assigned counsel and free transcripts (in some jurisdictions the right to a free appeal is offered to all children, regardless of indigency).

9. If needed, the right to free assistance of an interpreter. This right is fully respected by American courts. The denial of an interpreter, which would inhibit or prevent the child from participating and assisting in his or her defense, would clearly be invalid.

10. The right to have his or her privacy fully respected at all stages of the proceedings. Privacy of juvenile court proceedings, including delinquency actions involving violations of the penal laws, has been a hallmark of American juvenile justice. Most states provide for closed hearings, i.e., the public and the news media are barred, and only those persons who have a legitimate interest in the specific proceeding may attend.[16] Although the issue has been litigated in recent years, and some exceptions made, there is no doubt that privacy is presumed and that the court may, and usually does, conduct private proceedings. Similarly, the records and files concerning juvenile proceedings are ordinarily confidential, and access is limited strictly. Several states have statutory provisions for the sealing and, in some cases, the expungement of records, whenever appropriate.[17] The only exception to the stringent privacy standards is when an older child who is charged criminally is transferred to the adult courts. In these cases, which are numerically limited, there is a presumption in favor of open proceedings, although the court may generally conduct closed hearings when the interests of the child so require.

C. Diversion and Alternatives to Institutional Care

A major trend throughout the American juvenile justice system has been the proliferation of alternative programs, whereby a case involving a child accused of infringing the penal law is "diverted" or "adjusted" without formal proceedings. In most states, the large majority of children accused of committing less serious offenses, such as property crimes, are not formally charged. Diversion techniques may involve counseling, rehabilitation programs, community service or restitution. American law is accordingly in agreement with article 40's call for appropriate measures without resort to judicial proceedings (§3(b)).

Article 40 also suggests a variety of dispositions as alternatives to institutional care. Specific examples include supervision orders, counseling, probation, foster care, and educational programs. Individualized dispositions have been a hallmark of the American juvenile justice system, and the range of available dispositional alternatives include all the examples cited in the Convention. Further, in choosing a disposition, the judge or hearing officer is

Juvenile Justice

often bound by the "least restrictive available alternative" doctrine, which favors non-institutionalization, and dispositional decisions are appealable. If an older child has been transferred to the adult criminal court, usually because of the commission of a very violent offense, or the juvenile court's jurisdiction terminates below age eighteen, the range of dispositional alternatives is narrowed. However, probation supervision, counselling and rehabilitative programs are almost always available and are used extensively. United States laws and practices generally conform to the Convention, regardless of the age of the child or the specific provisions and practices of each state.

D. Loss of Liberty

The United State is also generally in compliance with the Convention's provision that detention or imprisonment be a last resort and for the shortest appropriate period. First, for the reasons outlined above, pre-trial detention is limited, both in scope and in duration. Second, loss of liberty or confinement after trial is generally limited. In many states, the doctrine of "least restrictive alternative" is applied.[18] In imposing a disposition, the court must order the least restrictive one consistent with the needs and interests of the child and the protection of the community. Thus, probation supervision or rehabilitative services are favored and confinement permitted only when there is no viable less restrictive alternative. Third, the length of time a child can be confined is limited, and ordinarily shorter than that of an adult (at least for the more serious offenses).[19] The only exceptions are "transfer" cases, in which a juvenile case in most states may be transferred to an adult court, usually when the child is over the age of fourteen and has been charged with a serious and violent crime, and those few states which restrict the age of juvenile court jurisdiction to sixteen or seventeen (rather than eighteen), thereby permitting the longer imprisonment of older juveniles. For the most part, imprisonment is permitted only for the appropriate time span contemplated by the Convention.

Children deprived of liberty in the United States must be treated with humanity and dignity and in a manner which takes account of their age, as envisioned in article 37 (section "c"). A substantial body of case law has evolved concerning the incarcerated child's right to be free of cruel or degrading treatment. Cases have also held, *inter alia*, that the child deprived of liberty possesses a constitutional right to decent accommodations, education, and supportive services.[20]

E. Separation of Juveniles from Adults

Children who are deprived of liberty are almost always housed in facilities or homes devoted solely to juveniles, and, hence, are completely separated from adults, as contemplated under article 37. In the relatively rare event when children are placed in a facility which also houses adults, federal law mandates that the juveniles be completely separated from any adult inmates.[21] The only minor exception may be the older youth whose case was transferred to the adult criminal court and who is subsequently incarcerated as an adult. All children in placement, including those few who may be imprisoned with adults, maintain the right to family visits and correspondence, save in exceptional circumstances.

Conclusion

The American Juvenile Justice system has pioneered many of the principles incorporated in the Convention articles devoted to juvenile delinquency and the treatment of children accused of or found to have engaged in criminal activity. Federal legislation mandates several Convention principles and state legislatures and courts have applied constitutional and statutory standards. The United States is, accordingly, in general compliance with the Convention.

Footnotes

[1] *See, e.g.*, Nelson v. Heyne, 491 F.2nd 352 (7th Cir. 1974), *cert. denied* 417 U.S. 976 (1974).

[2] Thompson v. Oklahoma, 108 S.Ct. 2687 (1988).

[3] Stanford, v. Kentucky, and Wilkins v. Missouri, 109 S.Ct. 2969 (1989).

[4] *See, e.g.*, CAL. PENAL CODE ANN. §190.05 (h)(9)(West 1988).

[5] As of July 1989, twenty-eight persons were under sentence of death for crimes committed below the age of eighteen, only 1.3 percent of all per-

sons under sentence of death; it is probable that the sentence of many of the twenty-eight will be reversed or commuted.

[6] *See* Schall v. Martin, 105 S.Ct. 2403 (1984).
[7] *See, e.g.*, N.Y. FAM. CT. ACT §340.1.
[8] New York, for example, has established a minimum age of seven; N.Y. FAM. CT. ACT §301.2(1).
[9] *See, e.g., In re* Causey 363 So.2d 472 (La. 1978).
[10] United States Constitution, Article I, §9(3).
[11] *In re* Winship, 397 U.S. 358 (1970).
[12] 387 U.S. 1 (1967).
[13] *See, e.g.*, N.Y. FAM. CT. ACT §312.1.
[14] United States Constitution, Amendment VI (1791).
[15] *See, e.g.*, N.Y. FAM. CT. ACT §340.1 and §350.1.
[16] *See, e.g.*, TEX. FAM. CODE ANN. §54.08.
[17] *See, e.g.*, N.Y. FAM. CT. ACT §§375.1 - 375.3.
[18] *See, e.g.*, Glenda Kay v. State, 732 P.2nd 1356 (Nev. 1987).
[19] In New York, for example, the maximum time a juvenile can be placed in a residential facility is limited to eighteen months for most felony cases ; see N.Y. FAM. CT. ACT §353.3.
[20] *See, e.g.*, Inmates of Boys' Training School v. Afflack, 346 F. Supp. 1354 (DRI 1972).
[21] 42 U.S.C. §5633(a).

CHAPTER 17

Involvement of the Child in Armed Conflict
Article 38

Thomas A. Johnson*

Introduction

On the cover of the June 18, 1990 edition of *Time* magazine, a very small thirteen year-old Burmese child holds a very large assault rifle next to the title "Child Warriors" and a caption declaring that "kids like him" are fighting and dying in war zones around the world. In the lengthy cover article which follows, there are graphic descriptions of seemingless endless armed conflict situations in different parts of the globe which are often characterized by the heavy involvement of children in one way or another. A media spotlight on such situations is encouraging in and of itself and may ultimately help generate sufficient international pressure to bring about change in the conduct of those who intentionally utilize or otherwise involve children in armed conflicts. However, virtually no remedial measures were proposed in the aforementioned article. Moreover, there was no mention whatsoever of the most recent effort of the international community to address the problem of the child involved in armed conflict, either as a participant (voluntary or not) or as a non-participant affected directly or indirectly.

That multilateral effort, of course, eventually produced article 38 of the Convention on the Rights of the Child and occurred in the Working Group of the United Nations Commission on Human Rights, which is open to all U.N. Member States, official observers and accredited non-governmental organizations. Whatever the opinions of individual members of the Working Group on the wisdom (or not) of including a provision on armed conflict in the Convention, the absence of any reference to the Convention generally, and article 38 in particular, in a relatively comprehensive news article on the subject of children in armed conflict might not surprise many of them. However, it would undoubtedly be somewhat discouraging, in view of their hard work to negotiate the consensus language on this difficult subject, which was adopted by the U.N. General Assembly during its 1989 session.

Armed Conflict

Notwithstanding the reasons for despair due to the continuing real-world involvement and victimization of children (by any definition) in numerous armed conflicts and for annoyance due to the lack of widespread knowledge about the Convention as a potentially effective remedial device, an important first step in improving any such situation is to increase government, media and public awareness of the basic problem(s). With regard to the tragedy of children involved in armed conflict, there appears to be growing awareness and concern about this problem in multilateral forums, and many individual countries among government officials, media representatives, charitable and human rights organizations, and individual citizens. Actually doing something about such a problem is another matter, but article 38 of the Convention is at least a good faith, widely-accepted step in the right direction.

In the formulation of any lengthy and complex multilateral instrument, which must finally be considered and adopted by more than 150 sovereign States in the United Nations General Assembly, there are bound to be particular topics and draft provisions which arouse strong feelings on all sides of the question at hand. As is well known, that was the case with the question of children in armed conflict, which is dealt with in article 38 of the Convention on the Rights of the Child. When a consensus at long last emerges on such a controversial matter, however, the chances of avoiding difficulties during each country's ratification process are often enhanced because of the thorough analysis and various compromises entailed in the consensus text achieved. For these reasons, that is likely to be the case with regard to article 38 in any future ratification process for the Convention in the United States and elsewhere. On the other hand, experience with multilateral treatymaking also shows that provisions which were not at all controversial, and were adopted relatively quickly during the drafting process, may later be major obstacles to ratification for one country or another, perhaps because of inadequate discussion and analysis in the first place.

■ BACKGROUND INFORMATION ON ARTICLE 38

In any event, whatever one might wish to say about article 38, it cannot accurately or fairly be asserted that the final text is the result of overly hasty drafting and cursory debate in the Working Group. On the contrary, some

Armed Conflict

might argue that a disproportionate amount of the Working Group's limited resources were devoted to article 38. This is not the place to review exhaustively, and perhaps comment on the legislative history of, article 38. That would literally be merely an historical exercise, since the language that now comprises article 38 is clear and unambiguous enough to render unnecessary a resort to the legislative history for "statutory" interpretation purposes.

Suffice it to say that the positions articulated throughout the debate on draft article 20 (renumbered as article 38 in the final text of the Convention) were sincerely held and well presented. A threshhold question was whether or not the Convention should even address the subject of armed conflict. Some Working Group participants with particular expertise in international humanitarian law maintained that existing international instruments in that field provided adequate protection for children if States would only adhere to those existing standards and that a Working Group made up primarily of generalists should not venture into such a highly specialized area of international law. However, many other participants argued that, in view of the real-world problems in this area, the Working Group would be remiss if it failed not only to emphasize or reinforce existing standards, but to improve upon those standards.

Obviously, the Working Group decided to proceed with the drafting of an article on children involved in and/or victimized by armed conflict. Without going into great detail, a draft article was adopted on first reading during the Working Group's 1986 session that (upon reflection) pleased no one because, *inter alia* it established no lower age limit for recruitment into military service. That oversight was remedied without significant controversy at the end of the first reading by utilizing language on recruitment from Additional Protocol I of 1977 to the 1949 Geneva Conventions.

It was during the second reading of the draft Convention that serious disagreement arose within the Working Group over what later became article 38. Some delegations wished to break new ground in the field of international humanitarian law by, for example, establishing eighteen as the minimum age for direct participation in armed combat. Other delegations, for reasons ranging from national security policies to religious principles, favored retention of the existing standards and considered the Working Group to be an inappropriate forum in which to revise the international humanitarian law

Armed Conflict

principles formulated in diplomatic conferences (notably those concluded in Geneva in 1949 and 1977) by the leading diplomatic, military, and security experts in the field at the time. This sometimes heated dispute continued throughout the second reading in late 1988 and remained a controversial matter during the 1989 sessions of the Commission on Human Rights and the General Assembly.

In both the Commission and General Assembly, however, a basic desire among all interested delegations to achieve consensus on the entire Convention text, combined with the realization that a public debate on the terms of article 38 (or any other provision of the text forwarded by the Working Group) could prove contagious and spread to several other articles of the then-draft Convention, resulted in adoption of the present version of article 38 and the Convention as a whole. Although extensive informal consultations were held among interested parties, no amendments or revisions were ever formally proposed in the Commission or General Assembly to the language adopted by the working group during its second reading.

Once again, not all delegations were happy with the final text, since it does not go beyond existing international standards and, in one narrow area (minimum age for participation in non-international armed conflicts under article 4 of Additional Protocol II), does not meet them. In its statement just before consensus adoption of the draft Convention by the Commission on Human Rights in March 1989, for example, the International Committee of the Red Cross [ICRC] (a recognized authority, to say the least, in the field of international humanitarian law) went so far as to suggest that deletion of paragraphs 2, 3, and 4 of article 38 would produce a better result than adoption of the full text.[1]

It should be noted, however, that the leading proponents of inclusion of an article on armed conflict in the Convention repeatedly rejected proposals to bring the article precisely in line with existing international standards by making the same distinction as the 1977 Protocols between international and non-international armed conflict, and then incorporating the language from each Protocol on the minimum age for participation.

Clearly, the ICRC's advice was not followed, and, accordingly, the United States and all other Member States of the United Nations now have before

Armed Conflict

them a Convention on the Rights of the Child which includes the same four-paragraph version of article 38 originally adopted by the Working Group at the end of its second reading of the draft Convention.

In the case of the United States, it is highly unlikely that, either within the Executive Branch or in the Senate, the final version of article 38 would provoke significant debate or controversy, precisely because the controversial issues that arose during the drafting process were resolved to the satisfaction of the U.S. Delegation. In view of the fact that U.S. legislation, policy and practice meet higher standards than those set forth in article 38, the possible obstacles to Executive Branch endorsement of the Convention and/or Senate advice and consent to ratification which may be present in other articles should almost certainly be totally absent from article 38. Stated differently, the United States Government is already fully in compliance with the terms of article 38, and it should thus be a non-issue during any consideration of signature and ratification of the Convention.

A. General Rules of Humanitarian Law: Paragraph 1 of Article 38

The basis for optimism concerning article 38 begins, appropriately enough, with paragraph 1, which declares:

> *States Parties undertake to respect and to ensure respect for rules of international humanitarian law applicable to them in armed conflicts which are relevant to the child.*

This provision expresses fundamental U.S. policy and practice in not only respecting applicable international humanitarian law in armed conflicts as a government, but in taking measures to ensure that individual U.S. military personnel exhibit such respect in the conduct of hostilities and in dealing with all persons involved in or affected by armed conflicts. During the last fifty years, the United States has been a driving force behind the development of international humanitarian law in a variety of ways, including the playing of lead roles in the post-World War II war crimes trials, the drafting of the four 1949 Geneva Conventions and the 1977 Protocols Additional thereto, and the formal training of U.S. military personnel concerning the law of war. This approach manifests itself not only in the law of war training received by U.S. military personnel and the actions taken against those who fail to comply, but in the allocation of people and materiel to activities (e.g., civil affairs units) that provide humanitarian relief and other forms of assistance to the civilian population in areas of armed conflict. The U.S. policy and practice of promoting respect for international humanitarian law includes, of course, the rules applicable to the United States in armed conflicts which are relevant to the child.

In addition to the foregoing points, another consideration that renders the possibility of controversy within the U.S. government over paragraph 1 of article 38 quite remote is that the obligations in the paragraph relate only to rules already applicable to the United States, such as the provisions of the Convention Relative to the Protection of Civilian Persons in Time of War (more commonly known as the Fourth Geneva Convention of 1949).[2] Other, more controversial, international instruments such as Additional Protocol I of 1977 to the 1949 Conventions are thus not covered by paragraph 1 of article 38 for the United States, although (as noted below) the United States considers some of the provisions of Protocol I to be principles of customary international law in their own right.

B. Participation in Hostilities: Paragraphs 2 and 3 of Article 38

Paragraphs two and three of article 38 are taken almost verbatim and certainly without any substantive distinctions from article 77, paragraph 2, of Additional Protocol I. Under the terms of paragraph 2 of article 38, States Parties are required "to take all feasible measures to ensure that persons who have not attained the age of 15 years do not take a direct part in hostilities." Paragraph 3 obligates States Parties to refrain from recruiting any person under the age of 15 into their armed forces and to give priority to the oldest in recruiting persons between ages 15 and 18.

As indicated above, Protocol I, as a whole, is unacceptable to the United States Government. President Reagan declared it to be "fundamentally and irreconcilably flawed" in his letter of January 29, 1987, transmitting Protocol II to the Senate for its advice and consent to ratification, but noted in the same letter that Protocol I has "certain meritorious elements."[3] In like manner, Secretary of State George Shultz (in his December 13, 1986 letter submitting Protocol II to the President) reported the conclusion of the inter-

Armed Conflict

agency review process that "Protocol I suffers from fundamental shortcomings that cannot be remedied through reservations or understandings," but he acknowledged "that certain provisions of Protocol I reflect customary international law, and others appear to be positive new developments."[4] It is unnecessary to debate how to categorize the virtually identical language in paragraphs 2 and 3 of article 38 on the one hand and paragraph 2 of Protocol I's article 77 on the other hand (i.e., customary international law or a positive new development or something else). It is sufficient to note that, whatever difficulties the United States Government has with Protocol I, they do not emanate from the article 77 language in question, as the U.S. Delegation made clear in the following statement to the Working Group concerning the text which was ultimately adopted as article 38 of the Convention:

> Not coincidentally, this text faithfully adheres to the language of Article 77 of Protocol I to the Geneva Conventions of 1949. Article 77 resulted from a long debate in the Diplomatic Conference convened to draft the Protocols only last decade. The United States does not believe that the Working Group is the appropriate forum to tamper with existing international law in this area.[5]

In short, paragraphs 2 and 3 of article 3 contain language that the United States accepted during the negotiations on the Convention, despite the fact that it is borrowed from an international instrument which, overall, is unacceptable to the United States.

Notwithstanding that paragraphs 2 and 3 of article 38 come from a controversial source, the fact remains that the language therein is fully consistent with the unilateral policy and practice of the United States. This language should pose no problems during any inter-agency or Senate deliberations on the Convention, because the Department of Defense actually maintains a higher standard than that required by paragraphs 2 and 3. U.S. Army Regulation 601-210 of 1 December 1988,[6] for example, states clearly that waiver requests for age requirements will not even be considered. Applicants are only eligible for enlistment if they are not less than 18 years of age. The only exception to this rule is in the case of persons not less than 17 years of age who are able to obtain the written consent of parents or legal guardians or who have no parents or legal guardians or who are married, legally separated, or divorced. Written consent must be submitted and

331

verified before any enlistment processing occurs, and enlistment is not authorized if either parent objects. In cases of custody by reason of divorce decree, desertion by one spouse, incapacity of one spouse, and so on, consent may be given by one parent with a detailed written explanation by that parent and either a notarized signature or one witnessed by an officer or noncommissioned officer. In all cases, age must be verified by documentation such as a birth certificate or passport.

With regard to participation in armed combat, the Department of Defense has frequently stated that every effort is made to ensure that no one is placed in a combat situation before age 18. According to Department of Defense policy, in those cases where someone 17 years of age enlisted during an armed conflict, every effort would be made to prevent participation of that individual in the conflict prior to attaining age 18. An absolute guarantee on this point is clearly not possible, especially during peacetime, when, for example, a ship with some 17 year-old crew members might, unexpectedly, become engaged in hostile action.

In terms of both policy and practice, to sum up, it is fair to assert that the United States presently meets and exceeds the standards set in paragraphs 2 and 3 of article 38, and there is no reason to believe that the the language therein would pose significant problems during any future consideration of the Convention by either the Executive or Legislative Branches of the United States Government.

E. Protection of Civilians in Paragraph 4 of Article 38

Paragraph 4 essentially reaffirms already existing obligations for States Parties to the Convention by providing that States Parties shall take all feasible measure to ensure protection and care for children affected by an armed conflict, "(i)n accordance with their obligations under international humanitarian law to protect the civilian population in armed conflicts." As a State Party to the Fourth Geneva Convention of 1949, the United States has already assumed many obligations with respect to children involved in armed conflict. Paragraph 4 of article 38 merely emphasizes these longstanding obligations and, thus, should not in any way cause difficulties for the United States Government.

Readers familiar with the 1949 Geneva Conventions will no doubt agree with commentators who have outlined the protections to which children are entitled under the Fourth Convention.[7] First, children benefit from the general protection accorded by the Fourth Convention to all civilians in the territories of the parties to the conflict. Second, if they qualify under a particular category of protected persons (e.g., residents of occupied territory, internees, etc.), children benefit from the protections connected with each category. Third, certain provisions of the Fourth Convention benefit children, including eligibility for refuge in safety zones (article 14), evacuation from besieged places (article 17), reception in neutral countries (article 24(2)), entitlement to relief supplies (article 23), receipt of special care, maintenance and education (articles 24, 50, 76(5), 94), and so on. Such specific obligations under U.S. treaty law, combined with relevant principles of customary international law that, for example, ban military attacks on the civilian population as such, make it difficult to imagine that any problems would arise for the United States in connection with paragraph 4 of article 38.

Conclusion

For the reasons set forth above, the language of article 38 should not constitute an obstacle to signature and ratification of the Convention on the Rights of the Child. Some may criticize article 38 for not setting new international standards. Others may criticize it for failing to include specific language prohibiting certain kinds of unacceptable actions directed against children by some governments in armed conflicts during the last decade (e.g., intentional targeting of children in one regional conflict by means of explosive devices that appeared to be toys and use of food as a weapon in another regional conflict by diversion of supplies from civilian populations with a high percentage of children).

However valid these and other criticisms of article 38 might be, they, nevertheless, would normally not be a basis for hesitating to sign and ratify this Convention, particularly in light of the fact that there are no inconsistencies between article 38 on the one hand and U.S. law, policy, and practice on the other hand. In short, it is unlikely that article 38 will be a significant factor one way or the other in the final United States Government decision on whether or not to sign and ratify the Convention on the Rights of the Child.

Footnotes

[1] Statement of the Representative of the International Committee of the Red Cross, United Nations Commission on Human Rights, March 8, 1989.

[2] 6 U.S.T. 3516. T.I.A.S. 3365, 75 U.N.T.S. 287.

[3] Letter of January 29, 1987 from President Ronald Reagan to the Senate of the United States transmitting Protocol II Additional to the Geneva Conventions of 1949, U.S. Senate (100th Congress, lst Session, Treaty Document 100-2).

[4] Letter of December 13, 1986 from Secretary of State George Shultz to President Ronald Reagan submitting Protocol II Additional to the Geneva Conventions of 1949, U.S. Senate (100th Congress, lst Session, Treaty Document 100-2).

[5] Report of the Working Group on a Draft Convention on the Rights of the Child, UN Commission on Human Rights, UN Document E/CN.4/1989/48 of 2 March 1989, Paragraph 603, Page 112 (summary of U.S. Delegation statement).

[6] Regular Army and Army Reserve Enlistment Program, Army Regulation 601-210, Headquarters, Department of the Army, 1 December 1988, Chapter 2.

[7] MICHAEL BOTHE, KARL JOSEF PARTSCH AND WALDEMAR A. SOLF, NEW RULES FOR VICTIMS OF ARMED CONFLICTS, [1982], pp. 473-479; INTERNATIONAL COMMITTEE OF THE RED CROSS, COMMENTARY ON THE ADDITIONAL PROTOCOLS OF 8 JUNE 1977 TO THE GENEVA CONVENTIONS OF 12 AUGUST 1949, (1987).

*The views expressed herein are those of the author and do not necessarily reflect those of the Department of State or of the U.S. Government.

AFTERWORD

Sanford N. Katz

The United Nations Convention on the Rights of the Child is a statement of ideals. It could have special influence on some developing nations, on other countries undergoing radical shifts in political ideology, and on nations that are looking toward new constitutions.

But what effect will the Convention have on American law? The authors of the essays in this volume have explored this question point-by-point and in depth. Their tasks were extraordinarily difficult. Mainly, the difficulties arise from our unique political and legal system, our Constitution, our intricately developed statutory and case law, our multi-layered language, and our lack of homogeneity in ethnic backgrounds.

Any international treaty or charter in the area of domestic relations creates problems for an American audience. To begin with, our federal system of government, unlike most others in the world, consists of complex relations between the federal government and the states. There are, however, fairly clear lines of jurisdiction. The federal, not state, government deals with foreign relations. State law, not federal, applies to the areas of domestic relations conveyed by the Convention. The question of domestic implementation of the U.N. Charter itself has been, from the inception of the United Nations, a matter of great complexity and controversy. This is no less true with the Convention on the Rights of the Child. Article 1, for instance, defines a "child" as a "human being below the age of eighteen." Article 6 states that "States Parties recognize that every child has the inherent right to life." The problems presented by these apparently self-evident statements is nearly a perfect microcosm of the difficulties presented by many of the articles in the Convention. They mirror problems in our domestic life. Currently in America, a major political, social, and legal debate centers around the very question of when a human being becomes a person who should be legally protected and which branch of government—legislative or judicial, federal or state—has the authority to make that determination.

Afterword

Article 2 goes on to state: "States Parties shall respect and ensure the rights set forth in the present Convention to each child within their jurisdiction without discrimination of any kind, irrespective of the child's or his or her parent's or legal guardian's race, color, sex, language, religion, political or other opinion, national, ethnic or social origin, property, disability, birth or other status." Discrimination continues to be a major problem for American society. After well over 200 years since our Declaration of Independence pronounced that "All men are created equal," we have not yet sorted out what equality means and the methods to achieve it. It is only in 1990 that the federal Congress legislated to prevent certain kinds of discrimination against the handicapped. We are still in unclear waters as to the status of illegitimate children in America. Although a great deal of progress has been made since the time when illegitimate children were considered the children of no one, these children have not yet achieved full equality with legitimate offspring in every legal aspect.

Article 12 speaks of assuring that "the child who is capable of forming his or her own views [has] the right to express those views freely in all matters affecting the child [and that] the views of the child [are] given due weight in accordance with the age and maturity of the child." And in the second part to that article, the Convention states: "For this purpose, the child shall in particular be provided the opportunity to be heard in any judicial and administrative proceedings affecting the child, either directly, or through a representative or an appropriate body, in a manner consistent with the procedural rules of national law." Once again, the Convention deals with a controversial subject.

The famous cases of *United States v. Kent*[1] and *In re Gault*[2] established the right to counsel in juvenile delinquency proceedings, and a number of states have legislation which provides that the wishes of the affected children of certain ages should be accorded some recognition in child custody cases (divorce). Nevertheless, courts and legislatures have been reluctant to mandate the right to legal counsel or the privilege of standing to children in every kind of juvenile proceeding, including divorce, child dependency, termination of parental rights, incorrigibility proceedings, commitment to a mental institution, etc. If mandatory legal counsel for children were required in all such legal proceedings, we would have a major crisis in the courts for a variety of reasons, financial and social. Increasingly, the high costs of procedure, including legal representation, is seen as competitive with the delivery of child welfare services. Therefore, a movement can be detected away from mandating an absolute right to legal counsel in all cases. Instead, new consideration is being given to considering the allowance of parents and non-professionals to assume the role of children's representatives in judicial proceedings.

A number of articles in the Convention address social responsibilities. For example, article 27 states: "States Parties recognize the right of every child to a standard of living adequate for the child's physical, mental, spiritual, moral and social development." And article 18 states: "For the purpose of guaranteeing and promoting rights set forth in the present Convention, State Parties shall render appropriate assistance to parents and legal guardians in the performance of their child-rearing responsibilities and shall ensure the development of institutions, facilities and services for the care of children." At a time in American history when more than 12 million children live below the poverty line, when it seems impossible to enact a national health care program, when pre-natal and post-natal programs are underfunded or non-existent in many states, when day care is at a premium and often too expensive to be within the reach of many American working families, this article would be particularly difficult for our Congress to fully implement. Even if those political leaders who are skeptical of government intrusion into family affairs were convinced by the article, the costs of complete compliance with the article might be overwhelming at a time of a shrinking economy.

Article after article refers to words and concepts like "inherent rights," "privacy," "freedom," "family," "family members," "best interests of the child," and so forth, which are not easily defined in American law, nor is there necessarily a national consensus on their meaning. For example, even after the United States Supreme Court case of *Griswold v. Connecticut*[3] established that there was a right to privacy protected under the American Constitution, a debate is still being waged as to whether such a concept is a 20th century idea rather than one from the 18th century. In a less theoretical vein, the term "family members" has created a controversy in the courts. Who are such members? Must family be defined in terms of biology? Sociology? Legal doctrine in a particular context?

Afterword

The articles whose difficulties have been discussed and the general observations on possible problems in terminology by no means cover either the full range of complexities or the enormous benefits at which these articles aim. As the authors in this volume have pointed out, many state and federal laws (statutes and cases) conform to the spirit and often to the letter of many articles. A few of such articles are of immediate importance, because of current national and international attention to their underlying issues: articles 19, 20 and 21.

Articles 19 and 20 provide for the protection from all forms of physical or mental violence, injury or abuse, or exploitation. Most state laws in America are in conformity with the provisions of article 19. For instance, where a child is being abused by its parents or other primary caretakers, there are provisions for placing the child in an alternative setting where the child will be protected and, hopefully, will find a nurturing affection. Of course, any system—any bureaucracy—has holes through which some victims will disappear.

Article 21 builds a hedge around adoption, both national and international, for the protection of the adopted child. Here again, the United States has stringent laws aiming at the same result. All adoptions in the United States are subject to some kind of administrative or judicial evaluation either during the placement process or just before judicial approval. The days of the private handing over of children by relatives, friends or strangers without any legal action approving the placement are over. However, there are some exceptions to this, such as the case where the prospective adoptive person or couple never seeks court approval and lies about the child's real identity, how the child was obtained, and the child's legal status. Article 21 promotes the careful legal regulation of adoption as a means to secure a child's protection and advance the child's welfare.

In spite of considerable difficulties, sometimes only verbal, which the articles present for the American context, taken as a whole this Convention does point the way to a brighter future for the world's children.

Afterword

Footnotes

[1] 383 U.S. 541 (1966).
[2] 387 U.S. 1 (1967).
[3] 381 U.S. 479 (1965).

Appendix

Appendix

Guide to Chapters Containing References to Articles of the Convention on the Rights of the Child

Article Number	Chapter Number(s)
Preface	3, 5, 7
Article 1	3, Afterword
Article 2	5, 6, 10, Afterword
Article 3	1, 5
Article 4	3
Article 5	2, 5, 13, 15
Article 6	3, 5, 11, Afterword
Article 7	5, 6, 10, 13
Article 8	6, 13
Article 9	1, 5, 6, 8, 13
Article 10	5
Article 11	5
Article 12	8, Afterword
Article 13	5, 7, 14
Article 14	5, 7, 13
Article 15	5, 7
Article 16	3, 5, 7
Article 17	7, 14
Article 18	1, 5, 10, 13, Afterword
Article 19	5, 13, Afterword
Article 20	6, 13, Afterword
Article 21	13, Afterword

Appendix

Article Number	Chapter Number(s)
Article 22	6
Article 23	3, 5, 11, 12
Article 24	3, 6, 11
Article 25	5, 6, 8, 11, 12
Article 26	6, 10
Article 27	6, 10, Afterword
Article 28	3, 6, 9, 14
Article 29	6, 9
Article 30	3, 6, 13
Article 31	14
Article 32	5, 14, 15
Article 33	15
Article 34	3, 5, 7, 15
Article 35	5, 13, 15
Article 36	15
Article 37	16
Article 38	17
Article 39	3, 12, 15
Article 40	1, 6, 16
Article 41	3
Article 42	---
Article 43	3
Article 44	3
Article 45	3